CONTENTS

CHAPTER

THE DESPOTISM THAT FAILED (1603-1642)

The Responsibility of James I.—Elizabethan Survivals: Cecil and Bacon—Charles I. and Buckingham; the End of Parliamentary Despotism—Charles I. and the Agents of Personal Government—The Responsibility for the Collapse of Prerogative Despotism; Laud, Strafford, Henrietta Maria—The Responsibility of Charles I. for the Civil War

The Main Cause: Suspicion—The Composition and Grievances of the Opposition—Economic Grievances—Religious Grievances —The Importance of strictly " Constitutional " Grievances—The Opposition Split (1641); Radicals and Conservatives

THE REVOLUTION THAT FAILED (1642-1660)

The Cause—Military Resources and Organisation—The Strategy of the First Civil War—The Spoils and Quarrels of the Victors (1646-9)—Cromwell and the Puritan Victory

The Great Puritan Split (1644-9)—The Disintegration of Independency (1649-53)—The Failure of Union by Dictatorship (1653-8)—The Disintegration of the Army (1658-60)

THE COMPROMISE THAT FAILED (1660-1688)

The Work of the Restorers; the National Settlement of 1660—The Work of the Restored: the Party Settlement of 1661-2—The Testing of the Restoration Settlement

Contents

ABBREVIATIONS

The following abbreviations are used, in footnotes, for works to which frequent reference is made :

Adam Smith :	Adam Smith : *The Wealth of Nations*
Bland : *Docts.*	Bland, Brown and Tawney : *English Economic History, Select Documents*
Burnet :	Burnet : *History of My Own Time*
Clar. : *Hist.*	Clarendon : *History of the Great Rebellion*
Clar : *S.P.*	Clarendon : *State Papers*
C.M.H.	*The Cambridge Modern History*
D.N.B.	*The Dictionary of National Biography*
D. Nichol Smith	D. Nichol Smith : *Characters of the Seventeenth Century*
E.H.R.	*The English Historical Review*
Evol. Plt.	Pollard : *The Evolution of Parliament*
Pol. Hist. Eng.	Pollard : Longman's *Political History of England* (Vol. VI)
Feiling :	Feiling : *History of the Tory Party* : 1640-1714
Firth : *House of Lords*	Firth : *The House of Lords in the Civil War*
Frere : *H.E.C.*	Frere : *A History of the English Church* : 1558-1625 (Vol. V, ed. Stephens and Hunt)
Gardiner : *Docts.*	Gardiner : *Constitutional Documents of the Puritan Revolution* (3rd edition)
Gardiner : *Hist.*	Gardiner : *History of England* : 1603-1642
Grant Robertson :	Grant Robertson : *Select Statutes, Cases and Documents* : 1660-1832 (3rd edition)
Holdsworth :	Holdsworth : *History of English Law*
Hume Brown :	Hume Brown : *History of Scotland*
Hutton : *H.E.C.*	Hutton : *A History of the English Church* : 1625-1714 (Vol. VI, ed. Stephens and Hunt)

Lucas :   Lucas : *Historical Geography of the British Colonies*

Ludlow :   Ludlow : *Memoirs*

Prothero :   Prothero : *Select Statutes and Constitutional Documents* : 1558-1625

Ranke :   Ranke : *The History of England Principally in the Seventeenth Century*

R.H.S.T. :   *Transactions of the Royal Historical Society*

Stone :   Stone : *England Under the Restoration*

Tanner :   Tanner : *English Constitutional Conflicts of the Seventeenth Century*

Trevelyan : *E.U.S.*   Trevelyan : *England Under the Stuarts*

Trevelyan : *Select Docts.* Trevelyan : *Select Documents for the Reign of Anne*

BOOKS OF GENERAL REFERENCE

GENERAL WORKS

Outline Histories :

DAVIES, G. : *The Early Stuarts.* (O.U.P., 1959)
CLARK, G. N. : *The Later Stuarts.* (O.U.P., 1956)
TREVELYAN, G. M. : *England Under the Stuarts.* (Methuen, 1904)
RANKE, L. VON : *The History of England Principally in the Seventeenth Century.* (O.U.P., 1875)
POLLARD, A. W. : *The Evolution of Parliament.* (Longmans, 1926)
HILL, C. : *The Century of Revolution.* (Nelson, 1961)
McELWEE, W. L. : *England's Precedence.* (Hodder and Stoughton, 1956)
AYLMER, G. E. : *The Struggle for the Constitution, 1603–89* (Blandford, 1963)
WILLEY, B. : *The Seventeenth Century Background.* (Chatto, 1934)
KENYON, J. P. : *The Stuarts.* (Batsford, 1958)

Constitutional, Legal and Administrative :

THOMPSON, M. A. : *Constitutional History of England : 1642–1801.* (Methuen, 1938)
KEMP, B. : *King and Commons : 1660–1832.* (Macmillan, 1957)
TANNER, J. R. : *Constitutional Conflicts of the Seventeenth Century.* (C.U.P., 1928)
DODD, A. H. : *The Growth of Responsible Government.* (Routledge, 1956)
HOLDSWORTH, W. S. : *History of English Law,* Vol. VI. (Methuen, 1937)
HUGHES, E. : *Studies in Administration and Finance, 1558–1828.* (1934)

Social :

COATE, M.: *Social Life in Stuart England.* (Methuen, 1924)
NOTESTEIN, W.: *English People on the Eve of Colonisation.* (Hamilton, 1954)
WILSON, C.: *England's Apprenticeship, 1603–1763.* (Longmans, 1965)

Collections of Documents :

PROTHERO, G. W.: *Select Statutes and Constitutional Documents, 1558–1625.* (O.U.P., 1913)
TANNER, J. R.: *Constitutional Documents of the Reign of James I.* (C.U.P., 1930)
GARDINER, S. R.: *Constitutional Documents of the Puritan Revolution.* (O.U.P., 1906)
FIRTH, SIR CHARLES and RAIT, R. S.: *Acts and Ordinances of the Interregnum.* 3 Vols. (1911)
BROWNING, A.: *English Historical Documents, 1660–1714.* (Eyre and Spottiswoode, 1953)
COSTIN, W. C. and WATSON, J. S.: *The Law and Working of the Constitution,* Vol. I. (Black, 1952)
GRANT ROBERTSON, C. G.: *Select Statutes, Cases and Documents, 1660–1832.* (1935)
TREVELYAN, G. M.: *Select Documents of the Reign of Queen Anne.* (C.U.P., 1929)
BLAND, A. E., BROWN, P. A., and TAWNEY, R. H.: *English Economic History, Select Documents.* (Bell, 1914)

AUTHOR'S PREFACE

THIS book does not attempt to provide exhaustive treatment or fresh historical material; it is a work, not of research in the strict and august sense, but of introduction and interpretation. It is based on the material that the student who is beginning a serious study of history is expected to read—the standard histories, modern monographs, and the more accessible documents and contemporary works. It is intended to encourage students to read widely in the great historical literature of the seventeenth century, and to guide them by suggesting certain problems and explanations. The book assumes in the reader a knowledge of the outlines of Stuart history, and consists mainly of analysis and commentary on the chief events of the period. I hope also that it will not be found too technical or detailed to interest the general reader, if that elusive person still reads history.

I wish to express my sincere thanks to Professor R. B. Mowat, to Mr. F. R. Worts and to Mr. J. D. Griffith Davies for their encouragement, advice, and valuable criticism. I owe to Professor Barker, not only the *Introduction* which adorns this book, but whatever I may possess of the method and spirit of historical interpretation.

I. D. J.

Oxford, 1930.

PUBLISHER'S NOTE

IN the 1966 reprint all the book lists, for reference books and suggestions for further reading, have been brought up to date.

INTRODUCTION

By Ernest Barker, D.Litt.,

Formerly Professor of Political Science in the University of Cambridge

I have sampled the wine of this book on *The English Revolution*. But I knew the vineyard from which it has come even before I sampled the wine. Indeed, I may be said to have had something to do with the planting of the vineyard; or to speak more exactly, and to limit my claims with a nicer regard to truth, I may be said to have "spread a compost o'er" its tender shoots. In other words, and without more beating about the bush, I had once the honour, and the excitement, of being Mr Deane Jones' tutor. But all that happened in a previous life and " another place."

Now it is said that " good wine needs no bush "; and it may also be said, with even more justice, that a good book needs no preface. But you may set up a sign outside a good inn; and I am therefore venturing to try my hand at painting the sign of *The Seventeenth Century*.

In which century would you have chosen to live if you could have had your choice about the date of your coming into the world? We should all give our different answers; but in England at any rate there is a good deal to be said for the seventeenth century. An Englishman born about 1625, and living until the " glorious Revolution " had come and he could say *Nunc Dimittis*, might have passed through many memorable moments. He might as an undergraduate, in 1643, have watched Henrietta Maria riding into Oxford, " by her husband's side, amidst the ringing of bells," to make her home in Merton College. A few years later he might, as a soldier in Cromwell's army, have sat on his horse at sunrise on a September morning near Dunbar, halted for a moment by the Lord General's command to sing Psalm cxvii (it has only two verses, but there was no time for a longer Psalm), before he swept down on the flying

Scotch. If he had come back to Oxford again for a visit, forty years after his going down, he might have stood in the Bodleian Quadrangle in 1683, and smelled the pungent reek of " certain pernicious books " of a radical tendency (Milton's writings were among them), which a loyal University had condemned to the flames. And if he had retired in his old age for the benefit of his health to Torquay, we can imagine him standing on a cliff, on a Monday noon in the beginning of November, 1688, while " a soft and happy gale of wind " carried the whole fleet of William the deliverer, under his eyes, into Torbay. For the seventeenth century was an exciting time ; and on whichever of the two sides a man stood—Roundhead or Cavalier ; Whig or Tory—he might be certain that he would alternate between victory and defeat, despondency and exultation.

The seventeenth century was not only a time of excitement : it was also a great and decisive century in our national development. In the previous century England had been living—for the first time since 1066, and for the last time till the twentieth century—under a native dynasty. If that dynasty had not been star-crossed by the cruel fate of an empty nursery ; if Anne Boleyn had given to Henry VIII a son as vital and as powerful as his father : if Elizabeth, again, had married Leicester, and had left a son as politic and as popular as his mother ; if, in a word, a new dynasty from Scotland had not succeeded to the throne—what would have been the future course of English history ? Would England have been guided by a patriot and Protestant king into the Thirty Years' War ; would Germany have been saved from her sufferings and devastation ; would France have been debarred from her period of subsequent ascendancy ? Or would much of what actually happened when a Scottish dynasty sat on the throne have happened under any dynasty ? Hypothetical questions only admit of equally problematical answers ; but the odds are perhaps in favour of the second of the answers suggested. Men, individual men, matter ; a family or a dynasty matters ; but what matters more than individual men or particular dynasties is the interests, the ideals and the ambitions of groups or masses of men. This is not to say that movements make history, and not men ; for men make movements, and there are no movements which are not started and directed by men. It is only to say that what makes national history most is the action not of lonely leaders, but of big battalions ; and by big battalions I mean social groups, and by social groups I mean professions, classes, occupations and " confessions." What made English history in the seventeenth century was the legal profession (always a great shaper of our constitutional development) : it was the landed gentry, increased and enriched by the confiscations of the Reformation, enthroned in the government of the English counties by the extension of the powers of the Justices of the Peace, and resolved to exercise a voice in the central government of England: it was the seafaring and cloth-weaving occupations, resolved to fare and to weave with as much liberty and to as much advantage as they possibly could : it was the English Church and the Puritan sects, both anxious to shape the commonwealth according to their ideas. It was the assembling of these factors at the beginning of the century, and it was the action and interaction of these factors during its course, that made the century momentous. By the beginning of the century the elements of a fresh social grouping, richer and more various than the old mediaeval grouping, had appeared. By the end of the century a system of balance between these elements—a system which adjusted them all to one another and to the monarchy —had been achieved ; and that system was to endure until 1832.

A Scottish dynasty, of the tragic and perennially fascinating Stuart house, was thus mixed with English common law and its lawyers ; with the English landed gentry ; with the English commercial and industrial classes ; with the English Church and the English Free Churches. The cauldron boiled and bubbled during a turbulent and creative century. Now this shape and now that seemed to emerge from the wreathing vapours as the form and figure of the new England that was to be. Now it was the face of " Black Tom Tyrant " and his system of Thorough : now it was a Republic governed by a unicameral Parliament ; now it was a dictatorship under the great Oliver, keeping England in order as if it were a " poor parish," and he its constable ; and now there seemed to be the menace (but did it ever exist ?) of a " second Stuart despotism." The shape that eventually emerged by 1714 was more prosaic than some of these, but it proved to be steady and

permanent.   There was a constitutional monarchy, with its powers
now canalized in legal channels—able indeed at times to exert what
Blackstone calls the "persuasive energy" of its influence, but
running for the most part quietly along formal and predetermined
ways.   (The lawyers, from Coke to Somers, had not been idle:
they had "legalized" the monarchy—and for that matter the
Army, the Budget and as much of the national system as they could
get into their frame-work.) There was, by the side of the monarchy,
a sort of diarchy of the landed and commercial classes (Disraeli
called it a Venetian oligarchy) ruling through the Houses of Parliament, and gradually feeling its way to a cabinet system.   The
English Church remained established, but the Free Churches had
won toleration by the Act of 1689 ; and anyhow there was a lull
in the religious fervour which at one time had seemed likely to
enthrone bishops as royal coadjutors, and at another time to insti-
tute a theocracy of the Saints.   It was a system of prose, property,
common sense and compromise.   There was one golden thread
shot through it, and that was an ideal of "civil and religious
liberty."   It was an ideal very imperfectly realised ; but at any rate
after 1695 there was no Licensing Act, and an Englishman could
print what he pleased—subject always to the law of libel and the
stolid sense of an English jury on the point of propriety.

But the ferment of the seventeenth century had produced results
outside the area of England.   It had produced a United Kingdom
of the island of Great Britain : it had produced a British Empire
across the seas.   Incidentally, and as it were, by the way, the
factors of sea-faring and Puritanism, added to the land-hunger of
the Eastern counties (from which came much of the stock that went
overseas), had settled the American plantations, and laid the foundations of the United States.   All this was a great and sufficient
achievement for the period of the Stuart dynasty ; and the last of
the Stuarts, if ever she meditated in one of her long silences on the
great growths which had attended the rule of her line, may well have
murmured, "Enough."

Perhaps there were two great things which a sagacious and impartial European, looking across the narrow seas about 1714, might
have said of the island we inhabit.   "First," he might have said,

" this English constitution is a remarkable thing, which seems to guarantee a good deal of liberty, and about which we on the Continent might well begin to think." This is the sort of thing which Montesquieu was actually saying in the middle of the eighteenth century; and the development of parliamentary government on the Continent in the next century shows that the English example had really started a good deal of thought. "Secondly," he might have said, " this expansion of England is another remarkable thing. Who knows where it will end, or to what remote continents and islands in the Southern Seas it may not take this wandering stock? Ought not we on the Continent to be taking some note of this movement?" The history of France in the eighteenth century, and the history of both France and Germany in the latter half of the nineteenth, are both, in their ways, a commentary on such a saying.

Hic desinit. I leave the reader to the story of *The Seventeenth Century.* I do not know that I have painted a good sign. It is enough if I have whetted an appetite. Perhaps I shall best succeed in leaving the reader with an eager zest if I cite two passages from this book, and ask a question about each. "History," the author says, "is a mere rattling of dead men's bones unless we breathe into the memories of the past the life of our personal sympathies and judgments." Are you bringing the life of your own experience, reader, to breathe upon this record of human experience? And again, "Most wars," says the author, " begin as a Crusade, but all end as a business." Would you reply, dear reader, that our Civil War, unlike most wars, began as a business, but ended as a Crusade?

ERNEST BARKER.

PROLOGUE

I. Omissions

In a short introductory work on the Stuart period it is fair and necessary to begin with the omissions that must inevitably be made. First, it is obviously impossible within such limits to treat adequately the literature and art of the period because of their very importance and variety. Such an omission has its dangers, for the divorce of the history of politics from the history of culture not only distorts the picture but deprives historical studies of a large part of their educational value. On the other hand, guides to literature are best avoided by the student; they either tantalise by their inadequacy or tempt with their short cuts to knowledge, and the busy candidate for examinations is often content to proceed no further than the substitute. Are guides to history, then, any more useful or less dangerous ? No student can claim any understanding of the seventeenth century without reading something of the histories of Clarendon and Burnet, the sketches of Dryden and Halifax, the diaries of Laud, Evelyn, Pepys and Swift, the speeches of Cromwell and the political reflections of James the First, Bacon, Hobbes, Milton and Locke. There can be no substitute for these, for they combine the real stuff of history with the quality of great literature. If an introductory survey attracts the attention of students to them, and is promptly discarded as a result, it has its reward.

Yet it has a useful function of its own. Milton's literary virtues are not affected by his religious prejudices, but Clarendon's historical value is seriously impaired by his misunderstanding of Puritanism as a factor in the Civil War. Anyone who begins to study the period needs a guide to save him from confusion and loss of time by pointing out where contemporary bias exists, and where the contemporary antidote can be found. It can indicate the central

problems and suggest methods of approach and various interpretations, so that the student may avoid uncritical and desultory
reading.

Secondly, this book is mainly confined to a central theme and
must pass over many important subjects except in so far as they
bear on this theme ; for example, the great economic developments,
the story of Scotland, Ireland, and the plantations are only men-
tioned for their connection with, and influence on the evolution of
English government and society. Similarly, it is impossible to
compress further and difficult to improve upon Professor Trevelyan's account of English social life in the first two chapters of his
England Under the Stuarts and in the first four of *Blenheim*, or upon
Macaulay's account of England in the third chapter of his *History*.
All that can be attempted here is to provide a guide to wider reading
and a general background for detailed and separate studies.

II. THE CENTRAL THEME : THE VICTORY OR OLIGARCHY

There is an initial difficulty in defining the main subject. The
seventeenth century is the century of revolutions in English history ; it is perhaps the most dramatic century of all. Many Englishmen place the dramatic climax in 1649 and consider the years that
follow as an age of spiritual reaction, declining in interest to the
anti-climax of the Hanoverian succession. They would treat the
history of England in this period as the " Decline and Fall " of the
Stuarts. This is a view which rightly emphasises the importance
of persons, and royal persons in particular, in an age when most
men held government to be a matter for princes rather than for
Royal Commissions. Nevertheless it is an inadequate view, a
historical half-truth only. 1714 is no anti-climax in English
history. The enthronement of George I. marks the political and
constitutional climax of the period 1588-1714 ; for it seals the
definite triumph of the idea of Parliamentary supremacy based on
the political rule of the propertied classes. From this aspect the
drama of 1649 and the surrounding years of war and change are
only an interlude, which left few permanent effects on English
society ; for it produced a violent break in the development of

English government which had to be repaired by an equally violent reaction. Except for these twenty years, there was one prevailing ideal ;—the joint and harmonious rule of the King and his Parliament. Any other permanent solution was steadily rejected by the nation, and in 1588 and 1714 the nation saw its ideal embodied. All that lies between these years serves to explain why and how Elizabethan and Hanoverian unity of government differ in their elements and spirit ; and this process of change or evolution must be the central theme in a study of the seventeenth century. The attempt to define and divorce the powers of King and Parliament produced the Civil War ; the failure to govern by two separate bodies—Protector and Parliament—made the Restoration inevitable ; the failure of the Restoration compromise to remove division and distrust led to the second revolution of 1688 ; and from 1689 to 1714 unity and efficiency were gradually restored and tested by war, party faction and a disputed succession. Thus after a century of insecurity, stable government was assured as before 1603 by the close fusion of the powers of Crown and Parliament in united control.

It is the historian's task to trace the path of the cycle of sovereignty through the processes of definition, division, experiment and reunion ; it is then the moralist's pleasure to assess whether it be a cycle of progress or of degeneration. Many will urge that it was no gain to replace monarchy by oligarchy : that the septennial Parliaments were as irresponsible and as tyrannical as a dynasty : that the overthrow of Stuart despotism was the work of feudal reaction : that a national paternal policy was discarded for a corrupt and greedy class domination : and that from 1660 onwards there was less government, and worse government in all that concerned the social and economic welfare of the people. These are pertinent moral criticisms ; but they judge the results of the age in isolation and omit the vital consideration that, whatever might have been, English democracy and prosperity are in fact based on the foundations laid by the politicians of the reigns of William III. and Anne. These men re-discovered the Tudor secret of governing that the Stuarts could never find—a link to co-ordinate scattered departments into an organic whole. It was not the same link, nor was the co-ordination so complete ; the essential difference was between the Tudor council and the modern cabinet. Elizabeth spread her councillors everywhere—in both Houses, in courts both central and local, lay and ecclesiastical : George I. found the Whig party in control of both Houses, the Bench of bishops, London and the banks, and all the sources of patronage. Party had succeeded Court ; forced loans gave way to the " spoils system " ; influence and not Prerogative was the " great mystery of State " ; the Commons rose from their place as occasional and submissive partners to the height of a practical monopoly of power.

With these differences in method, there is a fundamental similarity of principle ; and it was a principle that secured strength in action at the expense of neat theories and political formulae.   De Tocqueville might with some truth apply to both régimes his maxim that the English Constitution does not exist.[1]   The ambiguities that exercised the minds of Coke and Bacon are, if anything, less baffling than the contradictions between the written constitution of the Bill of Rights and of the Act of Settlement and the conventions that modified it in practice.   For the experience of a century of disorder had proved the necessity of sacrificing constitutional tidiness to the greater gain of flexibility ; history had justified the aims, though not the methods of Strafford, and had shewn the theories of Pym and Coke to be suitable only for obstruction—what Mr. Feiling calls " the constitutionalism of the ostrich." [2]   The mainspring of both systems is the indefinable, almost mystic conception of the King-in-Parliament—an indivisible institution, the elements of which are so fused that the one is meaningless without the other.   " The Crown had never been sovereign by itself, for before the days of Parliament there was no real sovereignty at all ; sovereignty was only achieved by the energy of the Crown in Parliament, and the fruits of conquest were enjoyed in common." [3]   But such powers cannot be restricted by rule or definition ; there is nothing they cannot do or undo ; the constitution becomes an infinitely elastic body of statutes and

[1] *La Démocratie en Amérique* (Bk. I, ch. 6) : " En Angleterre la constitution peut donc changer sans cesse, ou plutôt elle n'existe point."

[2] Feiling, K. : *England under the Tudors and Stuarts*, p. 134 (Thornton Butterworth).

[3] Pollard, A. W. : *Evol. Plt.*, p. 230.

conventions, controlled only by the responsibility of the legislators to the electorate.

Neither Elizabeth nor the Whig leaders had an exacting standard of responsible government. The Tudors in general have finer instincts on the question, if the preambles to their statutes are taken at their face value, and if their attitude to enclosures and Poor Law administration is compared with that of the Whigs. Wolsey, Somerset and Cecil framed and actively enforced a national and almost popular economic policy which was quietly let die by the Whig landlords and merchants. But the Hanoverian settlement had the confidence of the dominant interests and classes, so that the governors represented fairly well all that was articulate in the nation. The theory, at least, of representation and responsibility was ineradicably there, however much neglected in practice ; and the settlement, for all its imperfections, was the only basis on which constitutional progress could be combined with stable government.

III. The Legacy of the Tudors

In order to understand how this settlement was reached and how the roles of the Crown and Parliament were reversed in the process, the student must begin by examining the last fifteen years of the reign of Elizabeth, for here he will find the key to many Stuart problems. After 1588, when the sharpest domestic and foreign crises were over, Tudor administration, built to face successive emergencies, was applied to more or less normal conditions and was too cumbrous and conservative to adapt itself in face of growing discontent. When James succeeded, there was no break in the administration ; even after the death of Salisbury in 1612 the younger Elizabethan officials, such as Coke and Bacon, filled the less decorative posts ; Buckingham was no new portent to a generation that remembered Leicester and Essex. The first four years of Charles' reign have a similar character ; the dissolution of Parliament in 1629 is the first fatal breach in the old Tudor system. The years 1588-1629 form a historical unit, and represent a distinct phase of the relations of Crown and Parliament ; they witness the gradual breakdown of an organisation that had been largely created for the purpose of national defence in the period 1529-1588. Therefore any enquiry into the causes of the breakdown must begin before 1603 ; it must begin when pre-Armada methods of government clash with post-Armada requirements.   The causes of most of the quarrels are the same before and after 1603, though the temper of them may differ ; for instance, monopolies, impositions, Parliamentary privilege, royal marriages and succession, control of the Church and foreign policy.   It is as untrue to blame the Stuarts solely for provoking them as to describe their rule as a mere continuation of Tudor administration.   They did indeed attempt to continue Elizabeth's methods, but that is not all they did.   Mr. Feiling contrasts the old Queen, strong in word and action, with the Stuarts' fatal combination of strong words and weak actions,[1] and points out that they lacked the indispensable qualities of " constant strength, skill and sympathy," [1] by which alone paternal authority can be preserved in times of national growth.   Yet he asserts that " if legality could excuse incompetence, the Stuart cause was impregnable." [1]

The student must turn first, then, to Elizabeth's legacy to James. The basis of her power was her popularity and utility to the nation.   She and her father had, with the aid of many new and sharp weapons of government, preserved the independence and increased the wealth of England at the expense of medieval immunities and some medieval institutions.   Their rule was such that coercion and persuasion, force and sympathy were as a whole nicely balanced, and when they resorted to ruthless and arbitrary measures they were often no more than the instrument of the dominant passions and interests in the country.   When Sir Thomas Smith, Elizabeth's Secretary, describes the functions of the Justices of the Peace in these words ;—" There was never in any commonwealth devised a more wise, a more dulce and gentle, nor a more certain way to rule the people," [2] we are inclined to be incredulous of their gentleness to recusants, vagrants and sectaries ; but there is no reason to suppose that the gentry, yeomen, merchants, artisans, or even discreet Catholics felt as oppressive the rule of their neigh-

---

[1] Feiling, *op. cit.*, pp. 132, 130, 116.
[2] Smith, Sir T. : *De Republica Anglorum*, ed. Alston, p. 89.

bours, who represented in their midst the central government
without professional status or salary. The middle classes in town
and country regarded Tudor penalties as intended for other people
who fully deserved them, and did not inquire too closely into their
legality ; for the only alternatives were internal anarchy, foreign
conquest and Romanism with the fear of the Inquisition. Elizabeth's opportunist policy, with its ingredients of audacity, caution
and luck, somehow averted the twin dangers of invasion and
rebellion in an age that saw them ravage nearly the whole of
Europe : the miracle justified the methods and sanctified the
Queen.

After 1588 there was less need for miracles. The defeat of the
Armada brought confidence if not arrogance ; the execution of
Mary Stuart removed the chief centre of domestic and foreign
intrigue, and opened up the prospect of a peaceful and Protestant
succession. Hence after the heroic age came reaction. The
national coalition for defence was weakened when men turned their
thoughts to internal organisation and reform. The Queen and
some of her ministers were old and tired, but the energy of the
middle classes was unimpaired ; they were the richer for the wars
while the Crown was poorer. The House of Commons reflected
this change of the balance of power in its new claims and criticisms.
Friction increased and sympathy lessened ; the Crown seemed to
draw apart from Parliament and turn for support to the Church.

There were earlier signs of this dissolution of partnership.
Before 1585 Bishops rarely appeared in the Privy Council, for
" Queen Elizabeth herself was the great-great-granddaughter of a
citizen of London ; her Privy Council was of like descent, and its
members were given precedence of peers of the realm." [1] But from
1585 Whitgift was a regular member, and symbolises " the new
alliance of Church and Crown against Parliament which took
the place of Henry VIII.'s alliance with Parliament against the
Church." [1] It was Whitgift who organised Laud's engine, the
Court of High Commission, in 1583. In 1585 the Commons
registered their first protest against this new prerogative weapon
of the Crown, and in 1588 the Martin Marprelate tracts began to

[1] Pollard, A. W., in *E.H.R.*, vol. 38, p. 54.

shew the rising opposition to the Royal policy of isolating and sterilising English Protestantism.	In 1593 Elizabeth attempted to restrict the too free speech of the Commons on religious matters and an imprisoned Member cried ; " From the tyranny of the clergy of England, good Lord, deliver us." [1]	She turned the weapon, forged to crush Catholic traitors and assassins, against Protestant extremists who were politically insignificant and owed no foreign allegiance ; in 1593 she hanged two Brownists for seditious writings against the Prayer Book, the sacraments and the Queen's power to make laws concerning religion.	In controversy and in discipline Whitgift and Bancroft were strengthening the defences of the Church against Puritan rather than Papal attacks, and in this atmosphere Hooker's " Ecclesiastical Polity " came to educate English churchmen along the conservative lines of historical tradition.	The quarrels were not yet exacerbated by doctrinal differences, for Whitgift was as rigid a Calvinist as his opponents ; but the field was set, and the rulers of England took their sides— the Queen and her Bishops against the Commons and the majority of her lay Councillors.

Herein lies the political importance of these religious disputes. They brought to a head an issue which was created by the special character of the English Reformation.	Henry VIII. brought it about in the interests of Royal supremacy, but he found it necessary to use a not always subservient Parliament as his accomplice ; by 1603 the accomplice was taking all the credit for the change and claiming the rightful guardianship of its handiwork.	Parliament resented the plot to withdraw the Church from its supervision and to make the Church a royal and not a parliamentary organ ; the Queen wished to use the Church as a check and balance to an unruly Parliament.	Neither side cared anything for clerical independence ; both accepted the Tudor principle of the subordination of religion to the interests of the State.	This was the most urgent question in men's minds at the end of the sixteenth century, and it was complicated by their memories of the past and their fears for the future. In an age which had no census, they magnified the numbers and cohesion of the English Catholics, and they could not be expected

[1] Pollard, A. W. : *Pol. Hist. Eng.*, Vol. VI, p. 463 (Longmans).

to gauge correctly the extent of the decline of Spain. Protestantism seemed much less secure than it was. It was supreme only in England, Scotland and North Germany; in Holland the struggle was still uncertain and in France it relied on the word of the leader who had deserted it; in the rest of Europe the Jesuits were inciting popes and princes to the work of the Counter-Reformation. The threat and the fact of the Thirty Years' War must never be forgotten by students who wish to understand and criticise the Puritan attitude to "Papists and Arminians." Already in 1600 the danger was visible to all in Ireland. The Irish rebellion was ascribed to Papal and Spanish machinations, and it infused into English politics that atmosphere of racial and religious fears which made compromise and moderation in religion repugnant to the Protestant majority.

In this inflammable atmosphere other grievances were likely to take fire. The Commons granted more and more subsidies for naval and Irish campaigns and the Queen granted more and more monopolies. She had to plead for her Prerogative, " the fairest flower in her garden," and in 1601 Londoners cried: " God send the Prerogative touch not our liberty." [1] Elizabeth saved face by the Tudor art of gracious and timely submission, and the Commons did not press her hard; for she was old and worn in England's service, and her quarrels with them, though frequent and serious, could not destroy the mutual trust and respect born of common aims and risks.

Yet the cleavage of interests was real and deep, though disguised by personal factors of sympathy which must die with the old Queen. The only hope of averting a complete breach was that her successor would grasp the psychological basis of Tudor strength and not be deceived by Elizabeth's tactics in her weakness. For her reliance on the Church was a sign of failing powers and judgment, since it needed a strong hand and judicious whip to drive a turbulent Commons' team. Tudor strength lay, not in Divine Right or a standing army, but in a sitting Parliament. Her father declared: " We be informed by our judges that we at no time stand so highly in our estate royal as in the time of Parliament, wherein we as head

[1] Pollard : *Pol. Hist. Eng.*, p. 474.

and you as members are conjoined and knit together in one body politic, so as whatsoever offence or injury during that time is offered to the meanest member of the House is to be judged as done against our person and the whole Court of Parliament." [1] This is high doctrine, which no Tudor observed without lapse ; but their victories were won this way. The secret of their success is that they were strong and wise enough to use and guide the rising political forces of the nation in government, and did not sterilise any through fear and distrust. Henry VIII. " did not minimise but magnified Parliament. Under his rule its privileges were consolidated, its personnel was improved, its constituency was enlarged, its political weight enchanced in foreign eyes, its authority increased, its sessions made more frequent and prolonged." [2] Few speeches are more moving than Elizabeth's words to her last Parliament : " Yet this I count the glory of my crown : that I have reigned with your loves . . . a queen over so thankful a people . . . That my grants should be grievous to my people, and oppressions privileged under our patents, our kingly dignity shall not suffer it . . . I was never so much enticed with the glorious name of a king or royal authority of a queen, as delighted that God had made me his instrument . . . to defend this kingdom from peril, dishonour, tyranny and oppression." [3]

The true Tudor ring is in this confident appeal ; the monarchy so rests on the broad foundations of popularity and utility. If James I. could have inherited the Tudor art of government, as well as its machinery, he would have had a fair chance of settling with honour, though not with ease, the inevitable conflicts over religion and finance. But Elizabeth's difficulties were more easily transmitted than her personal advantages. The problems of State showed signs of increasing, rather than decreasing, in complexity ; and some of them were such as no personal qualities of tact and charm could solve. Feminine arts of procrastination, the policy of turning the blind eye, were possible no longer. The growth of the Counter-Reformation called for urgent and delicate decisions ; for Elizabeth's unique religious settlement, with all its virtues, left England isolated in Europe between two arming groups. And

[1] *Evol. Plt.*, p. 231.   [2] *Evol. Plt.*, p. 215.   [3] *Pol. Hist. Eng.*, p. 475.

this problem was bound up with one more insoluble. Policies demand money, if they are to command respect ; and not all the economies of the Queen could check the growing impoverishment of the Crown. Her long struggle for solvency was finally defeated by the expense of the Irish campaigns, and James succeeded to a Crown in debt, with no prospect of increasing assets. The radical evil was the depreciation of coin through the flooding of Europe by Spanish bullion from America ; hence the fixed rents of Crown lands and the fixed subsidies from Parliament were halved in value during the sixteenth century, and were to sink still lower. Neither King nor Commons understood the process, but blamed each other for greed, extravagance, or meanness ; economic ignorance was a large and permanent factor in the Stuart tragedy. For these reasons, besides religious and constitutional questions, the task of James I. would have tested a political genius, and it is only fair to distinguish, among the causes of his failure, the obstacles already existing from those he created himself.

IV. METHODS OF ENQUIRY

The history of Stuart England can conveniently be examined under four headings : the failure of James I.'s and Charles I.'s version of Tudor sovereignty (1603-1642) : the age of civil war and republican experiments (1642-1660) : the experiments and collapse of the restored Monarchy (1660-1688) : the consolidation of the supremacy of Parliament (1689-1714). After the student has obtained some knowledge of the principles by which the Tudors governed England and of the new conditions that made some of those principles obsolete and unacceptable to the middle classes, he will be able to see why the accession of a new dynasty in 1603 was such a critical turning-point in English history ; · and he can hope,with the aid of the clues he has found in events between 1588 and 1603, to unravel the causes of the violent changes and experiments of the seventeenth century. In this book a method of enquiry is suggested by which various historical factors—personal, religious, constitutional and economic—are examined separately. It is a method which makes for clearness, but it has dangers of its own. It tends to simplify too much the complex processes of history and to organise men's lives and motives into unreal watertight compartments. No one historical force ever acted alone, as in a vacuum; politics and religion react and interact on each other in a way that defies scientific analysis. The study of history can never be an exact science, for there are too many unknown factors; and when all appears to be accounted for, the mystery remains.

To this warning another must be added. He who would understand how the foundations of English greatness were laid in the seventeenth century must at first concentrate his attention on the main constitutional and religious struggles and put aside for a time many fascinating aspects of the history of the period. But one thing he must never forget—to see his picture of English life in due historical perspective. The picture is falsified if taken from its European setting, for history knows no such thing as splendid isolation. Therefore even a preliminary survey must include some account of the relations with Scotland and Ireland which led to the establishment of the United Kingdom, of the place of England in contemporary European civilisation, and of the part she played in the European exploitation of Asia and America. Otherwise it is fatally easy to think of Stuart England as dominating Europe in England's best nineteenth century manner; to treat the problem of Ireland in terms of the present ratio of population in the two countries; and to read back modern Imperialism into the treatment of the plantations. It is a good exercise in historical truth and in patriotic humility to remember that England was once a second-rate power, maintaining an obscure and at times precarious independence outside the main current of the life of Europe, until she was raised to greatness by the labours of three men—the rebel Cromwell, the foreigner William, and the traitor Marlborough.

The last warning is this. All the views expressed in this chapter and those following are personal, tentative and should be regarded with suspicion. They are meant to invite criticism and suggest it by example. Fortunately there can be no infallibility in historical interpretation. The fascination of the study of history is that it resembles the art of mosaic; from an infinite number of pieces

can be constructed an infinite variety of patterns. These essays
are intended to sketch the designs of a few simple patterns, and to
help the student to see as a whole the intricate mosaics of the art of
Ranke, Gardiner and Macaulay. But let him, as he reads, begin to
trace his own designs, however imperfect ; for history is a mere
rattling of dead men's bones unless we breathe into the ghosts and
memories of the past the life of our personal sympathies and judgments.

SUGGESTIONS FOR FURTHER READING
FOR THE PERIOD 1588–1603

*The Eli*ʒ*abethan Background*

ELTON, G. R. : *England under the Tudors.* (Methuen, 1955)
   The Tudor Constitution. (C.U.P., 1960)
BLACK, J. B. : *The Reign of Eli*ʒ*abeth.* (O.U.P., 1959)
ROWSE, A. L. : *The England of Eli*ʒ*abeth.* (O.U.P., 1959)
BINDOFF, S. T. : *Tudor England.* (Pelican, 1950)
NEALE, J. E. : *The Eli*ʒ*abethan House of Commons.* (Cape, 1949)
FRERE, W. H. : *The English Church in the Reigns of Eli*ʒ*abeth and
   James I.* (Macmillan, 1904)
HILL, C. : *The Economic Problems of the Church from Whitgift
   to the Long Parliament.* (O.U.P., 1956)
KNAPPEN, M. M. : *Tudor Puritanism.* (Chicago U.P., 1939)
SCOTT PEARSON, A. F. : *Thomas Cartwright and Eli*ʒ*abethan
   Puritanism.* (C.U.P., 1925)
THIRSK, J. : *Tudor Enclosures.* (Historical Association Pamphlet)
TAWNEY, R. H. : *The Agrarian Problem in the Sixteenth Century.*
   (Longmans, 1912)

I

THE THEORY AND PRACTICE OF DESPOTISM:
1603-1642

THERE are two questions which the historian must attempt to answer in order to understand the first forty years of Stuart history. Why did the Tudor system collapse ? Why was there a Civil War after that system had been abolished ? These two issues must be separated with care ; for it is too often assumed that the Civil War was the logical result of the opposition to Prerogative rule. In fact it was a sudden catastrophe which changed violently the steady course that English politics had taken for the preceding generation. The old system fell before a climax of national union in 1640—a movement that could be traced back to the later years of Elizabeth ; war was the result of a swift national cleavage, of which there was no sign before the summer of 1641. There were two distinct crises with distinct causes and contradictory results. The second —though it arose from the first and could not otherwise have occurred—is the more remarkable. It takes two armies to make a war ; how, then, did Charles learn so late the art of making friends, and how did he raise an army from a nation that had united to pull down his power ? In the first crisis it is easier to explain the fall of despotism than its duration for nearly forty years with such mismanagement and such slender resources ; the historian's chief task is to decide whether the fall was due mainly to pressure from without or to weakness within. The purpose of this chapter is to discuss the weakness within, and to assess the responsibility of the rulers, first for the collapse of their system, and secondly for the outbreak of war.

14

I. The Responsibility of James I

James I., on his accession to the throne of England, had to face two handicaps : he was a foreigner, and he was a man. He had no experience of English society ; he was ignorant of the habits and pecularities of the governing classes among whom Elizabeth lived as one of themselves. Thus the fragile personal links between Crown and subjects were broken, and would need careful repairing. Moreover chivalry ceased to soften the demands of the Commons. Englishmen looked on James as he was, whereas they had seen and thought of Elizabeth transfigured as the fair Gloriana. It was an unfortunate contrast, for their friendly but critical eyes did not find Majesty in imposing guise ; they found it hard to respect a King in stiletto-proof clothing, " his breeches in great pleats and full stuffed." He was irresolute, petulant and fearful. " He naturally loved not the sight of a soldier, nor of any valiant man." [1] There was worse to follow. James was a learned King, proud of his erudition and " content to have his subjects ignorant in many things." [2] If he was despised as a coward, he was even more disliked as a pedant.

Both James' cowardice and his scholarship had important results. In two respects his cowardice was beneficial to the nation. In home affairs he could be intimidated by persistent opposition, and he thereby saved his throne and averted revolution for his lifetime ; in foreign affairs his passionate dislike of war preserved England from serious entanglement in the futile ravages of the Thirty Years' War. " He was infinitely inclined to peace, but more out of fear than conscience." [3] Yet fear overrode conscience at times with evil results ; fear of assassination led to a vicious policy of alternate persecution and conciliation of Catholics, while the bogey of Scotch Presbyterianism dominated his treatment of English Puritans.

James' learning gave him a theory of despotism which is often held to be the main cause of the fall of the Stuarts. He had early adopted the traditional doctrine of the Divine Right of Kings as an invaluable " anti-clerical weapon of independence " against his Presbyterian chaplains in Scotland ; [4] and in 1599 he published to

[1] D. Nichol Smith, p. 5.   [2] *Ibid.*, p. 1.   [3] *Ibid.*, p. 8.
[4] Figgis, J. N. : *The Divine Right of Kings*, p. 257.

the world a full statement of his political ideals in the " Trew Law
of Free Monarchies." Four years later he hailed England as a
Promised Land where ideals might blossom into realities. He
came to his new realm rejoicing in his new opportunities, over-
flowing with paternal wisdom and benevolence. He was eager to
teach, but he would not learn, nor admit a partner in the high task
of government ; for he had worked alone for twenty years and had
succeeded by no efforts but his own. He had the rigid and com-
placent convictions of prosperous middle age, and he warned his
servants in the Star Chamber :

" If there fall out a question that concerns my prerogative or
mystery of State, deal not with it, . . . for they are transcendant
matters. . . . That which concerns the mystery of the King's power
is not lawful to be disputed." [1]

Unfortunately for his hopes of " Free Monarchy," his new subjects had an inveterate distaste for general theories, and put their
trust in the principles set forth by the Common Law and Statutes
—principles which James could only regard as a freakish collection
of precedents and accidents. Thus England provided him with
unfamiliar obstacles to his ambitions ; for in Scotland the Parliament was a pliant tool, the law was Roman and adaptable to despotism, and the only effective opposition came from the General
Assembly of the Church. In these new conditions the anti-clerical
King of Scotland became the priest-loving King of England ;
since the English clergy were submissive while laymen were
refractory, he sought ecclesiastical support and claimed abstract
and spiritual sanctions for his power. He declared his responsibility to God alone, and admitted no other check : " He that hath
the sovereignty may bind all his subjects but cannot bind himself
. . . the laws of a sovereign prince depend on nothing but his mere
and frank good will." Therefore " it is presumption and high
contempt in a subject to dispute what a King can do." [2]

This theory involved a complete dissolution of the old Tudor
partnership at the very time when the Commons, as junior partners,

[1] Prothero, G. W. : *Statutes and Constitutional Documents*, 1558-1625, p. 399.
[2] King James I. : quoted from Miss H. M. Chew's article in Hearnshaw's *Social and
Political Theories of Sixteenth and Seventeenth Centuries*, pp. 115 and 119.

were beginning to resent their subordinate position and were claiming a larger share in the direction of policy. It continually threatened them with degradation and the loss of initiative, while at the same time James' record of almost unrelieved failure as a statesman belied the theory and justified their protests. They were ordered to stand by and see the Hampton Court Conference wrecked by the King's arrogant temper; their religious principles were offended by his uncritical support of an unreformed Episcopacy, and by his spasmodic leniency towards his Catholic subjects; their national prejudices were flouted by the wealth showered on Scotch favourites, and by the admission of foreigners to the commercial and legal privileges of Englishmen;[1] their commercial instincts were outraged by the growth of impositions[2] and monopolies which were not used to further production, but either to satisfy the greed of courtiers or to give the King financial independence. Both religion and patriotism resented the continual and humiliating failure of James' foreign schemes. Only in 1609 and 1624 did he fulfil their desires by appearing as a vigorous Protestant leader. Between these years he tried, without men or money, to check the flood of religious war and hatred by a counter-flood of words and intrigues; and the Commons watched with impotent rage the Dutch alliance weakened, Denmark betrayed, the Palatinate overrun, and the name of England used and contemned for the ends of France and Spain. Gondomar's advice was taken when their own was rejected; Ralegh, last of the Elizabethan adventurers, was sacrificed to their old enemy; and Prince Charles was exposed, as they thought by James' folly, to the dangers of the Inquisition and to the greater risks of Jesuit blandishments.

Intellectually, James was often right and his critics both ignorant and wrongheaded. He was not responsible for the reckless stupidity of his son-in-law and the rash romanticism of his son; and he was right in abandoning the Spanish vendetta, in refusing to waste English resources on Frederick and Christian, and in saving his country—though by ignoble means—from the fruitless devastation that crippled Northern Europe for a century. But politically

---

[1] Calvin's Case in Gardiner's *History of England*, I, pp. 355-6.
[2] Bate's Case in Gardiner's *History of England*, II, pp. 6-11.

he must be condemned for his methods, if not for his motives ; his mysterious diplomacy and his refusal to take the nation into his confidence vitiated his policy and weakened his power as a mediator. Even the respectful forms of Parliamentary petitions cannot conceal the growing uneasiness and exasperation ; in 1621 the Commons declared that " Your Majesty's goodness hath been requited by princes of different religion, who even in time of treaty have taken opportunity to advance their own ends, tending to the subversion of religion, and disadvantage of your affairs and the estate of your children : by reason whereof your ill-affected subjects at home, the Popish recusants, have taken too much encouragement and are dangerously increased in their number and in their insolencies."[1] They demanded a Protestant marriage for Charles, the persecution of recusants, and an immediate war with Spain. The King replied by imprisoning some of the " fiery and popular spirits " and threatening the retrenchment of the Commons' privileges on the grounds of abuse, and the quarrel flared up into the great Protestation of the Commons of Dec. 18, 1621,[2] which James tore from the Journals of the House. The breach was clear and serious ; the Commons claimed that the liberties of Parliament were independent of the Royal grace, and maintained the right of general criticism and of full and free inquiry into government ; James denounced these claims as " an usurpation that the majesty of a King can by no means endure."[3] That they were revolutionary in law is hardly doubtful, and James in his defence shrewdly fell back, not on general theories of an ideal despotism, but on the historic practice of his great predecessor. Yet he never understood that Elizabeth's strength lay less in her constitutional rights than in her political wisdom ; that the true sanction of Tudor powers was not a set of precedents that other precedents might cancel, but in their necessity and utility to carry out a policy that had the confidence of their subjects. In 1621 this confidence was entirely lost ; twice previously, in 1611 and 1614, it had been weakened by James' unpopular measures, and particularly by his open contempt for his subjects' protests and advice. When at last experience convinced the Commons of the folly of their King's principles of government, respect

[1] Prothero, p. 307.   [2] *Ibid.*, p. 313.   [3] *Ibid.*, p. 316.

for his Prerogatives disappeared; it was a natural and almost unconscious step from criticism of national policy to demanding the control of it.

Yet we must not exaggerate the extent or the finality of this breach, for within three years James reached a height of popularity such as he had not attained since his accession, and when he died he was probably more popular than Elizabeth had been in her last years. For he was at last forced to recognise the collapse of his plans for peace, and he reluctantly submitted to Buckingham's war policy, which was inspired equally by a personal hatred of the Spanish grandees and by a desire to play the part of a national Protestant leader.

This belated popularity makes it difficult to assess James' part in perverting and weakening the national monarchy which had served England's needs since 1485. On the one hand, he did not know how to yield with grace or without loss of prestige, and he diminished the sympathy and confidence of Englishmen in the system they had accepted for over a century; yet he frequently yielded in time to avoid disaster and, except in 1621, he avoided any crisis of immediate danger to his throne. He left the control of affairs to a minister who had the support of a large party, and he left the throne to a King who had the popularity of youth and the good repute of being a devout Protestant and a sound hater of Spain. Yet though the dynasty in 1625 seemed to be firmly established, the course of James' reign had shewn that the monarchy had made its choice of favoured instruments and had cut itself off from half the institutions of government. James had ranged the Bishops, the Privy Council and the Prerogative Courts against the House of Commons, the Common Law and the Puritan congregations. His chief achievement was to narrow the basis of the Tudor monarchy; but like all his work, the achievement was incomplete. His laziness and cowardice in action allowed some relics of the old system to be preserved; it needed a King like Charles, who was as brave and obstinate as he was pious, to complete the process and convert the monarchy from a Parliamentary into an ecclesiastical institution. James was saved as Charles was ruined, by his characteristic weaknesses; but he did enough in isolating the Crown and in arousing opposition to justify Gardiner's harsh obituary notice : " James sowed the seeds of revolution and disaster." [1]

II. ELIZABETHAN SURVIVALS : CECIL AND BACON

Which of James' servants deserve to share the burden of responsibility ?   Buckingham did not so much influence as supersede James in 1624, and his responsibility is linked closely with that of Charles ; but the work of Salisbury and Bacon must be examined in connection with their master's, since they represent the attempt to adapt the methods and system of Elizabeth to a new dynasty and a new generation.   Their partial failure proves that even if James had had the genius of Elizabeth he would have found the old machinery unsuited to new conditions and obstructed by new forces.

Salisbury had been executant of Elizabeth's later policy—the policy that had irritated Puritans, Parliamentarians and merchants alike ; though he could teach his new master prudence, he could not guide him into sympathy with his subjects.   He must be held responsible to some extent for the quarrels that arose out of the administration of government as distinct from those provoked by the theories imported by James.[2]   He cannot be said to have had a policy : in foreign affairs he was, despite a Spanish pension, mildly Protestant, but he insisted on peace for economy's sake.   He served James faithfully in providing for his increasing debts, and doubled the ordinary revenues of the Crown; he tried to free him from financial dependence on Parliament by the Great Contract of 1610. But he was not as skilled in managing the Commons as his father had been, and the piocess of bargaining aroused the tempers of both sides ; the result was a general explosion of grievances that produced in 1611 the first open rift in the partnership of Crown and Parliament.   Salisbury had earned widespread unpopularity for James and himself by his insistence on peace abroad and by his extension of monopolies and impositions at home, and his critics

[1] Gardiner : *Hist.* V, 316.
[2] Nor can Salisbury be blamed for the troubles caused by James' extravagance.

opened a general attack on favourites, Proclamations, Prerogative Councils and Church Courts—an attack which was not closed until 1688.

If Salisbury's failure illustrates the obsolescence of the Tudor machinery on its practical side, Bacon's more tragic career reveals that Elizabethan ideals were no longer acceptable to English minds. Bacon was disgraced, not because he took bribes, but because he held the Tudor doctrine that public servants were directly responsible to the Crown and not to Parliament :—" God forbid also, on pretence of liberties or laws, government should have any head but the King.[1]   He could recognise, as few Englishmen could, James' intelligence and the wisdom and benevolence of many of his aims ; and he saw him as a national reforming monarch—uniting Catholic and Puritan, Englishman and Scot, Privy Councillor and Member of Parliament in a common endeavour to remove poverty and excess, and to restore the " true greatness of kingdoms and estates." [2] Bacon, unlike James, saw the necessity of co-operating with the Commons and tried, though without success, to revive the Tudor practice of initiating policy through Privy Councillors seated in the Lower House.[3]   In 1614, at the height of his favour with James, he induced him to give another trial to Parliamentary monarchy ; but he only succeeded in widening the breach of 1611.   From that time his influence gave way to that of Buckingham and Gondomar on the main issues of foreign policy, and his efforts were confined to defending the financial exactions of the Crown and to extending the sphere of Chancery at the expense of the Common Law.   As Lord Keeper he considered himself overseer of all the King's Judges and he used his authority to prevent the rigid legality of the Law obstructing the necessary work of government ; for he likened the judges to the lions under Solomon's throne, and warned them not to " check or oppose any points of sovereignty." [4] Bacon's theory of the Judiciary forms his chief contribution to

---

[1] Gardiner, S. R. : *Dictionary of National Biography* : article on Francis Bacon. Cf. also Sir William Holdsworth's analysis of Bacon's legal and political theories, in his *History of English Law*, Vol. V, pp. 238-254.

[2] Cf. Bacon's *Essay* with this title.

[3] Gardiner : *Hist.* II, 191-9.   Sketch of Bacon's principles.

[4] Cf. Bacon's *Essay on Judicature.*

the downfall of the Stuart despotism, and its disastrous effects were magnified by his personal quarrel with Chief Justice Coke, the champion of the "Rule of Law." As a consequence the Common Lawyers under Coke's leadership broke away from their long subservience to monarchy. Previously, Coke and the Judges had supported the Exchequer in Bate's case and had held Salisbury's impositions to be legal; in future, though Judges might be cozened or intimidated, the weight of the legal profession was on the side of Parliament and fortified the opposition with its knowledge and ability.

So by 1621 James and his advisers had split the institutions of law and government neatly in two. The immediate result was that the excluded bodies, Parliament and Common Law, combined to attack the Royal system by reviving the old weapon of Impeachment; they set up the alternative ideal of the medieval limited monarchy which had come to ruin in the Wars of the Roses. James had failed to convince the dominant classes in England of the beneficence of his principles of Kingship, while Salisbury and Bacon had not convinced them of the continued utility of the Tudor régime; nor had they succeeded in harmonising the new and the old. On the contrary, Salisbury's financial schemes, Bacon's judicial theories and James' religious and diplomatic policies are the chief causes of the conversion of Parliament from a submissive agent to a rival competitor in government.

III. Charles I. and Buckingham; The End of Parliamentary Despotism

Charles, though in general a simpler and stupider man than James, presents a much more difficult problem of analysis. It is easy to distinguish the ideas and motives of James from those of his councillors, for he had a mind that was both independent and suspicious; but it is impossible to examine Charles' career at any point apart from those to whom he gave his confidence.[1] There is the further difficulty that no Englishman or Scot can discuss his character without bias, conscious or unconscious, although there are two

---

[1] Cf. Ranke's comparison of James I. and Charles I. : II, 64-6.

obvious extremes which can be avoided. Sentimental Jacobitism, such as afflicted George III. and Dr. Johnson, is blind to the political stupidity and moral casuistry of the man who accepted and evaded the Petition of Right : who made England ridiculous in the eyes of Europe : who reduced most Englishmen to pray for the success of a Scottish invasion, and united his own subjects in the task of destroying the whole machinery of Tudor government. On the other hand, the ardent Whig forgets that Charles was the last English King who governed in the interests of the whole nation, as distinct from those of a class, and that with him collapsed all the machinery for the protection of the peasant and artisan : that he was soured from the beginning of his reign by the savage attacks on his personal and religious loyalties : and that his father's political legacy, the poverty of the Crown and the irresponsibility of the Commons' opposition might easily have driven a wiser man to desperate measures. It is also necessary to remember that Charles, like all the Stuarts with the possible exception of James II., was something of a foreigner ; neither his virtues nor his defects are typically English. Clarendon records that " He was always an immoderate lover of the Scottish nation, having not only been born there but educated by that people and besieged by them always, having few English about him till he was King." [1] Clarendon saw him from both sides, but though he actively helped to destroy his secular powers and servants, he cannot write of him after his death save in terms of the " blessed martyr." He guardedly admits his formality and reserve, which prompted a Venetian critic to remark : " This King is so constituted by nature that he never obliges anyone, either by word or deed." [2] This aloofness from his subjects was in strange contrast to his unreserved dependence on the few to whom he gave his heart. As a young man he was slow of speech, unless he talked with artists and scholars ; he was diffident of his own opinion and had no experience of public affairs. The rule of Buckingham was a natural consequence, and it produced the first crisis of his reign and the first stage in the development of his character as a ruler.

The influence of Buckingham on the course of events is in some

[1] D. Nichol Smith, p. 51 ; cf. Clar. : *Hist.*, IV, 488-92.   [2] Gardiner : *Hist.*, VII, 142.

respects contradictory. He was not afraid of Parliaments; he desired to use them and had full confidence in his power to do so; he was more willing than James or Charles to explain his policies to them and to adapt himself to their moods. Even when his party in the Commons turned against him, the monarchy was not necessarily endangered; for when once the " cause of all miseries, the grievance of grievances " was removed, Parliament and country looked hopefully to the rule of the young and popular King. Buckingham, in fact, gave James a belated popularity and Charles a fresh start. But there his services to the monarchy end, and his disservices to Charles' interests are many. His foreign policy, if whims and spites can be so dignified, had disastrous effects on Charles' position at home and abroad. First, he was responsible for the French marriage. He cannot be blamed for Henrietta's character, nor for reviving the traditional Elizabethan alliance with France; but the articles of the marriage treaty committed Charles to tolerate Catholics in the country and priests in the Queen's household.[1] The King and his Court were in future never free from suspicion of Popery—suspicion confirmed by the neglect of Denmark and the use of English ships against the Protestant fortress of La Rochelle, " to the great scandal and dishonour of this nation." [2] Secondly, a personal quarrel with Richelieu led Buckingham to engage England in war with the two strongest European powers at once, and his ill-prepared attacks on Cadiz and the Isle de Rhé exposed the national weakness and invited invasion. While English pride was outraged and her independence endangered, domestic grievances multiplied apace—forced loans, illegal tunnage and poundage, the hardships of pressing and billeting, the mutinies and depredations of unfed and unpaid troops. Under this provocation, Parliament broke away from its temporary alliance with the Crown and renewed the general attack upon its policy and ministers. Charles lost his popularity, and was forced to defensive obstruction to save " the man whom the King delighteth to honour." [3] Death, and not Charles, saved Buckingham from

---

[1] Gardiner : *Hist.* V, 258-60, for the treaty.
[2] Eighth Article of Impeachment (1626) of Buckingham; Gardiner, *Docts.*, p. 16.
[3] Gardiner, *Docts.*, p. 3.

disgrace, but Buckingham could not save Charles from the humiliations and restrictions of the Petition of Right. Its clauses could be twisted or evaded, but just as Magna Carta signified the end of Angevin despotism, so did the Petition of Right lay down fundamental principles of government by which sovereignty must pass, sooner or later, from the King and his Courts to the Parliament and their courts.

It was not only the Commons who were alienated ; not the least of Buckingham's achievements was to unite the two Houses of Parliament. His sudden rise to power and wealth, and his zeal for his family and dependents, in which "he was guided more by the rules of appetite than of judgement," [1] offended both the economic sense of the gentry and the pride of place of the Peers. Digby, Earl of Bristol, and Williams, Bishop of Lincoln, formed an alliance with the leaders of the Commons in 1626 and again in 1628, and that alliance carried through the Petition of Right after an ominous series of conferences between both Houses. The combination was not lasting, but the precedents were there, and the Houses had learned to work together despite the King's prohibition. In future, the Puritan middle classes could always rely on an active minority of lay Peers ; for the Lords feared, as did the French nobles, the levelling effects of the new despotism. But, whereas in France the Fronde failed in isolation, the English Lords, by lending their aid and prestige to the Commons, proved one of the chief factors in the success of the Rebellion in its early stages.

The breach made by Buckingham's policy became irreparable with his death. Charles never forgot the fierce outburst of joy and never forgave Parliament for inciting the attacks on his friend. Henceforth he trusted no one fully, and determined to be his own minister, owing an account of his actions to God alone. If his subjects did not agree with his acts, he would neither explain nor modify them ; where James would have temporised out of fear or prudence, Charles remained obstinate in the conviction of his own righteousness. It was in this mood that he faced his critics in the second session of his third Parliament in 1629. He had to meet a fresh assault on his Royal rights, when his ecclesiastical appoint-

[1] D. Nichol Smith, p. 12 ; Clar. *Hist.*, I, 12.

ments were questioned.   After Buckingham, his closest friends belonged to the small Arminian party in the Church, which appealed to him both by their liberal doctrine and their political exaltation of monarchy.   These two aspects of the movement equally exasperated the Commons, and the strained political atmosphere was further charged with doctrinal intolerance.   The nature of the three resolutions against Arminians and those who either collected or paid Tunnage and Poundage, and the violence used upon the Speaker in passing them, were both frankly revolutionary ; and Charles was quick to seize upon the tactical advantage, though he was blind to the strategic danger of the situation.   He was able to make one of his rare appeals to public opinion with a show of injured right and legality, and in order to preserve the Royal control of the Church, he dissolved the Parliament and threatened to call no more until his people should acknowledge the wisdom and justice of his aims.[1]

The importance of this quarrel can hardly be over-emphasised, for 1629 marks one of the few definite breaks in English history.   It ends the epoch of Parliamentary monarchy which lasted from 1485 to 1629 ; in this respect it is a far more decisive date than 1603. The disputes between Charles and the leaders of the Commons were a logical culmination of the crises of 1611, 1614, 1621 and 1626 ; but in 1629 a new and ominous feature emerged.   Hitherto, though words had been sharp, constitutional forms had been observed ; now, in the attack on the Speaker, and in the refusal to accept a Royal Dissolution, the opposition showed a new temper, and a readiness to appeal to force ; while the King in reply determined to reject compromise and to cut at the roots of the obstruction.   In this fashion and with these omens the Tudor experiment of a popular despotism on a Parliamentary basis passed finally away.

IV. Charles I. and the Agents of Personal Government

For the next eleven years Charles strove to mould England after the seventeenth-century fashion of autocratic states, and he felt sure

[1] Gardiner : *Docts.*, pp. 83 ff.   The King's Declaration, March 10, 1629.

of success, once the factious obstructors were silenced and sent to sulk in their country houses : " Be assured that we shall find honourable and just means to support our estate, vindicate our sovereignty and preserve the authority which God hath put into our hands." [1]   He failed because the conviction grew on his subjects that his means were neither just nor honourable, and because, while he himself and most of his advisers were unfitted for so great a task, two of them—Laud and Strafford—threatened the nation with only too complete success.   He began, however, with certain advantages.   When the Commons dispersed there was no organised opposition and no strong feeling in the country.   Of their two most forceful leaders, Eliot lay in prison till his death in 1632, and Wentworth had already taken service under Charles after Buckingham's removal and the Commons' " blow at Government." [2]   The Common Law judges were tamed by the fall of Coke, and abandoned their claim to question " matters of state."   Local and sectional discontent could be crushed by such organs of Prerogative as Star Chamber, High Commission or the Council of the North.   Common Law and Prerogative together could discover revenue in the old feudal dues, forest fines, customs and shipmoney, without an open violation of the Petition of Right ; a King as economical as Charles could live on such proceeds, provided that he abandoned any effective schemes in aid of his foreign relatives and co-religionists, and refrained from driving any considerable body of his subjects in the three Kingdoms to armed opposition.

The first condition was present after the general pacification of 1630 ; the second operated until 1638, when he and Laud tried to include the Presbyterians of Scotland in the English Counter-Reformation.   Between 1630 and 1638 Charles was able to govern England as he pleased, undisturbed by serious financial drain or foreign emergency ; peace brought a revival of commerce which filled the Exchequer and broke down the merchants' resistance to non-Parliamentary taxation.   In many respects he pleased to rule well.   Measures were taken to regulate the sale of corn, to restore the vigour of the Tudor Poor Law and wage-fixing system, to check the alarming growth of London, and to preserve common

[1] Gardiner : *Docts.*, 98.   [2] The Petition of Right.

land from enclosure. Most of the notorious exactions fell mainly on the wealthy classes, though the merchants passed their share to the consumers and many of the new " corporation " monopolies fell heavily on the necessaries of life. The country was too prosperous to care much for Charles' pinpricks, and there was no organised oppression except of religious dissenters ; political agitation could not thrive steadily on the petty annoyances of a half-hearted tyranny. Its typical agents were the Treasurer Portland, a secret Catholic and open monopolist : the mediocre Secretaries, Cottington and Windebank, busy with Court intrigues and schemes of reunion with Rome : and Noy and Finch, experts in ancient precedents and Prerogative arguments. These men provided that mixture of legal chicane and irresolute action which drove Laud and Strafford to despair.

What, then, is the responsibility of Charles' two great servants ? It is an insult to Strafford's abilities to hold him responsible for absolutism as it was, although his words and acts suggest a terrifying picture of what it might have been. It is true that he exercised considerable influence on occasion by his correspondence with Charles and Laud ; but he was not at the centre of affairs till 1639, and his methods of rule in Ireland and the Council of the North were never fully applied to the rest of England. Though Parliament singled him out as the chief agent, almost the personification of the eleven years' tyranny, this prominence was due mainly to memories of his apostacy in 1628 and to his leadership in the crisis of 1639-40. If he had had a free hand in the favourable conditions of the previous eight years, the Long Parliament would have found its task of destruction far more formidable than it was.[1] To modern eyes Laud's would seem the greater share of responsibility, because of his presence at Court and Council and because of the religious passions he provoked ; and when we examine the central and most flourishing period of Charles' personal government, it can be seen to coincide with the period of Laud's greatest influence.

On succeeding to Canterbury in 1633, Laud as Primate became the King's chief official adviser, as he had been unofficially for some

---

[1] Cf. Clarendon's character sketch in D. Nichol Smith, pp. 61-3 ; Clar. *Hist.*, I, 340-2.

years. When Archbishop Abbot's prudence and Portland's timidity were removed by death, both Church and State felt the spur of new energy. James had feared and distrusted his restless spirit, which " loves to toss and change, and to bring things to a pitch of Reformation floating in his own brain, which may endanger the steadfastness of that which is in a good pass." [1] In England he used mainly two instruments in his work—High Commission and the Metropolitan Visitation. Clarendon describes how " Persons of honour and great quality were every day cited into the High Commission Court, upon the fame of their incontinence or other scandal in their lives." [2] He used it to enforce morality on laymen and uniformity on clerics, and he tried to raise the spiritual and social level of the parish clergy by strengthening their authority over their parishioners, rich and poor. He left mere doctrine alone, provided it was discreetly expressed and not carried into controversy or practice ; but his Courts defined discretion so as to muzzle the Calvinist majority and protect the Arminian minority. While his genuine toleration in matters of thought shocked the country, his autocratic control of morals and ceremonial made him the best hated man in England. By 1639 he claimed to have secured an obedient and reformed clergy, but it was at the expense of reinforcing the Puritan sects, and of alienating not only the best, but the worst sort of laymen.

The Puritans hated Laud because he was in character one of themselves. He enforced the Book of Sports, not because he liked Sunday games, but because they provided a useful test and antidote for Puritanism ; he insisted on ritual, not because of its emotional and popular appeal, but because it was an essential part of a logical theory of religion. He agreed with their conception of a comprehensive Church supporting and guiding the State ; like them, he allowed no compromise on the fundamentals of religion. His Church would not endure any loosening of its two great bonds of union—sacrosanct Monarchy and ceremonial uniformity. Laud's contention was that though ceremonies cannot replace inward devotion, yet inward devotion can hardly exist without the " beauty

[1] Tanner, p. 83, note 3 (from Hacket's *Life of Williams*).
[2] D. Nichol Smith, p. 102 ; cf. Clar. *Hist.*, I, 125.

of holiness " ; for " ceremonies are the hedges that fence the substance of religion from all the indignities which profaneness and
sacrilege too commonly put upon it." [1]   Since the forms of worship
have a spiritual meaning and function, they cannot be left to the
anarchy of individual tastes ; they must be ordered and enforced
by one supreme authority, for " unity cannot long continue in the
Church where uniformity is kept out at the Church door." [2]

Such reforming ideals do credit to Laud as a Churchman, and
make him worthy to rank as a great spiritual leader ; but his
methods and political activities are more open to criticism.   There
are two main indictments against him : that of " over-meddling in
State matters," [3] and that of " appealing to Caesar " to carry out
his religious schemes.   It is difficult, and perhaps unhistorical, to
treat them separately, for in using the Star Chamber to protect the
Church and the Church to protect the Monarchy, he so confused
the functions of Church and State that he bound the fate of Charles
to his own, and brought upon both institutions the odium incurred
separately by each.   The ordinary layman, whether Puritan or
not, hated to see Bishops dominating the Council, Star Chamber
and Treasury, and interpreted the portent as a sign of the sacrifice
of State to Church; he felt what Chief Justice Richardson expressed
in 1633, that England was being " choked with a pair of lawn
sleeves." [4]

Laud undoubtedly sealed the fate of Star Chamber by converting
it into an ecclesiastical Court.   In this Court were inflicted the
savage punishments that made popular martyrs of Leighton,
Prynne, Burton and Bastwick; and Laud "was observed always to
concur with the severest side, and to infuse more vinegar than oil
into all his censures." [5]   In 1633 he used the Exchequer to suppress
Puritan lecturers by dissolving their endowments, thus offending
the formidable combination of Puritanism and property.[6]   He was
not less zealous in secular business, which he did not consider incompatible with his episcopal charge.   As a member of the Trea-

---

[1] Hutton : *H.E.C.*, p. 53.   [2] Tanner, p. 80.
[3] Fuller in D. Nichol Smith, p. 103.   [4] Gardiner : *Hist.*, VII, 320.
[5] Fuller in D. Nichol Smith, p. 102.
[6] Gardiner : *Hist.*, VII, 258-9.—Feoffees for Impropriations.

sury Commission he overhauled the Exchequer in a vain attempt to reduce extravagance and corruption ; and when this failed through the indifference of Charles and the resistance of Henrietta and Cottington, he threw all his energies into increasing the revenues by forest fines and the regular levy of shipmoney, and he thereby added to the Puritan charges against the Church that of complicity in financial oppression. The growing resentment began to receive public expression in 1637 in London riots against Star Chamber trials and in widespread refusals to pay shipmoney ; and this was the time that Laud chose to turn his " restless spirit " to Scotland.

V. The Responsibility for the Collapse of Prerogative Despotism ; Laud, Strafford, Henrietta Maria

Laud was a religious imperialist : he intended to confer on all subjects of the King, whoever and wherever they were, the blessings of uniformity. Foreign congregations in England, English congregations abroad, all received his correction and were ordered to conform. Strafford, with his encouragement, had improved the resources and morality of the Irish Church and had enforced Laud's Canons on the Irish Convocation in 1634. In the same year Laud made a beginning of reform in Scotland. James had done little after restoring a limited Episcopacy with two High Commission Courts in 1610 ; he had introduced some English customs in the Five Articles of Perth (1618), but he had expressly warned Bishop Williams against allowing Laud to " make that stubborn Kirk stoop more to the English pattern." [1] In 1634 Williams was in disgrace, and Laud would have no half-measures ; in three years he established one vigorous Court of High Commission, filled the Bishoprics with his own followers, and dominated, by means of the Bishops, the Scottish Privy Council and the "Lords of the Articles" who controlled the proceedings of the Scottish Parliament. The machinery of revolution was complete ; the revolution itself took the form of new Canons and a new Prayer Book authorised by the Royal Supremacy alone in 1637. The Book was denounced as

---

[1] Trevelyan : *England Under the Stuarts*, p. 186.

invalid without the authorisation of Parliament or General Assembly of the Church, disliked as a foreign imposition, and rejected as being even more Papistical than the English Book. It was Laud's ideal conception of a form of worship, but in impatiently grasping at his ideal he brought to a common destruction the episcopate and monarchy of three Kingdoms.

The events of 1638 in Scotland decided the fate of Charles' system for two reasons : they gave the English Puritans an example and they gave the English Parliament a weapon. First of all, the success of illegal resistance was fatal to the myth of absolutism ; it proved that a united nation could wrest almost any concessions from Charles, and that he had no solid force behind his show of of power. If the Scots, a people far less homogeneous than the English, could create an Assembly, executive and army within a year, then the English nation could use its Parliamentary experience and adaptable county organisation to forge far more easily a weapon of resistance.

Secondly, the Scottish rebellion destroyed the two props on which Charles' precarious despotism rested—small expenditure of revenue and the apathy of his subjects. Charles' resort to force was a desperate step for a King who had little surplus revenue and no standing army, whose only personal weapons were the ship-money fleets and the distant Irish troops of Strafford. Such forces could not reduce a nation ; he was helpless without the money and service of London, the Lords and the counties—that is, without the aid of those who had endured his government with patience at best. So far the apathy of the nation had been his best safeguard, but apathy does not produce generous loans or high-spirited soldiers.

Moreover the apathy that Hampden first challenged was now shattered by appeals from both sides—Charles hoping to arouse the feelings of outraged patriotism, and the Scots demanding sympathy for a common religion. The national awakening was decisive ; London rioted and refused aid, the army was mutinous and a body of Peers negotiated with the Scots. Charles was left with no choice but to make what terms he could with the angry nation in Parliament.

Thus Laud must take the full responsibility for the collapse of

Royal power in Scotland and for the exposure of its real flimsiness in England, but Strafford must share the blame of provoking the immediate catastrophe. Laud's miscalculation of the strength of Scottish opposition was balanced by Strafford's fatal delusion that the English Parliament could still be used as a tool of monarchy. He thought that, even if Parliament failed in its duty, public opinion would acquit Charles " before God and man " and sanction every means necessity demanded, " loose and absolved from all rules of government." He must be condemned for failing to see that the King had no resources left but the goodwill of his subjects, and that such goodwill could only be gained by a sacrifice of the men and methods of " Thorough." The utter ruin of his plans can be judged by Gardiner's summary of the results of the Short Parliament : " It made England conscious of the universality of its displeasure." [1] Pym beat him in tactics at every point ; by the moderation of his demands, the obstruction of supplies and the petition for peace he deprived the King of any moral or financial support. Pym forced the dissolution of the Short Parliament in order to inflame public opinion, and ensure the recall of a more organised Parliament on its own, not Strafford's terms ; he had to give Charles time to put himself more completely at the mercy of his subjects.

The process did not take long. Strafford's threats of an Irish army " to reduce this Kingdom," Convocation's futile grant of supplies, the Scottish invasion of the North—all made the issue clear ; a half-Papist Court and Church were plotting to enforce a suspect religion against the publicly declared protests of two peoples. In this chaos and panic the only safety lay in the return of the Parliament, and public petitions from the Counties, cities and Lords revealed to Charles the isolation of his position. What Englishmen petitioned for, the Scots enforced. Ranke points out the historical irony of the situation in November 1640 : the monarchy, which had for forty years striven to impose union on England and Scotland, submitted in the end to a revolutionary union symbolised by the Scottish demand for an English Parliament to settle the troubles affecting both nations.[2] Three hundred members of the Short Parliament, reinforced by new Puritan and

[1] Gardiner, *Hist.*, IX, 118.   [2] Ranke, II, 215.

constitutionalist members, came to Westminster with powers no
previous Parliament had possessed. They were secure in the
support of public opinion, in the organisation of Pym and in the
protection of a victorious army. On their assembling, most of
Charles' servants fled abroad ; Laud and Strafford were imprisoned,
and Charles, for the first time in his reign, was left virtually alone
to face the consequences of his acts and to come to terms with his
new rulers.

From this time Laud and Strafford ceased to be authors of the
drama they had created and became mere symbols of the King's
weakness or the Commons' vengeance. In the year between the
arrest of Strafford and the Grand Remonstrance Charles was given
the opportunity to show his own abilities ; for, with the clean sweep
of his agents, none but he could save the relics of his Royal dignity.
He had a difficult, but not impossible task. Parliament was willing
to acquit him of all crimes except that of being misled by evil
counsellors, and was prepared to welcome his rule within the limits
they prescribed. The habit of reverence for Kings was deep-
rooted in the conservative gentry, who came, not to destroy monarchy, but to rescue it from perversion. Even after a year's bitter
disputes the Grand Remonstrance [1] traced all evils to a " corrupt
and ill-affected party," who used every means " to maintain continual differences and discontents between the King and his
people " ; and it claimed that " we have ever been careful not to
desire anything that should weaken the Crown either in just profit
or in useful power." [2] But Charles could not frame a policy of his
own, nor could he avoid evil counsellors ; except when defending
his religion, he could not deliberate or act without the decisive
intervention of another person ; and in this critical year the
dominating influence was more ruinous than any before—the
influence of his Catholic Queen.[3]

Henrietta Maria was trained in the ways of despotism and reared
in the memories of civil war, but she had no experience or understanding of the conditions of Parliamentary monarchy. As Queen

[1] Gardiner : *Docts.*, pp. 202-232.   [2] Clause 156.

[3] Ranke, II, pp. 154-6, dates her active intervention in politics from the Scottish
crisis of 1637-8.

she had grown from a frivolous girl to an ignorant and masterful woman ; in the process she had slowly won Charles' deep affection and the deep distrust of the Puritans.   They saw her chapel thronged with English worshippers ; they saw priests, if discreet, freely moving over the country, while crypto-Papists like Laud were expelling the true Protestant element from the Church.   Reunion was in the air, and was openly advocated by Secretary Windebank and Bishop Montague ; there was a Papal agent at the Queen's Court, and an agent of the Queen at Rome.   It is not hard to see why popular report implicated both Charles and Laud in a Catholic conspiracy of Pope, Court and Bishops, " waiting for an opportunity by force to destroy those whom they could not hope to seduce." [1]   Yet in fact the Queen cared little for affairs of State until her family and her personal pride were threatened.

She proved only too prompt and resolute in the crisis.   Whether inspired by instinct, or by memories of her father's career, she saw but one issue of the quarrel—war : and but one remedy—foreign arms.   She gave Charles a fatal confidence in her reckless and futile intrigues ; he resisted and irritated Parliament while she promised him the aid of the Pope, Spain and France, the Irish Catholics and the English officers in the Northern counties.   She fully justified the old suspicions, and united Lords, Commons and London on the safe ground of anti-Popery in the solemn Protestation of May 1641. [2]   Her Army Plots drove Parliament to secure itself by taking from the King the right of dissolution, and Charles had to sacrifice Strafford to save his Queen from a London mob.   The attack was closing in.   First, the King's public powers were in danger, but now his family was exposed to correction ; in June 1641 the Ten Propositions demanded that the Queen's household be purged of Catholics, and that Protestant nobles be introduced to restrict her communications and superintend the education of her children. [3] Finally in November the news of a wholesale massacre of Protestants in Ireland seemed a terrible fulfilment of Puritan prophecy and vindicated their attacks on the Queen and Strafford.   The King too was implicated in this last and worst plot ; reports came that

[1] Gardiner : *Docts.*, p. 219 : cf. clauses 87-94 of the Grand Remonstrance.
[2] Gardiner : *Docts.*, pp. 155-6.   [3] Gardiner : *Docts.*, p. 165.

the rebels acted under the protection of the Royal Seal.[1]   Charles
heard of secret conferences discussing the impeachment of his wife,
and his fears for her safety, together with the spur of her taunts, led
him to the desperate step of counter-attack.   His attempted violence upon the five Members in the precincts of Parliament invited
and justified violence in return, and the clumsy failure of the attempt
encouraged his enemies to drop all pretence of deference and to
seize the power of the sword which he had half-heartedly drawn.
In January 1642 the Commons fortified themselves in London and
assumed control of the militia, while the King and Queen were
forced to retire from Whitehall to Windsor.   But for an absolute
surrender by the King, civil war was inevitable ; it was only delayed
by lack of military organisation and by the reluctance of both sides
to force the outbreak when they were uncertain which of them
the inarticulate majority of the nation would support.

VI. The Responsibility of Charles I. for the Civil War

Yet Henrietta cannot with justice be accused of causing the
Civil War.   If we take the results, without the motives, of her
actions, we must give her credit for coming very near to prevent it.
The net result of her policy was that she drove from the King's side
all parties except her own household and the scattered Catholics of
the countryside, and that she provoked the Parliament to deprive
the King of the last relics of his secular powers.   There could be
no Civil War if the King had neither men nor weapons to fight with.
The Queen, far more than Pym, kept unity among her opponents
and inspired them to make steady and relentless progress towards
the supremacy of Parliament.   But even she could not preserve
unity for ever ; the revolutionary demands of the ' Root and
Branch ' men forced moderate Churchmen and constitutionalists,
despite themselves, to the side of the King, in order that the ancient
structure of the Church might not be destroyed.   The Grand
Remonstrance, by combining a programme of religious revolution
with fresh constitutional claims, made the conservative party in

---

[1] Cf. *Cambridge Modern Hist.*, Vol. IV, ch. 18, for a good discussion of Charles'
responsibility for the Irish Rebellion.

religion extend its policy to include the defence of the remaining secular powers of the King.   Thus the Episcopal party became the Royalist party, and Popish plots lost their magic as bonds of Protestant unions.   So wide was the breach that not even the danger from Ireland could bring Hyde and Pym together, and nearly half the Commons saw a darker menace in Puritanism than in the armed irruption of the King into their midst.   It was this fear, and this fear alone, that gave Charles a party and kept it for him through the Irish and militia crises; and with its emergence the period of Henrietta's unchecked control of the King was ended.   Charles' policy henceforth, though subject to the vagaries of his own irresolution and his wife's importunities, was framed as a whole by English, Protestant and constitutionalist advisers, such as Falkland and Hyde.

At the end of 1641 Charles emerged for the first time as a leader of men.   He must share equally with the Queen and Laud the blame of causing the fall of the Tudor system, but he alone caused the Civil War.   At the climax of Parliament's supremacy he made of his own accord a decisive stand for his Church, freeing at last his personality from entangling influences.   In October he gave the Lords a plain declaration to " assure all my servants that I am constant to the discipline and doctrine of the Church of England established by Queen Elizabeth and my father, and that I resolve, by the Grace of God, to die in the maintenance of it." [1]   In these words he pronounced his death-warrant and created a cause which won half-England to his side.   He had failed as King to give to English political life anything of permanence or utility, and he had discredited by abuse many necessary powers and forms of government.   But he now ensured victory for his party, though his death proved more servicable to it than his life.   The work of his opponents was doomed within a generation, once they began to uproot the fundamental institution of the national Church.

It did not mean that Charles would cease to make mistakes— mistakes which entailed defeats and death for himself and for his followers : he was no more resolute or trustworthy as a leader than before : but he fought for a greater thing than his own fate, for a

[1] Gardiner, *Hist.*, X, p. 39 : cf. *Docts.*, pp. 201-2 (Speech to Recorder of London, Nov. 25, 1641).

cause whose strength was not exhausted with the defeat of Royalist arms nor crushed by the armed garrison of Puritanism. Though in life he was but the leader of a party, he became by his death a part of our national tradition. Elizabeth had typified the England of arduous triumph, and though Charles could not bear comparison with her in active courage, he had a passive kind of courage and a steadfast devotion to his faith which made him a noble representative of a Church in adversity.

SUGGESTIONS FOR FURTHER READING

GARDINER, S. R.: *History of England, 1603–42.* (Longmans, 1883–4)

WILLSON, D. H.: *James VI and I.* (Cape, 1956)

McILWAIN, C. H.: *Political Works of James I.* (Harvard, 1918)

TAWNEY, R. H.: *Business and Politics in the Reign of James I.* (C.U.P., 1958)

TREVOR ROPER, H. R.: *Archbishop Laud.* (Macmillan, 1962)

WEDGWOOD, C. V.: *Thomas Wentworth, 1st Earl of Strafford, A Revaluation.* (Cape, 1961)

GIBB, M. A.: *Buckingham.* (Cape, 1935)

AYLMER, G. E.: *The King's Servants: The Civil Service of Charles I, 1625–42.* (Routledge, 1961.) See also *E.H.R.*, lxxii.

ASHTON, R.: *The Crown and the Money Market, 1603–1640.* (O.U.P., 1961)

DIETZ, F. C.: *English Public Finance: 1558–1642.* (New York, 1932)

WORMUTH, F. D.: *The Royal Prerogative, 1603–1649.* (O.U.P., 1939)

MOIR, T. L.: *The Addled Parliament.* (O.U.P., 1958)

NICHOLS SMITH, D.: *Characters of the Seventeenth Century.* (O.U.P.)

BACON, FRANCIS: *Essays.* (Everyman)

For further works on this period see also the list on pp. 62–3.

II

THE ORGANISATION OF OPPOSITION (1603-1642)

I. The Main Cause—Suspicion

When Strafford at his trial made his moving confession of political faith :

"I did ever inculcate this—that the happiness of a kingdom consists of a just poize of the King's prerogative and the subject's liberty ; and that things would never go well till they went hand in hand together," [1]

there was little to distinguish his views from those of the judges who were bent on his death ; his fate was determined, not by his theory, but by their memories and fears of his practice. By the same rule the whole Stuart system was condemned—on suspicion. The votes of the Long Parliament were votes of ' no confidence ' in the acts and intentions of Charles and Henrietta, rather than in the theories of Bacon and James. Monarchy was the only workable solution offered by either side between 1603 and 1647, and the Stuart ideal of government, apart from the ecclesiastical trimmings, was not denied in general until men saw the extreme conclusions and gross abuses derived from its application by a particular set of men. Both sides drew their inspirations from, and claimed adherence to the traditions of Elizabeth, and the idealised memory of her reign survived even the Civil War to influence Cromwell and Clarendon. No doubt there were wide differences in interpretations of the same theory, and it was the business of lawyers and theorists to emphasise the differences ; but these were mere skirmishes compared with the main battle of grievances. In every crisis it was not the theory, nor even the overt acts of the govern-

[1] Holdsworth, Vol. VI, p. 78.

ment that evoked the fiercest outcry ; it was the growing suspicion of sinister forces and motives at work in Court, Council and Church.[1] It is no defence for the suspects that the accusations were often absurd ; it is an added condemnation of their statesmanship that they had so isolated Crown and people as to make such misunderstanding possible. Suspicion was fatal to the Tudor structure which was cemented by national sympathy ; without that cement the complex framework fell to pieces almost before the Long Parliament set upon it.

II. The Composition and Grievances of the Opposition

What men, or classes of men, formed the driving force of opposition and organised discontent and suspicion into action ? How should the grievances and the efforts to remedy them be classified in order of historical importance ? What were the conservative and what the revolutionary elements in the movement ? In what sense, and to what degree, did the opposition represent the majority of the nation ? All these questions are of vital importance, not only to the historian, but to anyone who would understand the basis of modern English politics. This chapter does not pretend to answer them, but is meant to indicate some of the decisive factors that any solution must take into account, and to provide one method of analysis and approach.

The task of examining the nature of the opposition is more complicated than that of assessing the responsibility of the rulers. The first chapter dealt with a known and limited set of men and institutions and with views and motives publicly and securely expressed, but this method will not suffice for the present purpose. If the historian confines his attention to outstanding figures like Coke, Eliot and Pym, he falls into the error that Charles made in 1626, when he thought to get rid of ' factious interests ' by barring Arundel and Bristol from the House of Lords and by disqualifying Coke and five others from the Commons by pricking them as sheriffs. Next,

---

[1] There is one striking instance of a general principle arousing the whole nation, and that is the declaration of the Judges in favour of Shipmoney. Cf. *infra*, p. 44 ; Clar. *Hist.*, I, 87 ; Holdsworth, VI, 28.

classification according to forces—Parliament, Common Law, Commerce and Puritanism, involves a false separation; for the lawyer and merchant were often both Puritans and Members of Parliament. Though the Parliament had a force of its own through its traditions and statutory powers, yet its real strength came from other forces; it was, after all, only the place where lawyers, merchants, landowners and Puritans met to talk under special conditions of privilege and procedure. The Common Law, too, had an innate strength in tradition and in the organisation of its professors, but its chief importance in the struggle was as a method used by forces which were far stronger because they represented much wider interests. If Parliament and the Common Law had not been closely connected, they would have both been destroyed; the history of the times was full of the destruction of isolated assemblies and legal corporations; the Common Law was only saved by Parliament, and Parliament was only saved by its close connection with local organisation and legal ability. The decisive factor in the failure of the eleven years' tyranny was that the same class of men filled the posts of Justice of the Peace and Member of Parliament, and that, though their Parliamentary activities might be cut off, they and their kind could not be replaced in the necessary and continuous work of local government.[1] Now these men were far less influenced by governmental pressure than by the fears, prejudices and ambitions of the propertied classes of town and country. It is difficult to define this ' middle class '—for so it may be roughly described; it included both the families ennobled and enriched by Tudor policy and the struggling yeoman and shopkeeper, and had no clean edges of demarcation above or below; it had within it many cleavages of social and economic interest which accounted for the difficulty of concerted action and the impossibility of permanent union; but it had certain characteristics in common— conservatism: individualism: a jealous regard for property: a strong commercial sense: a constitutional belief in the trinity of King, Parliament, Common Law: and an uncompromising Protestantism.

The student, therefore, must fix his attention on this one historical

[1] Holdsworth, VI, 55-66.

—the middle class; having recognised this central source
opposition, he can proceed to distinguish its instruments and
grievances and to estimate its strength. Though the complaints
of the subjects were as varied as the offence of the rulers, the root
causes of discontent were religious and economic; many of the
legal and constitutional grievances arose as a consequence of religious or economic disputes. The political effects of these two main
causes must be separated and compared with care; for the student's
picture of Stuart England depends largely on whether he
ascribes greater importance to Puritanism or to shipmoney as
historical factors; whether he accepts the religious or the economic
interpretation of Stuart history.

III. Economic Grievances

(a) Revenue

A detailed catalogue of Stuart financial expedients reveals that
fatal mixture of ingenuity and stupidity which was the characteristic feature of the system; many of them, such as fines in distraint
of knighthood, violated the first maxim of taxation in being both
vexatious and unproductive.[1] Moreover the plurality of taxes
yielded surprisingly small results; it is doubtful if the first two
Stuarts ever succeeded in raising in any one year as much as was
annually granted by post-Restoration Parliaments. It is to their
credit that the incidence of taxation, except that of monopolies, was
rarely oppressive; even the forced loans of 1626-7 were fixed
according to the light assessment of the subsidies that Parliament
had refused to grant. The nation could well afford to pay, particularly in the fat years of peace between 1630 and 1640, and the
Crown had some justification for its demands, since the steady
depreciation of bullion was diminishing its ordinary revenues.
The rents of Crown lands, feudal dues and the profits of justice
were seriously affected by the fall of money values.[2] Even apart

[1] Cf. short summary in Tanner, pp. 73-9; full account in Dowell: *History of Taxes
and Taxation*, Vol. I, book 8, and Appendices IV and V.

[2] Cf. Prologue, p. 11, and Cunningham, *Growth of English Industry and Commerce*,
Vol. II, pp. 164-180. Harrington, alone of contemporary observers, saw the significance of the contrast between the impoverishment of the Crown and the growing

from this, they had rarely sufficed for any monarch; Parliament had risen to power through the fact that the King had not enough to live on, coupled with the theory that he should, except in emergency, live of his own. The problem was aggravated by Elizabeth's debts and James' extravagance. James' resolutions of economy were broken before they were made, and his demands of regular Parliamentary grants, culminating in the Great Contract of 1610-11, met with peremptory refusals owing to the ignorance and distrust of the Commons. If the Commons must be blamed for ignorance, both James and Charles are responsible for their distrust, in refusing to enlighten or compromise with the Commons on questions of policy; the typical remarks addressed by James to Parliament in 1610 fully explain the difficulty which he and his son had in extracting the free and cheerful grants of their subjects.[1] Elizabeth's pride was not incompatible with tact, but Stuart arrogance never failed to give offence.

When Parliamentary subsidies were lacking, the Crown was forced to desperate remedies, in squeezing the last penny from the traditional sources of revenue, and in demanding new supplies on plea of emergencies. The methods adopted fall into two main classes: those that revived old claims of Common Law and Statute, and those that depended on Prerogative extension of the Law. The antiquarian revivals were a fair retort to the obsolete theories of government to which the opposition clung; medieval England may have been a Paradise in the eyes of seventeenth-century lawyers, but it provided some lucrative compensations for Stuart Kings. Nevertheless, these fines, though they irritated important persons and classes, were not more than occasional expedients compared with the attempt to secure a permanent and independent income by the doctrines of absolute power. There were four kinds of revenue that aroused the whole nation to anger and fear of worse to come. Of these the least important, because the most violent, was the use of benevolences and forced loans. They could only

wealth of the middle class; to this cause he ascribed the inevitable decline of monarchy, on the principle that: "As is the proportion or balance of Dominion or property in land, so is the nature of the Empire." Cf. *Harrington and His Oceana*, by H. F. Russell Smith, p. 23.

[1] Prothero, pp. 293-5.

be used sparingly from their very nature, and the first large demand in 1626 produced within two years their death-warrant by the Petition of Right.

Shipmoney, impositions and monopolies inflicted heavier burdens, and were a more serious menace because they were screened by Law. The perversion of the old duty of maritime defence to an annual money payment by the whole country very nearly succeeded in nullifying the Petition of Right and in removing the need of any future Parliament ; it completely succeeded in dissipating the lethargy of a prosperous community and in convincing them of the urgency of resistance. Clarendon remembered vividly the prevalent wrath and anxiety,[1] and a country knight declared : " Trewly the common people had been so bytten with shippe money they were very averse from a cowrtyer." [2] The nation knew as well as Strafford that " the debts of the Crown taken off, you may govern as you please " ; and the finances which had begun to make up arrears in 1635 showed a surplus in 1638.[3] But that was the peak ; Scotland soon absorbed the surplus and the rest, while very few local officials could be forced to collect shipmoney, and London followed Hampden's lead in resistance. The propertied classes saw that the law as interpreted by subservient judges " left no man anything which he might call his own "[1] ; they also saw that, though the law knew no " King-yoking policy," the Scots appeared to have found a way. " In Hampden's case . . . the logical consequence of this theory of the prerogative was reached. . . . And there is no doubt that the clearness with which it was expounded had not a little to do with the completeness of its overthrow." [4] The Royal Judges made it clear to subjects that the law, their last guardian, was turned against them ; the failure of Hampden's legal appeal and of St. John's purely legal arguments proved the futility of such safeguards without political power over the Executive.[5] Consequently legal protests were abandoned for political resistance : first, passive resistance to shipmoney which

[1] Cf. Clar. *Hist.*, I, 87.   [2] Holdsworth, VI, 28, note 6.

[3] Tanner, p. 77.   [4] Holdsworth, VI, p. 28.

[5] Hampden's Case should be studied in : Gardiner, *Docts.*, pp. 105-124 ; Tanner, Appendix IV ; Holdsworth, VI, 49-54.

wrecked the Royal finances and made the return of Parliament inevitable, and then open support of the active resistance of the Scots. Yet it should be marked that the conversion of passive to active resistance was due to religious, not economic factors.

(b) Stuart Economic Policy

Even as the Judges used the magic phrase of " the defence of the Realm " to cover a system of direct taxation, as early as 1606 they had discovered the financial possibilities of the King's powers in " the regulation of trade." [1] It provided the one way in which the King could share the nation's growing wealth ; by impositions Salisbury cleared a debt of £700,000 in four years. The Judges in Bate's case had admitted that no new duties could be imposed on subjects for revenue purposes without the consent of Parliament ; but they also laid down that the King could impose regulating duties on foreign imports in the interest of national commerce. It was a fine, but sufficient distinction ; merchants like Bate and Chambers appealed in vain to the Courts, while the Commons made angry protests in 1610 and 1629, and attempted to revive their control of indirect taxation by refusing to pass the Tunnage and Poundage Act in 1626 ; Charles levied the duties none the less, and the merchants, after a short period of self-denying non-importation in 1629-30, admitted the King to a share of their profits. Their failure reveals the weakness of a legal opposition by an isolated section, and proves, what the Parliamentary lawyers were slow to grasp, that interpretation is nine-tenths of the law.

The Crown was less successful with its revenue from the grant of monopolies, which provoked wider and fiercer resentment. Elizabeth had been forced to withdraw her grants, and James in 1624 agreed to a Statute prohibiting the sale of a monopoly in any commodity except new inventions.[2] But since the Statute excluded corporations from its restrictions, what Charles was not allowed to give to individual courtiers he gave to groups of courtiers as a chartered corporation. When, however, Charles extended the scope of these corporate monopolies to the staple articles of

[1] Cf. Bate's Case in Prothero, pp. 340-353, and Holdsworth, VI, 42-8.
[2] Prothero, p. 275.

domestic trade, such as bricks, soap, coal and malt, not only the excluded merchants, but the main body of consumers were outraged by these " plagues of Egypt " ; hence the first concession he had to make was the revocation of commissions, patents and monopolies in April 1639, " of his mere grace and favour to all his loving subjects." [1]

There was, nevertheless, a genuine policy of regulation, which created a less vocal but equally dangerous opposition. Though none of the economic measures of James and Charles can be entirely freed from suspicion, owing to their deliberate confusion of principle in shipmoney and impositions, they made a praiseworthy effort to preserve the balance of interests in commerce, industry, and agriculture.[2] The danger was that in every case of intervention they supported the losing side against rising economic forces. They upheld the craftsman and small manufacturer against the encroaching control of commercial capital, and this accounted for many of their monopolist charters ; as between capitalists, they backed the producer against the middleman beloved of the Commons ; in the disputes of capital and labour, their partiality for their poorer subjects is shown by the frequent appeal of artisans to the Star Chamber and the steady flow of Orders of the Privy Council regulating wages and prices. The fixing of minimum wages and maximum prices, the careful guard on corn and wool supplies, the employment of the able-bodied poor and the relief of the impotent poor, all embodied an active policy of paternal socialism ; and it is significant that all these activities except poor-relief, ended abruptly with the fall of the Prerogative system, not to be revived till the nineteenth century.[3] Constant reproofs and fines were needed to compel local Justices and employers to observe these humanitarian restrictions on economic freedom. The fate of the best side of Stuart rule makes it clear that the Star Chamber was abolished for

---

[1] Bland, Brown and Tawney, *English Economic History*, pp. 472-5.

[2] Cf. Unwin, *Industrial Organisation in the Sixteenth and Seventeenth Centuries,* *passim,* and the caution in Tawney, *Religion and the Rise of Capitalism,* p. 169 :— " The Governments of the Tudors, and still more of the first two Stuarts were masters of the art of disguising commonplace, and sometimes sordid motives beneath a glittering façade of imposing principles."

[3] Cf. E. M. Leonard, *The Early History of English Poor Relief,* chs. 9-14.

its virtues as well as for its vices—because it oppressed not only the poor Puritan, but also the rich merchant and landowner, the " engrosser " of corn and the encloser of common land.

Enclosures provide a good example of Stuart aims and difficulties. Charles and Laud worked hard, in the Tudor tradition, to prevent landed capital absorbing smallholders, evicting tenant farmers and depopulating the countryside ; but where the Tudors had met with their most marked failure, the Stuarts were not likely to succeed. The fatal obstacle was that the laws against enclosing were administered by the offenders themselves ; the unpaid Justices of the Peace rewarded their invaluable services in other spheres by appropriating the neighbouring commons. Long lists of fines for depopulation,[1] and the high rank of some of the delinquents, for instance the Earls of Northumberland and Manchester, testify partly to the needs of the Treasury, but also to the real effort to preserve the class of peasant proprietors. Nevertheless, Charles did not secure the united support of the yeomen and mastercraftsmen in the Civil War, while a large minority of their oppressors served him to the last. The London prentice mobs and the troops of the Eastern Association are a sufficient proof that religious passions often overrode economic interests in the final alignment of parties.

IV. Religious Grievances

Eliot declared that " It is observable in the House of Commons as their whole history gives it, that wherever that motion does break forth of the fears or dangers in religion, and the increase of Popery, their affections are much stirred ; and whatever is obnoxious in the State, it then is reckoned as an incident in that." [2] This maxim is applicable to the opposition outside, as well as inside Parliament during this period, and explains why economic grievances must be considered as subordinate causes of the rebellion. Economic power was a decisive factor in the victory, but material

[1] Cf. Bland, Brown and Tawney, *op. cit.*, pp. 276-7, for a complaint against Laud's activities on the Depopulation Commission.

[2] Holdsworth, VI, 122, quoted from Eliot's *Negotium Posterorum*, I, 69.

injuries could never have welded and inflamed the opposition to
united action. The conviction that drew together varied and dis-
cordant interests and classes in the work of destroying the foundations of absolutism was that there was no alternative way of saving
the Protestant religion in the British Isles.

(a) *Popery*

The bogey of Popery is a vital factor of the religious opposition
which must be examined. What were its sources and justification ?
How far was it exaggerated ?

The English Catholics were a small and dispirited body, scattered
by geography and divided in policy and organisation. The
Jesuits tried to link English Catholicism to the plots and aims of
the Counter-Reformation, but they were quite willing to betray
the clumsy and amateur intrigues of their rivals, the English
secular priests.[1] The majority of lay Catholics wished to preserve
a discreet effacement and to find a compromise over the Oath of
Allegiance which would reconcile their national and religious
loyalties. Yet in the absence of a census, nervous Protestants
magnified their numbers, ascribed to the whole body the acts and
intentions of a few, and saw in them a potential Spanish army ;
for the plots of the first two years of James' reign obliterated the
memory of Catholic patriotism in 1588[2]. With this unknown
quantity in politics, suspicion could easily be transformed into
panic wrath, inflaming all public issues. Parliament steadily
demanded from James the stern enforcement of the Recusancy
Laws, and as steadily refused supplies except for a naval crusade
against Spain ; James' efforts to preserve peace and a balance of
power united all his critics in the general attack of 1621, and the
movement forced on him a Protestant war in 1624 ; Buckingham's
failure to fulfil national and Protestant expectations drove Parliament to a second general attack which broke finally its Tudor
tradition of co-operation with the Crown. Anti-Popery had

[1] As in the Bye Plot, 1603 : cf. Trevelyan, *E.U.S.*, pp. 82-98.

[2] The diocesan returns of 1603 record 8570 recusants and 2¼ million communicants ;
the recusants are found mainly in the northern dioceses, *e.g.* 2442 in Chester, 720 in
York. But the returns were incomplete, and give no guide to the numbers of
" Church Papists." Cf. Frere, *H.E.C.*, pp. 289-290.

become a permanent political force, a rallying cry for opposition ;
but before 1629 its influence was mainly confined to foreign policy.
It was left to Charles to inflame it to the point of danger and to
divert its attack to the heart of the Monarchy. By his Catholic
marriage and by his support of the Arminians in the English Church
he drew the suspicion of Popery on the Royal Court and the State
religion.[1] Henceforward ardent Protestants feared hidden Popery
in the government more than open Popery in the countryside or
abroad. It is this fact that explains the bitterness of the constitutional quarrel of 1629 ; the Monarchy was assailed at its vital spot,
the Royal Supremacy over the Church. The anti-Papal movement was complicated by the identification of a section of the
English clergy as hidden Papists ; and this identification, however
false, is the real starting-point of the Puritan Revolution, and the
vital clue to the understanding of the success of the opposition to
the Stuarts. The student must examine carefully the reasons for
such a remarkable and fateful belief. For though in 1629 it was
the belief of a minority—and this explains the success of Charles'
coup d'état—it accounts for the unity of the triumphant opposition
of 1640, and it helps to explain the split between moderate and
radical Churchmen in 1641.

(b) *The Arminian Clergy*

The new storm-centre was the small, but learned and able group
of clergy, of whom Andrewes and Laud were the most distinguished
and Montague and Mainwaring the most vocal members. They
needed Charles' political support, and he gave it them without discretion in return for satisfying his religious needs of liberal doctrine and dignified devotion. Andrewes and Hooker gave them
their belief in the Catholic continuity of the English Church, Cosin
their liturgy, and Laud their theory of Church government and
their political influence. They came with a programme of much-
needed reform, and though their aims were diametrically opposed to
Puritan ideals except in the sphere of morals, they also regarded

[1] The name " Arminian " was applied to Laud and his fellows by their enemies,
since their rejection of Calvinist predestination was similar to the views of Arminius,
a Dutch theologian who was condemned at the Synod of Dort in 1619 for advocating
the doctrine of Free Will.

the Elizabethan settlement as an unsatisfactory intermediate stage, imposed by political necessity. Their religious theory was eclectic—neither Protestant nor Romanist by nature ; their political views on Monarchy were uncompromisingly Protestant ; [1] and yet from 1629 onwards ' Papist ' and ' Arminian ' were considered by growing numbers of Englishmen to be convertible terms.[2] The accusation was rightly directed against two Bishops—Goodman and Montague ; and though its absurdity in Laud's case seems manifest to-day, it must be remembered that the Pope fell into the same confusion as the Puritans when in 1633 he offered Laud a Cardinal's hat. Only Henrietta knew the full extent of his obstinate Protestantism.

The Arminian complication brought about a concentration of forces and reduced politics to the simplicity of a duel between Laudian and Puritan reformers. Laud had the advantage of time through his influence with the King and his presence in the central government ; by 1637 he had attracted in a fatal alliance an Arminian King and Church, a Papist Queen and a corrupt Court. His enemies had to recover from the blow they had received in 1629 ; but though their gathering was slower, it was more formidable. Far from the Court, they concentrated in the local centres of society and government ; Bishop and parish priest were isolated amid the hostility of religious and economic malcontents. The French Queen's Court, Laud's Scottish Prayerbook, and Strafford's Irish Army convinced them that Arminian and Papist were working hand in hand.

It was the imaginary Popish plot of Laud and Strafford, together with the staffing of an English army by Catholic officers, which made London, the counties and the Short Parliament refuse all loans and supplies ; and the new policy of destruction, as distinct from obstruction, of Royal power was inspired by the very real Catholic intrigues of Henrietta after the fall of Laud and Strafford. " The general hope and expectation of the Romish party, that their

[1] Cf. Figgis, *The Divine Right of Kings*, ch. 8 ; Prothero, pp. 435-9.

[2] " For an Arminian is the spawn of a Papist . . . and if you mark it well, you shall see an Arminian reaching out his hand to a Papist, a Papist to a Jesuit, a Jesuit gives one hand to the Pope and the other to the King of Spain." Rouse, M. P., in 1629, in Tanner, 68, note 1.

superstitious religion will ere long be fully planted in this kingdom again " [1] could only be defeated by the removal of all autocratic rights and weapons of a susceptible King and a corrupted
Episcopate.

Yet though the national fear of Popery destroyed the Prerogative, the Puritan identification of historical Anglican institutions
with Roman Catholicism offended in the end the good sense of
conservative Englishmen and thereby produced the Civil War.
There was general agreement in " clipping of these wings of the
Prelates by which they have mounted to such insolencies " [2]; such
was the purpose of the impeachment of Laud, the abolition of High
Commission and the removal of the Bishops from the House of
Lords. But the conservative party in both Houses would go no
further in Church reform than suggesting some Parliamentary and
lay checks on Episcopal authority. The question that divided
England after the political settlement had been completed in August
1641 was: where lay the greater danger to true religion—in
" Jesuiting Popery " or in the " raging sects " of Adamites,
Brownists, Baptists, and the Family of Love ? Strafford's last gift
to Puritanism, the Irish Rebellion, provided the answer for a bare
majority of the Commons, and drove moderate Puritans like Pym
and Hampden to accept the radical programme of the younger
Vane, Cromwell and St. John. The result was the Grand Remonstrance against " the malignant and pernicious design . . . of the
Bishops and the corrupt part of the clergy, who cherish formality
and superstition as the natural effects and more probable supports
of their own ecclesiastical tyranny and usurpation." [3] But moderate Churchmen saw greater danger to the Church in the remedies
proposed and they finally rejected the identification of the English
Church with Rome. The Remonstrance did not create the two
parties of the Civil War, but it defined their attitude to all the issues
in addition to religion, and it finally separated the conservative from
the revolutionary elements in the opposition.

[1] Root and Branch Petition, Dec. 1640—Gardiner, *Docts.*, p. 143.

[2] Lord Digby, Feb., 1641 ; cf. Tanner, p. 102.

[3] Gardiner, *Docts.*, pp. 202-232.

(c) *The Grievances of the Puritans.*

What sort of men and what ideals provided the lead and driving force of the opposition ?   It is not an easy task to define the character of Puritanism in the first half of the seventeenth century.[1] The name of " Puritan " was too frequently used as a term of abuse, like that of " Lollard " in the later Middle Ages and that of " Communist " to-day, to serve as an accurate classification, and yet it meant something more than a morality of disapproval.   Before 1603 it included two well defined groups—the Presbyterians of Cartwright and ' Martin Marprelate,' and the Separatists of Browne and Barrow ; the same clear division reappears between 1647 and 1662.   But in 1603-47 the sects were insignificant until Laud began to fill them in the years of his Visitation, and they were hated by all parties in the Church ; while the Puritans within the Church cannot strictly claim the name of Presbyterian, although their Calvinist doctrine was unimpeachable.   Even under the influence of the Covenant they set up a poor imitation of Genevan theocracy (what the Scots dismissed as " a lame Erastian Presbytery "), and without that external pressure they were content with modification of the existing system.   James made one of his worst mistakes in identifying the authors of the Millenary Petition with his late masters in Scotland ; for the Hampton Court Conference reveals the moderate and compromising spirit of the English Puritans, by which he might have profited if he had listened to Bacon instead of to Cecil and his own fears.   The Puritans were not distinguished by fundamental differences of doctrine until Charles took up the Arminian cause ; before then the majority on both sides accepted Archbishop Whitgift's Lambeth Articles of 1595 and the anti-Arminian decrees of the Synod of Dort (1619).   Though there was a fundamental distinction between the Puritan insistence on the exclusive authority of the Bible and the Anglican belief in Divine sanction for the historic forms and traditions of the Church, the moderate party consented to tolerate " things indifferent " and

---

[1] A modern large-scale history of Puritanism is badly needed : there is nothing of great value since Neal's *History of the Puritans* (4 vols., 1732-8), except Mr. Tawney's brilliant, but too brief remarks in *Religion and the Rise of Capitalism.*

reserved their opposition for customs and ceremonies which, in their opinion, violated the letter or spirit of Scripture.[1]

It must be admitted that James and Bancroft were highly successful in breaking up the organised Presbyterian party among their clergy, and that, for all James' threats of " harrying them out of the land," they secured their end with a minimum of vigour and a maximum of tact. The historical prominence of the " Pilgrim Fathers," who escaped from England in 1608-9, has obscured their original insignificance in influence and number, and similarly the number of clergy who suffered deprivation for refusing Bancroft's compromise of subscription without total conformity has been greatly exaggerated.[2] In fact James pursued the policy of Elizabeth and Whitgift with marked leniency ; there were no new penal laws and far less banishment and imprisonment. One reason may be that the need was less. The Presbyterians had dominated the Universities, found strong protectors at Court in Leicester and Essex, powerful advocates such as Peter Wentworth in the Commons ; they had even won the sympathy of many Bishops and of Archbishop Grindal. But the reaction against their system and methods led by Andrewes, Hooker and Bancroft made them unfashionable at Court and University, and since 1593 they had been fighting a losing defensive battle with little public support. In this respect the Hampton Court Conference signifies the decline rather than the beginning of a movement.

James could defeat a weakened clerical enemy, but he stirred to action a new force—lay Puritanism. One of the most striking features of the victorious Puritan movement is the absence of prominent divines until the rise of the chaplains of the New Model Army. A lay attack on a clerical State succeeded a clerical attack on a secularised Church. The lead was taken by country knights, city merchants and Common lawyers, and their weapons were not the pulpit or theological controversy, but the Law Courts and the Commons in Parliament. They did not try to revive the " Classes " and " Prophesyings "[3] of the previous generation ;

---

[1] Cf. Millenary Petition and Summary of Hampton Court Conference in Prothero, pp. 413-7.

[2] Frere, *H.E.C.*, pp. 320-1.

[3] Cf. Prothero, pp. 196-9, 205-9 ; Classis, pp. 468-70, and Scott Pearson.

they restricted their aims to secure a "preaching ministry," the reform of the ecclesiastical courts and the enforcement of Parliamentary control over the pretensions of Convocation and Catholic activities. They chiefly objected to Bancroft's elevation of Bishops by Divine Right above the lay control of Parliament, to the expulsion of clergy for nonconformity, to the Canons of 1604 (which were not submitted to Parliament), and to the employment by Church Courts of secular judges and secular penalties. Excommunication by lay officers " for trifles and twelve-penny matters," [1] and the oath " ex officio," " whereby men are forced to accuse themselves," were the two most unpopular features of the Court of High Commission, which by its arbitrary procedure and comprehensive jurisdiction smelt strongly of a Papal Inquisition.[2] For ten years Chief Justice Coke attempted to restrict the activities of Church Courts by the Common Law writ of Prohibition, in face of the wrath of James I.; but after his fall in 1616 the Puritans found no Judge anxious to befriend them at the cost of the Royal displeasure.[3] Their other hope was in Parliament's resentment of the claims of Convocation and High Commission. However, the debates and obstructive methods of the Commons brought little concrete results. James' early Parliaments were more concerned with Recusants, privileges and Proclamations, and the later Parliaments, although they ostentatiously avoided Communion at Westminister Abbey " for fear of copes and wafer cakes and such other important reasons," [4] were ineffective except in foreign policy. The most striking Puritan success—the abandonment of the Declaration of Sports of 1618—was won outside Parliament, and even amid the Protestant fever of 1621-4 James was able to veto two Bills for stricter observance of Sunday.

What was needed for effective action was a general stirring of the nation. It came with the participation of England in the Thirty Years' War and the rise of Arminianism; Buckingham and Laud provided Puritan leadership with a solid following of anti-

[1] Cf. Millenary Petition of 1603 and Commons' Petition of 1610 in Prothero, pp. 413-6 and 302-7.

[2] Cf. High Commission of 1611 in Prothero, pp. 424-434.

[3] For Coke and Prohibitions, cf. Holdsworth, V, 429-432.

[4] Frere: *H.E.C.*, p. 376.

Roman nationalists. Events from Charles' accession justified Brooke's diagnosis that Puritanism was " the root of all rebellion and disobedient intractableness, and all schism and sauciness in the country " ;[1] the movement which had risen from the remains of Elizabethan Presbyterianism and had survived its defeats in James' reign attracted, between 1624 and 1628, the leading spirits of the opposition (except Wentworth and Selden), and was organised into a definite Parliamentary party with a clear programme and a large body of public opinion behind it. Its leaders, Phelips, Eliot, Strode and Pym, planned the first sustained and comprehensive attack on the powers, in addition to the abuses of the Crown ; they abandoned the defensive for the initiative, and presented the nation with an alternative set of political and religious principles. In 1629 political Puritanism was fully developed and defined as a result of the quarrel with political Arminianism ; the era of personal government created no new parties but compelled all men and classes in the nation to make their choice between the two. When Laud's ecclesiastical system began to operate in full force, an ever increasing number of Englishmen turned to the Puritan minority for leadership, and the history of Puritanism became for a time the history of England.

V. The Importance of Strictly " Constitutional " Grievances

The holy alliance of Puritanism and Capitalism was the decisive factor that united unorganised discontent into systematic and purposeful opposition ; the grievances and ambitions of the two allies gave that opposition its driving force and its programme.

If, then, religion was the chief issue and property a close second, are there any constitutional questions of vital importance which do not arise from these two sources ?

(a) *The Local Roots of the Commons*

From 1603 to 1629 most of the religious and economic quarrels had a constitutional setting in the Courts or in Parliament ; since

---

[1] Hutton : *H.E.C.*, p. 34.

the methods were legal and Parliamentary, the whole issue can be called constitutional, in contrast to the period 1629-40, when the opposition could not appeal to Parliament and ceased, save in Chambers' and Hampden's cases, to appeal to Law.   Yet the contrast is not so great as it appears.   After 1629 the Parliamentary opposition transferred its obstruction from the central to the local constitution, and this local constitutional struggle was in fact, though not in reputation, more important than that at Westminster.   It proved that the Royal victory over Parliament was illusory ; when the central assembly was suppressed, Charles found his schemes " wrecked on the rocks of the county organisation." [1]   It was useless for purposes of absolutism to resolve Parliament into its constituent parts of Shire and Borough, when the parts were more firmly rooted than the whole ; the only hope of permanent control lay in the substitution of a professional bureaucracy, after the manner of Richelieu or Napoleon, for the amateur rule of local magnates ; and such an experiment was impossible without vast revenues and a standing army.[2]   Nevertheless the local institutions could not organise national control as they could preserve national resistance ; hence the chief importance of the Parliamentary history of this period is that it concentrated the agents of local government, and gave them a common policy and a common allegiance.   The quarrel between King and Parliament also represented the quarrel between the central and local administration.

(b) The Work of the Lawyers in the Commons

This close connection of the Commons with the local organs of government was a source of both strength and weakness to the Parliamentary opposition ; it gave it a representative character and it gave it a parochial and unsympathetic attitude to national and foreign problems.   Moreover, as it was stamped with provincialism, so did the co-operation of the Commons' lawyers imprint upon it the stamp of legalism.   Consequently the medievalism of the squires and the technicalities of the lawyers turned the fight for

[1] Tanner : p. 78.

[2] Cromwell's Major Generals were the nearest English equivalent to such a system before the nineteenth century.

liberty and religion into wrangles over procedure and privileges ; much of the fiercest debate was on points of law and custom which had very little relation with any important issue. The Commons assumed all the airs and jealousies of a Court which was both autonomous and arbitrary,[1] and built up at their will a body of law which formed the basis of the outrageous claims of the irresponsible Hanoverian Parliaments. Yet a bristling fence of Committees, Orders of the House and Protestations was their sole protection against the overriding demands of Royal sovereignty ; in answer to James' theory, based on Roman Law, which derived the rights of Assemblies or Diets solely from the concession of the Prince, the Commons asserted that their powers had sturdier roots than Royal condescension : " Our privileges and liberties are our right and due inheritance, no less than our very lands and goods. . . . Our making of request in the entrance of Parliament to enjoy our privilege is an act only of manners." [2] This was the challenge which faced the first Stuart at the beginning of his reign, and the same challenge of the combined rights of Property and Parliament drove the last Stuart King from his throne. James I. saw that its implications reduced Monarchy to a legal fiction, even though the challengers denied them ; it was " as if a robber would take a man's purse and then protest he meant not to rob him." [3] It is not hard to imagine the apoplectic wrath of Henry VIII. or Elizabeth if they had heard such insolent words, and it is but fair to James to ascribe some of his high claims to the Commons' aggression as well as to his own vanity. Privileges could wax as mightily as Prerogative, if the Commons were allowed to control and define their nature and extent ; a comparison of the Apology of 1604 with the Protestation of 1621 shows how fast the Commons' claims had grown. They claimed in 1621 freedom of speech, not only on questions put before them by the King, but on all " arduous and urgent affairs " of State, Church and Law ; they recorded the new claim " that the Commons in Parliament have like liberty and freedom to treat of these matters in such order as in their judgments

[1] Cf. Floyde's Case, 1621, Prothero, pp. 337-9.
[2] Apology of the Commons, 1604 : Prothero, pp. 286-293.
[3] James' answer to Commons, 1621 ; Prothero, pp. 312-3.

shall seem fittest " ; and all this with no check but the " censure of the House itself." [1] When an elaborate system of procedure was evolved in the hands of the opposition for the chief purpose of obstructing Government business,[2] there was no Government possible until the obstruction was removed ; and when in 1629 the opposition seized upon the person and powers of the Speaker and made him a servant of the House instead of the chief servant of the Crown in the House, the process of self-determination was complete ; and the Commons were entrenched in a position which made Parliament useless as an aid to Royal government. Charles declared justly that " under pretence of liberty and freedom of speech . . . they take liberty to declare against all authority of Council and Courts at their pleasure . . . and to erect an universal over-swaying power to themselves." [3]

Yet paralysing tactics do not make a substitute for government, nor do obstructionists make good statesmen. The leaders of the Commons always exposed themselves to the criticisms of constructive reformers such as Bacon and Strafford, because, while they refused to the Crown the necessary discretion to provide for emergencies or for new conditions not foreseen by old laws, they did not see that such a refusal threw back the responsibility for government on themselves. Coke and Eliot did not want to govern, and they had no adequate theory of modern government ; their attitude was more reactionary than conservative, more legal than political. Though they revered medieval precedents they learned no lessons from the medieval " lack of governance " which accompanied those precedents. Their disregard of Tudor experience, save when it favoured Parliamentary privilege, led them to advocate the division and strict definition of the twin powers of Parliament and Crown, and to set above them as arbitrator the Courts of the Common Law. They were blind, until the Common Law was used against them, to the necessity of a political theory ; they clung to the " rule of law " until the events of 1629-40 proved that it really meant the rule of men who interpreted the law. Nothing but a series of political

[1] Prothero, pp. 313-4 : Protestation of 1621.

[2] Redlich, *Procedure of the House of Commons*, and Holdsworth, VI, 88-103.

[3] The King's Declaration showing the causes of the late Dissolution, in Gardiner : *Docts.*, pp. 83-99.

shocks compelled the Long Parliament to seize sovereignty for itself. It was Henrietta, and not a reasoned theory, that made English Parliaments undertake the business of government; although, as early as 1610, the full theory of the supremacy of the King-in-Parliament, as it is understood to-day, was proclaimed in the Commons by Whitelocke.[1] With this exception, the opposition leaders accepted the views of Coke and Selden, which amounted to a negation of government; for though the Prerogative that they denounced sounds a monstrous tyrant, it means nothing more than discretionary executive power, which is essential to any sound Constitution. "The King had no prerogative, but that which the law of the land allows him," held the Judges in the Case of Proclamations (1610),[2] and Selden believed that Prerogative " is something that can be told what it is, not something that has no name . . . the King's prerogative is not his will, or—what divines make it—a power to do what he lists. . . . The King's prerogative, that is the King's law . . . the law that concerns him in that (*i.e.* any given) case." [3] Above that law rose, in the embodiment of Edward Coke, the spirit of Magna Carta, who " is such a fellow that he will have no sovereign." [4] It is therefore not surprising that the fight of the lawyers ended in immediate defeat, although they forged the weapons and returned to guide the victorious party of 1640. There are two outstanding causes of their failure. First, Charles and his Privy Council weighed the balance in favour of the Prerogative Court and, after Coke's dismissal, destroyed the nuisance of two parallel and rival Judicatures by a careful selection and discipline of the Common Law judges. The ' Rule of Law ' was unattainable until the tenure of judicial office was freed from Royal pressure. Secondly, the Commons could never carry through a programme of reform until they controlled their own dissolution, directly or indirectly, and safeguarded their members from arrest

---

[1] Prothero, p. 352 : " The sovereign power is agreed to be in the King ; but in the King is a twofold power ; the one in Parliament, as he is assisted with the consent of the whole state ; the other out of Parliament, as he is sole and singular, guided merely by his own will." Cf. Holdsworth, VI, pp. 84-7.

[2] Bicknell, *Cases on the Law of the Constitution*, 7 : cf. Holdsworth, IV, pp. 296-7, and VI, p. 31.

[3] Prothero, p. 412.   [4] Holdsworth, V, p. 451, note 2.

at the close of their sessions.   These indispensable powers were lacking to the opposition of 1603-29, and the want of them made failure inevitable.   It became obvious that no legal or constitutional tactics would ever secure them ; it needed the revolutionary force of national indignation, backed by the threat of arms.   So at last militant Puritanism, after exhausting its patience with the traditional remedies, turned to the Scottish army and the London mob as the necessary instruments of correction.

VI. The Opposition Split (1641); Radicals and Conservatives

The student of Stuart history must always keep in mind one fundamental fact : that both parties of the Civil War, and both parties of the Restoration and 1688 Revolution sprang from the opposition formed against the system of the first two Stuart Kings. The Cavaliers of romance—the Courtiers and Catholics—were a source of weakness rather than of strength to Charles I. ; the men who made his resistance possible were the men who broke the unity of the opposition in November 1641, when they divided against the Grand Remonstrance.

The Remonstrance revealed to all those incompatible elements which had existed in the opposition from the beginning of the struggle.   The violence of the rupture is less to be wondered at than the long life of the coalition.   Nothing but the folly of Charles and his Queen, and the panic fear of Popery and evil counsellors could preserve harmony between the radicalism of the Puritan middle class and the conservatism of nobles like Digby, lawyers such as Hyde, and devout and cultured landowners of the type of Falkland.   By August 1641 the destruction of political abuses was complete, and the masses of men whose politics consisted of negatives—no Star Chamber, no High Commission, no Popery—were satisfied.   But when they found that others valued the work done only as a preliminary to revolutionary reconstruction, they began the weary fight against innovation over again ; they entered upon the unending struggle between the radical and conservative forces of the nation—a struggle which took its first shape in civil war and assumes to-day the less dramatic form of a General Election.

Partisans, both modern and contemporary, tend to regard Hyde, Falkland, Culpeper and Digby either as repentant sinners or as apostate wretches. Yet in fact, while conditions had changed around them, the Anglican constitutionalists stood where they had always stood ; they merely faced about to resist innovation from below in the same spirit in which they had resisted it from above. They had attacked and removed abuses of Monarchy and Episcopate because they loved the institutions themselves ; they were faithful, both in attack and in defence, to their antiquated theories. They rejected the pleas of Charles and Pym alike that the complex business of government could not always be carried on within the strict bounds of legal cases and precedents.

The futility of this attitude is best illustrated by Hyde's confession of the opportunity lost by Charles and his new advisers in the summer of 1642. When the King, by a timely show of force, could have crushed the dilatory preparations of the Parliament, " these men still urged the execution of the law," thinking " that what extravagance soever the Parliament practised, the King's observation of the law would, in the end, suppress them all."[1] This policy lost the war, and the same policy was responsible for the failures of the constitutional protests against the Stuart despotism. The student must look elsewhere for the secret of successful opposition in 1640-2 ; he must look to the ruthless ability of the Puritan minority, to suspicion of the Court, to fear of the Counter-Reformation which united even Englishmen and Scots, to the greater fear and hate of Ireland. Despotism fell because, for a few vital months, the fears and suspicions of the majority supported the schemes of the minority. Neither radicals nor conservatives could have succeeded alone ; but they had one strong link—a common Protestantism. That link was forged by the real and imaginary dangers to Protestantism caused by Charles and his servants ; that is, unity and success was imposed on the opposition from without. For this reason, the historical verdict on the deaths of Laud and Strafford must be, not judicial murder, but political suicide.

Yet if victory did not come from within, the Civil War did. The catastrophe of the Ulster massacre undid all the labours of the

[1] Clar. *Hist.*, II, p. 250.

summer of 1641 ; for it rendered the constitutional settlement null and void. That settlement had two main features : one, a division of powers between King and Parliament—a division that greatly favoured the Parliament, but a division none the less : the other, a weak and crippled Executive. There was no provision for unity and strong administration in an emergency ; Charles had cried " Wolf, wolf," too often. So when a real, as distinct from a " shipmoney " emergency arose, when an army was needed to save the Protestant settlers and punish the Papist rebels, Parliament saw that the King could claim lawful control of an instrument by which he might restore the whole apparatus of despotism.[1] The dilemma exposed the fundamental political cleavage in addition to the existing religious cleavage, between Puritan and Anglican. The conservatives were prepared to face the risk of despotism rather than abandon the Monarchy to complete domination by a Parliament controlling its own army ; they preferred the possibility of a new Strafford to the certain destruction of the old English constitution. The radicals saw nothing but their labours jeopardised and their future reforms denied them ; they could not trust a Popish Court to deal adequately with a Popish rebellion, which it had probably encouraged.[2] While conservative principles remained untouched by the crisis, the Puritans advanced to the new revolution which they saw looming before them.

SUGGESTIONS FOR FURTHER READING

In addition to books suggested at the end of the first chapter, the following are recommended :

AITKEN, W. A. and HEMMING, B. D. : *Conflict in Stuart England.* (Cape, 1960)

MOSSE, G. L. : *The Struggle for Sovereignty in England.* (Michigan, 1950)

RELF, F. N. : *The Petition of Right.* (Minneapolis, 1918)

[1] For the Militia Ordinance of March 5, 1642 and its consequences, cf. Gardiner *Docts.*, pp. 245-7, 248-9, 254-261.

[2] Cf. *C.M.H.*, Vol. IV, ch. 18.

Judson, M. A. : *The Crisis of the Constitution, 1603–42.* (Rutgers, 1949)

Notestein, W. : *The Winning of the Initiative by the House of Commons.* (O.U.P.)

Hulme, H. : *The Life of Sir John Eliot.* (Allen and Unwin, 1957)

Bowen, C. D. : *The Lion and the Throne.* (Hamilton, 1957)

Hill, C. : *The Economic Problems of the Church from Whitgift to the Long Parliament.* (O.U.P., 1956)

Puritanism and Revolution. (Secker and Warburg, 1958)

Haller, W. : *The Rise of Puritanism.* (O.U.P., 1938)

Mathew, D. : *The Jacobean Age.* (Longmans, 1938)

Stone, L. : *Social Change and Revolution in England, 1540–1640.* (Longmans, 1963)

Adair, E. D. : ' The Petition of Right '. *History,* v.

Gordon, M. D. : ' The Collection of Ship Money in the Reign of Charles I '. *R.H.S.T. 3rd Series,* iv.

Hinton, R. W. K. : ' Government and Liberty under James I '. *C.H.J.,* xi.

Keir, Sir David : ' The Case of Ship Money '. *Law Quarterly Review,* lii.

Usher, R. G. : ' James I and Sir Edward Coke '. *E.H.R.,* xviii.

Willson, D. H. : ' Salisbury and the Court Party in Parliament '. *American Historical Review,* xxxvi.

' Summoning and Dissolving of Parliament, 1603–1625 '. *American Historical Review,* xiv.

For books on economic problems, see pp.317–18.

III

THE PURITAN CONQUEST

THE aim of this chapter is to account for the victory of the Puritans in war and politics between 1642 and 1651. The conquest contains two clearly marked stages, divided by the events of 1647. The first stage consists of the conquest of the Royalist and Anglican party by the uneasy alliance of Englishmen and Scots, Presbyterians and Independents; and the second consists of the conquest of three nations, with their diverse parties, by the single-minded force of the Independent Army.

I. THE CAUSE

The first and most obvious question is—what was the " Cause " which drew men either to the Royal Standard or to " live and die with the Earl of Essex " ? What was it that prevented the continual negotiations from ever restoring the peace that all men longed for? At Colnbrook in November 1642, at Oxford in 1643 and Uxbridge in 1645 peace was nearly in sight, and if one examines the professed " war aims " of each side, it is difficult at first to find any serious bar to agreement. The King took his stand for " the true reformed Protestant religion, the known laws of the land, the liberty and property of the subject, and the just privileges and freedom of Parliament " ; [1] while the Parliament at Westminster raised an army " for the preservation of the public peace, and for the defence of the King and both Houses of Parliament." [2] The popular terms " Cavalier " and " Roundhead " are not very helpful,

[1] Clar. *Hist.*, II, p. 312.

[2] Clar. *Hist.*, II, p. 178 : The Royalists satirised these mental acrobatics in a ballad with this refrain : " 'Tis to preserve his Majesty, That we against him fight."

for the King's Court was ruled at first by grave and sober men like Falkland, who disliked war and frivolity equally ; nor was the army of Essex distinguished as a whole by its religious fervour or shorn locks.[1]   It cannot be called strictly a war between King and Parliament, unless a majority of the Commons and a minority of the Lords at Westminster without the King constitute a Parliament more than a minority of the Commons and a majority of the Lords with the King at Oxford.   Even the religious breach was not irreparable until 1643, when the need of outside help tied the reluctant Puritans to the rigid Presbyterian system of the Scots and drove Charles to compromise his Protestantism by making truce with the Irish Catholics.   The true cause of division must be found, not in the professions of the politicians, but in the motives which inspired large numbers of non-political Englishmen to risk their lands and lives in the quarrel.

(a) *The Ideal of Allegiance*

The Royal Army was created by two national instincts—conservatism and loyalism.   No doubt zest was added to loyalty by the general hate and fear of Puritan severity ; men who had not endured the arbitrary rule even of an anointed King would not stomach it from fanatical Parliament-men.   But stronger than this was the fear of anarchy ; when Parliament made laws at its fancy and destroyed all certainty in institutions, property and religion, the conservative element turned back to the Crown as the one fixed star in a madly revolving universe.   There was a Royalist doggerel which vividly expresses this feeling :

> " The mitre is down,
>   And so is the Crown,
>   And with them the coronet too ;
>   Come clowns and come boys,
>   Come hobber-de hoys,
>   Come females of each degree,
>   Stretch your throats, bring in your votes,
>   And make good the anarchy." [2]

[1] Firth, C. H. : *Cromwell's Army*, p. 231.
[2] Firth, *Royal Historical Society Transactions*, 1912, p. 61.

Charles appealed to such men to defend two of their fundamental institutions—the Church and Property. He won their sympathy in adversity, as he had failed to do in prosperity, since his fate was linked with that of the national Church : " The crown was crucified with the creed." [1] He won their respect because he stood in 1642, as Hampden in 1637, for the rights of Property. The King had his rights no less than his subjects—rights that the Law protected and on which the Law depended : rights that Parliament ought to respect and every man was sworn to defend—and if they were taken from him, the foundations of justice and property fell with them. Doubts and theories were over-ridden by the urgent duty of personal allegiance ; Lord Paget spoke for thousands whom the Militia Ordinance of March 1642 turned against the Parliament :

" When I found a preparation of arms against the King under a shadow of loyalty, I rather resolved to obey a good conscience than particular ends, and am now on my way to His Majesty, where I will throw myself down at his feet and die a loyal subject." [2]

(b) *The Ideals of Rebellion*

The gathering of loyal subjects to defend their King was natural enough ; it would have been a historical miracle if it had not occurred. What is more surprising is the strength of the party which rose at once for the Parliament in armed defiance of traditional loyalty. The name of Essex had not the magic of the King's, nor had the wordy appeals of the Parliament the force of a personal summons ; " Privilege of Parliament " was not such a stirring battle-cry as " Dieu et Mon Droit." Yet the response was immediate. Even the fleet, which Charles had raised with such trouble, deserted him for the men who had refused to pay for it ; despite the King's appeal, Warwick the Admiral and almost all his ships took their orders from Parliament, " by whose authority the Kings of England have ever spoken to their subjects." [3] The rising was not against the King—regicide was far distant—but

---

[1] Firth, *Royal Historical Society Transactions*, p. 60.

[2] Firth : *House of Lords*, p. 114. Cf. also May : *History of the Long Parliament*, pp. 270-1 for the effect of Edgehill in driving neutrals to the side of the King, " to whom it proved a kind of victory."

[3] May, *op. cit.*, p. 209 ; cf. also Clar. *Hist.*, II, pp. 215-225, on the loss of the Fleet.

against the "malignants" who surrounded and corrupted him, whose "traitorous counsels" would deliver them into the merciless clutches of foreigners and Papists; they knew that the Queen was seeking help abroad, and they were convinced that the King's advisers were in league with the Irish rebels.

The Parliamentary "Cause" contained complicated, and often conflicting sets of ideals. There were three chief groups—the religious enthusiasts, the mere Parliamentarians and the democratic republicans. The first class was inspired by a devotion to a spiritual ideal—the Kingdom of God upon earth; they set up against the creed of personal loyalism the creed of the fear of God, which casts out all earthly fears—even the fear of Rupert's cavalry charge.[1] Such men formed the backbone of the Eastern Association and the New Model armies, and proved themselves the natural leaders of the struggle. They fought for Parliament, not as an end in itself, but as a means for attaining the true end of pure religion; yet neither they nor their allies realised at first that their support of Parliamentary institutions was strictly conditional.

The bulk of Charles' opponents can be included in the second class—the unqualified Parliamentarians. Their views had a Puritan tinge, but their main object was to preserve the Parliamentary gains of 1640-2 from Royalist reaction; they were ever ready for a compromised peace and would have gladly ended the war in 1643, and again in 1645—between Marston Moor and Naseby. Despite their Presbyterian beliefs, they were fundamentally conservative in politics; though they feared absolutism, they respected Monarchy as a pillar of society like unto themselves. Such views led the great corporations, London above all, to throw their decisive influence on the side of Parliament, and such was the spirit which animated the old "country" nobility.

The third class, composed of those who wished to complete the work of secular reform by establishing a representative republic, more or less democratic, with or without a nominal King, only came to prominence as a result of the confused passions and debates of

---

[1] Some of them derived great comfort from denunciation of malignants; cf. Sergeant Nehemiah Wharton's views on "Goddam blades, hatched in Hell," in Firth: *Cromwell's Army*, p. 280.

the period of settlement (1646-9). Their leaders—Marten, Lilburne, Overton and Rainborough—were more noisy than influential, except on the occasions when they won the favour of Cromwell's troopers or the London apprentices; they were, in general, politically insignificant and served only as a source of irritation and reproach to the Puritan and Parliamentarian interests.[1]

(c) Mixed Motives

Neither side could have won without the determination and leadership of its enthusiasts, and yet minorities cannot maintain a prolonged contest with their own lives and purses unaided. Both parties claimed to be protecting the liberties of the people and both had to force men to be free. Both King and Parliament took to impressment by the end of 1643; half of the New Model infantry consisted of pressed men until the army was placed on a more or less " peace establishment " in 1651, and though the cavalry of both sides usually attracted sufficient volunteers (largely because of the greatly superior pay), most of the horses and arms were supplied after the first rally by requisition or confiscation. Similarly free gifts soon failed to bear the expense of war, and forced loans, confiscations, free quartering, and taxes, direct and indirect, provided the main revenues of the military chests. Thus a good deal of party unity and strength depended on discipline by " force majeure " of the vast mass of wavering or indifferent neutrals; even so in the separatist West of England there arose in 1645 organisations of Clubmen prepared to resist the intrusion of national problems and demands into their local interests.[2]

There were two other factors, important if not decisive, which determined the choice of many. The local influence of great Lords and landowners, quasi-feudal in its character, decided, as it had done in the Wars of the Roses, the political complexion of large

[1] Cf. Gooch: *English Democratic Ideas in the Seventeenth Century*, chs. 4 and 5.

[2] Gardiner: *History of the Civil War*, Vol. II, pp. 264-7 and 305-7. In the winter of 1642-3 the counties of Devon and Cornwall drew up a treaty of neutrality for " an honourable and firm peace between the two counties of Cornwall and Devon," as if they were sovereign States; and there were similar movements in Yorkshire and Cheshire. Cf. Clar.: *Hist.*, II, pp. 459-461. It is difficult to find a parallel to this provincialism except the treaty between the Earls of Chester and Leicester in the reign of Stephen.

districts; *e.g.*, the Newcastle and Stanley interests held the North for the King, except Hull and the West Riding where the Fairfaxes were strong, while Hertford and Hopton controlled the South-West; for the Parliament, Manchester and Cromwell dominated the Eastern Counties, Lord Saye and Sele held Banbury and Oxfordshire, the Earls of Warwick and Holland held Essex and Berkshire respectively. Where territorial influence was divided, as in Lincolnshire between the Royalist Earl of Lindsey and Lord Willoughby of Parham, or in Warwickshire between the Earl of Northampton and the Puritan Lord Brook, the general issue was subordinated to a bitter family quarrel such as reminds the historian of the days of Stephen or Henry VI.[1]

To counterbalance these anarchic tendencies, there was one centralising factor in English life which favoured the Parliament. Since it was in possession of the regular machinery of government, many were unconsciously influenced by the habit of obedience to the commands of London, rather than those of York or Oxford. Such men tended to regard the rule of Parliament as normal and regular, a rule that prudent and peace-loving men should obey, and they had an inbred distrust of a King who did not act " in a Parliamentary way." [2] Hence, in the " Paper War " of March-August 1642,[3] although Parliament was more aggressive in the exchange of manifestoes, Charles' designs on Hull and Portsmouth convinced many hitherto indifferent spectators that he was threatening to disturb the peaceful routine of their ordinary daily lives. They did not make stout partisans, but they formed a useful reserve for the party that held London and the State offices; hence the strategic and political importance of London in the war.

Most wars begin as a Crusade, but all end as a business. From the beginning of the Civil War both sides had to supplement enthusiasm by material offers of reward. Now, though the English

[1] Cf. May, *op. cit.*, pp. 213 ff.; and Firth, *House of Lords*, p. 123 : " The more the local history of the Civil War is examined, the more evident becomes the survival of feudal traditions and feudal feeling."

[2] Coke's phrase in the debates of 1628 : " We cannot take the King's trust but in a Parliamentary way "—*i.e.* on record in Statute (Gardiner, *History*, VI, 274).

[3] Cf. Gardiner, *Docts.*, and Clar., *Hist.*, Vol. II; especially the Nineteen Propositions of June, 1642.

are an incurably civilian race, they have always produced a quota of adventurers and soldiers of fortune. It was men of this type who provided the rudiments of military experience for the amateur armies of 1642. The same spirit attracted veterans of the Dutch and Swedish armies, squires and undergraduates to serve under Rupert ; while apprentices, yeomen and unemployed were tempted by Parliament's more tangible offers of pay and by the prospect of confiscated lands. As the war dragged on and the King's poverty became more manifest, this factor proved one of the chief advantages of the Parliament, whose pay, though always in arrear, was higher and more certain ; it accounted, with impressment, for the rapid formation of the New Model Army, since many Royalist prisoners preferred to continue their profession in their late enemies' service rather than languish in prison.[1]

II. MILITARY RESOURCES AND ORGANISATION

Since the war was mainly a conflict of ideals common to all Englishmen, it was impossible that there should be any neat division of districts or classes ; there were two parties in every city or county, even in Parliamentary London and in Royalist Oxford. However a certain set of religious and political convictions seemed to attract large groups of men with similar occupations. In general, the extremes of rich and poor followed the King, though of the Peers, the richest and most distinguished—Northumberland, Bedford, Essex and Pembroke—stood by the Parliament and continued the medieval tradition of rebellious " overmighty subjects." [2] The backbone of the Parliamentary cause was provided by the freeholder and lesser country gentleman in the county, and the rising tradesman and apprentice in the town ; [3] very few towns of importance save dignified or uncommercial towns such as Chester, York

[1] The early chapters of Firth's *Cromwell's Army* give the best short account of the personnel and organisation of the forces of both sides.

[2] Cf. Firth : *House of Lords*, pp. 115-120, for the views of the Parliamentary Peers, and Clar. : *Hist.*, II, pp. 537-541 for characters of Pembroke and Northumberland.

[3] Cf. Clar. : *Hist.*, II, p. 296, on the division of forces in the West: " Gentlemen of ancient families and estates " were for the King, but " people of an inferior degree, who by good husbandry, clothing and other thriving arts, had gotten very great fortunes " supported the Parliament. Cf. also Tawney : *Religion and the Rise of*

and Oxford turned voluntarily to the King, owing to " that factious humour which possessed most corporations, and the pride of their wealth " ;[1] and the Eastern counties, where the freeholder was strong, were the solid and unswerving allies of the Parliament. This superiority can be shown by a short comparison of the rival resources and organisation. The number of combatants was fairly even ; Sir Charles Firth estimates it at roughly 60,000 on each side. Parliament's advantage lay in the concentration and availability of their troops, and after 1644 in better discipline ; but both sides suffered from desertions and the policy of detached garrisons, and the decisive battles, except Marston Moor, were fought by comparatively small armies.[2] Numbers depended largely on pay, and Parliament had by far the richer war chest. It could draw by gift, loan or tax on most of the circulating wealth of the nation and on all the profits of foreign trade ; by 1644 it had a regular income from customs, excise and levies from the counties (the " monthly assessments " for the New Model), and it possessed the central machinery of collection at London. Charles, on the other hand, relied mainly on his private wealth, the gifts of his wealthy supporters, and the forced contributions of the country districts which his garrisons controlled ; consequently his revenues declined from the first and were doomed to rapid exhaustion.[3] The two decisive weapons in revenue as in strategy were the Fleet and London. The ships of the Parliament kept open the seas and the ports, revictualled and reinforced Hull, Plymouth and Gloucester, and gave Parliament the outer lines of communication and the power of outflanking their enemies ; Charles, without a fleet, was unable to touch the wealth and arsenals of the ports, was cut off from Ireland and abroad, and exposed to attack from the more mobile forces of the Parlia-

Capitalism, pp. 198-211 on " Puritanism and Society," especially a description of Bristol in 1645 : " The King's cause and party were favoured by two extremes in that city ;- the one, the wealthy and powerful men, the other of the basest and lowest sort ; but disgusted by the middle rank, the true and best citizens " (p. 202).

[1] Clar. : *Hist.*, II, p. 470.   [2] Cf. Firth : *Cromwell's Army*, pp. 22-35.

[3] The Marquis of Worcester was believed to have spent £900,000 for the King, and the Marquis of Newcastle £700,000 (Firth : *House of Lords*, p. 24). Firth also shows (*Cromwell's Army*, pp. 26-29) that financial needs, rather than strategy, split the Royal armies into isolated garrisons ; large numbers of troops were used as tax-collectors, with disastrous results to their discipline and popularity.

ment.   London, above all, clinched the superiority of the Parliament.   London not only gave it its vast wealth, credit, and the machinery of government, but it had in August 1642 the only effective military organisation in the country.   While the " trained bands " of the counties were soon discarded as useless by both sides, or, if used, would not venture beyond their shire boundaries, London's 18,000 citizens and apprentices formed a comparatively well-drilled unit, steady under fire and stout in morale ; they saved their city from Charles at Turnham Green in November 1642 and they saved Gloucester in 1643.[1]

Finally, the radical weakness of Charles' position was the geographical grouping of his supporters.   Although he had friends in large numbers everywhere except in London, the East and South-East, his strength lay in the poorer and isolated corners of his Kingdom, where provincial feeling was keenest.[2]   His most solid block of territory was in Wales and the Marches ; the Royalist North was threatened by the Scots, Fairfax and Hull, and the Royalist South-West was masked by Plymouth, Taunton and Gloucester.   As long as these obstacles remained, it was impossible to entice his followers from their homes, and it was equally difficult to maintain communications between his scattered armies.   The Parliamentary districts had a centre in London and a circumference in the Fleet ; they consisted mainly of a solid block of the richest and most populated counties in England—Surrey, Middlesex, Kent, Essex, East Sussex and the Eastern Association.   Geography was on the side of rebellion.

III. The Strategy of the First Civil War

In summarising the campaigns of the Civil Wars, it is necessary to begin with two warnings.   First, the student must not expect nor imagine too much pure strategy in a war directed largely by amateurs and politicians ; secondly, though he must concentrate on the

[1] Firth : *Cromwell's Army*, pp. 13-18, illustrates the defects of the militia in the Bishops' and Civil Wars.   Cf. Beaumont and Fletcher, *The Knight of the Burning Pestle*, Act V, for some lively satire on the City Bands.

[2] Cf. p. 68, note 2.

decisive battles of the field armies, he must remember that they
comprise only a small proportion of the fighting. The war was
mainly a mass of local sieges, raids and feuds ; it is significant that
when one side evolved a professional army in 1645, it ended the war
within a year and held down three hostile nations for fifteen years.[1]
Both Cavaliers and Roundheads were nearly ruined by local and
personal factions ; but while the latter secured military unity for
the critical period of 1644-6, the Royalists never healed the breach
between civilians and soldiers. Clarendon confesses that :

" Want of discretion and mere folly produced as much mischiéve
as the most barefaced villainy would have done . . . and the King
suffered as much by the irresolution of his own counsels, and by the
ill-humour and faction of his own counsellors . . . as by the indefatigable industry and the irresistible power and strength of his
enemies." [2]

However, amid a great deal of aimless fighting, there are two main
offensives which must be examined—the Royalist offensive of
1642-3 and the Parliamentary offensive of 1644-5.

(a) The Royalist Offensive, 1642-3

The King's first need was a central base in the Midlands as a
concentration-point for his scattered allies, and his first task was to
remove the local obstacles which detained them ; when once the
concentration was effected, he must advance on London, whose
wealth and organisation could alone restore him to power and
respect. His first mistake was to make Oxford his base and the
home of his Court. Oxford was too far removed from the Royalist
strongholds and was always an exposed outpost, threatened by
London, Banbury and Hampden's country ; it was in the end fatal
to Charles, since fear for his Court led him, after his capture of
Leicester in May 1645, to return towards Oxford—into the arms of
Cromwell and Fairfax at Naseby. Oxford was only useful as long
as he held to his first plan of campaign, which was to surprise
London, without waiting for his full supports, before Parliament had

[1] The only historical works that deal exclusively with the Civil War are County
histories ; cf. list in Firth : *Cromwell's Army*, p. xi.
[2] Clar. : *Hist.*, IV, 2.

organised their defence ; but his own preparations were too slow, and though Essex opened the way to London after Edgehill, the City Bands closed it effectually at Turnham Green. After this half-hearted effort, which hardly deserves the name of offensive, he was compelled to adopt a more ambitious scheme, and that quickly. Time fought against him ; if his enemies could avert disaster and preserve their spirits on the defensive, they would drain his resources and wreck his improvised government while reserving and perfecting their own.

Thus Parliament was thrown on the defensive under the cautious guidance of Pym and Essex. Later, the Parliamentarian leaders were severely blamed by Cromwell for their Fabian strategy ; but what may have been a fault in 1644 was a saving virtue earlier.[1] Apart from considerations of military prudence, the psychological effect of an early victory might have been a dangerous reaction in favour of the outraged King, similar to the effects of Edgehill, but on a much larger scale ; Manchester saw the danger when he declared :

" That war would never be ended by the sword but by accommodation, and that he would not have it ended by the sword, and that if we should beat the King ninety-nine times, and he beat us but once, we should all be hanged." [2]

The urgent tasks were to secure the defences of London and to maintain local resistance in Royalist districts in order to prevent an overwhelming concentration in the Thames valley.

Hence the decisive events of the first stage of the war were the repulse of the first attack on London in November 1642, the consolidation of the Eastern Association and its extension northwards in 1643 to Lincolnshire and Hull, and the relief of Gloucester in September 1643.[3] The second and more dangerous design on London by three armies from Oxford, Yorkshire and the West never matured, because Plymouth, Gloucester, Hull and Lincolnshire immobilised the Royalist forces. There was a temporary balance of success for the King in territory gained, but the indecisive nature of the success was a great triumph for his opponents ; for it meant

---

[1] Cf., p. 77.   [2] Firth: *House of Lords*, p. 145.
[3] Cf. Clar.: *Hist.*, II, pp. 394-8 and III, pp. 165-170 for London and Gloucester.

that the Parliament could in future take the offensive against a divided and weakened foe.

(b) The Parliamentary Offensive, 1644-5

In 1644 the war was approaching its climax ; there was a hardening in temper and an extension of area. In both camps the professional soldiers began to chafe under the prudence of the politicians and demand a fight to a finish. Whereas in 1642 and 1643 both sides vied in their professions of desire for peace, so that " whoever opposed it would be sure to be by general consent a declared enemy to his country," [1] after Uxbridge the pretence was abandoned, the lists of proscribed persons grew longer, and the mention of peace brought on the offender the suspicion of treachery. At Oxford the dominance of the Queen and Digby in the King's counsels stiffened the resistance and led to the Cessation of Arms in Ireland which released the Royal troops for English service ; in London the signing of the Covenant with the Scots on September 25, 1643, put a further bar in the way of compromise and restored the martial spirit of the Commons and citizens ; both alliances inflamed the struggle with renewed and increasing religious passion.[2] In January 1644 the Irish force landed in Cheshire and began to clear up the Parliamentary outposts, such as Nantwich, which hampered Royalist communications between North and West ; and at the same time Leslie, with a much larger force, crossed the border to co-operate with Fairfax in Hull, and so to take the Royalist North in the rear.

Thus began the Parliamentary offensive, and its first-fruits was the destruction of the Irish reinforcements by Fairfax at Nantwich ; by this victory the Cavalier North and West were separated by Fairfax's army and garrisons. All that the King gained by his Irish policy was the exasperation of his enemies (who killed, as at Naseby, any Irish of either sex), and the general reproach of sacrificing his religion to military necessity.[3]

---

[1] Clar.: *Hist.*, II, p. 303. [2] Gardiner : *Docts.*, pp. 267-271. (Covenant.)

[3] Clar. : *Hist.*, III, p. 315 ; for his discussion of the political effects, cf. III, 268, and 486-490 (Uxbridge). Clarendon blames the Parliament for refusing to send forces to crush the Irish rebellion, and asserts that in the reinforcements, there was " not an Irishman among them."

The intervention of the Scots was far more effective, if not decisive. Their services to the Parliament have been, and still are weighed in the partisan balance of nationalist and religious prejudice; even Clarendon, who suffered less from Scottish than Cromwellian hostility, records with an Englishman's glee how Leslie " fled ten miles and was taken prisoner by a constable " after Marston Moor, while the English Puritan cavalry " charged on that side so well, and in such excellent order, being no sooner broken than they rallied again and charged as briskly." [1] However there can be little doubt that the Scots gave the Parliament a needed margin of numerical superiority and provided, besides mere numbers, a trained and experienced force, even though the price in cash and commitments was heavy. Without such aid the Parliament would hardly have had time and security to reorganise its scattered and dispirited troops into the formidable machine of the New Model Army, which alone could render Scottish help as unnecessary as it was unwelcome. [2]

Taken by itself, the campaign of 1644 was no more decisive than that of 1643; it did little more than restore to the Parliament some territory and advantages equivalent to those lost in the previous year. Yet the lack of decision in 1644 was not fatal to the Roundheads in the sense that the partial successes of 1643 had ruined Charles' hopes; for the superiority in morale, numbers and wealth was still increasing, and they still held the initiative. They had only to proceed warily—avoiding still the risks of any desperate battle which might expose London to a sudden change in the fortunes of war—and they could isolate and round up their opponents in the separate corners of England; then, when Charles could no longer bring up his reserves, they could surround him and his Court, and force him to accept their terms without the risk and shame of a violent assault upon his person. Such appears to have been the plan of Essex, Manchester and Waller, the leaders of the main Parliamentary armies. But there arose a more vigorous and less cautious party which demanded, through the voices of Cromwell and Vane, an immediate trial of force with the King's field

[1] Clar. : *Hist.*, III, pp. 374-5.
[2] *I.e.* unwelcome to the Independents and moderate Puritans.

army.[1]   This division of policy, which became acute after the deaths of Pym and Hampden in 1643, was reflected in the military operations of 1644.   Manchester was given the united forces of Essex, Waller and the London bands in October 1644, 16,000 in all, with " positive orders to fight the King as soon as was possible." [2] He had a golden opportunity to end the war when he caught the inferior field-army of Charles at Newbury, cut off from its Oxford base ; but he missed his chance, partly through poor tactics and chiefly through his political fears of the results of a decisive battle. It was clear to the militant party that the complete victory they desired could never be attained until the whole spirit of the leaders and " storm-troops " of the army was remodelled, as well as its organisation.   Hence the failure of the second battle of Newbury discredited the "half-measures" party ; the results were the "Self-Denying Ordinance " [3] and the creation of a central striking force, with the power and the will to strike hard and strike home.

Apart from this abortive campaign, the main operations of the Parliamentary offensive were carried out on the old lines, and produced a lucky success and a glaring, though not disastrous failure. Marston Moor destroyed the Royalist control of the North, which Rupert and Newcastle had secured in 1643 ; but this " sudden and unnecessary engagement," as Clarendon calls it, was only made decisive by Rupert's and Newcastle's desertion of their men after the battle.   On Newcastle's flight abroad his personal following dispersed and left no rival to the Fairfax interest in the North, while Rupert's horse did not again " ever bring any considerable advantage to the King's service, but mouldered away by degrees." [4] This collapse exposed the whole Royalist position ; for there was nothing to detain the armies of Leslie and Cromwell from marching South and driving the King into Cornwall or Wales.

Against the loss of the North and the material losses of infantry and artillery must be put the defeat of Essex's attempt to break up

[1] Cf. Ranke, II, pp. 417-422; cf. also Firth's *Cromwell*, and Gardiner: *H.C.W.*, Vol. II.

[2] Clar. : *Hist.*, III, p. 432 ; account of 2nd Newbury, pp. 432-441.

[3] For the two Ordinances, see Gardiner: *Docts.*, pp. 287-8, and Firth : *Cromwell's Army*, pp. 31-3 ; *House of Lords*, pp. 144-151.

[4] Cf. Clarendon's mournful analysis of the results of the battle, *Hist.*, III, pp. 372-384.

the Royalist hold on the South-West. Lostwithiel was as inglorious for Essex as Marston Moor for Rupert, but its effects were both minimised and localised.[1] Plymouth still threatened the victorious Royalists, while the drunkenness of Goring allowed the Parliamentary horse to escape ; the captured infantry had to be turned loose, since prisoners were an expensive luxury, and the only real gain was 38 pieces of artillery. So 1644 ended with the King clinging precariously to Wales and the West with diminished and mutinous forces, while the Parliament was made to set its House and Army in order under the stern and confident leadership of the Independents.

The campaign which was crowned with the victory of Naseby of June 14, 1645, differs in two important respects from those of preceding years. First, the King received new and surprising support from Scotland ; Montrose created a dangerous diversion in the absence of Leslie's first-line troops, and threatened to restore a balance of forces in the North.[2] If Charles had struck North after the storming of Leicester, the New Model might have found a much more determined and a more united foe ; but the opportunity to regain Scotland and the North of England was entirely neglected. The second and decisive new factor was the appearance of Cromwell and a well-trained, well-paid, and mobile army, 21,000 strong. Though half the army was at first composed of pressed men, they were reliable because of the organised pay and equipment, and their freedom from political and religious intrigues ; moreover, the whole force was leavened and stiffened by the religious enthusiasm of its Independent commanders, officers and cavalry units. This spirit is well illustrated by the declaration of 1647: "We were not a mere mercenary army, hired to serve any arbitrary power of State, but called forth and conjured by the several declarations of Parliament, to the defence of our own and the people's just rights and privileges."[3]

---

[1] Cf. Clarendon's account of Lostwithiel, *Hist.*, III, 398-405.

[2] John Buchan's *Montrose* gives a vivid and sympathetic sketch ; for the Royalist failure to see their chance, cf. Clar.: *Hist.*, III and IV.

[3] Firth: *Cromwell's Army*, p. 354; for summary of New Model, cf. pp. 66-7 . For the new spirit: " a spirit that is like to go as far as a gentleman will go," cf. Cromwell's reminiscences in his speech to Parliament of April 13, 1657; against " gentlemen that have honour, courage and resolution in them," he raised " such men as had the fear of God before them, and made some conscience of what they did."

A single ideal united these men against Cavaliers whose personal allegiance was by now rent by personal ambitions; and to direct them there was for the first time unity and freedom of command. Both the Parliament and the Committee of both Kingdoms reluctantly surrendered control of strategy and appointments to the Commander-in-Chief; thus England obtained, as a rod for her back, her first Regular Army.

The struggle of amateurs against professionals, especially when the amateurs had not the advantage of morale, was hopeless and short. Fairfax sought the King wherever he lay—before Taunton, in Oxford and in Leicester, while Charles, ignorant of his enemy's movements and new designs, exposed his person and his only mobile army in the East Midlands, since his one chance lay in preserving contact through the Midlands with his widely scattered supporters. But as Charles divided his inferior forces, by garrisons at Leicester and Oxford, Fairfax concentrated the armies of the Parliament; and at last (despite Presbyterian hostility), he secured the services of Cromwell, the one man who could stand the shock of Rupert's attack. In the fateful battle of Naseby the King and his troops bowed before the irresistible attack of the man who from the first declined to hamper his acts by the pretence of fighting for " King and Parliament," the man who had declared that " if the King chanced to be in the body of the enemy that he was to charge, he would as soon discharge his pistol upon him as at any other private person."[1] The complete victory of Independent discipline over Cavalier rushes in the fiercest hand-to-hand combat of the war is best explained in the words of Clarendon:

" And that difference was observed shortly from the beginning of the war, in the discipline of the King's troops and of those which marched under the command of Cromwell (for it was only under him, and had never been notorious under Essex or Waller), that though the King's troops prevailed in the charge, and routed those they charged, they never rallied themselves again in order, nor could be brought to make a second charge again the same day : ... whereas Cromwell's troops, if they prevailed, or though they were beaten and routed, presently rallied again, and stood in good order till they received new orders. All that the King and prince could do could

[1] Clar.: *Hist.*, IV, p. 305. For Naseby, cf. IV, pp. 40-47.

not rally their broken troops, which stood in sufficient numbers upon the field, though they often endeavoured it with the manifest hazard of their own persons. So that in the end the King was compelled to quit the field, and to leave Fayrefax master of all his foot, cannon and baggage ; among which was his own cabinet, where his most secret papers were, and letters between the Queen and him ; of which they made that barbarous use as was agreeable to their natures, and published them in print, that is, so much of them as they thought would asperse either of their majesties and improve the prejudice they had raised against them, and concealed other parts which would have vindicated them from many particulars with which they had aspersed them."

The victory of Naseby was decisive both in strategy and morale. The isolated garrisons fell helplessly in their turn, while even Rupert urged peace, and the local forces melted away in disorder. Goring disappeared into France ; Greenville turned to pure plundering ; Rupert finally crushed Charles' unyielding spirit by surrendering Bristol in four days after promising to hold it for four months ; Poyntz broke up the King's last body of horse at Rowton Heath and destroyed his forlorn hope of joining Montrose ; Montrose himself was being surprised and crushed at Philiphaugh by Leslie's returning troops. Between two enemies Charles chose those of his own nation, and his surrender to the Scots at Newark began his last fight for his throne, in which diplomacy and the divisions of his enemies proved stronger weapons than the arms of his friends.[1]

IV. The Spoils and Quarrels of the Victors : 1646-9

The direct effect of Naseby was to demoralise and discredit the Royalist party, but it was not long before it produced equal confusion among the victors. The diplomatic campaigns of 1646-9 make the military campaigns of 1642-5 appear simple by comparison ; their abortive schemes and quickly changing combinations provide an almost impenetrable maze for the historian. All the waste of men and treasure seemed to have settled and created

[1] For the Royalist collapse and recriminations, cf. Clar. : *Hist.*, IV, pp. 48-154.

nothing. A long search for " settlement " was begun which led England through Regicide, Republic and Dictatorship back to Monarchy again. King, Parliament and Army àdvanced successive schemes until the solution that the Army adopted and enforced put an end to all the others and completed the Puritan conquest. However, the soldiers had no full and distinct programme before 1647 ; at first they were content to let Parliament make a general settlement with the King, provided they were assured of their two main interests—arrears of pay and religious toleration. The student must therefore begin with the first attempt at settlement, the failure of which brought the army into action.

(a) *The Failure of the Parliamentary Scheme for Settlement* : 1646-7

The negotiations at Newcastle, where Charles remained in Scotch custody, broke down because Charles, unlike his captors, had a single aim which he would not compromise. He fought no longer for power, throne or life, but for a Church he had sworn to preserve ; for her he would make any concession except a compulsory Covenant, embrace any ally, and refuse any terms that did not give him some hope of restoring Episcopacy and the Prayerbook. The immediate result was that the Scots surrendered their recalcitrant King to the English Parliament, on payment of debts and the condition of Charles' personal safety ; but Charles had more to hope from the moderate English Presbyterians than from the rigid Covenanters. By offering temporary concessions he tempted the moderate party led by Holles and Waller to renew their allegiance, and he created an immediate division in the Parliament.[1] The Presbyterian leaders hardly knew, between Charles and Cromwell, which man to fear and which to trust ; both threatened their religious supremacy, but Charles at least accepted the principle of a national religion and had a dislike equal to theirs of the religious anarchy of the sects. So in 1647 a section of the party was drawing unhappily and secretly to the leadership of their prisoner, and was prepared to sacrifice the gains of war through fear of religious and civil anarchy.

[1] For the Propositions of Newcastle and the subsequent negotiations, cf. Gardiner : *Docts.*, pp. 290-316 and xliii-xlv.

But their decision came too late ; their " distracted and divided counsels " ruined them.   Clarendon aptly contrasted their methods with those of the Independents :

" The Independents always did that which, how ill and unjusti-fiable whatsoever, contributed still to the end they aimed at, and to the conclusion they meant to bring to pass; whereas the Presby-terians, for the most part, did always somewhat that reasonably must destroy their own end, and cross that which they first and prin-cipally designed." [1]

The crisis came when in May 1647 Parliament ordered the New Model to disband without pay, without religious security, and before an open settlement with the King was made.   The soldiers sus-pected treachery and foresaw persecution ; they mutinied, and won their Generals to their side.   In two strokes they asserted their latent supremacy—by the capture of the King and the march on London.   They now determined to dictate a general settlement, in addition to securing their particular interests.   Ostensibly they came to London as the protectors of a " Free Parliament " which had been outraged by London Presbyterian mobs ; but in fact Parliament, as well as Charles, had found a stern master, and the sign was the Army's first purge—the expulsion of eleven Presby-terian leaders from Parliament.

(b) *The Army's Settlement* : 1647-9

The intervention of the Independent Army in politics in August 1647 is the watershed of the Puritan Revolution.   It was the cul-mination of revolt and the beginning of reaction ; it put old causes out of date and set before the nation new and urgent issues.   One example must suffice to show the change.   The First Civil War had been fought to preserve the powers and dignity of the Parlia-ment ; in 1647 both Presbyterians and Independents showed an utter disrespect for it—abused it, intimidated it, and abandoned it for the King to serve their ends.   Pure constitutionalism was dead ; while Charles and the Presbyterians conducted debates on the Parliamentary or Royal control of the sword, the object in dispute took control of them.

[1] Clar. : *Hist.*, IV, p. 303.

Two factors postponed the full effects of this intervention. First, the Army had to define and agree upon its political programme, and agreement was only reached after protracted debates and the suppression of a second mutiny in November 1647. Ireton's " Heads of Proposals " was balanced against the more radical " Agreement of the People " drawn up by the regimental representatives or "Agitators";[1] Cromwell was forced to sharper words and sharper deeds before he could restore unity and discipline. Then, once unity was won, the Army leaders, with their recent experience in mind, showed more caution and respect in their negotiations with authority. They treated patiently, and even hopefully, with Charles, and they allowed the chastened Parliament to renew its proposals in the modified form of the Four Bills of December 1647.[2] But a second crisis forced them to action again and ended their hesitation. Charles had scattered the seeds of dissension far and wide, and they bore unexpected fruit in Scotland. In December 1647 he concluded a secret "Engagement" with the moderate party of Hamilton, who led the third Scottish invasion of England within ten years and provoked the Second Civil War.[3]

The war of 1648 has not the dramatic interest nor the complexity of the great Civil War ; it consisted of small and scattered risings in Wales, Kent and Essex, and a half-hearted Scottish raid ; it was crushed by the prompt action of Fairfax and Cromwell at Colchester, Pembroke and Preston. Yet in a sense the second war was more decisive than the first. It finally showed the Army leaders what they must do. They were challenged by a joint movement of Cavaliers and Presbyterians for a complete restoration of the Monarchy ; their answer was to abandon compromise and decide on the complete abolition of the Monarchy. The issue was clearer than in 1642, and the temper more savage; deportations and executions followed, and Charles was no longer the King but the " man of blood." Some of the results of 1648 were distinct from, and even contradictory to the results of 1645. The first contest secured the gains of the English and Scotch Parliaments and created an evangelical alliance of the two peoples ; the second broke this

---

[1] Gardiner : *Docts.*, pp. 316-326 and 333-5.   [2] Gardiner : *Docts.*, pp. 335-347.
[3] Gardiner : *Docts.*, pp. 347-352.

alliance, destroyed the Presbyterian experiment in England, and began the Cavalier-Presbyterian combination which was to effect the Restoration of 1660. Above all, the second war decided, far more than the first, the destinies of the two protagonists, Charles and Cromwell. Naseby had cost Charles his power, but Preston lost him his throne and life ; the first war had produced Cromwell the General, the second, Cromwell the Dictator.

The reckoning of the victorious and exasperated soldiers was swift. First, the treacherous Parliament must be disciplined. It had no claim on their forbearance, since it had always been hostile to Dissent, and even in 1647 had wasted valuable time in preparing a penal code against heresy. It was not an object of adoration, but a means to an end : " the rights and privileges of the people and the safety of the whole." [1] When, in neglect or defiance of the lesson of 1648, it reopened negotiations with the blood-guilty King, Pride's Purge fell upon it in December 1648 and expelled all save a hundred resolute Independents and Republicans. The pitiful remnant of the Lords was left to sit forgotten around their fire a few weeks longer, but in March 1649 the House of Lords was abolished as " useless and dangerous to the people of England." [2]

But the settlement of institutions was incidental to the main task the Army set before it ; their real quarrel was with a man—Charles Stuart. They demanded justice for blood shed and security for the work of reconstruction ; they saw no way but a clean cut—the head of Charles " with the Crown upon it." [3] Although the death of Charles would make an irreparable breach between them and two nations, their convictions or delusions drove them to seal their conquest by the execution of " the occasioner, author and continuer of the said unnatural, cruel and bloody wars." [4] It need hardly be said that the trial and execution of the King by a handful of his subjects were illegal to a farcical degree ; even had it been the act

[1] From the Army Remonstrance of June 1647, quoted in Firth : *Cromwell's Army*, p. 354. It declared that " Parliamentary privileges as well as Royal prerogative may be perverted or abused."

[2] Gardiner : *Docts.*, p. 387.

[3] Trevelyan : *E.U.S.*, p. 289. Pp. 289-291 contain a good discussion of the significance of Charles' death.

[4] Gardiner : *Docts.*, p. 380 (from the Sentence of the High Court). For documents connected with the trial, cf. pp. 371-380.

of a genuine Parliament, the King could not be condemned for " high treason," which is an offence against the life and safety of the King. It was, whether justifiable or not, an act of revolutionary violence. Yet illegality is not a sufficient indictment in such circumstances ; the true judgment on the regicides is that they doomed their own work with the same fate of violent destruction. Despite their appeal to moral law and popular rights, they stood in fact by force alone, and they ranged against them all the law-abiding and traditional beliefs of a civilian nation.

V. Cromwell and the Puritan Victory

As Charles on the scaffold symbolised the liberties and traditions of England, so the rise of Cromwell contained in essence the spirit of the conquering Army. He forged and maintained that unity of purpose which enabled the Army to hold its conquests for eleven years and to extend their power over the British Isles, the surrounding seas and the New World ; it was therefore natural for his enemies to see in all events the signs of his ambitious cunning working to a preconceived plan.[1] Yet it is incorrect, though tempting, to ante-date either Charles' halo or Cromwell's ascendancy.

His speeches and letters show his difficulty in reaching decisions and his reluctance to assume responsibility ; he had not the mind that could plan ahead, but the genius that acted on impulse. He originated none of the many schemes of his party ; he took fire from the ideas of others, such as Ireton, Harrison and Lambert. He waited, often in agonies of indecision, for guidance from " Providences "—the hand of God revealed in events ; he read the omens like a Roman Consul. This, alone and adequately, explains his sudden adoption of the extremists in May 1647 and December 1648, and his final decision on Charles' death : " If any man had deliberately designed such a thing, he would be the greatest traitor in the world, but the Providence of God had cast it upon them." [2] Without these revelations he was by nature conservative

[1] Clar. : *Hist.*, IV, pp. 223 and 305-8 ; Ludlow, *Memoirs*, I, pp. 365-6 and 376-7 ; Tanner, *op. cit.*, pp. 159-161 and 185.

[2] Firth : *Cromwell*, p. 216.

and diffident in politics ; he was reluctant to put pressure on the civil authority of Parliament, for his sense of discipline foresaw anarchy in military pronunciamientoes and rash experiments. In May 1647 he said of Parliament : " If that authority falls to nothing, nothing can follow but confusion " ; [1] and he told the Agitators in July 1647 : " That you have by force I look on as nothing." [2] But once he put " fleshly reasonings " behind him, and surrendered to Divine guidance as revealed in his own victories, then he bound up with his own fate the fate of the Army, of Independency, and of the Nation. The head of one monarch fell because another and greater had arisen ; the shadow of Hobbes' Leviathan fell across the land.

However, the " chief of men " was not moved to wield his political power directly for some years ; he left to the Independent provisional government the preparation of a permanent settlement while he ensured its acceptance at Drogheda, Dunbar and Worcester. He was not moved to intervene by secular issues, except the threat of anarchy ; as late as 1651 he allowed the Rump to engage in a Dutch war of which he disapproved. He had little interest in a millennium of political liberty ; his maxim for the government of men—" what's for their good, not what pleases them "—was closely similar to Charles' last charge to his subjects ; [3] he would only use force upon constituted authority in the sacred interest of religious liberty, to protect " the chosen people of God." [4] Two events—or " Providences "—removed his diffidence ;—the " crowning mercy " of Worcester and the backslidings of the Rump. All others had failed to set religious freedom on a safe foundation, and he was the chosen instrument of God ; it was both cowardice and sin to refuse " the power God had most clearly by his Providence put into my hands." [5] He convinced himself, though not others, that he had neither planned nor desired the consummation :

" And indeed this hath been the way God has dealt with us all along ; to keep things from our eyes all along, so that we have seen

[1] Firth : *Cromwell*, p. 161. [2] Firth : *Cromwell*, p. 169.
[3] Cf. Trevelyan : *E.U.S.*, p. 289.
[4] Cromwell's speech to Parliament on April 3, 1657 best describes his views on civil and religious liberty ; cf. passage in Tanner, *op. cit.*, p. 169.
[5] Firth : *Cromwell*, pp. 335-6 ; speech of Sept. 12, 1654.

nothing in all his dispensations long beforehand—which is also a witness, in some measure, to our integrity."[1]

It was in this spirit of ecstatic confusion and great expectations that the Puritan conquest was accomplished and symbolised in the rule of Oliver Cromwell. He and his officers had led " the people of God " out of bondage to the threshold of freedom; they had employed and of " cruel necessity " rejected all methods until the sword alone remained; they had sacrificed institutions, law, popularity and civil liberty for their high end. They failed because the people of England were not, and did not wish to be the people of God, and because their attempt to put their ideals into practice led to the degradation of their aims and the disintegration of their instrument. They produced a violent reaction which not only swept away new reforms but endangered the national gains of 1640-2; their fight for toleration engendered nothing but intolerance; the Army, their chosen weapon and the terror of Europe, left nothing permanent in English life except " a rooted aversion to standing armies and an abiding dread of military rule."[2] All this was because the means falsified the end; the ruthless conquest carried within it the seeds of violent dissolution. Yet their battered enemies watched their triumphs with reluctant admiration, and foreign States treated them with obsequious respect. History cannot pay them less honour, nor can Englishmen allow partisan feeling to belittle the men who made the first effective union of the British Isles, and first made England a great maritime and European power. They are above our pity or reproof, for they were in truth independent. It was to God, and not to men, that they offered their work for judgment; Cromwell dissolved his last Parliament with the words that all Puritans would echo: " Let God be judge between you and me."

[1] Firth : *Cromwell*, p. 331 ; cf. speech of Sept. 12, 1654 : " I called not myself to this place ; of that, God is witness."
[2] Firth : *Cromwell's Army*, p. 385.

SUGGESTIONS FOR FURTHER READING

CLARENDON, EARL OF: *History of the Great Rebellion.* (O.U.P.)

VERNEY, LADY FRANCES: *Family Memoirs*, Vols. I and II. (Longmans)

LUDLOW, EDMUND: *Memoirs.* (O.U.P.)

EVELYN, JOHN: *Diary.* (Everyman)

BAXTER, R.: *Autobiography.* (Dent)

WEDGWOOD, C. V.: *The King's Peace, 1637–41.* (Collins, 1955) *The King's War, 1641–7.* (Collins, 1958)

WORMALD, B. H. G.: *Clarendon.* (C.U.P., 1951)

HEXTER, J. H.: *The Reign of King Pym.* (Harvard, 1941)

BRUNTON, D. and PENNINGTON, D. H.: *Members of the Long Parliament.* (Allen and Unwin, 1954)

BURNE, A. H. and YOUNG, P.: *The Great Civil War.* (Eyre and Spottiswoode, 1959)

WOOLRYCH, A. H.: *Battles of the Civil War.* (C.U.P., 1958)

FIRTH, SIR CHARLES: *Cromwell's Army.* (Methuen, 1921) *The House of Lords in the Civil War.* (Longmans, 1910)

YULE, G.: *The Independents in the Civil War.* (C.U.P., 1958)

FEILING, K.: *History of the Tory Party, 1640–1714.* (O.U.P., 1924)

PEARL, W. L.: *London at the Outbreak of the Puritan Revolution.* (Hart-Davis, 1961)

YOUNG, G. M.: *Charles I and Oliver Cromwell.*

CARLYLE, THOMAS: *Cromwell's Letters and Speeches.* 3 Vols. (Methuen)

ABBOTT, W. C.: *Writings and Speeches of Oliver Cromwell.* (Harvard, 1947)

GOUGH, J. W.: 'The Agreements of the People'. *History*, xv.

HEXTER, J. H.: 'The Problem of the Presbyterian Independents'. *American Historical Review*, xiiv.

IV

THE DISINTEGRATION OF THE PURITAN EMPIRE

By January 1649 the Independent section of Puritanism had cleared the way for its great experiment; all internal opposition had been crushed and all obstacles removed—except the impassable chasm between their ideal and its execution. They set out to combine a religious settlement which must be enforced on an unwilling nation with a political theory which derived the authority of the Commons from the sovereignty of a free people. They began with the confident and ludicrous claim that the Rump was chosen by and represented the people, and whatever it enacted had the force of law, " and all the people of this nation are concluded thereby." [1] The failure of the experiment was shown by Cromwell's despairing cry in 1656: "I am as much for government by consent as any man, but where shall we find that consent? Amongst the Prelatical, Presbyterian, Independent, Anabaptist or Levelling parties?" [2] The purpose of this chapter is to show how the attempt to find an ideal settlement of religion and liberty resulted, first in ever widening divisions among the idealists, secondly in the degradation of the ideals, and thirdly in the rejection by the nation of the settlement and its authors.

The decisive factor of failure was the marked tendency of Puritanism to disintegration—a process which began long before the Puritan conquest was complete. Between the death of Pym and the rise of Cromwell there was no unifying influence among the sects and factions that supported the Parliament, and a deep rift in Puritanism began to appear as early as 1644. The quarrel between Manchester and Cromwell was more than a strategical dispute; it was a trial

[1] Cf. the Commons' Declaration in Firth : *Lords in Civil War*, p. 208.
[2] Ludlow, *Memoirs*, II, p. 11.

of political strength between Independents and Presbyterians, soldiers and civilians, radicals and conservatives. The victory of the Independents made them an autonomous power; the Self-Denying Ordinance gave them control of the Army and put the Presbyterians as well as the Royalists at their mercy. From 1644 onwards the New Model Army, like the army of Gideon, proceeded to shed by degrees all unworthy comrades, until by 1660 a few righteous men alone remained. The winnowing process can be examined in four stages : the split in the general body of Puritans (1644-9), the disintegration of Independency (1649-53), the failure of Cromwell to find new bonds of unity (1653-8), and the final disintegration of the Army (1659-60).

I. The Great Puritan Split: 1644-9

One of the most remarkable features of the First Civil War is that, when both sides suffered from internal dissensions, the side that suffered most secured the victory. The disputes of the Royalists were due to personal factions, not fundamental principles ; but the followers of the Parliament only maintained an outward unity, based on compromise, so long as the rift between Puritan and Episcopalian was deeper than that between Presbyterian and sectary— that is, until 1647. The history of Puritanism in 1644-9 turns on the conviction of the Puritan majority that Puritan and Anglican must work together against the danger of the militant sects ; that conviction was formed in 1647 and confirmed by the events of 1648-9. In their hatred of toleration the Presbyterians " gave up the attempt to coerce Charles . . . and fell back on the principle of re-establishing his authority as it was in August 1641, in return for the concession, scarcely more than nominal, of a three years' Presbyterianism." [1]   The Scots were even more decided ; the Engagement of 1647 was directed less in aid of Monarchy than for the " Suppressing the opinions and practices of Anti-Trinitarians, Anabaptists, Antinomians, Arminians, Familists, Brownists, Separatists, Independents, Libertines and Seekers." [2]

[1] Gardiner : *Docts.*, Introduction, p. xlv.
[2] Gardiner : *Docts.*, p. 348.

The issue that split Puritanism was toleration. From 1647 the fundamental question in politics was no longer King or Parliament, but uniformity or diversity in religion. Charles even turned to the radical Army for a time, because he saw more hope of saving his Church through its liberal views on religion.[1] The Army, in all its proposals, laid down one " Fundamental " which no human power, neither King nor Parliament, must alter :

" That such as profess faith in God by Jesus Christ, however differing in judgment from the doctrine, worship or discipline publicly held forth, . . . shall not be restrained from, but shall be protected in the profession of their faith and exercise of religion according to their consciences, in any place except such as shall be set apart for the public worship." [2]

This was an ultimatum, affecting both religion and politics, which Charles and the Presbyterians alike rejected, and their refusal exposed them both to the Army's anger ; for it soon appeared that there was a limit to the Army's toleration in practice. And once the Army made its forcible intervention in politics, it created immediately new causes of division in Puritanism.

One of these new factors was the radicalism which permeated the ranks and even the staff of the Army ; their proposals for sweeping democratic changes alarmed the conservative and propertied instincts of the Presbyterian Lords and merchants.[3] But a far more universal feeling was the civilian fear of arbitrary militarism. This was the issue which Charles defined at his trial—the issue for which he died :

" It is not my case alone, it is the freedom and liberty of the people of England. . . . For if power without law may make laws, may alter the fundamental laws of the Kingdom, I do not know what subject he is in England that can be sure of his life, or anything that he calls his own." [4]

Charles raised the same cry for " Fundamentals " as the soldiers —not the reformers' Fundamental of toleration, but the citizens' Fundamental of legality, which alone brings stability. Both his

[1] Cf. Gardiner : *Docts.*, pp. 326-7 (Charles' answer to Parliament in Sept. 1647).
[2] Gardiner : *Docts.*, p. 370 (Second Agreement of the People).
[3] Cf. Gooch : *English Democratic Ideas*, ch. 4.   [4] Firth : *Cromwell*, p. 221.

death and the rising of 1648 were civilian protests against military
rule ; he and his allies, new and old, strove ineffectively to stop an
armed attack on the whole framework and spirit of English institutions.　Their defeat made the victors still more intolerant of the
old forms, still more confident in the sacred mission of the sword ;
but the military violation of the foundations of government in the
winter of 1648-9 completed the Puritan split together with the
Puritan conquest.　The issue was made perfectly clear ; Independency stood for toleration, radicalism and militarism, while the
rest of the nation longed for religious uniformity, conservatism
and their civilian institutions.

II. The Disintegration of Independency : 1649-53

Four years of negotiation and intrigue had not only divided the
Presbyterian party from its Independent allies, but they had also
ruined its internal unity.　Part of it turned to the King, part sulked
in isolation, part followed with misgiving the Independent lead.
But in the same period the various sects which dominated the New
Model achieved, though painfully, unity and a common policy.
War had welded them, and peace nearly dissolved them in the
quarrel between officers and men in November 1647 ; but war came
again to the rescue in 1648 and united oligarchs, Levellers and Fifth
Monarchists in the work of vengeance.　The blood of the King
sealed their unity and set them apart as a marked people, cut off from
the world by general detestation ; and the task of crushing Royalism
in Ireland and Scotland preserved the spirit of unity and discipline.[1]
While that remained, they had little to fear from external foes ;
Charles II., though a devout Covenanter for the occasion, could
not unite the Scottish factions of Argyle, Hamilton and Montrose ;
Ormonde in Ireland could not maintain for one year the precarious
alliance of Protestants and Catholics ; in England the old and new
Royalists were paralysed by feuds, distrust and poverty, and showed
no enthusiasm for a Stuart Prince surrounded by Covenanting
clergy.

[1] Three regiments mutinied at Salisbury in March 1649 for " England's freedom,
ɔldiers' rights," but they were promptly suppressed and aroused no general support
ɪor Levelling principles.

Yet Independent unity thrived only on opposition; when the sects had the time and power to devise each their own Utopias, Independency tended to return to its natural anarchy. All they had in common was a hate of their late persecutors and an unbounded confidence in their mission to reform abuses; but unity depended on leaving undefined the goal of the mission.

The Independent party was composed of four main groups: the Parliamentary Republicans who filled the Rump: the religious fanatics who proposed the exclusive rule of Saints and canonised themselves for the purpose: the political Levellers who demanded pure democracy: and the social Levellers, who demanded free land and economic communism.

These last, the " Diggers " of St. George's Hill, were too few to have any influence, but their repression by the Independent leaders throws an important light on the economic views of Cromwell and his kind.[1] Simple men like Winstanley imagined that the fall of the Stuart tyrant would bring with it the fall of the economic tyranny of lawyers, clergy and nobles; they forgot that enclosures, tithes and Court fees were the perquisites of the new masters of England, and they found that Cromwell revered private property only less than religious liberty. " A nobleman, a gentleman, a yeoman," he said, " that is a good interest of the land and a great one ";[2] his conservative and orderly instincts were shocked by the Levelling outbreaks, both at St. George's Hill and at Salisbury, and he began to ponder a settlement which should combine liberty with order. The " Diggers " have this historical importance, that they helped to turn Cromwell away from political radicalism towards strong government " with somewhat of monarchical power in it."

The political Levellers caused graver anxiety to the new government, for they had as a mouthpiece that great and noisy Englishman, John Lilburne, whom no London jury would convict. The

[1] Cf. Gooch, *op. cit.*, ch. 6; *Clarke Papers*, Vol. II, pp. 215-224; and Trevelyan, *E.U.S.*: note to p. 282.

[2] Firth: *Cromwell*, p. 248. Cromwell's defence of existing common rights at Huntingdon and Ely is quite consistent with his attitude towards the Diggers; in both cases he upheld concrete legal rights against encroachment, whether of greed or of revolutionary theory.

very act of taking office had divided Independency into government and opposition, the placed and the placeless. The Rump naturally regarded the establishment of a Republic under its control as the climax of its efforts, but to the democrats the Republic was not so much an end but the means of urgent reforms. While the *Eikon Basilike* revived Royalism, Lilburne harried the government from within, and denounced it for its activity in repression and its slowness in reform. The reformers gave the Rump no thanks for weathering the Royalist reaction and prosecuting the Irish and Scotch campaigns ; they attacked its emergency measures, particularly the elastic Treason Act of July 1649, and accused it of corrupt dealings over Royalist confiscations. These attacks soured the temper and undermined the authority of the Rump ; they increased their unpopularity by a Dutch war, an ill-managed prosecution of Lilburne, a severe censorship of the Press, and a grudging concession of private worship.[1]

Nevertheless the real danger to Independent unity was in religious radicalism ; the chief disruptive force in Puritanism was not social or political unrest, but the old heritage of the Reformation —the search for a pure Christian State. It was the guiding spirit of the Army, leaders and men alike ; their victory led them to expect " the dawnings of the gospel-day," for it was to this end that God had blessed them in " that which is falsely called the chance of war." [2] When they returned from their battles in 1651 and found that the men who should have revived a " godly ministry " had done little or nothing to arrest the collapse of organised religion, they became the natural leaders of the general discontent and turned to their favourite peace-time occupation of petitioning Parliament. But the high Commons rejected the petitions as insubordinate and shelved the scheme of John Owen, Cromwell's chaplain, for a voluntary national Church ; and when the pressure grew, it threatened to perpetuate obstruction by refusing to dissolve itself.

The Rump, as nominal rulers, made the same fatal mistake that King and Presbyterians had made ; it defied the wishes of the sovereign Army on the vital question of religious reform. The

[1] For the legislation of the Rump, cf. Gardiner : *Docts.*, pp. 381-399.
[2] Firth : *Cromwell*, p. 252.

effect followed precedent; it passed with its predecessors into the limbo of discarded institutions. Once more the Army crushed the Parliament; but in April 1653 there was this difference, that an Independent Army crushed an Independent Parliament. Henceforth Independency was split into a civilian and a military faction; Puritanism fell into further confusion and disintegration.

III. THE FAILURE OF UNION BY DICTATORSHIP: 1653-8

(a) Cromwell and the Rule of the Saints (April–December, 1653)

The expulsion of the Rump left no authority in the land but the orders of the Captain-General of the Army. Cromwell had a boundless and arbitrary power, limited only by the religious principles of his troops. Yet though his Puritan critics accused him of planning for the Crown as early as 1651, he did not seize this occasion for his own ambitions; fired with the enthusiasm of his followers, he delegated his powers to the " Saints." He and his Council declared that " since this Parliament, through the corruption of some, the jealousy of others, the non-attendance and negligence of many, would never answer those ends which God, His people, and the whole nation expected from them," they would appoint with the Lord's blessing an assembly of " men fearing God, and of approved integrity," who should " encourage and countenance all God's people, reform the law, and administer justice impartially."[1] In place of a secular Republic, they set up a spiritual Commonwealth; in place of representatives chosen by fallible men, they called the elect of Heaven from the Independent congregations.

This is the most amazing experiment of an age of surprises. The despised sects were given arbitrary powers over their persecutors and were ordered by a confiding but impatient Army to establish the Kingdom of Heaven upon earth. Some of them came to their task with modesty and even reluctance; but Harrison and his Fifth Monarchist group came full of revelations and revenge, determined to share their sacred business with no worldly men; for

[1] Cf. Declaration of April 22, 1653, and Summons to "Barebone's" Assembly in Gardiner: *Docts.*, pp. 400-5.

" the saints shall take the Kingdom and possess it." Harrison distrusted possible rivals like Cromwell and Lambert, who sought to dilute sanctity with property ; far from being grateful for their support, he rejoiced that God had " made the General instrumental to put the power into the hands of His people contrary to his intentions." [1] Clarendon called them " a pack of weak senseless fellows," the tools of Cromwell, who put them in office to discredit all alternatives to his personal rule ; but, as with Lilburne, he underestimated their autonomous influence and exaggerated the influence of his arch-villain.[2] Gardiner rightly judges that Barebone's Assembly represented " the high-water mark of Puritanism in Church and State " before the worldly reaction of the Protectorate.[3] Though their work, if ephemeral, was not without merit, its chief importance was that it aroused the conservative instincts of the Army leaders to moderate their religious fervour. For the Saints, instead of making peace, were setting all England by the ears in their lust for removing everything that conflicted with the pure law of Moses ; their apocalyptic spirit brought a Terror in the air, and Royalists, Presbyterians, lukewarm clergy and pagan Universities were only saved by Cromwell's repentance of his enthusiasms.

Once again the soldiers turned against their civil representatives, and the Saints in December 1653 were sent to join the growing and motley opposition. Their dismissal created a more dangerous rift in Independency than any before—a rift in the Army. The Army was their home from which they could not be expelled—unless only Cromwell could find in the nation other supporters for his government. In the meantime Independency was split asunder between idealists and realists, between strict Republicans like Vane and Ludlow and virtual Monarchists who turned to Cromwell and the strong hand in government. Cromwell had to find new bonds of unity by which he could control his Army, conciliate his opponents, and satisfy the majority of men who longed for order and settlement under any system.

---

[1] Gardiner : *Commonwealth and Protectorate*, II, p. 274.

[2] Cf. Clar. : *Hist.*, V, pp. 274-286.

[3] Gardiner : *Commonwealth and Protectorate*, II, p. 340 and II, pp. 290-324 for their legislation. Cf. also Tanner, lecture XI.

(b) The Protectorate : 1654-8

No summary can do justice to the achievements of the Protector ; his greatness cannot be assessed without the aid of Carlyle, Clarendon, Gardiner and Firth. This chapter deals only with the reverse side of the picture—with the problem of the permanent failure of his aims and system.

All the blame cannot be put upon Richard Cromwell ; his very incompetence is a reflection on Oliver as a judge of men, or at least of kinsmen. Sir Charles Firth ascribes the fall of the Protectorate to the moral decline of Independency and to the rise of selfish factions that Oliver made use of and Richard failed to control.[1] Among contemporaries, Burnet wrote that " it was generally believed that his life and all his arts were exhausted at once, and that if he had lived much longer he could not have held things together " ; but Clarendon, who had waited patiently for Oliver's death, confessed his despair and surprise when " this earthquake was attended with no signal alteration," and when " his son inherits all his greatness and all his glory, without that public hate that visibly attended the other . . . so that the King's position never appeared so hopeless, so desperate." [2]

However, his critics were agreed on one point, that his motive in accepting the office of Protector was personal ambition.[3] Cromwell's own defence was that he, and he alone, was called by God to save religious freedom and social order by absolute methods, and that, after weathering the emergency of 1653, he made every effort to bridge the gap between military and civil rule by transforming his dictatorship into a legal constitution. This he regarded his supreme duty—to lead the nation back from despotism to constitutionalism, provided that the return was accompanied by orderly government. To fulfil this end it was imperative to widen the narrow basis of support for his rule ; he must attract civilian allies to rid himself of a total dependence on the Army.[4] Yet if

[1] Firth : *Cromwell*, pp. 446 and 484-6.
[2] Burnet, I, p. 68 ; Clar. : *Hist.*, VI, pp. 98.
[3] Burnet, I, pp. 79-81 ; Clar.: *Hist.*, V, pp. 287-8 ; Ludlow, *Memoirs*, II, pp. 9 and 29.
[4] Cf. Firth : *Cromwell*, p. 437 : " The history of the Protectorate is the history of the gradual emancipation of the Protector from the political control of the Army."

Cromwell's aim was material power, he was more absolute as General than Protector, and in the Instrument and Humble Petition he gladly accepted limits to his authority. Nor was he dazzled by titles and the names of things ; for he was no formalist and treated the name of King as no more than " a feather in a hat." But he grasped anything that might serve him in the heroic task of reconciliation ; he would use any weapon to unite " the interest of Christians and the interest of the nation." His optimism would not recognise that such union was politically impossible ; if " any whosoever " think the interests inconsistent, " I wish my soul may never enter into their secrets." [1]

His domestic rule consists of two experiments, separated by an interlude. The interlude of the Major-Generals was made much of by his opponents, and has received more attention from history than it deserves. It was but a temporary expedient in an emergency, to prevent a large-scale repetition of Penruddock's Royalist rising at Salisbury in March 1655. The crisis was real, despite the ease with which Penruddock was crushed, for it coincided with a movement of his own high officers against the Protectorate.[2] " It was a bold enterprise, and might have produced wonderful effects . . . but they did nothing resolutely after their first action " ; so Clarendon accounted for the failure, in words which apply generally to Royalist activities in this period.[3]

Military local government lasted from the autumn of 1655 until the spring of 1657 and was undoubtedly efficient—hence, indeed, its unpopularity. It is politically significant of two changes in Cromwell's policy. It ends the courting of the Royalists, who were made to pay for the system by " decimations " and were cut off from their social pastimes at races, cock-fights and taverns ; and it shows a renewed confidence in his officers, or at least a determination to divert them from politics by the cares of local administration. There is little doubt that Cromwell was attracted by their initial success to extend their powers ; he even saw in them a short

[1] Speech to the Committee of Second Protectorate Parliament, on April 3, 1657.

[2] Cf. the petition of the three Colonels in Ludlow, I, p. 406; Ludlow himself was hostile and turning to Harrison ; Overton was plotting against Monk in Scotland ; cf. I, pp. 400-435.

[3] Clar. : *Hist.*, V, pp. 377-8.

cut to religious reform, and defended them on the ground that they had been " more effectual towards the discountenancing of vice and the settling of religion than anything done these fifty years." [1] In this respect they reveal his political, and only too human failing —a passion for short cuts when his dearest ideal was in sight ; not all the lessons of experience could prevent his religion from occasionally overriding his worldly wisdom.   Yet in its administrative aspect the experiment is no historical monstrosity, but an attempt to revive the necessary central control of local officials which both Tudors and Stuarts regarded as the secret of good government ; it combined the powers of High Commission and Star Chamber, and was an English equivalent of Richelieu's system of Intendants. With its removal efficient local government and justice disappeared, except for capricious spasms of activity, until the nineteenth century.

Nevertheless it was a relapse in policy to the arbitrary methods of 1653—a relapse which Cromwell soon repented and the nation was long in forgetting.   Militarism cast suspicion on all his schemes of civil government ; no ingenuity could bridge the gap between soldier masters and civilian subjects.   Even the Humble Petition, for all its likeness to old monarchy, was but a flimsy sheath for the new sword ; and the brightness of the sword shone through it.

The Instrument of Government, the most pretentious of Cromwell's schemes, cannot be condemned for simplicity nor for plagiarism.   It embodied the " fundamentals " of the Agreements, the system of Councils evolved by the Army, and a thorough revision of the methods of Parliamentary representation.   It proposed to give a limited power of legislation to a single chamber, which was to meet at least once in three years for sessions of not less than five months, and was to be elected by persons of sound religion and two hundred pounds' worth of property.   Royalists, except Catholics and allies of the Irish, might elect or be elected for any Parliament after the first four Triennial Parliaments ; any person elected was subject to the approval of a majority of the Council before he could take his seat.   Such an approved body could pass laws which did not infringe the Instrument without the

[1] Firth : *Cromwell*, p. 352.

consent of the Protector ; and in session, it was to control the army, militia and taxation, and to nominate candidates to the Council.[1] Thus did Cromwell hope to combine representative government with the two elements that he held essential to a permanent stability : " somewhat monarchical " and " somewhat unalterable." No Parliament, or any other human power, was given the right to persecute peaceful dissenters—except of course Papists, Prelatists, and " such as, under the profession of Christ, hold forth and practise licentiousness." [2]   Nor could it hinder at every turn the actions of the Executive, although it was allowed ultimate control by cumbrous and indirect means.   The Council was the heart of the system.   Its members served for life and could not be removed even by the Protector ; it was to choose future Protectors, and the present Protector was bound to follow its advice on all important matters ; it could make war and peace, tax, and issue ordinances, subject only to the subsequent confirmation of a Parliament censored by its scrutiny.[3]

This was the new Magna Carta, the sure guardian of religious liberty and social order, the experiment to end experiment.   It embodies the aims, experience and commonsense of that brilliant company of officers Cromwell had picked and trained, and particularly of Lambert ; the military oligarchy decided that " it was high time that some power should pass a decree upon the wavering humours of the people, and say to this nation, as the Almighty Himself said once to the unruly sea : ' Here shall be thy bounds ; hitherto thou shall come and no farther '." [4]   They might have been less confident if they had heard of the legend of Canute.

Cromwell adopted the scheme, though on paper it might have made him as powerless as a Doge of Venice, because of its written guarantee that absolute power could no longer be wielded and abused by men.   He accepted cheerfully all its limitations, though his interpreting power was at times used to strain the spirit of the

---

[1] Gardiner : *Docts.*, pp. 405-417.

[2] Clause 37.   The vital religious clauses are pp. 35-38.

[3] Clause 21.   The Council interpreted the ambiguous qualifications of cl. 17 ; " known integrity " and " good conversation " were useful political, as well as moral, tests.   About 100 political opponents were excluded from each of the two Protectorate Parliaments.

[4] Firth : *Cromwell*, p. 341.

Instrument ; [1] and he gave all his energy to give it root in the habits and minds of the nation. He forgot that the only thing that can take root is the living and growing plant ; that the Instrument put a dead end to the constitutional growth of English society. No self-styled Parliament could accept as binding a private document without statutory confirmation, which necessarily involved the right of modification ; no large body, in the religious atmosphere of the century, could resign the right to define and repress " damnable heresies " ; and none who had fought for Parliament could fail to raise the cry of " Privilege " when duly elected representatives were barred from their seats by a Council that had no legal standing. The Instrument, as a consequence of its frontal attack on all English political instincts, revived in an aggravated form the old quarrel between an active Council and an obstructive Commons. After five " lunar " months of wrangling, and despite Cromwell's labours of mediation, friction ended in deadlock and dissolution, and sole power was restored to the Council, whence it had come. Thus the Protector's first constitutional experiment failed to heal the civil and military factions of his followers ; it was equally unsuccessful in uniting the excluded parties within its rigid embrace.

The Instrument left the Royalists still at the mercy of the Army, without Parliamentary hearing or liberty of public worship, subject to heavy " decimations." [2]   Theirs was the submission of despair ; the 1655 rising and the activities of Cromwell's spy service revealed them as irreconcilable at heart, and he soon gave up hope of support from this quarter.

The Presbyterians, as parliamentarians and persecutors, could not support veiled despotism and naked toleration ; yet they accepted a place with the Independent and Baptist clergy in the

[1] He defined " month " in the Instrument, cl. 8, as a lunar month, in order to dissolve a Parliament which claimed power over " fundamentals." This is a fair example to show that no scheme can provide exhaustively for all contingencies, and that even the most rigid is inevitably altered, if not by modifying machinery, by gloss, convention, and varying interpretation. There cannot be a " rule of law " which is not ultimately a rule of men.

[2] Cf. clauses 14, 15, 31, and 37 of the Instrument ; clause 40 protected the agreements of the Army with compounding or surrendering Royalists ; one of the causes of the expulsion of the Saints was their breach of such agreements ; cf. Gardiner, *Commonwealth, etc.*, II, pp. 305-6.

organisation of a national and voluntary worship set up by Ordinance in 1654, and they were suspected by the other parties of courting the Protector. But the merchants, from whom the strength of the party was drawn, resented the heavy taxation for the armed forces and the war with Spain,[1] and disliked sharing their monopoly with Scotch and Irish competitors ; the weakest side of the Protectorate, its financial extravagance, alienated the full support of economic interests, though they welcomed the benefits of peace and order.

Republicans denounced tyranny, Fifth Monarchists denounced heathenish monarchy and worldly qualifications, Levellers attacked a military and propertied oligarchy. The forbearance of Cromwell only encouraged them to plot his death, to intrigue with Papist Spain and " malignant " Charles Stuart against " that grand imposter, that loathsome hypocrite, that detestable traitor, that prodigy of nature, that opprobrium of mankind, that landscape of iniquity, that sink of sin, and that compendium of baseness, who now calls himself our Protector." [2] These somewhat vehement passions spread easily through the unoccupied troops, their original home ; it needed regular pay, constant watching and stern discipline to control the Army—the real " instrument of government." The high officers showed signs of ambition and faction ; Ludlow, Harrison and Overton were cashiered ; even Lambert fell into disfavour ; Cromwell turned the West Indies to account, both by deporting Royalists and by employing discontented officers like Penn and Venables in the ill-prepared and ill-conducted expedition against Hispaniola. Thus the Instrument won neither the respect of the rulers nor the obedience of subjects ; it acted only as another factor in the disintegration of Independency. By converting the General into the Protector, by sending Cromwell from the camp to the Court, it deprived him of that close touch and sympathy with his troops that had been his chief support and inspiration. When he at last began to distrust his army, the end was in sight ; there was nothing to do in his weary old age but to

---

[1] For the cost of the Army, cf. Firth : *Cromwell's Army*, pp. 184-5 ; despite the Protector's reductions, it did not fall below one million pounds annually.

[2] Clar. : *Hist.*, VI, p. 70 (1656, July).

safeguard the religious liberty of the few by accepting the political prejudices of the many. The fever of experiment and reform had exhausted both ruler and ruled ; the whole nation cried for " settlement "—in Cromwell's own words, " that we may know where we are." [1]

(c) *Cromwell and the Restoration of Monarchy*

The Humble Petition and Advice is Cromwell's confession of failure and the beginning of the Restoration. It set up a counterfeit monarchy which gave no security under the treason laws,[2] and an imitation House of Lords in which all but two Peers refused to sit.

The last remedy of Cromwell had all the defects of a sham ; it had not the virtue of the original, and it deceived and conciliated neither old nor new opponents of the Protectorate. It merely aroused fears and hopes of a genuine restoration. Vane asked : " Shall we be under-builders to supreme Stuart ? " and prophesied that " if you be minded to resort to the old government, you are not many steps from the old family." [3] While the Levellers and Republicans regarded it as the foulest apostasy of all, so foul that it made " killing no murder," the Commons, although they gained large powers at the expense of the Council, disliked what Cromwell called the " Christian and English interest " in the Other House— *i.e.* the number of soldiers and councillors and the lack of property and birth.[4] Cromwell and his nominees stood alone against the " tumultuary and popular spirit " of the Commons, and once more the energies that ought to have gone to government were wasted on wrangles between the Houses. The new constitution had not the saving merit of its predecessor, a strong and unified executive ; and though factions were willing to take advantage of it, there was no wholehearted devotion to it. It had, also, one fatal effect. It brought to a crisis the differences of the Protector and the Army grandees.

[1] Speech to committee of Parliament, April 11, 1657.

[2] By an act of Henry VII., obedience to a ' de facto ' King was not treason. For the Petitions, cf. Gardiner : *Docts.*, pp. 447-464, and Tanner, pp. 192-9.

[3] Tanner, p. 198.

[4] For the composition and temper of the House, cf. Firth : *House of Lords*, ch. 8.

The authors of the Instrument naturally resented the abandonment of their masterpiece, and only accepted the degradation of the Council because of the equivalent influence of the second chamber ; but their chief and unrelenting opposition was to hereditary Kingship, which would end the Council's control of an elective Protectorate.   All Cromwell's influence and entreaties could not move them.   He might safely dismiss Lambert, whose ambition isolated him from the rest ; but he was powerless without the advice and co-operation of the Major-Generals and the group led by Fleetwood and Desborough, who refused to serve him as King.   After a mental struggle more painful and prolonged than usual, he surrendered to the Army and gave up the one chance of a civil settlement that might possibly achieve in time national unity in acquiescence, if not in sympathy.   When Kingship was lost, the remaining changes were useless to him ; for the other House, besides drawing on his following in the Commons, accentuated party factions and raised them to the dignity of constitutional issues.   He gained ceremonial prestige and power independent of the Council ; he lost the unclouded confidence of his most trusted officers and broke the uninterrupted harmony of interests between him and them.   He was no longer the soul of the army, and he was not to be the head of the nation ; he fell between the General's saddle and the Royal throne.   He was still able to defeat the Republicans when they sought to turn the grievances of the soldiers to their use and he purged the army of open malcontents (Feb. 1658) ; in the summer of 1658 he seemed strong at home, but for financial deficit, and he was at the peak of his glory abroad.   And yet he was not sure of himself, nor of his work ; for the corporate spirit of the victors of Naseby and Worcester was gone for ever.

IV. The Disintegration of the Army : 1658-1660

(a) *The Fall of the Civilian Protectorate*

Cromwell towards the end of his life gave a modest estimate of his work : " I have, as before God, often thought that I could not tell what my business was, nor what I was in the place I stood in, save comparing myself to a good Constable set to keep the peace of the parish." [1]   Clarendon and Thurloe, Cromwell's Secretary, agreed that the peace seemed deeper after his death than before, but they both looked anxiously for a sign from the army.   The signs soon came—first prayer-meetings and then petitions.   The officers were wondering how to greet this strange portent, a civilian Protector ; reports came of " secret murmurings in the army, as if his Highness were not General of the Army as his father was." [2] The real head and unifying force of the army was removed ; could it either raise or receive another person or Cause to maintain that unity ?

The confused story of the months from October 1658 until March 1660 is the real tragedy of militant Puritanism : the story of a leaderless army that did not know what or whom it wanted, until in sullen despair it allowed the return of the one man it did not want.   The Army began by destroying the Protectorate which it had itself created, because, though Richard might still serve national ends, he refused to treat the particular interest of the soldiers as paramount.   They would not return to what Ludlow called their " proper station " ; they demanded political autonomy, with a Commander-in-Chief distinct from the Protector.   When Richard resisted this fatal division of power, which meant virtual abdication, they allied with the Republicans to dissolve his packed Parliament and to enforce his deposition in April 1659.[3]

England thus reverted to the constitutional vacuum of 1653, and " settlement " was more remote than ever ; the Army once again could indulge without limit in its favourite pastime of constitution-mongering.   Yet 1659 was not 1653, nor was Lambert for all his talents a Cromwell in greatness and influence ; the union of a high mission was replaced by the schism of interested factions.   The fate of Richard Cromwell revealed the decay of the Army's unity ; while a few English officers and the majority of the Scotch and Irish officers unconditionally accepted his rule, the grandees of Walling-

[1] Speech to Committee of Parliament, April 13, 1657.

[2] Tanner, p. 201 : "Oliver was Protector because he had been Lord General ; Richard was only Lord General because he was Protector."

[3] Cf. Firth : *Cromwell*, p. 446 : " The Protectorate fell before that alliance between the Republicans and the malcontents in the Army which Cromwell had always been strong enough to prevent."

ford House, led by Fleetwood and Desborough, deserted him for
their own mysterious ends, and Ludlow's party revived the pure
Republican movement.   As 1647 had proved, nothing could keep
the army together but a common enemy and a strong commander;
it was in fact the futile Cheshire revolt of Sir George Booth in
August 1659 which alone postponed the clash between the English
and Scotch armies.

(b) The Generals and the Rump

It would be falsifying history to bring order out of the confusion
of the year between the fall of Richard and the return of Charles II.
There is no logic nor reason in it.   The resurrections and re-burials
of the Rump : the meteoric energies and extinction of Lambert,
now a Fifth Monarchist, now considered an eligible father-in-law
to Charles Stuart : the cryptic evolution of Monk from Cromwellian, Republican, Presbyterian to Royalist : the alliances of
Fleetwood with Ludlow, Lambert, the Anabaptists and the Rump
—all these events produce a tangled skein of desperation, irresolution and treachery which needs a psychologist's rather than a historian's analysis.   Yet one thread may be traced.   The English
officers, with the exception of Ludlow's following, were bent on
finding a civil government which should secure their military careers
and political independence in perpetuity, while the civilian parties,
whether Cromwellians, Republicans, Presbyterians or Royalists,
were determined to reduce both the numbers and political claims
of these " overmighty subjects."   Lambert stated the issue when
he attacked the Rump which he had restored in May : " I know not
why they should not be at our mercy, as well as we at theirs." [1]
He and his fellows had forgotten the proud boast of the New Model
that their being soldiers had not deprived them of the rights and
feelings of Englishmen ; they had won their victories by their
soldierly qualities for their English ideals, and they undid their
victories by sacrificing the Englishman to the soldier, the nation to
the regiment, their public ideals to their private careers.   The
Cause of Liberty degenerated into the cry for " liberties " like those
of a feudal baron ; they became a political anachronism similar to

[1] Ludlow, II, p. 100.

the Free Companies of Italy or the Huguenot fortresses of France—an excrescence that no civilised society of whatever structure could endure.

The first revival of the Rump (May-October 1659) was a sign of the Army's political sterility; the Generals, save always Lambert, had no more constructive ideas to offer and fell back upon old remedies. They hoped to satisfy the universal cry for a Parliament, while using it for their own purposes. But the remedy failed either to placate the nation or to restore order, for it created two irresponsible powers instead of one, two bodies whose claims were mutually incompatible and jointly inimical to a national settlement. The Generals and the Rump were unnatural allies, who were only brought together by a common fear of losing their particular privileges; soldiers and civilians soon fell out on the old scores, until their futile wrangling was cut short by the armed intervention of Lambert and Monk.

(c) *The Duel of Lambert and Monk*

These two men of genius and of action, who with Blake represent the greatness of Cromwell's military training, simplified the political chaos from September 1659 to April 1660 by their personal duel for supremacy. Lambert's aims were the more clearly defined of the two, and that fact was one of the causes of his defeat. As Cromwell's natural successor, he determined to revive the elective Protectorate and the principles of his own Instrument. In this spirit he crushed first the Royalists and then the Commonwealthmen; he drove out the Rump in his master's manner and proposed in its stead a rigid constitution of two chambers and a strong Council of State. Monarchy was in sight once more—the monarchy of a General, not of a King, when Monk made the first and most decisive of his mysterious moves.

No man knew—no man will ever know—what Monk intended; history cannot judge whether instinct, chance or Machiavellian design led him on the path of Restoration. One of his motives may be deduced with safety. He was a professional soldier, careless of politics and insistent on discipline; if he reluctantly interfered in politics, it was to prevent any future interference of the Army, since such activities led not only to disorder in the nation, but also to disturbance in the regiments. He would have no sectarians in his ranks, and had built up a non-political army, animated by the two sentiments proper to the soldier—a belief in regular pay and a blind confidence in their General. He embodied that spirit himself; he served Oliver without question, and he served his son until, as he said, " Richard Cromwell forsook himself, else I had never failed my promise to his father on regard to his memory." [1] But the fall of the Protectorate left him free from allegiance and engagements. It was not a freedom he relished ; he had no mission, no political ideals or ambitions ; he was a man who needed a master to give him orders and relieve him of responsibility and initiative. Hence he obeyed the Rump, until the Rump also " forsook itself " under Lambert's threats ; hence the long delay before he ventured into the whirlpool of party intrigues and paper constitutions.

He came into England, ostensibly to restore the Rump, in reality in search of a master. The ambiguity of his intentions was his chief recommendation to all parties which hoped to use him ; his caution gave confidence to all non-party men who saw in him the last chance of " settlement " ; he convinced civilians, as well as his own troops, that " he was a man in whose steps we may follow in safety." [2] Against Lambert's brilliance and impulsiveness he had overwhelming advantages in his own caution, the fidelity of his troops and in popular sympathy. He avoided the mistake of fighting Cromwell's ablest lieutenant ; he did not so much defeat him as give him time to defeat himself. While the rivals negotiated at Newcastle, the Rump profited by Lambert's absence to return to office under the penitent protection of his military rivals ; while in the North, Lambert's funds ran out and his troops slipped away to their homes or to Monk's well-supplied paymasters. Monk's army marched unopposed on London, while the English army melted away, its leaders quarrelled among themselves, and Presbyterians and Cavaliers were stirring under the banner of a " free Parliament." [3] After twenty years the last remnant of

[1] Ranke, III, p. 265, n. 1.   [2] Guizot : *Monk's Contemporaries*, p. 146.
[3] Cf. Clarendon : *State Papers*, Vol. III, *passim* ; especially the letters of Mordaunt, pp. 642-3 and 649, 667, 707 ; Mordaunt saw that Monk would not be hurried and was very apprehenisve of Royalist indiscretions.

organised Puritanism was the force of 7000 men and £25,000 that Monk controlled ; the master of that force was the master of three nations.

Monk used the Parliament to coerce the City, and then used the City to coerce the Rump ; he forced it to admit the exiled Presbyterians, the " Secluded Members " of 1648 ; he removed the English regiments garrisoning London, and by the pressure of his own troops and the use of popular agitation he forced political Puritanism to commit suicide by dissolving the Long Parliament. A " free election " was proclaimed, in which Cavaliers might vote, though they were in theory ineligible as representatives.[1] This revolution of a few weeks was Monk's most miraculous achievement ; he succeeded, where Cromwell and Lambert had failed, in securing the dissolution of the perpetual Parliament with its own consent—and that without bloodshed and against the wishes of a much larger military force. The miracle cannot be explained completely by the divisions that paralysed the English Generals. Though Overton meekly surrendered Hull and Harrison was captured ingloriously by militia, though Ludlow retired to prudent obscurity, the utter failure of Lambert's last appeal to arms in April 1660 needs a separate explanation. Lambert gave a lead to the militant Independents against the old foes, Royalists and Presbyterians ; but the fanatics rallied not, and he was rounded up with ease by Ingoldsby, a repentant regicide.

(d) Officers and Men

The fundamental cause of the Restoration was that the rank and file of the English army deserted their officers, as they had tried to do in 1647 and 1649 ; so that generals without an army found themselves as helpless as the politicans they had bullied. The reasons for this fatal split in the instrument of conquest are political and financial. The lower ranks, with the Colonels, had no enthusiasm for the would-be Protectors who inspired them with no ideals and failed to satisfy their anxiety on the vital questions of indemnity and pay ; they grew less and less eager to endanger their lives and to incur popular hatred and legal penalties for the selfish aims of

[1] Actually many, though still a minority, were elected ; Ranke, III, pp. 301-2.

their leaders.   They realised that a Parliament alone could provide
for their arrears of pay and indemnify their many illegal acts.[1]
When the grandees tried to rouse their professional jealousy against
the Scotch army, they refused to stir and allowed Monk to purge
the officers' ranks at his pleasure ; thus regimental morale was destroyed and the Independent storm-troops accepted Presbyterian
and even Cavalier commanders.

The divorce of interests between officers and men was made
final by differences over pay.   The officers as a whole were well
paid, the high officers extravagantly so ; therefore the pressure of
continual arrears was not so hard as on the ranks, whose pay did not
greatly exceed the wages of the agricultural labourer.[2]   The officers
often received estates of land, and saw visions of themselves as
country gentry on retiring from service ; the men who received
debentures on " the public faith " instead of cash were forced to
sell their prospects at large discount to their officers.   The corporate
spirit and community of interests disappeared when the natural
guardians of the troops were transformed into greedy land speculators, exerting economic and disciplinary pressure despite ordinances of Parliament.   The men grew poorer and saw their officers
grow rich on their poverty ; it was small wonder that capitalists
like Lambert found little support from the victims of their exploitation.   While the speculators had everything to lose from the
Restoration, the soldiers had the promise of Charles II. to pay their
long-delayed wages and to grant them indemnity.   Thus when
religious passion was exhausted and political Utopias were discredited, the economic factor was supreme.   Moreover, the New
Model had always placed regular pay second to sound religion in
their ideals, and under the Protectorate Cromwell had of set policy
accentuated its professional, at the expense of its " Crusading "
character.   At the end, after the purgings of Monk, the professional
element was dominant, and awaited under strict discipline the
arrival of the King who had promised to pay them for their past
services in prolonging his exile and harrying his supporters.

[1] Cf. the petition of May 1659, Ludlow, II, p. 87, and Ranke's comments on
the restoration, III, pp. 270-3.

[2] Cf. Firth, *Cromwell's Army*, ch. 8, for the whole subject of rewards, pay and
debentures.

Cromwell had said in 1647: " That you have by the sword I look on as nothing." Militant Independency fulfilled the prophecy. All that remained of its ideals and victories was the Declaration of Breda, of which the one concession of principle was never observed; their only guarantee the word of a Stuart. All that survived of their conquering unity was the unquestioning obedience of mercenaries to Monk the paymaster. All their weapons turned against them; the wonderful discipline which had broken Cavalier charges now served to help the shattered and vindictive Cavaliers back to power, and the corruption and faction which had crippled their enemies spread to their own ranks. They took the sword, and if they had perished by the sword, it would have been a just and noble end. But the Regicides alone had the privilege of martyrdom; their less fortunate comrades lived to see the violation of their principles and the disgrace of their country, knowing that they had made no effort to prevent it. No one who reads the querulous and spiritless reports of Hyde's agents in the *Clarendon State Papers* will believe that Royalists or Presbyterians, separately or together, had the energy or ability to restore Charles of themselves; nor is it likely that Monk would have triumphed over determined opposition as he did over divided leaders and indifferent followers.[1] Monk, the last of Cromwell's Generals, does not represent the spirit of victory; he is the incarnation of defeat. The heroes had ended as mercenaries and abdicated in shame and self-disgust; the Londoners grew bold and hissed them in the streets. " They are become vile in the eyes of the people," said a spectator; but that was not the tragedy. They had become cheap in their own eyes, and sold their Empire for a few weeks' pay.[2]

[1] The collapse of Republicanism can best be seen in Ludlow's *Memoirs*, while Evelyn's *Diary* reflects the despair and the passive role of the Royalists in the Restoration preliminaries. Cf. Ludlow, II, pp. 355-7, for his final summary of the causes of the fall of the Commonwealth.

[2] " And all this was done without one drop of blood shed, and by that very army that rebelled against him "; Evelyn, May 29, 1660.

SUGGESTIONS FOR FURTHER READING

AIRY, O. (Ed.): *History of My Own Time, by Bishop Burnett*, Vol. 1. (O.U.P.)

MILTON, JOHN: *Prose Works.*

HUTCHINSON, MRS.: *Memoirs of Col. Hutchinson.* (Dent)

FOX, GEORGE: *Journal.* (C.U.P.)

THURLOE STATE PAPERS.

FIRTH, SIR CHARLES: *Oliver Cromwell.* (O.U.P. World's Classics, 1953)

GARDINER, S. R.: *History of the Commonwealth and Protectorate.* (Longmans, 1903)

ASHLEY, M.: *Oliver Cromwell and the Puritan Revolution.* (E.U.P., 1958)

Cromwell's Generals. (Cape, 1954)

The Greatness of Oliver Cromwell. (Hodder, 1957)

HILL, C.: *Oliver Cromwell.* (Historical Association Pamphlet)

HARDACRE, C. H.: *The Royalists During the Puritan Revolution.* (The Hague, 1956)

HUTTON, W. H.: *History of the English Church, 1625–1714.* (Macmillan, 1910)

SHAW, W. A.: *History of the English Church, 1640–1660.* (Longmans, 1900)

JONES, R. A.: *Mysticism and Democracy in the English Commonwealth.* (O.U.P., 1932)

NUTTAL, G. F.: *The Visible Saints.* (Blackwell, 1957)

BRAITHWAITE, W. C.: *The Beginnings of Quakerism.* (C.U.P., 1955)

WHITELY, W. T.: *A History of the British Baptists.* (Griffin, 1932)

FIRTH, SIR CHARLES: ' Cromwell and the Expulsion of the Long Parliament in 1653 '. *E.H.R.*, viii.

' Cromwell and the Crown '. *E.H.R.*, xvii, xviii.

See also p. 88.

V

THE RESTORATION SETTLEMENT : 1660-7

THE historian must beware of taking the Restoration too seriously ;
he should remember that its chief figure, the restored King, was
highly sceptical about it, though he acted his part skilfully enough.[1]
To begin with, a complete restoration of the past is historically
impossible—a truth of which Victorian Gothic architecture is an
ever-present reminder. The student must expect and watch for
revolutionary elements in the Restoration settlement ; he must
distinguish what was preserved from the Interregnum and what was
originated in 1660 from what was restored from 1642. He must
guard against accepting the formal theory that all public history
since 1642 had been washed out as if the Flood had come again ;
he must remember that though old institutions might be revived,
the generation that had worked them had vanished and a new generation had arisen on which eighteen years of Revolution had left
an indelible mark. It is true that the violence of the reaction of
1660 was of the nature of a deluge ; the sudden and surprising
miracle of national unity threw a nerve-strained people off its
balance.[2] The feeling of release after fears and uncertainty had a
hysterical quality ; in fact, national hysteria was one of the more
lasting effects of the Restoration, and later Stuart history cannot be
understood without taking it into account.

But the Restoration was not all emotion ; it is necessary to separate its emotional and political aspects. Its first stage was a national
act of welcome to its King. Here the only expressed conditions
were those of the Declaration of Breda : a general pardon, liberty

---

[1] Cf. Trevelyan : *E.U.S.*, p. 330, for a brilliant account of Charles' return : " The
comic spirit had landed on our coast."

[2] Evelyn's *Diary* and the *Verney Memoirs*, Vol. III, provide many illustrations.

to tender consciences, the confirmation of titles to property, and the Army's arrears ; and on all these points " the word of a King " sheltered behind the future decisions of a " free Parliament." [1] There were, thus, no binding terms, no foreign allies to recompense, no concerted Royalist effort to reward ; Charles entered his Kingdom at the invitation of his opponents and without the aid of his friends.   A nation united by common oppression seemed about to revive the Tudor foundations of government—sympathy and confidence.   Burnet in retrospect declared : " To the King's coming in without conditions may be well imputed all the errors of his reign." [2]

Yet there were conditions, real though not expressed, more binding than those of Breda ; for the whole movement was not for absolutism, but against it.   The second stage of the settlement includes the political Restoration, the work of parties, which between 1660 and 1662 consolidated and in some respects perverted the national Restoration.   Exaltation and harmony could not last ; when their fever was spent, the politicians could no longer be thwarted from the task of avenging wrongs and satisfying partisans.

There was still a third stage which the student must consider with the others.   Harrington, the Republican theorist, prophesied that the Monarchy would not retain its ascendancy more than seven years :

" Let the King come in and call a Parliament of the greatest Cavaliers in England, so they be men of estates, and let them sit but seven years, and they will all turn Commonwealth's men." [3]

It was seven years from 1660 to the fall of Clarendon, the great engineer of the Restoration settlement ; in 1667 the period and spirit of Restoration reached its end.   The student must apply the seven years' test to the settlement, and must judge it, less by the bonfires of 29th May, 1660, than by the results and repute it achieved in the years that followed.

[1] Cf. Gardiner : *Docts.*, pp. 465-7.   [2] Burnet, I, p. 89.
[3] Trevelyan : *E.U.S.*, p. 375.

I. THE WORK OF THE RESTORERS; THE NATIONAL SETTLEMENT OF 1660

Two bodies share the doubtful honour of setting Charles Stuart on his father's throne—Monk's Scottish Army and the Presbyterian Long Parliament. The Cavaliers had no real share in it; they were not the restorers, but the restored,—and at that reluctantly restored as a concession to the wished-for King. All the voluminous correspondence and the business of agents does not hide the fact that the Royalist role was passive, and their only possible contribution, discretion.[1] They did not play their part well, as Monk's irritated delays and the shyness of the Presbyterian Lords attest; but for Royalists like Booth and Mordaunt Charles might have been King in 1659.

(a) *The Contribution of Monk*

Monk was the military agent of Restoration; but he had no political ambitions, and kept aloof from politicians and parties. That was the secret of his immediate success and of his subsequent insignificance. For his reward he was satisfied, whether through avarice or stupidity,[2] with the Royal favour, a title and estate, a deciding voice in the Council on military affairs, and the just treatment of his men. His permanent influence on the settlement was to prevent the revival of the Treaty of Newport of 1648 as the terms of settlement. Hyde was resigning himself and his King to make dangerous though temporary concessions, when he heard that Monk opposed the proposals of the Presbyterian Junto, and had put pressure by a show of arms on the Convention to cut short its debates and proclaim the King before the fanatics seduced the soldiers.[3] Nothing came of the Convention's plans save a resolution for toleration and for a national synod to settle religion, and even that was subject to the decision of a free Parliament. Thus the last act of Cromwell's repentant General was to administer a final defeat to Presbyterianism and so to complete the good work begun in 1644.

---

[1] Cf. Clar.: *S.P.*, Vol. III, docts. for March and April 1660.

[2] Burnet, I, p. 89.

[3] Cf. letters between Charles and Monk, Clar.: *S.P.*, III, pp. 745-6; and Speaker Lenthall's advice to the King, III, p. 712.

(b) The Contribution of the Presbyterian Party

The Presbyterian party, under Monk's rude guidance, carried through all the formalities of restoration,—faithful to their habit, which Clarendon observed, of succeeding only in attaining the opposite of all they desired and intrigued for. Their guiding motive was the conviction that, while the Covenant was their goal, Parliament and constitutional methods were the proper weapons; therefore while they intended to restore Presbytery in in some form, they did restore Parliament in complete form. Their battle-cry never altered from "King and Parliament," their policy was always "accommodation"; their true enemies were Papists, malignants and sectaries—never the King, Lords and lawyers. Holles had urged Charles I. in 1644 to put himself at the head of the Parliament, and gradually softened his party's terms as his hatred of Cromwell grew fiercer;[1] Manchester had been deprived of his command for respecting the King's person, and of his seat in Parliament for trying to save his life; Fairfax had refused to serve either Commonwealth or Protectorate, and had taken Lambert's army in the rear when it threatened Monk's advance; the money of Presbyterian Scotland had furnished Monk with the tool that blunted English swords. These four men, and this money, brought Charles back to England.

The temporary alliance of Presbyterian and Cavalier, begun in the Second Civil War and cemented by eleven years of oppression or exile, was based on certain common interests as well as common enmities. The Scotch had noted with disfavour from the first that men like Manchester, Hollis and Waller were gentlemen first and Covenanters afterwards, and that they intended nothing but "a lame Erastian Presbytery." In religion, they had in common with the Anglicans a belief in a national and compulsory Church, and an even greater horror of toleration. In politics, their instincts of privilege, property and place were violated no less rudely than the Cavaliers' by the intrusion of low-born merit into the hereditary art of government. They were members of the same social and economic caste; they shared the old English feudal tradition of

[1] Cf. Guizot's short sketch in *Monk's Contemporaries*.

respect for the laws they had made, and they inherited an inbred dislike of professional armies which they paid for and did not control. Hyde made co-operation easier by guiding the Royalists along constitutional lines after the failure of the swordsmen and of Henrietta's plots; he discouraged futile risings and foreign appeals and put his sole hope in a voluntary English Restoration by reunion.[1]

(c) *The Contribution of London*

The Presbyterians brought to the movement not only this large measure of agreed principles, but also the invaluable support of the merchants who ruled the Common Council of London. They hated the Army for its religion and expense, its unpopular Dutch peace and Spanish war, and its repression of the City's proper influence on politics. So, as a London petition sowed the seed of Civil War, London again led the reaction against military rule. Its Council refused in December 1659 to recognise or pay taxes to the Rump and its Committee of Safety; it began to treat with Hyde's agent Mordaunt and even with Monk, when he was sent by the Rump to destroy the fortifications of the City (February 1660).[2] London's decision cleared the situation; Monk came out openly for a "free Parliament" and rallied both Presbyterians and Royalists to the City's policy.[3] It had its reward in the restoration by Charles of its privileges and in the safeguarding of its economic interests. The King recognised that trade was the principal interest of the country; contract was sanctified by the Act ratifying private sales during the Interregnum, and monopoly was strengthened by the confirmation and extension of the Navigation Act.

(d) *The Restoration of Vested Oligarchy*

Interest, not ideals, was the keynote of the settlement; and where new and old interests conflicted a compromise was necessary.

---

[1] In June 1659 Hyde (who became Earl of Clarendon in 1661) hoped that the King " shall owe more to his own subjects for his restoration than to foreign princes " (Clar.: *S.P.*, III, p. 497).

[2] For Mordaunt's and Monk's dealings with the City, cf. Clar.: *S.P.*, III, pp. 643, 649, 690, 691.

[3] Mordaunt called London " the master-wheel by whose motion the successive rotations of all the lesser must follow " (Clar.: *S.P.*, III, p. 659).

Bishops, landowners, merchants, lawyers and soldiers claimed, like
the King, to enjoy their own again ; the ex-rebels claimed to retain
their own as the reward of repentance.   The public lands of Crown
and Church reverted of course, and the public confiscations by the
revolutionary governments were as naturally annulled ; this satisfied the King, Bishops and the exiled magnates.   The Puritan pro-
fiteers were protected by a legal fiction that " made the enemies to
the constitution masters, in effect, of the booty of three nations " ; [1]
it was held that the transfers of land from "compounding" Royalists were voluntary and therefore binding contracts, though in
fact the forced sale of land to raise fines and " decimations " was
virtual confiscation.   Thus the economic Restoration was the
return of a landed oligarchy, drawn from both of the sides of 1642,
which secured its power, with Monarchy as its ornament, at the
expense of the unprivileged of both sides.   The Puritan Lords
sacrificed the speculating officers and Presbyterian clergy and the
Cavalier magnates sacrificed the lesser gentry, while agreeing to
share the spoils of office among themselves.

The spirit of oligarchy informed all the acts of the Convention
Parliament.   It gave back the worthless militia to the King with
ostentatious loyalty, but allowed him no regular army; [2] it punished
the regicides and pardoned itself ; it confirmed the abolition of the
Crown's profits from feudal tenures, and it carefully refrained, with
Clarendon's connivance, from restoring to the King an effective
Council or an independent revenue. [3]   Neither Major-General nor
Star Chamber was to disturb the administrative slumbers and enclosing energies of the country Justices ; they would let the King
alone, provided he left them alone, but they reserved the ultimate
control of policy by monopolising the grant of all taxes, direct or
indirect.   Englishmen "went mad with joy" in 1660, but they
did not lose their purses in their excitement.   The restoration of
Royal power, as distinct from the Royal line, was not their aim ; it

[1] Feiling, p. 101, quoting Roger L'Estrange, a High Tory pamphleteer.

[2] The oligarchy controlled the militia in practice, for the Lords-Lieutenant nominated the officers and purged the ranks ; it was " an armed force of the wealthy
classes " (Gneist, *Constitutional History*, II, p. 278 and Tanner, pp. 223-4).   For
their dislike of a standing army, cf. Clarendon's Impeachment (Stone, p. 22).

[3] For Clarendon's views, cf. Feiling, pp. 102-5, and Burnet, I, pp. 159-160.

was no more than an ideal that Charles II. in spasms, and James II. wholeheartedly, planned in secret. The theory of the Restoration was that Charles II. resumed his father's powers from 1642 ; the facts show that the Convention meant to resume the powers claimed by the Long Parliament from the break of 1653—the powers of an irresponsible body in constant session with a final and decisive voice in government.

II. THE WORK OF THE RESTORED : THE PARTY SETTLEMENT OF 1661-2

Part of the work of Monk and the Convention endured for centuries, as for example Parliament's control of finance ; part lasted no longer than two years. This was natural in a settlement improvised by an irregular assembly ; the promises and moderation forced on the Cavaliers might well be swept away by a loyal, revengeful and legitimate Parliament. It was indeed remarkable that the Cavalier Parliament of 1661 did confirm the Acts and policy of the Convention's political settlement ; it was impossible that there should be continuity in religious policy. When Monk's army and the Convention disappeared, Puritanism had no safeguards but Charles' word and Clarendon's statesmanship ; and Clarendon could not prevent, even if he had tried, the breaking of the Presbyterian-Royalist alliance and the destruction of Presbyterianism as a political and religious force.

(a) The Destruction of Presbyterianism

The complete disappearance of the great Presbyterian party from English politics is one of the outstanding catastrophes of the seventeenth century. Some were absorbed in the sects they had despised, some returned to Episcopacy which, though " High," was impeccably Protestant ; but the rapid extinction of their organised influence needs further explanation.[1]

Their political defeat can be traced to three factors. First, they rose and fell with their Scottish connection. Scottish arms in 1644

[1] The career of Richard Baxter forms the most interesting and illuminating commentary on this question ; see list of books at the end of the chapter and Davis' *Bibliography*.

and Scottish money in 1660 put them in power ; as Cromwell broke the alliance in 1648, so Charles in 1660 on Lauderdale's advice abandoned the old Stuart policy of uniting the two Kingdoms and decided to foster division between them as a maxim of government. Thus by the separation of the countries both Presbyterian parties were left in helpless isolation.[1]

Secondly, the main body of English Presbyterians was left leaderless by the bribing of the grandees, and their past treatment of Anglicans exposed them to a logical system of revenge. They had proscribed the Prayer Book ; the Cavalier Parliament condemned the Solemn League and Covenant to be burned by the common hangman. They had attacked the King on the professed ground of seeking his true interests ; from 1661 the oath of non-resistance disqualified all officials, clergy and teachers who upheld " that traitorous position of taking arms by his authority against his person, or against those that are commissioned by him." [2] Because they had deserted the Elizabethan ideal of a comprehensive Church, the Act of Uniformity threw them into the outer darkness of Dissent ; even as they had defined citizenship by churchmanship, so did the Corporation Act of 1661 and the Five Mile Act of 1665 confine municipal franchise (which involved Parliamentary franchise) to loyal Anglicans. The toleration they had denounced was denied to them by the two Conventicle Acts of 1664 and 1670 " for providing further and more speedy remedies against . . . seditious sectaries and other disloyal persons, who, under pretence of tender consciences, have or may at their meetings contrive insurrections." [3] The next 150 years gave them ample leisure from the cares of government to reconsider the merits of religious liberty and the fallibility of Parliaments, and to prepare their next contribution to English history—the Industrial Revolution. [4]

What made their repression so complete was the dominance of the Commons in Parliament. The Cavalier gentry who filled the

---

[1] Cf. Burnet on the Scotch settlement, I, pp. 101-158 ; the Scots suffered most, since they had taken no active part in the Restoration.

[2] From Corporation Act ; cf. Grant Robertson, *Selected Statutes and Constitutional Documents*, p. 36.

[3] From Act of 1670 ; cf. Grant Robertson, *op. cit.*, p. 70.

[4] Cf. Tawney, *Religion and the Rise of Capitalism*, ch. 4.

Lower House had no respect for the great rebels in the Lords, and little reason to be grateful to their own leaders who seemed indecently eager to forget past crimes and to forgive the sinners. They set out, in defiance of Clarendon, to " expel the poison of sin and rebellion " out of the nation, and by their own power they forced on King, Council and Lords their savage " settlement " of religion. The Act of Uniformity of 1662 utterly undid the work of the Declaration of Breda and the Act of Indemnity. On Saint Bartholomew's day 1662 they finally broke the unholy alliance with Presbytery by expelling 2000 clergy from their livings, without compensation, just before their tithes were due. They not only made the laws, but they enforced them as local Justices; they applied their Code both to keep Puritans away from Church and to punish their absence; Burnet records of the execution of the Conventicle Act, " that if any doubt should arise concerning the meaning . . . it was to be determined in the sense that was most contrary to conventicles." [1] Organised Puritanism fell, as Stuart despotism had fallen, before the invincible combination of the Commons and the Commissions of the Peace.

(b) The Balance of Power in Parliament

The destruction of one of the great Restoration parties by the other, through the agency of the Commons, has a constitutional, as well as religious significance; it proved that the surface reaction towards Monarchy had not affected the supremacy of the Commons in Parliament. The House of Lords never recovered its lost prestige after eleven years' disuse; the wars had exposed the mediocre abilities of its members and had diminished their wealth; they had been gradually excluded from the inner councils of both sides, and their ornamental functions had not been needed. The younger Peers, therefore, grew up without the training or taste for office, and the active politicians among them preferred pulling wires in Court or Commons to reviving old and unpopular claims. The Upper House tacitly accepted the secondary position assigned to it by the political theories of the time—that of a revising and checking

---

[1] Burnet, I, p. 270; cf. also Stone, pp. 109-122.

Chamber ;[1] its only constitutional gain in 1660 was the revival, after a long lapse, of its function as supreme Court of Appeal from the English lay courts as a result of the abolition of Star Chamber.[2] In politics the country copied the King's neglect when he found that they had " little power to do him good or harm."

The King shared the active duties of government between his mistresses, his Council and his loyal Commons. His mistresses reserved for their part diplomacy and expenditure, and banished Clarendon when he meddled in their monopoly ; the Council had thrust on it the tangles and grievances so created, and busied itself with wars, trade and plantations, and the " management" of the Commons ; the Commons were undisputed masters of grants of supplies, ecclesiastical and local government.   Their Statutes over-rode Royal Ordinances, they had the initiative and deciding voice in domestic policy, and it was necessary either to deceive or placate them in foreign affairs ; they were the dominant partners because they were the paymasters on whom Court and Council depended for their necessary luxuries.   They preserved the Bates, Hampdens and Darnels of their time from Prerogative exactions ; for though they gave Charles tunnage and poundage for life and a hereditary excise, they fixed the rates by statute ; and their grant, generous as it was and ample as it might have been to an economical and unambitious King, was insufficient to meet Charles' past debts and ever present needs.   Like Clarendon, they had " no mind to put the King out of the necessity of having recourse to his Parliament " ;[3] and they extended their control to the grants of Convocation, which lost in 1665 its last relic of financial independence.[4] Their power was the more because in a venal age, Charles was no exception : "Charles Stuart would be bribed against the King."[5]

On two major points the Convention and Cavalier Commons were unanimous.   In finance Cavalier instinct reinforced Puritan

[1] Cf. the last chapter of Firth : *House of Lords*, for the restoration of the Lords; even Republicans admitted that " though their power and dependencies are gone, yet we cannot be without them " (p. 296).

[2] The Commons disputed this power in vain in 1675 in the case of Shirley *v*. Fagg.

[3] Burnet, I, p. 160.   [4] Burnet, I, pp. 197-8 ; Stone, p. 114.

[5] Halifax, sketch of Charles II.   For a short summary of the financial settlement of the Convention Parliament (confirmed by the Cavalier Parliament), cf. Tanner pp. 221-223.

policy; it was the Cavaliers who reversed the Darnel judgment of 1627, who claimed to audit and appropriate public monies and jealously maintained their sole right to initiate supplies. They had the same dislike of an active and meddlesome Executive; there was no halo round restored officialdom. In the heat of the regicide trials the Crown lawyers admitted that though " the law in all cases preserves the person of the King to be authorised, . . . what is done by his ministers unlawfully, there is a remedy against his ministers for it." [1] Because of this spirit, the Restoration of Charles II. did not bring England into line with the general European movement towards despotism, but preserved the unique English compromise of limited Monarchy. Ranke ascribed the exception to the fact that Charles was set on his throne " without the direct interposition of any of the great continental powers "; [2] but the fundamental reason was that the Restoration reflected, and was only made possible by, a change in tactics of the propertied classes. The knights and burgesses who ruled the vital centres of English government—the shires and corporations—saw that their ends could be better secured by using them than by opposing the Crown. It was a shrewd calculation, which experience had taught and the future confirmed; but it was upset for a time by the cunning of the restored King.

(c) The Restoration of the Anglican Church

The only institution that was fully restored in power and repute was the House of Commons, together with the local government and society which it represented; the only institution which approached the Commons in completeness of restoration was the Anglican Church. 1662 is the most decisive date in the history of English religion since the Reformation; it is far more important for the Church than 1660 is important for the State. Yet with Church as with Parliament, the attempt to abolish history and return to the conditions of 1641 was unsuccessful; and the clearest sign of revolutionary change is the name "Anglican," which replaces "English" as a fitting description of the new establishment. The religious

[1] Ranke, III, p. 330 : " It is this contrast between the inviolability of the King and the responsibility under the law of those who execute his commands which is the foundation and cornerstone of the English constitution."

[2] Ranke, III, p. 335.

as well as the political settlement was the work and triumph of a party, and party government was in itself a product of the revolution.

The Church had been the supreme issue in the Civil Wars; it should be the greatest gainer by the victory of its sworn defenders. The Cavaliers straightway restored the Bishops to Parliament and their lands; the Press and Universities were reserved for Anglican doctrine; all but Anglican orders were pronounced invalid; unconditional acceptance of the Prayer Book was imposed on all clergy, and the Anglican sacraments were made the test of office and good citizenship.[1] Episcopacy came back with "our most religious King "[2] at its head and Clarendon at its service; the connection with the Monarchy seemed closer than ever, and the *Eikon Basilike* was revered as a new Gospel. Its triumph over Puritanism was complete. The Savoy Conference of 1661 finally confirmed the decision of the Hampton Court Conference against any concession even to moderate Presbyterianism. Sheldon proved a harder judge than even James I.; he made no advances and allowed no discussion; for he was determined to secure purity of doctrine by exclusion, and he would have none of Clarendon's plan for a comprehensive Church uniting the two great parties in support of the Crown.[3] The Act of Uniformity was the seal of his victory; it split English religious life in half, and established not only Anglicanism but Nonconformity.

The sacrifice of comprehension involved a revolutionary change in the position and government of the national Church.

First the conception of an official religion which devoted all its energy not to include, but to exclude, large numbers of citizens was entirely new to English politics; it was utterly alien to the traditions of the English Reformation as understood by the statesmen, both lay and clerical, of Tudor and early Stuart times. Cranmer,

---

[1] For the Clarendon Code, cf. Grant Robertson : Tanner, pp. 225-230.   Cf. also the important Licensing Act in Grant Robertson, p. 61.

[2] Burnet, I, p. 183, wrote that this phrase in the Collects " gave great offence and caused much indecent raillery."

[3] Cf. Burnet's acid account of the Bishops and their policy, I, pp. 176-186.   The Presbyterian proposals, framed by Calamy and Baxter, were based on Archbishop Usher's scheme of a mixed government of Bishops and Presbyteries.

Burleigh, Whitgift and Laud would have condemned in unison the
political folly and doctrinal rigidity of the Restoration Bishops and
squires. The immediate victory was in reality a confession of permanent failure—a failure of the Church to satisfy the religious needs
of its people. It condemned itself from 1662 to an existence as the
Great Sect—powerful and privileged, but still a sect; and it was
soon forced to recognise the parallel existence of other sects. The
Toleration Act of 1689 was the logical consequence of the Act of
Uniformity. But as yet passion obscured logic; only Charles
and the Independents advocated religious toleration, and both
were impotent. Secondly, the Royal prerogative of ruling the
Church—the mainspring and keynote of Henry VIII.'s and Elizabeth's Reformation—was abolished when the Anglican Commons
overrode the Royal Declaration of Indulgence of December 1662,
and maintained that " Penal statutes in matters ecclesiastical cannot
be suspended but by Act of Parliament." [1] The Tory party assumed
the airs and duties of the " Defender of the Faith "; the Church
became the monopoly of a political party and passed out of the hands
of both King and people. It remains to discover what the Church
gained and lost by the revolution.

Pepys complained of " the height of the Bishops, who I fear will
ruin all again," [2] and Burnet records their laziness, born of good
living on the million and a half pounds that the renewal of the
Church land leases brought in.[3] Yet they were shadows of their
former selves, as Sheldon was a shadow of Laud. Death in exile
had removed Laud's school, except the amiable Juxon, who was a
mere figurehead at Canterbury. Clarendon was constantly worried
over the almost complete break in continuity of the Episcopate; [4]
the care of the Church was perforce entrusted to a bench of new and
inexperienced rulers. They were not entrusted with Laud's most
effective weapon; High Commission was gone, never to return
save as the signal for instant revolution; for the Statute which

[1] The phrase was used in the Common's protest against the Declaration of 1672,
but it applies equally to their attitude in 1662-3.

[2] Pepys' *Diary*, 30th June, 1662.　　　　[3] Burnet, I, p. 186.

[4] Clar. : *S.P.*, III, pp. 520, 570, 613 ; he feared the episcopal succession would die
out, and leave the way clear for Presbyterianism.

revived the ordinary Church Courts expressly excepted " the high-commission-court, or the new erection of some such like court by commission." [1] They lost an old power, used by Laud in 1640, when Clarendon persuaded Sheldon to accept Parliamentary taxation for the clergy ; and while the clergy gained in consequence a Parliamentary vote, their peculiar assembly, Convocation, was less respected by King, Parliament and Bishops after it ceased to be a source of supply.

There is no doubt that twenty years' oppression and exile had a disastrous effect on the vitality and prestige of the hierarchy. First, the restored Church, despite the Penal Code, played a less important and independent part in the life of the Court and the wider life of the nation. Charles I. had ennobled his Church by his dignity and sacrifice ; but while he was being canonised, his son was undermining the established religion by encouraging its enemies and arousing suspicion among its friends. Sheldon had no influence at Court comparable with Laud's, for his sober morality prompted him to reprove Charles II. for his vices, and finally to exclude the head of the Church from Holy Communion. Despite Clarendon's protests that Charles was " the most an Englishman and the most a Protestant," Anglicanism had little to hope for from Charles and his favourites—Buckingham and Bennet, the Castlemaines and Madam Carwells, from a Court where Nell Gwyn gloried in the name and popularity of " the Protestant whore," where the only serious diversions had a sceptical and scientific, rather than a devotional flavour.

The squire received the parish priest with a less ironic welcome than Charles received the Bishops, but even in the unchanging countryside men had developed a new temper. Though religion had been the main cause of the Civil War, it was not the main cause of the Restoration. The Restoration was at first an anticlerical movement against the chaos of religious fanaticism ; it demanded political and religious order, not a religious revival. The spiritual fervour of the early struggle had been exhausted, and only survived in the spirit of revenge ; the Restoration produced a revival of controversy and party politics rather than that of religious thought,

[1] Grant Robertson, p. 33.

except the Latitudinarian School of Cambridge theologians.[1] The Royal society reflects the temper of the age; 1660 begins the ascendancy of philosophy over theology, and heralds the eighteenth-century decline of organised religion. In this changed world the parish priest was subordinate to the squire; for the lay patron recovered his patronage at the same time as the parson recovered his tithes.[2] The squires in Parliament were careful not to revive Laud's ideal of an independent estate of the clergy correcting the spiritual failings of their parishioners without respect of persons or interests; the Restoration clergy had little of the moral authority and social prestige of the reformed Laudian priests. They were to be the squire's chaplains, zealous in his interests and tender of his peccadilloes; their thunder was reserved for Papists, sectaries, and the vices of the lower classes.

In brief, the restoration of the Church was only partial, and included two revolutionary features—the substitution of Parliamentary for Royal supremacy, and the substitution of an exclusive for a comprehensive system. While all the apparatus of Church life and power—doctrine, discipline, property and privileges—was revived, and even strengthened and embellished, its autonomy was not restored, and that by design. It was restored by lay politicians for political ends; it was fatally involved in the corruption and vicissitudes of the new era of party politics.

(d) *The Restoration of the Court*

One of the causes of the Revolution had been the unpopularity of the Court of Charles I. and Henrietta; one of the causes of the Restoration had been the dislike of the growth of the atmosphere and habits of a Court around the Protector. Puritans denounced the worldliness and intrigue which put a barrier between them and Oliver, while monarchists saw in it a ludicrous, almost blasphemous imitation of Royalty. Yet Restoration also brought in the inevitable Court. Foreigners must be impressed and Charles must be indulged after the hardships and humiliations of his exile—the

---

[1] Cf. Burnet, I, pp. 186-191; and Hutton: *H.E.C.*, ch. 18, for a favourable estimate of the state of the clergy.

[2] The parochial clergy were notoriously poor, and the Bishops notoriously rich. Cf. Hutton: *H.E.C.*, pp. 321-4, and Burnet, I, p. 186.

patched clothes, low fires and mounting debts. Moreover, a
Court was needed in the national interest ; for the King must marry,
to mend his ways and to secure the dynasty. So the courtiers
came thronging back, their greed and intrigues adding enormously
to Clarendon's worries. Yet it would be gross libel on the Courts,
either of Charles I. or the Cromwells, to assert that they were restored
in 1660 ; what came over the Channel was something far different.
They had been English in their sober dignity—perhaps a little
formal and dull ; in 1660 Whitehall became a shoddy imitation of
Versailles.

Charles II.'s Court reflects all that he and his companions had
forgotten of English life and all they had learned of Continental
life ; the one accusation that cannot be made against it is that it was
insular. There was as sharp and as unfortunate a break in the
traditions of the Royal household as there was in those of the
Church, and Clarendon's influence failed to bridge the gap in either.
He and his friends, Ormonde and Southampton, were equally
uncomfortable in the new atmosphere with the Puritan Lords like
Holles and Anglesey or the non-partisan Albemarle and Sandwich ; [1]
all alike found themselves gradually excluded from the King's confidence, while the King's private confidants such as Buckingham
and Bennet soon began to intrude into the public business of the
State. Thus in 1662, when men rested from their labours and
enthusiasms and began to take stock of what they had restored, they
discovered a force in politics that had crept in and taken root almost
unnoticed ; and they saw that, while they had been re-establishing
the foundations of Church and State, the Court had established
itself on no foundations but adultery and wit. [2] From 1662 to 1667
this discovery had two important results : the growing opposition
of the " country " to the Court, which quickly destroyed the unity
and submissiveness of the Cavalier Parliament : and the overthrow
of Clarendon's ministry by the courtiers, when they considered it
safe to annex all the public powers and offices. These five years
revealed the flaw in the hurried work of Restoration. The party

---

[1] These are the titles adopted by Monk and Montague (the commander of the fleet
which brought Charles II. home).

[2] Cf. Osmund Airy's lively sketch in his *Life of Charles II.*

which restored Parliament above the law and a monarchy limited by law, had safeguarded the nation against the worst dangers of Prerogative; but it had omitted to provide any but the clumsiest checks on the central executive, and was helpless against the new methods of the Court politely called " influence."

III. THE TESTING OF THE RESTORATION SETTLEMENT

(a) *The Double Attack on Clarendon*

As the Court flourished so the Chancellor declined.   Clarendon offended the Commons, insulted the mistresses and bored the King; his conception of his public duties was at once Utopian and antiquated.   He detested parties and bribes as tools of government; he relied on the known laws, the limited Prerogative, and above all the Privy Council: " the body of it is the most sacred and hath the greatest authority in the government of the State, next to the person of the King himself." [1]   He had a triple allegiance to the rights of the Crown, the sanctity of the Church, and the liberties of the people; and all that there was of compromise in the settlement is due to this fact.   But in an age of extremes, he invited the fate that threatens all moderate men; all factions united to remove the arbitrator, the one obstacle to their different aims. His fate closed on him when, at the end of 1662, his great friend Ormonde was removed to Ireland, and his faithful servant Nicholas was dismissed from the Secretaryship of State to make room for his open enemy, Sir Henry Bennet.[2]   His isolation was accentuated by two other causes, his pride and the marriage of his daughter to James, Duke of York.   James was as unwilling a husband as Charles was a reluctant son-in-law, while the Royal connection drew Clarendon still more above and aloof from his colleagues.   He was thus identified with the unpopularity of the Court that he disliked and that disliked him, and he became a convenient scapegoat for the men who ruined him and his policies.   It is difficult to judge whether men hated his uprightness or his arrogance the more, his refusal of unjust petitions, or his rudeness to the petitioners. " He was high," says Burnet, " and was apt to reject those who

[1] Feiling, p. 117.   [2] Better known as Arlington of the Cabal.

addressed themselves to him with too much contempt " ; as " the chief or the only minister . . . he was indefatigable in business . . . but with too magisterial a way." [1]   Such a man needed the firm support of the King to outweigh these disadvantages, and such a man deserved support, if only from regard to his unaided services during the exile and the work of restoration ; but gratitude had no place in Charles' mind, nor was it included in the scheme of restoration.   Charles soon found him irksome, " always pressing the King to mind his affairs " ; then ludicrous, as a butt for Buckingham's wit—" lively jests were at all times apt to take with the King " ; [2] and finally dangerous.

Burnet gives his opinion that " he never seemed to understand foreign affairs well, and yet he meddled too much in them." [3] It was the failure of the Dutch War that brought on his impeachment and banishment.   It was a golden chance for his enemies to remove the overmighty subject.   The judicial charge of treason was absurd, but the political accusation was justifiable on the same grounds as that against Bacon and Strafford—that the Minister had lost the confidence of, and had disowned responsibility to Parliament.   The chief contrast between their cases and Clarendon's was that their masters had tried to protect them, whereas Charles II. for personal ends was privy to a Parliamentary attack on a Royal Minister, and consequently on the Crown's freedom of choice and action.   Clarendon was accused of private corruption over the sale of Dunkirk, on the grounds that " he hath in a short time procured to himself a greater estate than can be imagined to be lawfully gained in so short a time " ; [4] he was accused of betraying the King's " secret counsels " to the Dutch in wartime,[5] of " designing a standing army to be raised and to govern the Kingdom thereby," and of advising the King " to lay aside all thoughts of Parliament for the future." [6]   In fact, he was disgraced for all the evils that he strove to check—evils which were only made possible by his removal.   The Commons, in blind fury at the humiliations of Dunkirk and the Medway, were hoodwinked by the true criminals

[1] Burnet, I, pp. 94-5.   [2] *Ibid.* p. 249.   [3] *Ibid.* p. 95.

[4] Eighth Article of Treasons alleged ; Stone, p. 23.   [5] Sixteenth Art., Stone, p. 23.

[6] First Art., Stone, p. 22.

into using their powers for their own discomfiture; Charles began his policy of allowing his servants enough rope to hang both their enemies and themselves. He retained himself against Clarendon " in his personal against his politick capacity " ;[1] he won an easy popularity and private relief from the complaints of the " buffoons and ladies of pleasure " by surrendering the one servant who made his return possible. But the tragedy of Clarendon is the tragedy of all king-makers, save Monk who was a king-maker by accident ; and this tragedy is redeemed by the nobility of the sufferer and the historical monument he erected to his name.

(b) Disillusionment and Revision

Clarendon's fall is of more than personal moment ; it signifies the fall of the Restoration compromise both in spirit and in machinery. The Tudor ideal of division of spheres and unity of purpose between King, Council and Parliament had proved incapable of resurrection. The new triumvirate was that of King, party and bedchamber ; the constitution had assigned no place to the two last, nor would they be content with anything short of sovereignty. For the rest of Charles' reign they fought each other for the power and profits of office, the one headed by Danby and Shaftesbury, the other by Barbara Castlemaine and Louise de Kerouaille ; while Charles and his hero, Louis XIV., made occasional interventions on either side without prejudice. It was a combination of Castlemaine and Danby (then Sir Thomas Osborne) that brought down Clarendon, and the unnatural character of the alliance is reflected in the absurd inconsistency of the charges made.

In five years the Bedchamber had pulled down the Council, and had ended the reign of the great administrative officers of State. Their place was taken by the party managers, and the two attempts at reviving government by public Council—Temple's scheme of 1679 and the Act of Settlement of 1701—conclusively proved its impracticability. For it needed a deferential, trusting and united people for its success ; and after the first raptures of 1660 that condition passed away, and division succeeded unity as the

[1] Halifax: *Life of Charles II.* Halifax's short sketch is a masterpiece of analysis and style ; any estimate of Charles' ability and aims must be based on its observations.

basis of government.   The real indictment against Clarendon is
that guided by " obsolete rules of law and conscience," [1] he did
not see the portents ; he did not gauge the violence of the emotional
reaction from the hysterical joy of 1660.   Papist and Republican
plots and rumours of plots, the Fire and Plague, the panic fear of
Dutch or French invasions, the distrust that magnified Charles'
guards into another New Model and converted incompetent
officials into wicked traitors—these were the influences that swayed
men's minds in 1667.   The cry " We are saved " was drowned by
the scream " We are betrayed " ;   and undiscriminating rancour
fixed on Clarendon, instead of on Charles, as the traitor to the settlement and the falsifier of its high expectations.

Finally, the dismissal of Clarendon by the King on charges that
could not be proved, confirmed the supremacy of the Commons
in Parliament.   Charles was temporarily freed, but permanently
enslaved—unless he could find a foreign master.   Even James II.
saw the true meaning of his father-in-law's fall ; from it " one may
date the beginning of all the misfortunes which happened since,
and the decay of the authority of the Crown ; he (*i.e.* Clarendon)
generally supporting that Prerogative, which his successors never
minded." [2]   The Commons had encroached on the rightful preserves of the Crown from the time that they had refused to allow
any Royal discretion in the execution of the Act of Uniformity ;
they had gone on to interfere in foreign policy ; they had taken the
management of war finance out of the proper channels by Parliamentary commissions, and at last they revived Impeachment as a
political weapon to secure Parliamentary control of policy.   Their
power and temper had intimidated the Lords and impressed the
King ;   Charles decided that it was imprudent to oppose or snub
them, but that it would be easy to share their spoils by judicious,
and not too scrupulous management.   If he was not to be a Grand
Monarch, " he might do well at least to be a partner." [3]   His
affable and familiar nature, his love of practical jokes, his talent for
dissembling and for winning over opponents, all inclined him to the

[1] Feiling, p. 115 ; Clarendon thus describes Bennet's view of his own maxims of
State.   Cf. also in Feiling, p. 121, a description by a Member of the Commons of
Clarendon's attitude towards them.

[2] Feiling, p. 122.   [3] Halifax, *Charles II.*

new game, and only his love of ease restrained him.   But Clarendon had to be removed before Charles could descend from the uncomfortable throne on which he had placed him, or put off the dignity of the King for the effusiveness of the political tout and the " common solicitor." [1]   Cromwell and Clarendon had both insisted that things should not be done in a corner ; but their day was gone, and the age of mean men and mean methods followed. Charles knew well their and his own degeneracy ; " they are men of no conscience," he said, contrasting the new generation with the " stiff and sullen " Essex and Holles, " so I will take the government of their conscience into my own hands." [2]

SUGGESTIONS FOR FURTHER READING

CLARENDON, EDWARD, EARL OF : *History of the Great Rebellion*, Vols. V and VI. (O.U.P.)
  State Papers, Vol. III. (O.U.P.)
AIRY, O. (Ed.) : *History of My Own Time, by Bishop Burnet*, Vol. I. (Dent)
  Charles II. (Longmans, 1904)
LUDLOW, EDMUND : *Memoirs.* (O.U.P.)
PEPYS, SAMUEL : *Diary.*
SAVILLE, CHARLES, EARL OF HALIFAX : *Works.* (O.U.P.)
FOX, GEORGE : *Journal.* (C.U.P.)
EVELYN, JOHN : *Diary.*
OGG, D. : *England in the Reign of Charles II.* 2 Vols. (O.U.P., 1956)
BOSHER, R. S. : *The Making of the Restoration Settlement.* (Dacre Press, 1951)
CRAGG, G. R. : *Puritanism in the Age of the Great Persecution.* (C.U.P., 1957)
  From Puritanism to the Age of Reason. (C.U.P., 1950)

---

[1] Burnet, I, p. 272 ; cf. Halifax's epigram on Charles' intrigues : " He did always by his Councils as he did sometimes by his meals ; he sat down out of form with the Queen, but he supped below stairs."

[2] Burnet, I, p. 272.

FEILING, K. G.: *History of the Tory Party, 1640–1714.* (O.U.P., 1924)
  British Foreign Policy, 1660–1672. (Macmillan, 1930)
BRYANT, A.: *Samuel Pepys.* 3 Vols. (C.U.P., 1947–9)
CARLYLE, E. I.: ' Clarendon and the Privy Council '. *E.H.R.*, xxvii.
WHITEMAN, A.: ' The Re-establishment of the Church of England 1660–3 '. *R.H.S.T. 5th Series*, v.
ABBOT, W. C.: ' The Long Parliament of Charles II '. *E.H.R.*, xxi.

See also pp. 159–60.

VI

WAS THERE A SECOND STUART DESPOTISM?
(1667-1688)

RESTORATION comedies are witty, gross and brutal; they are also prolix and involved, and sacrifice plot to dialogue. The comedy in which James II. was the buffoon and Charles II. the actor-manager had all these qualities, and one of them, complexity, to excess. The variety of motives, interests, plots and counter-plots is no less confusing than the twists and changes in policy of the leading actors. For when ability succeeds character as the criterion of statesmanship, opportunism at once replaces principle as the foundation of policy. The distinctive features of politics in this period are the lack of fixed loyalties and institutions, the fluidity of the party groups, and the superfluity of brilliant and insatiable personalities. Thus in an age of uncertainty and decaying tradition, personality is the supreme factor, and the student must begin by searching for the motives of the dominant politicians.

I. THE AIMS OF CHARLES II

Of the Royal brothers, James' motives were simple, direct and patent to all from 1673, when he resigned his offices under the provisions of the first Test Act; all men knew where he was and what he stood for—strong monarchy and Catholic toleration. But while there is no doubt about James' despotic inclinations, there is less certainty about Charles' intentions, as there was less persistency in his nature and less simplicity in his intellect. Burnet, who knew him well and, though missing the finer shades, made some shrewd judgments, declared that " the King loved the project " (of absolutism)" in general, but would not give himself the trouble of laying or managing it." [1] The evidence of Halifax, one of the wisest and sanest Englishmen that ever lived, is conclusive against a permanent absolutist policy : " He chose rather to be eclipsed than to be troubled : he loved too much to lie on his own down-bed of ease : in a man so capable of choosing, he chose as seldom as any man that ever lived." [2] We may safely accept Halifax's word that his great design was not despotism, but the preservation of his health ; " it had an entire preference to anything else in his thoughts."

However, the wish was there, if not the will : " he thought government was a much safer and easier thing where the authority was believed infallible, and the faith and submission of the people was implicit " : hence his political admiration of Catholicism and Louis XIV.[3] He resented the interference of the Commons in finance and foreign policy, in both of which he preferred a French to an English master ; yet his political prudence overcame his dignity, for he was a realist in politics, placing tactics before doctrine.[4] He was content if he could preserve the Stuart line with some relics of its old powers, and some profit from the new conditions. His policy was in general defensive, not aggressive ; Halifax in the conclusion of his " character " distinguishes " yieldingness " as Charles' chief political characteristic—and virtue, for it was " a specifick to preserve us in peace for his own time." He likens the foundation of Charles' power to a feather-bed : " As a sword is sooner broken upon a feather-bed than upon a table, so his pliantness broke the blow of a present mischief much better than a more immediate resistance would have perhaps done." This is a perfect analysis of the method by which Charles broke the force of the Exclusion Plot, and it fits the whole reign except for the burst of energy that produced the Treaties of Dover of 1670 ; but if it is accepted, the credit for a grand despotical design cannot

---

[1] Burnet, I, p. 269.   [2] Halifax : *Charles II*.

[3] Burnet, I, p. 93 ; cf. in the same sketch (included in Nichol Smith's *Characters*) : " The great art of keeping him long was, the being easy, and the making everything easy to him."

[4] Tanner, p. 233, quotes a remark ascribed to Charles II. by Burnet, I, p. 345 : " He did not wish to be like a Grand Signior, with some mutes about him and bags of bowstrings to strangle men as he had a mind to it ; but he did not think he was a King as long as a company of fellows were looking into all his actions, and examining his ministers as well as his accounts."

be given him ; for despotism is not built upon feather-beds. His whole life, apart from the formal public acts and declarations in which he acted the monarch with finished grace, illustrates that he was a creature of the new world, not of the old. He was not the reincarnation of Henry VIII. or Charles I. ; he was the incarnation of Party, the forerunner of Bolingbroke, Walpole, Canning and Disraeli. He did more to found His Majesty's Opposition than the second Stuart despotism.[1]

These psychological conclusions must be applied to the three crises of the Monarchy in the period : the first Popish Plot of 1670 and the Protestant reaction of 1673-8 : the second Popish Plot or Plots of 1678 and the Royalist reaction of 1681-5 : the third Popish Plot of James II. and the Revolutionary reaction of 1688. These three dominated English politics for fifty years ; from 1667 Popery superseded Puritanism as the national bogey. All three failed, but they produced by reaction results of vital importance ; the first caused the Test Acts and the Orange alliance, the second caused the collapse of the Whigs and the revival of Royalism, the third brought on the Revolution and the twenty years' war with France. Further, they ended the isolation of England which had marked Clarendon's purely English Restoration, and added to the internal confusion of English politics the new complications of European intrigue. England became the chosen battlefield of French and Dutch diplomats, and King and politicians obeyed the orders of alien paymasters, like the Polish and Swedish nobles of the eighteenth century. Religion was not the sole issue ; in many respects it declined as a motive force before trade. Shaftesbury and Charles himself were both sensitive to the influence of commerce ; Shaftesbury advocated toleration for Protestant Dissent as " good for trade," supported the French alliance because France was not a serious commercial rival of England, and worked to destroy Holland as the " Carthage " of the London merchants.[2]

[1] Seeley disputes this honour for Louis XIV. : *Growth of British Policy*, II, p. 241, a point noted by Tanner, p. 239.

[2] " *Delenda est Carthago* " was the text of his appeal for war supplies in the Parliamentary session of Feb. 1673 ; cf. Ranke, III, pp. 531-2.

II. The Great Design of 1670

Once freed from Clarendon's restraint, Charles plunged into the welter of religious, economic and national rivalries—to try his own skill, to seek what profit and amusement he could, and to find a short cut back to the uninterrupted pursuit of his pleasures. He picked his men with care, for their abilities and influence alike. There was Lauderdale for Scotland, Shaftesbury for Dissent and London, Buckingham for his wit and solid block of Commons' votes, Clifford for his Catholic influence and his absolutist views, and Arlington, the heart of the Cabal and the real confidant of the King. They were chosen partly for their common aims—toleration, commerce, hate of the Dutch : partly for their personal divisions which gave Charles leverage and control.

The new Ministry won immediate popularity by the Triple Alliance with Holland and Sweden in 1668, which brought Louis to his first check at Aix-la-Chapelle. This was nothing but a tactical move with a financial objective—to gain Parliamentary subsidies and to make Louis bid for their support ; their real aim from the start was to secure a profitable French alliance against the Dutch. The trick succeeded, for Louis was forced to buy off one of the maritime powers threatening his shores, in order to crush the other.[1] The Cabal had a useful stock of pretexts to justify their reversal of policy ; there was continual friction with the Dutch over trade and colonies, over the deposed Orange dynasty and the violation of the peace terms of 1667, while alliance with France was a traditional Elizabethan and Cromwellian maxim.[2] Even the Declaration of Indulgence of 1672 could be construed as a belated attempt to honour the promise of Breda. Yet there was a revolutionary factor—a secret Treaty that linked the French alliance, the Third Dutch war and the Declaration in a single policy of internal despotism under alien protection :

" The King of Great Britain, being convinced of the truth of the Catholic Faith, is determined to declare himself a Catholic . . . as

---

[1] Cf. Ranke, III, Bk. XV for a summary of the diplomacy ; Stone, pp. 25-40 for documents and illustrations.

[2] Stone, pp. 33-4.

soon as the welfare of his realm shall permit.   His Most Christian Majesty promises to further this action by giving to the King of Great Britain 2,000,000 livres tournois . . . and to assist His Britannic Majesty with 6,000 foot-soldiers." [1]

Here is a project of a real restoration of Monarchy, such as Clarendon had feared and averted ; the price was to be the destruction of the Dutch and Spanish colonial Empires and the subjection of England to the unchecked power of France.   The plan appears so fantastic that it is hard to believe that shrewd politicians like Charles and Arlington ever intended to carry it through.   One thing alone is clear in the obscurity of these intrigues ; Louis soon ceased to expect much from England, and Charles acted half-heartedly in all respects except his demands for money.   When both Louis and the English Commons grew suspicious and closed their purses, the plot at home and the war abroad fizzled out together ; its one concrete result, the first Test Act, was enough to extinguish it and its agents.   Charles and Lauderdale escaped the wreck of the Cabal ; Clifford and Arlington retired in disgrace, Buckingham fell out with the King for a spite or a joke, and Shaftesbury, scenting dark secrets behind and danger ahead, skilfully withdrew to manufacture plots of his own.

The utter failure of both designs, public and secret, reflects as much on Charles' intelligence as on his morality, unless the not improbable conclusion is drawn that Charles " double-crossed " Louis and betrayed French and Catholic interests more effectively than English and Protestant interests.   Though public rumour gave it a fictitious life, the great design was still-born ; Charles " disguised his Popery to the last." [2]   Yet the open policy of the Cabal was sufficient to arouse the nation to a sense of acute danger, and James' admission of Popery, together with his proposal to marry a Popish princess chosen by Louis, raised the succession question which had infuriated Parliaments and shaken thrones ever since the Reformation.   Pamphlets and satires inflamed public interest ; the coffee-houses hummed with rumours ; by-elections took place amid uproar and a new electioneering art sprang up ; the Commons dropped the docile lethargy that had lain upon it

[1] Stone, p. 28.   [2] Burnet, I, p. 93.

since the fall of Clarendon, and the divisions swelled in numbers and frequency.[1]   Before this outbreak a policy and a ministry that offended Parliamentary and national sympathy were doomed. Charles saved but one relic of his scheme, the fatal marriage of James of York and Mary of Modena; and this was countered by the emergence of Monmouth and William of Orange in the role of Protestant successors.

In 1674 Charles II.'s first experiment as the direct ruler of his people came to an end.   Before 1667 he had left government to Clarendon, and after 1674 he had a series of ministers and policies thrust upon him; but between these years he was undisputed master and had at his service what de Witt described as the ablest Ministry in Europe.[2]   He was master of everything but wealth, and that defect was the ruin of his plans.   The Stop of the Exchequer in 1672 was less an act of despotism than an admission of bankruptcy; it was the first sign of his inevitable failure.   It meant that his credit was exhausted with both his paymasters, and it meant his condemnation to eight years of opposition to his official advisers.

III. Royal Opposition and Party Government: 1673-1681

(a) *Opposition to Danby*: 1674-8

So far the King had provided the Cavalier Commons with leaders of his own choosing, such as Clarendon and Arlington; in 1674 they returned the compliment and virtually forced on him their own nominee.   Sir Thomas Osborne, a Yorkshire landowner devoted to wealth and titles—Danby was one of many—had as his programme the task of leading the King and nation back to the old Cavalier policy of economy, Anglicanism and independence.[3]   His chief difficulty was to reconcile party control with Royal dignity; he was officially the servant of none but the King, while in fact he was responsible to a critical and exacting Commons.   He could rely on steady support from neither side, for party ties were loose

---

[1] Cf. Professor W. C. Abbot's articles on the Cavalier Parliament in the *English Historical Review*, Vol. XXI.

[2] Abbot in *English Historical Review*, XXI, p. 263.

[3] Cf. Feiling, p. 154, for an analysis of the importance of Danby's administration.

and unrecognised, and Charles was an elusive and treacherous master. The new experiment was of great significance, but its immediate results were meagre—the completion of the Clarendon Code by the two Test Acts of 1673 and 1678, an economical administration which restored the Royal finances, and the Orange marriage of 1677.[1] The last was Danby's most popular, creditable and momentous achievement. It cemented the Dutch alliance against Louis' bribes and Charles' inclinations, it secured the religion and independence of two nations, and it brought Louis to his second check at Nymwegen in 1678. All Protestant England rejoiced at the betrothal of William and Mary Hyde :

" The whole night was spent in ringing of bells and bonfires, and the greatest expressions of joy which I believe ever were in England, except at the King's restoration." [2]

Yet all was not secure, Danby least of all. Charles' private policy ran counter to the public, and Danby was forced to carry it out through his office and beliefs ; for " the King's personal authority was still both theory and practice of Cavalier politics." [3] Charles was strong enough to paralyse Danby's Church policy and to commit him to the French connection simultaneously with the Orange alliance ; so that Danby, while organising armaments to crush France, was implicated in proposals for a separate peace with France that would have repeated the betrayal of 1670. However, in the contest of treachery Charles and Danby were this time outmatched, for Louis provided French money and French information for the righteous Protestants who impeached Danby in 1678 for receiving French bribes.[4] Thus Louis' revenge for the Dutch marriage turned Protestant rejoicing into panic wrath, and the minister who faced both ways followed Clarendon into exile as Charles' second scapegoat. But Louis was not prepared for the violence of the explosion he caused ; he was bent on teaching Charles a lesson and on getting

[1] For finance, cf. Feiling, p. 156 ; for Statutes, cf. Grant Robertson, pp. 80-92.
[2] Stone, p. 41.   [3] Feiling, p. 155.
[4] Stone, p. 42. Cf. also Articles of Impeachment, Stone, p. 47 ; Grant Robertson, pp. 566-9 ; Tanner, p. 243. Danby was accused of assuming regal power without the Council, of erecting arbitrary government with a standing army ; also " that he is popishly affected and hath traitorously concealed . . . the late horrid and bloody plot."

rid of the English army : he wished to embarrass, not to destroy the Monarchy. Though anti-Popish feeling was rising in the Commons and nation, the second Popish Plot came as an earthquake to all schemes and institutions :

" On the 10th of October came the first news of the Popish Plot, or a design of the Papists to kill the King. Nobody can conceive that was not a witness thereof, what a ferment this raised among all ranks and degrees." [1]

(b) The Three Popish Plots of 1678.

In 1678 not one, but three Popish Plots came to a head. There was Louis' successful plot with the Parliamentary opposition to disgrace the Protestant Minister and to humble the renegade Catholic King. The second was that of Coleman, James' secretary; his fanatic spirit conceived a plan with La Chaise, the confessor of Louis, for the " conversion of three kingdoms " and the " subduing of a pestilent heresy" by the joint agency of James and Louis; he told his correspondent that " there was never such hopes of success since the death of Queen Mary as now in our days." [2]   But this plot was mistimed, for Louis in 1678 was not bent on new designs, and had no romantic urge to revive the halcyon days of Mary Tudor with himself playing the thankless role of Philip of Spain. The third plot, born of Oates and nursed by Shaftesbury, was based, like the second, on a gross misjudgment of the patriotism and impotence of the English Catholics. Nevertheless, there was enough reality in the menace of French power and Catholic activity to make all Protestants ready to believe, or to act as if they believed, the concoctions of Oates, Dangerfield and Bedloe : " The plot must be handled as if it were true, whether it were so or no." [3]   The effects of this convergence of plots and scares coloured the whole of English life for generations. It provided the last chapter in the English " Book of Martyrs " ; it extinguished old, and created new

---

[1] Sir John Reresby: *Memoirs* (ed. Ivatt), p. 179.

[2] Trevelyan: *E.U.S.*, p. 388.

[3] A remark ascribed by Temple to Halifax, cf. Miss Foxcroft's *Life of Halifax*, Vol. I, p. 160. Yet Halifax asserted that the Catholics " had not put off the man in general, nor the Englishman in particular."

political forces ; it opened the second revolutionary era of the century. The Revolution of 1688 was conceived in 1679 ; such were the political consequences of Titus Oates.

One body that the Plot extinguished deserves an obituary notice. Charles dissolved the Cavalier Parliament to save Danby from impeachment, and so ended the age of " perpetual Parliaments." Yet there was nothing of senile decay about it ; it had received new blood from frequent by-elections, and from 1670 its members developed the electioneering methods which Shaftesbury was to raise to perfection.[1] They brought forward the great issue of the Protestant Succession ; they made the great revolution in foreign policy which linked England with her old rival against her old ally ; and they handed on to their successors their claim to dictate the King's choice of policy and ministers. Apart from lapses into generosity or laziness, such as those of 1661-2 and 1669-70, they were watchful and vehement critics of government, and they performed the invaluable service of maintaining Parliamentary claims in the interval between the two Parliamentary Revolutions.[2] They had their weaknesses ; they lacked cohesion and discipline, they were open to Court influence and corruption, they allowed their political sense to be overcome at times by waves of loyalism and their victories to be nullified by subsequent carelessness.[3] But they had this advantage over the succeeding Parliaments who surpassed them in organisation of policy and electoral machinery : their political conservatism and prudence consolidated their gains and invited no dangerous reaction. Their successors rose higher on the tide of national hysteria, but then sank lower in the slough of reaction ; while Danby did not reach far enough, Shaftesbury overreached himself.

[1] Compare Professor Abbot's account of the Cavalier elections in *E.H.R*, XXI. with Mr. E. Lipson's account of the Exclusion elections in *E.H.R.*, XXVIII.

[2] Cf. Abbot, *op. cit.*, p. 285 : " The history of the Cavalier Parliament modifies the idea that the Revolution of 1688 was in any sense a conspiracy of great Lords far in advance of their time, and more or less independent of popular sentiment."

[3] *E.g.*, the " clear and coherent programme " that Feiling (p. 154) ascribes to Danby was not carried out ; there was vacillation over the Dutch alliance and war credits in 1677-8, and over Crown rights when they allowed a dispensing clause in the Second Conventicle Act ; they allowed Charles to undo the Triple Alliance and to relax the Clarendon Code.

(c) Charles in Opposition to Shaftesbury : 1679-81

Shaftesbury follows Clarendon, Arlington and Danby as the key-man of a definite Restoration epoch ; he was the " daring pilot in extremity " of the Terror.[1] He represented the new spirit of party more closely even than Charles ; he was a man " for close designs and crooked counsels fit," [1] using patriotic and religious credulity for party ends ; in Dryden's words, he usurped " a patriot's all-atoning name " and shielded his ambition behind " the buckler of the people's cause." He won to his side the interests of commerce, London and Dissent ; from his house in Aldersgate and the King's Head Tavern, home of his Green Ribbon Club, he organised petitions, elections, debates and divisions, prosecutions and mob demonstrations—a revolutionary symphony under a skilled conductor. His ultimate aim was the establishment of a commercial oligarchy in control of Crown and Parliament, with the corollary of toleration of all Protestants.[2] His immediate objective was Exclusion—the Parliamentary alteration of the succession to ensure a Protestant heir and to remove James, the centre, passive or active, of all Popish Plots. Yet Limitation was as much a part of his policy as of his opponents'. Monmouth was to be no less a puppet King than James ; for he would be an elective King with a Parliamentary title and a party guarantee ; the result would be :

> " That Kingly power, thus ebbing out, might be
> Drawn to the dregs of a democracy." [3]

This was the sham Protestant plot which made the Catholics its victims and the Protestants its tools, which manipulated a genuine national emergency to the narrow interests of a party. The real attack was that against Danby's alliance of Court and Cavaliers by a revived alliance of great Lords, merchants and Dissenters—the malcontents of the Civil War. The spirit of '41 was abroad ; the preachers were out again with the cry of Popery ; the old Republi-

[1] Dryden, *Absalom and Achitophel*, indispensable for a study of the Exclusion Crisis.

[2] Catholic toleration was excluded, not on any religious principle of Shaftesbury the Deist, but because of its connection with France and the Court.

[3] Dryden, *op. cit.* (cf. selections in Nichol Smith's *Characters*). Cf. Feiling, p. 195, for the Tory suspicion of elective Monarchy.

cans reappeared, and associations sprang up that recalled the Covenant.[1] The turning-point in the direction of the attack came with the dissolution of the " Habeas Corpus " Parliament of 1679. The subsequent sweep of the constituencies by the Whigs filled the Anglican gentry with the fear that they were doomed to exclusion along with James, and that their enemies would make religion a pretext for political proscription as they had done in 1662. The Whig agitation for a speedy summoning of Parliament in the winter of 1679-80 finally converted the national crisis into a war of parties, " petitioning," and " abhorring " ; all that remained of the original problem was the succession question, and even that was used as a test of the new problem : whether the pressure of organised groups outside Parliament was to be allowed to dictate policy to both King and Parliament.

The new force in politics had two immediate effects. First, political groups coalesced into two organised parties, and Shaftesbury's machine was met by a combination of Court, manor and rectory. The organisation of both was indeed rudimentary and collapsible until after 1714 ; but from 1679 they had a permanent nucleus and an enduring spirit which survived the strain of political upheavals and the attacks of conservative statesmen like Halifax.[2] Secondly, their infant strength was proved by the utter failure of the conservatives to revive in 1679 the method of government by a national Council.[3] Temple devised a scheme, in the Burleigh and Clarendon tradition, for a Council of thirty, representing both parties as well as Crown officers ; it was to be the sole adviser of the Crown, replacing Cabals and first ministers. But whereas simple men like Evelyn saw in the plan a cure for national divisions, neither Charles nor the politicians were deceived. Charles vowed in private : " They have put a set of men about me, but they shall know nothing " ;[4] the Commons suspected " the old leaven " in the Council, and Shaftesbury, its President, soon abandoned it as

---

[1] Hence the name " Whig " from the Scotch Covenanters ; cf. Stone, p. 54, for the origin of party names.

[2] " The best party is but a kind of a conspiracy against the rest of the nation "— *Political Thought and Reflections.*

[3] Cf. Prof. R. Turner's article in *E.H.R.*, Vol. XXX, and Stone, pp. 50-1.

[4] *Memoirs of the Earl of Ailesbury*, Vol. I, p. 34.

useless for his purpose.   By 1680 the experiment was dead, while factions and cabals flourished anew ; the new parties had pronounced the death-sentence upon the old Constitution.

In the following year the Exclusion quarrel reached its climax. Perhaps the most remarkable feature of the crisis is that revolution was the subject of fierce debate for three years without any recourse to arms.   There were admittedly threats, mob excesses and judicial murders, but the nation retained a surprising measure of self-control. The party system provided it with an alternative to wholesale bloodshed, and may take some credit for diverting passions as violent as those which had caused the Civil Wars.   And when the Whig party went beyond the bounds of prudence and threatened in 1681 to repeat the catastrophe of 1641, its enemies were able to effect its immediate and complete downfall.[1]

Only less remarkable is the change in the public opinion concerning Monarchy and its powers.   Prerogative was dead ; even the King's mistresses went over to Exclusion.   Charles kept a discreet silence on Divine Right and exiled his fire-eating brother, who lamented that " the Monarchy is gone." [2]   Charles recognised this fact and let all things go except the succession.   He put his hopes in time, the mistakes of his opponents, and popular sympathy for his defence of his family's birthright ; he based his tactics, not on Prerogative, but on property—an appeal that aroused the strongest instincts of squire and parson.   Meanwhile Parliaments and coffee-houses probed into the fundamentals of Monarchy with the freedom of Levellers.   It became a commonplace that under certain conditions Monarchy must be reduced to a figurehead and surrender the sovereignty to Parliament, and that public utility must override indefeasible right.

Once the " mystery of princes " had been invaded by the profane hands of subjects only a miracle could restore it.   The defeat

[1] Cf. Reresby's account of the Oxford Parliament : *Memoirs*, p. 213 : " Many of the discontented members, of both Houses, came armed, and more than usually attended ; and it was affirmed there was a design to have seized the King, and to have restrained him till he had granted their petitions."

[2] Cf. James' letters, written in exile at Brussels, in Stone, p. 52 : " The Bill that was read against me . . . was against law, and destroys the very being of the Monarchy, which I thank God yet has had no dependency on Parliament nor on nothing but God alone, or never can, and be a Monarchy."

of Exclusion without the lesser evil of Limitation was in appearance a miracle of this nature.   The return of the Royal brothers to power and popularity, the return of the Cavaliers to non-resistant loyalism, both seem to imply a violent national revulsion of penitence and abasement.[1] Hysteria alone explains the extent and speed of reaction, but the root cause is clear—an uncertain succession involving certain civil war.   The Whig failure was the more inevitable through their disagreement on the choice of a Protestant successor ; the moderates preferred William of Orange to Shaftesbury's puppet, Monmouth.   Shaftesbury's policy sacrificed, not only the stability of a hereditary system, but the Protestant defences against France ; his choice of Monmouth was a personal move too flaunting and rash for the conservative middle class, and it led instantly to the adoption of James by the Tories as the lesser evil. For James, for all his Popery, was a Prince of rightful claims and a man of experience, sincerity and honour.   The last throw of the Whigs, the Protestant plots of 1682-3, served only to confirm the Stuart strength, to seal it with the blood of Russell and Sidney, and to increase the pace and rigours of reaction :

" The shattered remains of English liberty were then attacked on every side ; and some of the noblest blood in the nation was offered up a sacrifice to the names of the Popish martyrs and made to atone for the Bill of Exclusion." [2]

IV. CHARLES AND THE ROYALIST REACTION : 1681-5

In 1681 the fall of free institutions seemed to be involved in the fall of the men who had discredited them ; despotism seemed to be the one way of salvation for a faction-ridden nation.   Yet it is an open question whether English liberty was not more gravely threatened by the domination of Shaftesbury's party, engendered in the haste and heat of revenge, than by the measures taken by the King and Tories for precaution as well as revenge.   It is clear that

[1] Cf. the anathemas of the University of Oxford after 1681 and its insistence on " the badge and character of the Church of England, . . . submitting to every ordinance of man, for the Lord's sake, whether it be unto the King as supreme or unto governors as unto those that are sent by him " ; Feiling, p. 201.

[2] Stone, p. 65, from Wellwood's *Memoirs*.

the direct attack in 1681 was on party, not liberty; the flight of Shaftesbury (despite the protection of his London juries), the dismissal of the Whig Lords, the annihilation of the Exclusionist machine were just and natural consequences of the failure of a Terror.   Whether the result was despotism or not depends on an answer to this question : did the lion's share of victory fall to the King or to the rival Parliamentary party ?

(a) *The King's Share of Victory*

Macaulay declared without qualification that " The King had triumphed." [1]   Parliament was scattered and none petitioned for its recall ; the Whigs discarded it as a broken, and the Tories as a dangerous tool.   But Charles knew from his father's career that freedom from Parliamentary opposition gave no permanent security unless his opponents were dislodged from their local strongholds from which Parliament drew its lifeblood.   Therefore his real victory, greater than the Oxford Dissolution, was his purge of the Parliamentary boroughs of their Whig and Dissenting governors. London, with its Green Ribbon Club and its refractory juries, was deprived of its Charter, and this inspired a stampede of the other boroughs to surrender theirs for remodelling, lest a worse thing befall them.   In general they submitted to Crown nomination of their officers in accordance with the fate of London :

" That no Lord Mayor, Sheriff, Recorder, Common Sergeant, Town Clerk, or Coroner . . . shall be capable of or admitted to the exercise of their respective offices, before His Majesty shall have approved them under His Sign Manual." [2]

Thus opposition was crushed at its source, and the docility of future Parliaments seemed assured.

In 1683 Charles appeared to be in a far stronger position than in 1670 ; the Protestant opposition was divided, the Whigs were expelled from central and local government, the Tories professed unquestioning obedience.   It only needed French gold to complete the resurrection of the 1670 Monarchy ; and before the Oxford

[1] *History of England*, ch. 2.

[2] Stone, p. 62 ; cf. Reresby's *Memoirs*, pp. 230-1 and 255, for the surrender of the Charter of York and the part taken by Halifax.

Parliament Louis had decided to restore his penitent vassal to favour and to renew his pension. His conditions were easy : " *de ne point assembler son parlement, et favoriser mes intentions dans toutes les occasions qui se présenteraient* " ; and five million livres was generous pay for vague and mainly negative services.[1] However the pension was temporary, and was paid grudgingly and in arrears.

The fact that there was nothing permanent in this arrangement had an important effect on Charles' plans and power. French money by itself was inadequate for large schemes, either at home or abroad, as was proved by the evacuation of Tangier in 1683. No standing army was possible with such resources. Now the one recipe for despotism after 1660 was an army and the support of the Catholics and Dissenters ; and Charles had abandoned all three by his acts and alliances in 1681. He was still dependent on the support of a Parliamentary party. There is no evidence that he and his Tory advisers intended to rule permanently, or even as long as eleven years, without Parliaments ; the very care taken to pack the boroughs points to a revival of Parliament as soon as the frenzy had died down and the Tory machine was perfected. No doubt Charles was inclined to postpone the worries that even a loyal Parliament could cause, but the whole scheme bears the mark of a temporary respite.

There can be no despotism without the will to despotism. In 1681 Charles was tired of government ; he used his wits for a last effort, to secure not an aggressive tyranny but a political retirement, and he restrained the despotic desires of his impatient brother. The love of ease and pleasure resumed its normal sway in 1684 ; Halifax's diagnosis is confirmed by Reresby's account of Charles' life at Newmarket :

" He walked in the morning till ten of the clock ; then he went to the cockpit till dinner-time ; about three he went to the horse-races ; at six he returned to the cockpit, for an hour only ; then he went to the play, though the actors were but of a terrible sort ; from thence to supper ; then to the Duchess of Portsmouth's till bed-time ; and so to his own apartment to take his rest." [2]

[1] Ranke, IV, p. 136, note 1. Cf. his chapter on the Oxford Parliament for Charles' appeals to Louis (Bk. XVI, ch. 9), and Vol. IV, pp. 190-6 for French payments and policy in 1684.

[2] *Memoirs*, p. 251.

It was a programme that left little time or vigour for government, and his sudden death proves a greater exhaustion than his subjects were aware of.

(b) The Tories' Share of Victory

Despotism depends not only on will but on opportunity; the next question is whether Charles could have prevented the Tory domination to which he consented. He had nothing apart from their support but an inadequate French pension and the fickle affections of the populace.[1] Fulsome protestations of loyalty must have offended his taste without deceiving his reason; he did not need the warning that Bishop Morley sent in vain to James : " that if ever he depended upon the doctrine of non-resistance, he would find himself deceived." [2] Charles only saved the dynasty by swallowing whole the aims and prejudices of " the old Cavalier and truly loyal party." He had no option in 1681 but complete surrender—he had merely a choice of masters ; he could become either a Whig puppet or a Tory mascot.

Limited Monarchy was established in fact and denied in theory by the same men. The Tory monopoly of office, central and local, lay and clerical, established a despotism indeed ; but it was not Royal despotism, as James learned to his cost. If we discount men's words by their deeds, we must admit that a King who ruled with the Tory squire on one side and the Anglican priest on the other was not a King of the 1670 pattern ; " we must march together," said Charles, and it was the King who had to keep in step. His Tory ministers, the two Hydes and Halifax, quarrelled among themselves but combined against Sunderland, the last relic of Court government ; they were resolved to keep Charles, not without plain speaking, to lawful, Anglican, and eventually Parliamentary ways.[3] There was nothing sinister in their temporary aversion to

---

[1] The national sorrow at his death is dangerous evidence, for the obituary column daily proves that charity is evoked more readily by death than by life.

[2] Feiling, p. 201 ; cf. also pp. 203-4 : " No logical process could reconcile the Tory political theory with their constitutional sense or their religious convictions."

[3] Cf. Feiling, ch. 7, and Ranke, Vol. IV (Bk. XVI, chs. 11 and 12), particularly Ranke's judgment : " We may regard this as the first decidedly Tory government that ever existed " (IV, p. 158).

Parliaments.   They had as yet no machine or demagogic skill comparable to Shaftesbury's ; their strength was in the countryside, and their followers disliked frequent and expensive journeys to Westminster and all the discomfort and upsetting influences they found there.   A government without Parliament which did nothing, asked for no money, and supported local authority, was the ideal of a lazy and parochially-minded squirearchy.   Parliament was a weapon in reserve, to discipline a King who strayed from the narrow path of Tory Anglicanism.

(c) *Halifax and the Nation's Share of Victory*

The fear of '41 and another Long Parliament [1] was not wholly the fear of a selfish section, nor did the reaction serve party interests alone.   The defeat of Exclusion was a personal triumph for one man, George Savile, first Marquis of Halifax ; and his ascendancy in Charles' Council from 1680 to 1685 is a guarantee that there was no Royal despotism, and that even party despotism was tempered by national interest.   Burnet, with bewildered disapproval, described him as a man " who went backwards and forwards, and changed sides so often that in conclusion no side trusted him " ; he added that " He seemed full of Commonwealth notions, yet he went into the worst part of King Charles' reign." [2]   The truth is that Halifax only changed as men changed around him ; he was the proud and watchful " Trimmer," who balanced and saved the ship of State ; if he went into the worst part of the reign, it was to retrieve the nation's safety.   He acted as a check on Exclusion and reaction alike ; his acquiescence in the settlement is a sign of its soundness in the circumstances, and a proof that " moderate men had won what they desired." [3]   Though he was a unique and lonely figure—a true aristocrat in an age of oligarchs—he interpreted, both in conduct and in words of clear and virile English, the inarticulate desires of common men :

[1] Shaftesbury is reported to have attempted to deny the King's right to dissolve Parliament and to have made efforts to keep Parliament in session at Oxford despite the Royal Dissolution (Ranke, IV, p. 135).

[2] Burnet, I, pp. 267-8.   Burnet could not understand a " Christian in submission," who " believed as much as he could," and he suffered often from Halifax's ridicule (cf. Nichol Smith, pp. 318-9).

[3] The opinion of Professor Abbot, in *E.H.R.*, XXI, p. 285.

"Our Trimmer thinketh that the King and Kingdom ought to be one creature, not to be separated in their political capacity ; and when either of them undertake to act a part, it is like the crawling of worms after they are cut in pieces." [1]

Against faction and despotism he appealed to Law—" not the King's Laws, nor the Parliament's Laws, but the Laws of England " ; and he declared that " those who will not be bound by the laws rely on crimes ; a third way was never found in the world to secure any government." [2] His one aim was the restoration of national harmony, and his chief virtue was an amazing sanity in an age that infected most men with its madness.

His qualities deprived him of some influence ; he could not save Stafford or Russell, since he could not restrain the parties he despised and denounced ; his tenure of office depended solely on the favour of the King, a man of like penetration, if less honour. His influence died with the death of wisdom on the Throne ; not even Halifax could save James from his folly. Yet his imperishable achievement is that he prevented in 1680 a harebrained revolution which must have produced a worse and more lasting reaction than that of 1681 ; while saving the rights of William of Orange, he gave the Stuarts a last chance.[3] It was a wise forbearance which made possible the permanent success of the Revolution of 1688.

V. James II. and the Tory Despotism : 1685-8

(a) The Failure of the Royal-Tory Alliance : 1685-6

James set out, in blind confidence, to march together with his brother's allies. He had been their natural leader since 1681, when his qualities of pride and courage had appealed to the Tories in their

---

[1] " The Character of a Trimmer " (*Works*, ed. Raleigh, p. 56). Halifax has found, in the late Sir Walter Raleigh, an editor worthy of him. Raleigh's Introduction to his edition catches the spirit of the man, patricularly his sane patriotism. Raleigh would have given much to have written this : " But for the earth of England, tho' perhaps inferior to that of many places abroad, to him " (the Trimmer) " there is Divinity in it, and he would rather die, than see a spire of English grass trampled down by a foreign trespasser."

[2] *Political Thought and Reflections* (Works ed. Raleigh), p. 212.

[3] Cf. Dryden's panegyric in *Absalom and Achitophel* of Jotham, " of piercing wit and pregnant thought " (Nichol Smith, p. 319).

common danger. In the following years he had strengthened his position, with Charles checking his worst indiscretions; in 1685 he was at last free to take seriously both his own position and his party's protestations. A bigot succeeded a sceptic, an idealist succeeded a politician; James had the fixed ideas and the humourless pride that make up the common tyrant. He began by assuming that he could make Tory domination a basis for Royal despotism. His first Parliament, which he had made some attempt to pack, disillusioned him. Though it was acclaimed as the " most loyal and landed Parliament " since 1661, the dangerous cry of " free Parliaments " was raised by Edward Seymour, a great Tory magnate who regarded the West Country seats as a family preserve.[1] This was the first sign of distrust, which Monmouth's and Argyle's risings allayed for a while only; the uneasy alliance collapsed in the second session of the Parliament. The dismissal of Halifax in October 1685 was significant but not fatal, as long as James retained the support of his brothers-in-law, Rochester and Clarendon, who led the High Tories; but when he demanded a grant for a large army, to be officered at his discretion, Parliament met him with a blank refusal. It went further against him, to demand the rigorous enforcement of the Test Act and to attack the Royal prerogative to dispense from the laws.

The first revolution of the reign took place when James prorogued Parliament in November 1685 and turned to the Whigs— the party which he had helped to proscribe for their attack on him. " He was naturally eager and revengeful," wrote Burnet, " he was for rougher methods." [2] Since conciliation had failed, he turned naturally to force; he determined to make Prerogative instead of Parliament the basis of his power. His policy was declared by the Royal Judges in 1686 in the case of *Godden v. Hales*, upon which he based his attack upon the Protestant monopoly of civil and military office.[3] The significance of this case lies, not only in James' plan to create a Catholic army in defiance of the Test Acts, but in its threat to the Tory-Anglican supremacy as established by Parliament and accepted by Charles II.; it shows that before James could

[1] Cf. Feiling, pp. 205-7; Stone, p. 69; *Verney Memoirs*, Vol. IV, ch. 9.
[2] Burnet, I, p. 169.   [3] Grant Robertson, pp. 384-8, and Tanner, Appendix VIII.

found a real despotism, he must undo the work of his brother's last years, and it proves that the settlement of 1681-3 was not in design or effect a foundation for absolute Monarchy.

(b) The Improvised Despotism of James II. : 1686-8

James knew that, if his power was to last, there was one task more urgent than the creation of a standing army—the remodelling of the Tory fortresses of the Universities and the Commissions of the Peace. His attempt to convert Magdalen College and Christ Church into Catholic seminaries was a body blow at Anglican education, and his scheme to uproot the Tory monopoly of local government was even more dangerous, though it has received less attention.[1] In 1687 the last of the Popish Plots was in full swing. The Hydes were at last dismissed for putting religion before family ties ; a High Commission Court was set up, in defiance of the Act of 1661, to muzzle the Church ; [2] Whigs, and Dissenters freed by the first Declaration of Indulgence of April 1687, were restored to municipal office : and the bulk of the Tory Justices was dismissed for refusing to pledge themselves to a policy of toleration and repeal of the whole penal code of religion.[3] It was an attempt to reconstruct the shattered machine of Shaftesbury by a coalition of Catholics, Quakers and Independents.

The scheme went badly from the start. It was difficult to find candidates for the vacant posts ; for most of the Catholics, including the Papal Nuncio, disapproved, and the main body of Dissent, in spite of the appeals of William Penn for his Royal friend, was reluctant to abet Popery and invite fresh Tory reprisals. The immediate result was to reunite the cause of local oligarchy with the general causes of Parliament and Protestantism—Danby's combination of 1674 ; the local Justices appealed to Parliament, and Halifax and Danby opened negotiations with Dykvelt the Dutch Commissioner.[4] The doctrine of non-resistance was wilting under the test of events ; it was cruelly slain by its authors, the

---

[1] For the Universities, cf. Stone, pp. 74-8, and Hutton : *H.E.C.*, ch. 12.

[2] Cf. Ecclesiastical Commission Act, 1661.

[3] Cf. Feiling, pp. 218-221.

[4] Feiling, pp. 224-5 ; Ranke, IV, p. 311.

Bishops, when they refused to proclaim the second Declaration of Indulgence from their Churches in May, 1688.[1]

The trial of the Seven Bishops completed at once the failure of James' experiment and the union of the Protestant opposition. The Bishops turned Whig in friends and doctrine; they made Whig distinctions between passive and active obedience, between the personal and Parliamentary authority of the King; they too appealed to Parliaments, past and future, against "such a dispensing power, as may at pleasure set aside all law, ecclesiastical or civil." [2] They declared, in their extremity, for Parliamentary relief for Dissent; they were cheered by London crowds and James' troops, and a London jury acquitted them. But the greatest portent of all was that some of James' Judges, trained by Jeffreys, frankly engineered the verdict and summed up against the dispensing Prerogative:

"It amounts to an abrogation, an utter repeal of all the laws. . . . If this be once allowed of, there will need no Parliament; all the legislature will be in the King, which is a thing worth considering, and I leave the issue to God and your consciences." [3]

Thus was the issue made clear to all by a Royal Judge, speaking not as a servant of the Crown but as a citizen, laying aside his wig as the Bishops laid aside their theories.

On the night that the Bishops were acquitted, seven noble conspirators sent to William of Orange a definite invitation.[4] For the danger was not over; for the last three weeks the threat of a permanent Catholic dynasty grew with the growth of Mary of Modena's son. The birth of a Catholic heir on June 10, 1688, was also the birth of the Revolution. It forced the opposition to wrest the initiative from the King; they could no longer be content with defeating James' counter-revolution against the system of 1681; they must take away his and his son's title as well as his power. James' bid for power was doomed because he cast aside the two props of the old Monarchy, the gentry and the Anglican Church, and because Dissent rejected the unnatural alliance " between

[1] For the Declaration, Bishop's Petition and Trial, cf. Grant Robertson, pp. 388-406, and Tanner, Appendix IX.

[2] Grant Robertson, p. 392. [3] Grant Robertson, p. 404. [4] Cf. Stone, pp. 80-1.

liberty and infallibility " ; but his very throne was doomed when he upset the Protestant Succession of his daughters, Mary and Anne Hyde.   The national desertion was all but unanimous ; the most loyal of Cavaliers joined with the sects wooed by Halifax to force on James a Parliamentary settlement which would secure " religion and properties." [1]

(c) *The Revolution of* 1688

The protagonists in June 1688 were James and the outraged Tories led by Danby and Halifax ; but both sides had to call in allies, and success depended on a right choice and a skilful wooing. James lost his throne mainly because he offered no resistance to which supporters could rally ; the Tory leaders won because they secured the alliance first of the Whigs and Dissent, and secondly of William and Mary.

James, like Richard Cromwell, deserted himself ; his friends and servants followed his example with alacrity.   The obstinate courage of his early years was lacking ; he vacillated between Sunderland and Petrie, between Parliament and Louis ; he prepared to fight, then fled, returned to treat with William, and fled again. All he gained was the return of the Bishops to a qualified obedience ; what he lost was the aid of Louis.   It is to his credit as an Englishman that he refused French help as long as any hope of English support remained ; but he thereby lost his throne.   Louis, irritated by James' snubs, left his English protectorate to its fate and embarked on more promising conquests on the Rhine ; for a few critical months he left Holland unmasked, and this move alone made William's invasion possible.[2]

When force challenged force, the improvised despotism

---

[1] Cf. Feiling, p. 235 for the Cavaliers ; for Dissent, cf. Halifax's *Letter to a Dissenter* ; he urged on them " the duty . . . in Christianity and prudence, not to hazard the public safety, neither by desire of ease nor of revenge " (*Works*, p. 129).   Penn kept the Quakers loyal, and the appearance of Vane and Titus in the Privy Council suggests that James had some Independent support ; but the majority were satisfied by the Anglican promise of Parliamentary relief and suspected the protection of a Catholic King in the light of Louis' Revocation of the Edict of Nantes in 1685. Moreover the two pamphlets of Halifax, the *Letter to a Dissenter* and the *Anatomy of an Equivalent* had a wide influence.

[2] For the diplomatic history of the Revolution, cf. Ranke, Vol. IV, pp. 369-440. For a spirited defence of James as an " intense nationalist " cf. Mr. Belloc's *James II*.

crumbled at its foundations.   The fleet, James' especial pride, was faithful ; but he had neither the time nor the money to equip a fleet comparable to the fifty men-of-war commanded by William and the Whig Admiral Herbert, and at the decisive moment the winds blew against Popery as in 1588 and escorted the Protestant Armada down the Channel to Torbay.[1]   Yet there still remained an army of 40,000 men, a concentrated and overwhelming force.   Once again time was against him.   By 1688 he had introduced only a minority of Catholic officers—a leaven to ferment Protestant discontent, while the ranks, except for Sarsfield's 3000 Irishmen, were stout Protestants who cheered the mutinous Bishops.   Religious division paralysed James' striking force and saved William from the fate of Monmouth.   One of the first to desert was John Churchill, General and favourite of the King ; he not only broke up the army but he brought to William the invaluable support of the Princess Anne, whose claims James might have urged against those of her sister, Mary of Orange.   Thus James was stripped of all his weapons, material and diplomatic, and resigned himself amid a cloud of negotiations to that flight which eased the consciences of Tory revolutionaries.

The Tories were not much happier in their attack than James in his defence.   They had to admit Whig allies in increasing numbers ; they swallowed whole the Whig doctrine of Exclusion and conditional obedience ; they had to talk gracefully of toleration ; and they sacrificed their insularity to foreign aid and leadership—they accepted a Dutch Calvinist as saviour of the Anglican Church. Like the Presbyterians in 1660, they quieted their scruples by the formula of a " free Parliament," and they refused to look forward to the ultimate consequences of their acts.   If James, either by summoning Parliament or by resisting the foreign intruder in English and Royal fashion, had made a last appeal to the spirit of Cavalier loyalism, he would have found ample support, and William's following would have melted away as discreetly as it had gathered.   Only Halifax and Danby, the founder of the Orange alliance, were fully committed to William's venture ; typical Tories

[1] Cf. Macaulay's *History*, ch. 9, for a vivid account of the naval and military situation in 1688.

like Nottingham and the Hydes only supported it because James made no opposition, and on condition that William should call and protect a free Parliament which should itself decide between the children of Anne Hyde and Mary of Modena.

" The country is not fond of him," an observer wrote of William in November 1688 ;[1] but he had three claims on English parties, two of which appealed particularly to the Tories.   First, he was a Stuart by descent and marriage, and had as such a rightful interest in the English succession ; he had been the Regent proposed by the Tory Limitation scheme of 1679-81.   Secondly, he had refused to endorse James' and Penn's appeals for Prerogative toleration, and in 1687 he had proclaimed his belief in Parliamentary toleration, the maintenance of Tests and restrictions on Catholic worship. This declaration is one of the decisive factors in the success of the Revolution, since it gave both parties a common programme and a pledged leader.[2]   His third claim was that he was the acknowledged Protestant champion when all Europe feared the Franco-Jesuit offensive which had struck its first blow by the Revocation of the Edict of Nantes ; his cause was the cause of all Protestants, and it weaned the Tories from their Anglican prejudices and the Whigs from their commercial jealousies.

Nevertheless revolutionary unity was only maintained by a discreet silence about the final settlement.   A small section—some of the Whigs, Burnet, William himself and possibly his wife—had a definite plan for a dynastic change involving the instant deposition of James ; but that was not the main issue till after the Revolution, when it arose out of the difficulties of settlement.   Nor was toleration the " cause " ; for all agreed, from interest if not from conviction, on some measure of relief, and quarrelled only about the means.   The real " cause " was that of 1660—restoration ; the restoration of the vested rights of religion and property that James had attacked.   Parliament was again the means ; the end was to secure the propertied classes in the local government of State and

[1] Stone, p. 81.

[2] It is contained in an open letter of the Grand Pensionary Fagel ; cf. Ranke, IV, pp. 387-395 and Burnet, I, pp. 731-3.   Burnet was largely responsible for it, during his exile at William's Court in 1685-8.   He also had great influence with Mary, and persuaded her to tell William that she would not accept the English Crown without him or make him " his wife's gentleman-usher " (I, pp. 692-3).

Church. In this respect the binding force of opposition was economic interest ; Whigs and Tories united to recover from James the spoils that they were wont to dispute between themselves. Yet the "economic man" was not the whole Englishman, even in an age notorious for self-seeking ; it would be unjust, in reaction from Macaulay's glowing colours, to deny the reality of religious and patriotic motives in the rising. The connection of religious conviction with vested rights may be a sign, not of the shallowness, but of the depth of its roots. "No Popery" was not so much a cry of fear as the watchword of national pride and civic liberty, however imperfectly conceived ; it overrode party strife and insular prejudice, and it linked the patriots of two countries in a "general agreement of all thinking men, that we must no more cut ourselves off from the Protestants abroad, but rather inlarge the foundations upon which we are to build our defences against the common enemy."[1] The common enemy was not James, but Louis, yet the memory of Charles II. and the menace of Louis fixed on James the stigma of the tool of France and the traitor to national independence. In this sense the fall of James II. was the second Stuart tragedy of misunderstanding, and its most fitting epitaph is that of Halifax :

"A people may let a King fall, yet still remain a people ; but if a King let his people slip from him, he is no longer King."[2]

SUGGESTIONS FOR FURTHER READING

The works of Burnet, Fox, Evelyn, Halifax, Verney, Airy, Stone, Feiling, Russell Smith (as given under Chapter V).

DRYDEN, JOHN : *Absolem and Achitophel.* (O.U.P.)
The Hind and the Panther. (O.U.P.)
OGG, D. : *England in the Reign of Charles II.* 2 Vols. (O.U.P., 1956)
England in the Reigns of James II and William III. (O.U.P., 1955)
BROWNING, A. : *Thomas Osborne, Earl of Danby.* 3 Vols. (Jackson, 1944–51)

[1] Halifax, *Works*, p. 140.　　[2] Halifax, *Works*, p. 183.

KENYON, J. P. : *Robert Spencer, Earl of Sunderland.* (Longmans, 1958)

FOXCROFT, H. C. : *A Character of the Trimmer.* (C.U.P., 1946)

TURNER, F. C. : *James II.* (Eyre and Spottiswoode, 1948)

BELOFF, M. : *Public Order and Popular Disturbances, 1660–1714.* (O.U.P., 1938)

LIPSON, E. : ' Elections to the Exclusion Parliament '. *E.H.R.*, xxviii.

TURNER, R. : ' The Privy Council of 1679 '. *E.H.R.*, xxx.

DAVIES, G. : ' Council and Cabinet 1678–1688 '. *E.H.R.*, xxxvii.

CRAWFORD, C. C. : ' The Suspension of Habeus Corpus and the Revolution of 1689 '. *E.H.R.*, xxx.

See also pp. 133–4.

VII

THE CONSTITUTIONAL SUPREMACY OF PARLIA-
MENT: 1689-1714

I. THE REVOLUTIONARY " SETTLEMENT " OF 1689

WAS there a Revolution in 1688 and a final settlement in 1689 ?
Or has the importance of the crisis of 1688-9 been exaggerated ?
On the question of Revolution, the lawyers insist that there can
be no doubt; for England and Scotland had no King and no Royal
Seal from December 11, 1688, to February 13, 1689, and the Convention which called William and Mary to the throne had no legal
standing.[1] Even the Tories admitted at first a constitutional break ;
their excuse was that revolution was forced on them by the fact
of James' desertion : " We did not dispossess our King, but he
deserted us." [2] Their latest historian asserts that, " so far as lay in
his power, the King, its appointed guardian, had dissolved English
society." [3] Nevertheless, the interregnum was not anarchy, except
in London; for local society and government held together on
foundations that Laud and Cromwell, greater revolutionaries than
James II., had failed to shake. Halifax was sceptical of the amount
of change, or even of gain ; and there is much in the reigns of
William and Anne that confirms his belief in the continuity of
English politics, if not of English law.[4] A Court formed instantly
around the new Monarchs, with the old corruption, patronage and
pretensions. Prerogative was but scotched ; William at once
declared his intention " to maintain the lustre of the Crown " [5] and

---

[1] Cf. Maitland, *Constitutional History*, pp. 281-8.   [2] Cf. Feiling, p. 248.
[3] Feiling, p. 239.
[4] Cf. *Political Thoughts and Reflections* : " After a Revolution you see the same
men in the Drawing-Room " (of the Court) " and within a week the same flatterers.'
[5] Ranke, IV, p. 519.

soon revealed his congenital dislike of Republics and limited Monarchies ; Anne as late as 1714 scolded a Parliament for its lack of
" regard for my just Prerogative and the honour of my government." [1]   Suspensions of the Habeas Corpus Act, the unprece-
dented growth of taxation and the standing army might make simple
men wonder if William III. were not James II. in disguise.   The
Church was still in danger, if we are to believe Anglican clamour ;
patriots found that Dutch interests and Dutch guards had replaced
French interests and Irish guards ; secret Treaties still flourished
under Somers as under Arlington and Danby.

It is this conservative character of the Revolution which Macaulay
considered its chief glory ; [2] and conservatism is nowhere more
marked than in the " fundamental " document of the Revolution.
The Bill of Rights completed the constitutional trinity of English
freedom, and, like Magna Carta and the Petition of Right, it was a
statement of past wrongs to be redressed and " ancient rights and
liberties " to be regained ; it enacted no constitutional machinery
or sanctions, except a new Oath of Allegiance and a regulation of
the Succession.[3]   Therefore, if we are to find new elements in the
Constitution, we must look beyond 1689.   We must also remember
that the hasty arrangements of the Convention were but a provisional settlement, accepted by many " without prejudice " for
fear of anarchy and invasion.   Though Englishmen of the next
century regarded its work as a final solution of the problems of
Crown, Church and Parliament, though Bolingbroke and Burke
taught their parties the dogma of the " finality " of 1689, which
fixed and perfected for ever the British Constitution, nothing is
more certain than that the men of 1689 treated their work as a make-
shift, to be changed or disowned as interest required.   Hence their
work cannot be judged by itself; they started great things, but finished nothing ; to give it the dignity of a permanent settlement would
be to accept the legend of posterity in the face of contemporary

[1] Feiling, p. 472.

[2] Cf. Macaulay's peroration to ch. 10, written in Nov. 1848 : " It is because we had
a preserving revolution in the seventeenth century that we have not had a destroying
revolution in the nineteenth ; it is because we had freedom in the midst of servitude
that we have order in the midst of anarchy."

[3] Cf. Grant Robertson, pp. 129-138.

evidence.[1]   Uncertainty begat treachery, and treachery begat uncertainty.   Halifax was no exception, although he was more committed than most to the new King ; the man whom Macaulay singled out as the incarnation of the Revolution spirit told a Jacobite agent in February 1689 that " there were but small hopes of a lasting peace from this settlement." [2]   Despite his active services for William he wished it known that " he spoke always with great respect of King James," for, as he told Reresby, " we have wives and children, we must consider them and not venture too far." [3]   His correspondence with the Court of St. Germain is proof that the worldly-wise had little faith in the Constitution they bequeathed to a grateful posterity.

Yet, though for long after 1689 nothing was settled and anything might happen, a limit can be set to the age of experiment, a date can be fixed when the work and the misgivings ended and the legend and complacency began.   In 1714 " finality " seemed more distant than ever, but by 1727 settlement was proved by the peaceful accession of the second Hanoverian King and by the continuance of Walpole's soothing régime.   The crisis of 1714-5 was the last formative test of the Revolutionary structure, and produced the finishing touches ; the Peace of Utrecht, the death of Louis XIV., the failure of the 1715 rising, the Riot and Septennial Acts finally established a Protestant dynasty and a supreme Parliament.   Hence an examination of the character of the Revolution settlement must treat the period from 1689 to 1714 as a historical unit, and must link the provisional arrangements of 1689 with the subsequent modifications and additions.

II. Limited Monarchy

In 1689 the succession to the Crown was changed in order to preserve the Church by means of Parliament.   Of these three

---

[1] Cf. Evelyn's *Diary*, March 29, 1689 : " Things far from settled as was expected," and April 26, 1689 : " Confusion and dissension among ourselves . . . no person of public spirit and ability appearing, threaten us with a very sad prospect of what may be the conclusion."

[2] Reresby, *Memoirs*, p. 338.   Cf. Macaulay, ch. 11 ; " Our Revolution, as far as it can be said to bear the character of any single mind, assuredly bears the character of the large yet cautious mind of Halifax."

[3] Reresby, *Memoirs*, pp. 345 and 349.

institutions, the Crown must be considered first, since the regulation of its succession and powers was the most urgent task of the revolutionaries. How did the Revolution affect the English Crown either in abstract dignity or in concrete powers ?

(a) The " Mystery of Princes " Unveiled

Undeniably, Majesty was diminished. Its twin buttresses, personal loyalism and Divine Right, were torn from it, and under the Calvinist William it received only the qualified support of a divided Church. The King was an important State official, to whom every respect was due ; but, as Bolingbroke later taught the Tories, " the spring from which this legal reverence arises is national and not personal." [1] Both William and Anne, however, tried in different ways to revive the Royal dignity, and they were above all anxious to preserve its independence from the encroachments of parties.

William had the handicaps of alien birth, speech and interests, of a natural reserve and unimpressive person, but he was helped until 1694 by a wife devoted to him and acceptable to Church and nation. After Mary's death his personal unpopularity weakened the Monarchy, until the assassination plots of 1696 brought a reaction in his favour as the national leader against France ; the national Association to protect his life gave him the necessary support to obtain from Louis XIV. the recognition of his title at the Peace of Ryswick (1697).[2] Even in the violent reaction that followed the peace and the Whig abuse of the Association, William secured, at a cost of personal humiliation and concessions, the confirmation of the Protestant Succession by moderate men of all parties. The Act of Settlement proved that the Crown was a national necessity at the same time that its restrictive clauses provided a series of insults directed at the man who wore it.

Perhaps the chief success of William's domestic policy was that Anne ascended the throne by national agreement. The Whigs were committed to her as a Protestant, and the Tories rallied to

[1] *The Patriot King.*

[2] Cf. Evelyn's *Diary*, February 26, 1696 : " Though many did formerly pity King James' condition, this design of assassination and bringing over a French army alienated many of his friends."

her as a Stuart and a High Anglican.[1]   With the death of her father in 1701 and the suspect legitimacy of her brother, she had almost a clear hereditary title ; so Divine Right could revive for a space, and the unwelcome prospect of a German King was put out of mind by Queen and Tories.   Yet despite these advantages and for all her Royal pride, Anne found the task of preserving the Crown from becoming a party tool as difficult as William had found it.   She had her way, though not without many tussles, in ministerial and Church appointments ; but in the all-important sphere of foreign policy she was forced to rely on her Ministers and even on the parties she disliked.   Notwithstanding her appeal to her Ministers " to keep me out of the power of the merciless men of both parties," [2] her reign is remembered for the first appearance of complete party government.   Her beloved confidants, Sarah Churchill and Abigail Masham, were both partisans, and her piety made her a Tory despite herself.[3]   Yet Bolingbroke and Swift denounced her "confounded trimming and moderation," which led her to resist party extremes such as the Occasional Conformity movement in 1705 and Boling-broke's plot in 1714.[4]   Though she was a weak and changeable woman, not endowed with great gifts of intellect or self-reliance, she had almost a Tudor instinct for the national interest in a crisis ; even on her deathbed she saved the national settlement of 1689 and 1701.   By appointing Shrewsbury, the moderate Whig, instead of Bolingbroke to succeed Harley, she defied the claims of party in the joint interests of Crown and nation, and in the spirit of an indepen-dent ruler.

The maintenance of the Royal dignity was also due to the conservatism of the Ministers of both William and Anne.   Halifax, Danby, Marlborough, Godolphin and Harley, all disliked the insolence of party, though they were all compelled to bow before

[1] " My own principles must always keep me entirely firm to the interests and religion of the Church of England, and will incline me to countenance those who have the truest zeal to support it " (Feiling, p. 362).

[2] W. T. Morgan : *English Political Parties and Leaders in the Reign of Anne*, p. 196 ; cf. also Trevelyan, *Select Documents for Queen Anne's Reign* (1702-7), pp. 190-2.

[3] She wrote of William's reign : " Everything was leaning towards the Whigs, and whenever that is, I shall think the Church beginning to be in danger " (Morgan *op. cit.*, p. 165).

[4] Cf. Feiling, p. 444.

it. They turned to the Royal favour as a check to the raging Commons, and that favour was as vital to their position as was party support. " The Queen is the centre of power and union " was the guiding maxim of Harley ; nothing alarmed him more than a large Tory majority in the Commons, except a large Whig majority.[1] The influence of the Crown, both by patronage and by personal appeal, was a powerful, at times a decisive, factor in Parliamentary elections ; not once did Anne fail to secure a favourable verdict when she appealed to the country against presumptuous Ministers or arrogant party majorities. Thus, though the sting of Prerogative was drawn and even the Royal veto was discarded after 1707, the spirit of national Tudor Monarchy was not yet dead. Harley and Anne were faint shadows of Cecil and Elizabeth, but in 1714 the Crown was still worth the wearing, provided that the wearer was English, a sound Anglican, and graced with some measure of Tudor courage and tact.[2]

(b) The Powers of Utilitarian Monarchy

The Judges of the early Stuarts had made a distinction between the ordinary and the absolute Prerogative of the King ; such a distinction, though it was fiercely denied by Coke and Selden, serves to explain what happened to the powers of the King after the Revolution. High Prerogative, as a bottomless treasury of arbitrary powers, was buried with the suspending power and the Royal control of Army and finance ; but there remained definite prerogatives, as necessary discretionary powers of the Executive. It was of the essence of utilitarian Monarchy that the King should work ; in the division of labour between King and magnates, the King was assigned the irksome duties of central administration and the magnates reserved the more congenial task of managing their local estates and offices appurtenant.

There was nothing in the Bill of Rights to check the King's appointment and control of the important officials of State—being Protestant. William and Anne preserved for their own lives the

[1] Cf. Bolingbroke's bitter attack on Harley as a traitor to his party in his *Letter to Wyndham* in 1717.

[2] Anne in her first pronouncement as Queen declared : " I know my own heart to be entirely English " (Feiling, p. 364).

control of the Judges by commissions granted " durante bene-placito regis," [1] and they both chose servants to suit their personal likes or policy.   William, after dissolving the Whig Convention Parliament in 1690, formed a Tory ministry ; but that did not prevent him from consulting the old courtier Sunderland in face of all protests and complaints that " a Prince that chooses his enemies for his guards should disband his friends."   He promoted his Dutch friends, Bentinck and Keppel, to high rank and office ; [2] he was strong enough to save Somers and Montague from impeachment in 1701 and to create a Low Church Episcopate under Tenison and Burnet.   He submitted at times, as in 1695 and 1701, to party pressure ; but by the arts of compromise and by using the feuds of Whig and Tory, Lords and Commons, he preserved intact his Continental policy, with the exception of the Spanish Partition scheme.   In brief, his political opportunism had an element of real independence.

" In selecting Ministers Anne's motives were fundamentally personal " ; [3] her favour and displeasure were the decisive factors in the careers of Marlborough and Harley.   For all her Tory leanings, she never forgave the High Church leaders, Rochester and Nottingham, for pressing the Bill against Occasional Conformity against her wish in 1705, and she liked to keep in office such moderate Whig grandees as Shrewsbury and Somerset.   Her personal influence in Court and Church appointments was more marked than William's, for she had the jealousies of a woman and the touchy pride of a small mind ; she would stand no hectoring :

" Whoever of the Whigs thinks I am to be hectored or frightened into a compliance, though I am a woman, is mightily mistaken in me." [4]

Her bursts of self-assertion continually upset the calculations of

[1] The alterations of the Act of Settlement, which gave the Judges a commission " quamdiu se bene gesserint " and made them removable only by Parliament, were not operative until the Hanoverians succeeded.

[2] The Tories forced William to revoke his lavish grants of Irish Crown lands to his favourites in 1700.

[3] Morgan, p. 198.

[4] Morgan, p. 175. Cf. also p. 194, for her shrewd judgment on the Tories : "I can't for the life of me think it reasonable to brand all of them with the name of Jacobite."

the politicians; even Sarah Churchill confessed defeat.[1] Her last act
was a gesture of Royal independence at Bolingbroke's expense;
she escaped the party net in 1714 by obstinacy and her " incurable
disease of procrastination." [2]

(c) Constitutional Checks on the Crown

Nevertheless the indirect pressure of Parliament upon the Crown
was steady and strong; besides the clumsy method of impeachment, it took the form of administrative obstruction.   William
could usually be moved by a threat to cut off his war supplies and
troops; by limiting its grants in time and amount, by passing
Appropriation and Mutiny Acts for one year only, Parliament had
the King at its mercy, and it used its power to criticise administration by a growing use of Parliamentary committees.[3]   Whigs or
Tories might be silenced by office, though not both at once; but
there was besides a permanent " country " group hostile to Court
influence, an ever present weapon for disgruntled partisans.   The
" country " members, though they lacked the cohesion and discipline of a party, were formidable in a crisis, since they represented
the conservative commonsense of the ruling classes; they looked
with equal distrust upon party domination and Court influence.
They broke the Whigs over the Sacheverell case and the Tories over
the commercial clauses of the Treaty of Utrecht; but their most
striking triumph was the enforcement of their whole programme
in the Act of Settlement.   In it they secured at once the Protestant
Succession and the independence of Parliament.   Since even a
Triennial Parliament was not safe from Court influence, they removed all hope of patronage from the members of the Commons,
and deprived a foreign King of the power to place his officials in the
Commons, where they might defend or initiate policy by speech and
vote.   Since cabals and secret policies had reappeared, they revived
the old Privy Council, excluding all foreigners; it alone was to be

[1] Cf. Morgan, pp. 205-210, and Trevelyan : *Select Docts.*, Conduct of the Duchess
of Marlborough (by herself).

[2] Swift, *Memoirs relating to the Queen's Ministry of* 1710; cf. also Bolingbroke's
Letter to Wyndham on her " fatal irresolution."

[3] Cf. Parliamentary Board of Trade (Egerton, *Short History of British Colonial
Policy*, pp. 116-7).

responsible by the signature of its members, for " all matters and things relating to the well governing of this Kingdom which are properly cognizable in the Privy Council by the Laws and Customs of this Realm." [1]   An alien King was to be checked by an independent Commons and an English Privy Council, and he could not leave England nor engage the nation in war without the consent of Parliament.   It is true that few of these direct checks came into operation ; but their repeal was due, not to Anne's revival of Crown influence, but to the growing confidence of parties and to their desire to unite Parliament and a strong Executive under their own control.

The prime cause of the dependence of Royal policy was the existence of Parliaments in constant session, in accordance with the clause of the Bill of Rights that " Parliaments ought to be held frequently." [2]   Annual Appropriation and Mutiny Acts provided a sanction for the clause, and the Triennial Act of 1694 completed the structure of Parliamentary supremacy.   It ensured, not that Parliaments should be summoned regularly—that was already provided for, but that they should be dissolved regularly ; it was a safeguard, not against their disappearance, but against their servility.   A poor King could not hope to maintain control of the Commons and electorate, when every three years he must renew his efforts and ransack his purse.   And yet without the support of this changing Legislature he could do little of his own, nor could he avoid policies thrust upon him.   The Royal veto was an ineffective weapon ; it delayed, but failed to destroy unwelcome legislation like the Triennial and Place Acts.   The suspending power was gone, and the dispensing power was too dangerous to be used. [3] The Privy Council was regulated by Statute, and had no executive authority except over the overseas possessions of the Crown, while Parliamentary Statutes and Committees were encroaching in Imperial as well as domestic government.   The new Coronation Oath bound the Monarch in uncompromising terms " to govern the people of this Kingdom of Great Britain and the dominions

[1] Cf. Grant Robertson, pp. 155-6.   [2] Cf. Grant Robertson, p. 133.

[3] Cf. Bill of Rights, Sect. II (Grant Robertson, p. 137) ; later, Parliamentary Acts of Indemnity replaced Royal dispensations.

thereunto belonging according to the statutes in Parliament agreed on, and the respective laws and customs of the same." [1] On such terms there could be no successful administration unless Royal policy coincided with, or submitted to, the wishes of the dominant party in the Legislature. William bowed and Anne responded to the changes of public opinion; they had still the power to adapt and moderate other people's policies, but the initiative had passed from the Crown to its subjects.

William's career as King illustrates best the hard fate of independent Royal programmes. His ideal of religious union and equality was rejected both in England and in Ireland; the restrictions of the Toleration Act, the sharpening of the Recusant Code and its extension to Non-jurors, the violation of the Treaty of Limerick, the quarrels of Convocation, all proved the permanence, even the revival of religious divisions. His Irish policy was one long humiliation; though William won the Battle of the Boyne, all the fruits of conquest passed to Parliament. [2] His European triumphs, for which he sacrificed all other aims, were undermined by Parliament as soon as they had ceased to serve immediate English interests; after the precarious peace of 1697, his army was cut down with malicious economy to the level of September 1680—a carefully chosen date. His just and bitter comment was that " Parliament had accomplished a feat which the French had striven in vain to do for eight years." [3] Parliament went further to attack the Royal Prerogative of treaty-making, when William tried to secure European peace and balance by partitioning the Spanish Empire. It is probable that Parliament would have disowned the Partition Treaties if Louis had not saved it the trouble; in the end the blunders of Louis in 1701 did more than either English party to preserve William's life-work.

Where William failed Anne was not likely to succeed, in spite of her advantages of birth and sex. In her reign the initiative in foreign policy passed finally to political parties, and its direction to subjects who were party leaders by choice or necessity; Marlborough, Harley and Bolingbroke were the real successors of William in the business of settling Europe. Yet though Anne did

[1] Coronation Oath Act, 1689 ; cf. Grant Robertson, pp. 116-120.
[2] Cf. Ranke, V, 204-214, and below, ch. IX.   [3] Ranke, V, p. 174.

not make policy, she used her undoubted influence to check the excesses of partisan schemes when they deviated from the national interest. She supported the Whigs in a national war and a national union with Scotland, and she helped the Tories to make a national peace ; but she drove out the Whigs when they refused to make the peace the nation demanded, and when the Tories threatened in 1714 the national settlement of the Succession, she turned on them, as she had in 1705, and drove them into the wilderness of Jacobitism and opposition. Thus in the Revolutionary era the Crown was only effective as a check or balance in policy, and its chief function, as the repentant Bolingbroke expounded later, was to interpret and uphold the will of the nation against the blind zeal of party politicians.

III. Church and Constitution

(a) *The Supremacy of the Church over the Crown*

" The ecclesiastical element in English history appears at every step," wrote Ranke [1] ; it appeared at no time more forcibly than in this sceptical and corrupt generation. Religion made William unpopular and Mary and Anne popular, it made Defoe a Whig and Swift a Tory ; throughout the eighteenth century—the " Age of Reason "—no cry was so inflammatory as " Christianity and the Constitution " or " Popery and Wooden Shoes." As in 1660-7, so from 1689 onwards, far more labour and heat was expended on the fortification of the Anglican Church than on any other institution ; it was regarded as late as 1800 (by George III., then sane) as the fundamental and unalterable part of the constitutional settlement.

The Royal succession was bound to the re-established Church by the Coronation Oath, the Bill of Rights and the Act of Settlement. This union alone reconciled Englishmen to Dutch and German Kings and kept James and his son in exile ; for many Englishmen the recognition of the Protestant succession was the most valuable clause in the Treaties of Ryswick and Utrecht and the one adequate motive for renewing war in 1702. A monarch

[1] Ranke, IV, p. 523.

who could neither become nor marry a Papist, who must be a communicant of the State Church, who could alter nothing in religion by Royal Commission or Ordinance, was no longer the head but the servant of the Church. National allegiance to the King was relative to his absolute allegiance to the Church—such was the essence of the Tory social contract.

(b) The Church as the Keystone of the Revolutionary System

If then Royal Supremacy, the keystone of the Reformation, was now an empty form, did the Church find freedom or another master ?

The King of England was deposed because he dared to offend the Anglican Church ; therefore Parliament had no other course than to erect the exclusive authority of the Church as the bond of society in place of the tottering Crown. The King must swear at his Coronation to " maintain and preserve inviolately the settlement of the Church of England and Ireland and the doctrine, worship, discipline and government thereof as by law established," and to " preserve unto the bishops and clergy of England, and to the churches there committed to their charge, all such rights and privileges as by law do or shall appertain unto them or any of them." [1] The Toleration Act in one sense emphasised the exclusiveness of this authority, for all its grant of " some ease to scrupulous consciences " of Protestants ; for besides refusing relief to Catholics and non-Christians, it carefully omitted to give Dissenters political rights by any modification of the Test Acts.[2] Churchmanship was still the test of full citizenship, and the steady and successful attack upon ' Occasional Conformity ' was a logical result of this principle. The Church was in danger, and with it the foundations of government, when Dissenters crept into office and violated at once the sanctity of the Sacrament and the spirit of the Constitution.

[1] Grant Robertson, p. 119.

[2] Grant Robertson, pp. 123-128 ; cf. his preface to the Statute : " It is clear that it is a misnomer, for it is not based on the principles of Toleration, which it does not admit, but merely grants a very limited exception from the statutory penalties, under carefully defined conditions. . . . The two principles, (a) that religious beliefs other than those of the Established State Church involved civil disabilities, and (b) that the State was responsible for religious error which ought not to be left unpunished, continued to be the basis of the law . . . until 1828 and 1829."

In 1711 both parties agreed to restore and confirm the Revolutionary supremacy of Anglicanism.[1] Three years later the Schism Act proved that exclusion, and not toleration, was the dominant feature of the settlement; the Act "to prevent the growth of schism and for the further security of the Churches of England and Ireland as by law established" whittled toleration down to a bare and illiterate immunity, and gave the Anglican party not only the government of the adult but the education of the young.[2] But for its repeal in 1719 it would have driven Dissent into intellectual exile, and it may therefore be considered the English and Tory version of the Revocation of the Edict of Nantes. If these Acts are taken with the new penal Code against Catholics, the whole represents the political and social monopoly of Anglicanism, built up, added to, and zealously guarded throughout this period.

(c) *The Supremacy of Parliament over the Church*

Nevertheless the days of Laud had not returned; the men of 1688 did not plan nor build a theocracy. The Church as a political institution was set on high—but by laymen and for laymen, as the clergy found to their cost. Sacheverell's sermons not only voiced the vain expectations of undiscerning Churchmen, and their contempt for their time-serving brethren who were for tolerating deadly error, but they protested against persecution from above as well as insolence from below. He was impeached for " wickedly and maliciously insinuating that the members of both Houses . . . were . . . conspiring the ruin of the Church ";[3] and though the clumsiness of the Whig attack defeated its object, it reveals clearly enough the Erastian spirit and methods of the age. The most portentous political machinery was brought into action against a noisy priest who ventured to denounce lay control of the Church and blasphemed against the Original Contract.

Convocation was impotent, Parliament omnipotent; the poli-

[1] For the Act of 1711, cf. Grant Robertson, pp. 187-190. The Act against Occasional Conformity imposed penalties on Dissenters who took the Sacrament in order to qualify for public offices.

[2] Cf. Grant Robertson, pp. 190-4.

[3] Third charge against Henry Sacheverell, 1710; cf. Grant Robertson, pp. 421-437 and prefatory note : " Burke . . . was of opinion that the trial furnished the best statement of the doctrine and counter-doctrine of the Revolution of 1688."

tical failure of the one spontaneous clerical movement—that of the Non-jurors—shows the decline of the Church as an independent power. Sancroft, the idol of England in 1688, found but 400 clergy and scarcely a layman of importance save Clarendon to follow his punctilious respect for oaths sworn to James II; the Oaths Acts of 1689, 1696 and 1701 swept all such fanatics from office and exposed them, true Churchmen as they claimed to be, to a fate like to that of a Recusant and worse than that of a Dissenter.[1] Even among obedient clergy, few had wide influence, save Bishops like Compton, Burnet, Atterbury, or publicists such as Sacheverell and Swift. Swift himself begged in vain for preferment from the Whigs, and his services to the Tories in 1710-14 merited more than the Irish deanery Harley conferred on him. These men, too, were influential not as Churchmen but as partisans; for the clergy in general, Swift's comment is illuminating " that he does not see how that mighty passion for the Church, which some men pretend, can well consist with those indignities and that contempt they bestow on the persons of the clergy." [2] The real leaders of the Church were Harley the ex-Presbyterian, Bolingbroke the Deist, and Nottingham the Parliamentary lawyer; while Wharton and Walpole became the heirs of Pym, Hampden and Hollis as the guardians of Puritanism.[3] Such men had no care for religion except as a political asset; clerical independence, far less theocracy, was unattainable by a party Church in a Parliamentary State.

[1] Cf. Grant Robertson, pp. 121-3 (Act enforcing new oaths on all office-holders); pp. 144-7 (Act of Security extending oaths to all persons); pp. 160-1 (Abjuration Oath against all Pretenders, enforced on all office-holders and members of both Houses of Parliament).

[2] Swift, *The Sentiments of a Church-of-England Man.* Cf. also his *Letter to a Young Clergyman,* where he describes the lot of nine-tenths of the clergy, despite Queen Anne's Bounty: " They ... first solicit a readership, and if they be very fortunate, arrive in time to a curacy here in town, or else are sent to be assistants in the country, where they probably continue several years, (many of them their whole lives) with 30£ or 40£ a year for their support; till some bishop, who happens to be not overstocked with relations or attached to favourites, or is content to supply his diocese without colonies from England, bestows upon them some inconsiderable benefice, when it is odds they are already encumbered with a numerous family." Swift was describing the Irish Church, but it is not an unfair sketch of English clerical life at the beginning of the eighteenth century.

[3] Before 1711 " Whig " and " Presbyterian " were used as interchangeable terms : but the share of the Whigs in passing the Occasional Conformity Act and depriving Dissent of political power ended the Puritan stage of Whig development.

IV. The Balance of Power in Parliament

Since 1603 Parliament had advanced to examine and control all departments and policies of the State; its fiercest battle had been over the Royal Supremacy of the Church, and when in 1688 it secured victory there, Crown and Church fell together into its power. The King's Church became the Parliament's Church, and instead of a Royal Parliament there was a Parliamentary King. Legally and historically Parliament was incomplete and inconceivable without its authorised and authorising head; the King-in-his-Council-in-Parliament was the inseparable unit of government. Yet the revolutions of the seventeenth century had established the claim and fact of the two Houses to act without and despite their legal author; by their will the King had been expelled and recalled—he was the attribute and they were the substance of the sovereign body. Thus in 1689 the constitution-makers had a choice of principles: either to revive the union of King in Parliament or to frame a system on the base of a King out of Parliament. The one involved Parliamentary sovereignty and a figurehead monarchy, the other a division of functions between a limited Parliament and a limited monarchy. The latter was the theory of the Bill of Rights and the Act of Settlement, but the former was the final solution grafted by the parties and constitutional conventions upon the formal settlement.

(a) *The Impotence of the King in Parliament*

The two Acts assumed or defined a distinction between the duties of the King in Parliament and the King in Council. The King in Parliament regulated the Church, army, finance, trade, the succession to the throne, justice, and an infinite variety of domestic matters; a mass of private Acts replacing the old Orders in Council shows that the Legislature had become its own executive, and the scarcity of public Acts after 1715 indicates its preoccupation with the details of administration. The King in Council was left with the management of the Royal household, the Navy, plantations and foreign affairs; but in these he was subject to continual interference and obstruction from Parliament. Yet while Parliament steadily encroached on the powers of the Crown in Council, it would tolerate no interference of the King in Parliament, and was determined to make his Parliamentary functions purely nominal. The Act of Settlement was the most emphatic expression of this determination ; but the modification in 1707 of the clause which excluded Royal officials from the Commons must not be interpreted as a sign of weakening. It meant that the desire of Parliament to control Crown policy overrode the fear of Crown influence in Parliament ; the barriers between Crown and Parliament were removed because they impeded the free action, not of the Monarch, but of the political parties. The King was to be bound as before—not by the brittle chains of Statute, but by stronger though invisible bonds ; long before the death of Anne it was clear that the doubtful Succession would be settled in favour of the candidate who accepted unreservedly the programme of one or other of the Parliamentary parties.[1]

(b) The Decline of the House of Lords

The impotence of the King in Parliament cleared the way for a duel between the Lords and Commons for the vacant leadership. For some time after 1688 it seemed possible that the Lords might regain some of the ground lost since 1642. They alone of central institutions held together in the winter of 1688 ; they undertook to preserve order and to arbitrate between James and William, and they took the lead in arranging a settlement. Consequently, with the exception of the Commons' " country " group, parties and policies in William's reign were led, if not from the Lords, at least by the prominent Peers ; and their influence has marked the Revolution settlement with the stamp of aristocratic republicanism. Halifax had an equal contempt for the passions of the mob and the tinsel of monarchy ; Burke described England after 1689 as governed by " men of great natural interest or great acquired consideration." [2] But it was not by virtue of their rank, but of their territories and abilities, that Halifax, Danby and their kind ruled in Parliament and Court ; their chief care was management of the Commons rather than of their own House.

[1] As early as 1705 it was remarked : " They don't so much value in England who shall be King, as whose King he shall be " (Feiling, p. 382).

[2] Burke, *Thoughts on the Causes of the Present Discontents* (*Select Works*, ed. Payne, Vol. I, p. 11).

The House that had killed the Exclusion Bill was defeated in a series of decisive disputes with the Commons. Beginning with the Convention debates over the vacancy of the throne, the Commons imposed their views on the Lords with two exceptions— the "tacking" of a clause against Occasional Conformity to a money Bill in 1705 and the cases arising out of the Aylesbury election of 1702. These two rebuffs to the "horrid arbitrariness" of the Lower House proved that the combination of Royal Prerogative and Lords' privilege was still formidable against party extremes not backed by strong popular support.[1] But except on the dangerous ground of privilege and property, the "encroachments" and "innovations" that the Peers denounced were successful "in effect to subject the law of England to the votes of the House of Commons."[2] In 1689 the Commons insisted on James' "abdication" against the Lords' theory of desertion, and they summarily rejected the Comprehension Bill sent down to them; in 1694 the Lords reluctantly assented to the creation of the Bank of England in spite of their fears of its effect on land values, and in 1698 they submitted to the tacking of a clause disbanding the army to a money Bill. In 1699 the Lords made a stand, when the Commons in their attack upon William's grants to his Dutch friends tacked a Resumption Bill to the Land Tax Bill and rejected the Lords' amendments. The Lords thereupon protested that:

"The joining together in a money Bill things so totally foreign to the collecting of money, and to the quantity and quality of the sum to be raised, is wholly destructive of the freedom of debates,

[1] For the Aylesbury cases cf. Grant Robertson, pp. 408-420. Three great constitutional points were raised; (i) the limits of the Commons' jurisdiction in privilege; (ii) the omnicompetence of the appellate jurisdiction of the Lords; (iii) the rights of electors to the "freehold" of their franchise.

But although the Lords defeated the Commons' attempt to extend its privileges, it was not a decisive victory. Professor Turberville, in his *House of Lords in the Eighteenth Century*, p. 71, points out that the Lords did not again challenge the Commons' jurisdiction over elections; and the rights of electors were often infringed by the habit of deciding disputed elections as trials of party strength in the Commons (cf. Walpole and the Chippenham election, 1742). The Lords were more successful when they held up the Trial of Treasons Bill for several sessions, until in 1696 the clause securing the right of Peers to be tried by Peers was included.

[2] Grant Robertson, p. 413. Against this must be set the judgment of Montague (*Introduction to Bentham's Fragment on Government*) on the settlement of 1689: "What remains to the Crown and the House of Lords is just enough to make it incorrect to say that the House of Commons is fully sovereign."

dangerous to the privileges of the Lords and to the prerogatives of the Crown. For by this means things of the last ill consequence to this nation may be brought into money bills, and yet neither the Lords, nor the Crown, be able to give their negative to them, without hazarding the public peace and security." [1]

Yet for all these high words, they gave way, and the defeat was decisive; while their rights of Judicature and personal privileges remained unimpaired, their control of policy was at the mercy of the Commons' control of finance.

Finance is the key to the inferiority of the Upper House. In 1660 it was restored to social, rather than political power, and neither Charles II. nor William III. had any high opinion of its influence; what strength it had was based on its territorial influence, its corporate sense and its unity through intermarriage.[2] Against the advantages of a brilliant personnel, influence at Court, and the right of Peers of personal access to the Monarch, must be set this overwhelming disadvantage: that their House represented, on questions of policy and supplies, not communities, but persons only, however distinguished.[3] They had long ceased to initiate money grants, and after 1678 they no longer amended genuine money Bills sent up from the Commons; in 1699 they failed to stop the abuse of " tacking " non-financial clauses to money Bills. The urgent need of supplies between 1689 and 1714 converted the Commons' financial supremacy into a general domination, and confined the Lords to the defensive weapon of the veto. Burnet in 1700 confessed alarm at the consequences of the Revolution he had helped to engineer :

" We were . . . become already more than half a commonwealth, since the government was plainly in the hands of the House of Commons, who must sit once a year, and as long as they thought fit, while the King had only the Civil List for life, so that the whole administration of the government was under their inspection." [4]

---

[1] Turberville, A. S. : *House of Lords in the Reign of William III*, p. 207.

[2] Turberville, A. S. : *House of Lords in the Reign of William III*, p. 232.

[3] This inferiority was recognised as early as the fourteenth century; cf. Stubbs' *Charters* (9th edition), p. 504 : " Duo milites, qui veniunt ad Parliamentum pro comitatu, majorem vocem habent in Parliamento in concedendo et contradicendo " (sc. auxilium) " quam major comes Angliae " (from the " Modus Tenendi Parliamentum ").

[4] Burnet, II, p. 247.

In this duel the reign of William was decisive; under Anne the Lords regained no ground and won no lasting victory for their House, while Commoners even wrested the leadership of parties and policies from the class that had held it from 1660. Harley and Bolingbroke in their prime led their party from the Commons, and in 1711 inflicted on the Lords the crowning humiliation of creating a permanent nobility for the purpose of a single Act—the Treaty of Utrecht. The struggle of the Houses, which was almost the leading constitutional motif of William's reign, was finally settled and superseded by the all-engrossing party duel, in which the powers of the Crown and of both Houses were used and attacked without scruple by party manœuvres. Parties and economics together completed the fall of the Lords. Parties took their origin and strength, not from the dignified and judicial Upper House (though the party influence of individual Peers might be immense), but from the Commons and electorate. Quality bowed before quantity of interest; for all their great estates the Peers were out-weighted in property by the squires and merchants who filled the parties and provided the economic foundation of the Revolutionary system. Squire Walpole completed the work of Squire Harley when he defeated the Peerage Bill of 1719, which was to make the Lords an entrenched and exclusive body; he finally ensured that the leader of the Commons should be the leader of the nation.

(f) *The Supremacy of the Commons and the Economic Settlement*

Between 1689 and 1714 the functions of Crown and the House of Lords were defined and limited; but the body that prescribed the limits for others set none for itself. The all-embracing and encroaching activities of the Commons defy classification; there was little they could not and dared not do. Their powers are best seen through the life of the parties that animated them; but their relation to the economic forces of the country should be examined separately, since economic control was the secret of the Commons' supremacy.

Unkind critics of the Revolution assert that its chief result was to substitute the Divine Right of property for the Divine Right of Kings. There is much in the Revolutionary gospel according to

John Locke to justify the sneer ; *e.g.* " The great and chief end . . . of men united into commonwealths, and putting themselves under government, is the preservation of their property " : [1] and " The supreme power cannot take from any man any part of his property without his own consent." [2]   Men of property led and won the Revolution ; their victory was consolidated by attaching the Constitution to the economic powers of the nation.   As the landowners and merchants took upon themselves the burdens of government —customs and excise and the great Land Tax, they determined also to secure the spoils.   Hence the party history of the two reigns is largely the struggle of the landed and banking interests for the monopoly and perquisites of political power.   The Parliamentary establishment of the National Debt and the Bank of England wedded —the Tories said " enslaved "—the Constitution to the Whig monied interests ; in 1715 the Protestant Succession was ensured as much by fear of " repudiation " as by fear of Popery.   Land had to wait longer for constitutional consecration.   The first project failed ; the Land Bank of 1696, which was to " dish " the Whig Bank and bind national credit to the landed interests, was unable to mobilise its assets or to provide the government with quick and generous loans ; but in 1710 an Act was passed to restrict membership of the Commons to substantial landowners.   This Act was designed to serve the Tories as the National Debt served the Whigs, to give them a permanent hold on the Constitution.   Unfortunately for the Tories and fortunately for the nation, it proved impossible to enforce it.   If effective, it would not only have crippled the mercantile interest in the Commons, but it would have excluded such men as Burge and Fox from public life.   Evasion, however, was easy ; patrons and lawyers provided temporary or fictitious estates for the landless candidate.   Nevertheless the Act is historical evidence that Parliament was rooted in the land as deeply as in the stocks.[3] Thus the Constitution gained both credit and ballast ; the balance of power represented and was responsive to the balance of property.

The Commons, therefore, representing economic power, took from the Crown its Prerogative of economic regulation.   Men like

[1] Locke, *Of Civil Government*, Book II, ch. 9.   [2] *Ibid.* ch. 11.
[3] Porritt, *The Unreformed House of Commons*, vol. I, pp. 166-181.

Montague, Godolphin and Walpole became political leaders on the sole ground of financial genius ; economic issues decided the fate of nations and governments, as in the cases of the Scottish Union, the French Commercial Treaty of 1713 and the South Sea Bubble. No Dutch alliance or King could remove the economic barriers of the Navigation Acts ; no Crown Prerogative could stop the Commons from regulating Crown grants of land, from interfering in the government of colonies and Chartered Companies. The age of " Parliamentary Colbertism " had begun.[1] Industry was left to itself, but agriculture and commerce were nursed, assiduously if not wisely, by a landed and mercantile Commons. In 1689 an export bounty on corn was established in place of the export duties which threatened landowners with a glutted home market and low prices, and at the same time the heavy import duties of 1673 were maintained. Thus with State encouragement of corn-growing and protection of prices, with the removal of opposition to enclosing, and with the landowners' control of the Legislature, agriculture became both a fashion and a power in the land, and moved securely forward to the improvements and capitalisation of the eighteenth century. Large-scale commerce became likewise a power and complication in politics. Commercial pressure, such as that which ruined the Scotch Darien Company, played a large part in renewing the French war in 1702 after Louis' exclusion of foreign traders from the united Franco-Spanish empire, and in moulding the character of the Treaty of Utrecht. In William's reign the rivalry of two East India Companies decided the fate of governments ; in 1711 Harley farmed the National Debt to the South Sea Company and so linked its credit and destiny to the heart of the Revolutionary system. Speculation and lotteries were ennobled to be sinews of State, and the pervading and corrupting influence of money seemed to old-fashioned Tories to be destroying the ancient rock-like Constitution and casting the nation on the shifting sands of markets and exchanges. Yet for all their forebodings and the Bubble which confirmed them, the chief benefit of the Revolution was the opportunity it gave for the development of agricultural and commercial wealth under a stable and

[1] Cf. Cunningham, *Growth of English Industry and Commerce*, Vol. II.

sympathetic government. For this reason England from 1689 drew farther and farther ahead of her European rivals, who lacked the blessings of a capitalised Constitution. For the Commons, however ill they represented and served the people, were fully representative of the active oligarchy that governed and exploited the British Isles, India and America, at a time when European nobility was sinking into political paralysis and economic parasitism.

Each man must strike a balance-sheet of the Revolution for himself; any assessment of its gains and losses depends largely on the principles of the assessor. The politician will hail the birth of the party system; the moralist will note the decline of public morality that accompanied it. Against the rise of capitalism must be set the depression of the peasant and craftsman. The process of assessment is not easy, for some products of the Revolution had paradoxical effects; the National Debt, for instance, became a national asset. The fact that the Revolutionary system was so expensive as to involve the nation in heavy borrowing was one of its safeguards; the British Empire was built on the solid basis of overdrafts and credit. Similarly, the theory of limited monarchy as stated in the Bill of Rights and the Treatises of Locke, had a deep influence on the American and French Revolutions; but if we credit this to the Revolution, we give credit for a theory that was discarded in England almost as soon as it was made. To make a true valuation, we must base it on the conventions and external influences that breathed life into the forms of the Constitution; for the fundamental change was in spirit, not in form—not in the Constitution, but in the powers behind the throne. We must examine the aims and achievements of the political parties, if we would discover what the nation and the ordinary citizen gained from the settlement and experiments of the years 1689-1714; for both nation and individual were fed by the crumbs that fell from the party-managers' tables.

SUGGESTIONS FOR FURTHER READING
FOR THE PERIOD 1689–1714
(Chapters VII and VIII)

In addition to works cited previously (pp. ix, x, 133, 134, 159, 160), the great classic studies of this period are, of course, Macaulay's *History of England* (standard edition in 6 vols. by Sir Charles Firth), and Hallam's *Constitutional History of England*. (Dent)

The following works may also be consulted :

The Political Works of SWIFT (Bell), DEFOE (Bohn), and ADDISON (Bohn).

BOLINGBROKE : *Letter to Wyndham, Patriot King, Dissertation on Parties*. (O.U.P.)

OGG, D. : *England in the Reigns of James II and William III*. (O.U.P., 1955)

TREVELYAN, G. M. : *England under Queen Anne*. 3 Vols. (Longmans, 1930–4)

The English Revolution, 1688–9. (O.U.P., H.U.L., 1939)

CHURCHILL, SIR WINSTON : *Marlborough, His Life and Times*. 4 Vols. (Harrap, 1947)

FEILING, K. : *British Foreign Policy, 1660–72*. (Macmillan, 1930)

History of the Tory Party, 1640–1714. (O.U.P., 1924)

WALCOTT, R. : *English Politics in the Early Eighteenth Century*. (O.U.P., 1956)

TURBEVILLE, A. S. : *The House of Lords in the Reign of William III*. (O.U.P., 1913)

The House of Lords in the Eighteenth Century. (O.U.P., 1927)

HALEY, K. H. D. : *William of Orange and the English Opposition*. (O.U.P., 1953)

JONES, J. R. : *The First Whigs*. (O.U.P., 1965)

PARES, R. : *Limited Monarchy in the Eighteenth Century*. (Historical Association Pamphlet)

THOMSON, A. N. : *The Secretaries of State*. (O.U.P., 1932)

GILL, D. M. : ' The Treasury, 1660–1714 '. *E.H.R.*, xlvi.

PLUMB, J. H.: 'The Organisation of the Cabinet in the Reign of Queen Anne'. *R.H.S.T. 5th Series*, vii.

SYKES, N.: 'Queen Anne and the Episcopate'. *E.H.R.*, l.

For the economic settlement, see pp. 317–18.

VIII

PARTIES AND THE NATION: 1689-1714

I. PARTY GROWTH AND FLUX: 1689-1702

IT seemed a miracle to contemporaries that the fabric of English society was not rent asunder by the bitter and unscrupulous feuds of Whig and Tory; it would still seem so to us, did we not read back into history the genteel spirit and the sporting rules of the party game as played from 1832. It was not until the second half of the eighteenth century that Burke elevated parties to the dignity of national institutions:

" Party is a body of men united for promoting by their joint endeavours the national interest, upon some particular principle on which they are all agreed." [1]

Such may be the ideal party, but it bears little resemblance to the political groups that Bolingbroke led and Halifax detested. Bolingbroke made no such claims in 1710:

" I am afraid we came to Court in the same disposition as all parties have done—that the principal spring of our actions was to have the government of the State in our hands; that our principal views were the conservation of this power, great employments to ourselves, and great opportunities of rewarding those who had helped to raise us, and of hurting those who had stood in opposition to us." [2]

The spoils of office and the proscription of enemies formed an adequate programme to the Tories of 1710 as to the Whigs of 1696 and 1708; both gave a posthumous justification to the frequent denunciations of party by Halifax, who wrote just before his death:

[1] *Thoughts on the Cause of the Present Discontents*, 1770.
[2] *Letter to Wyndham*, 1717.

185

" Nothing is more evident than that the good of the nation hath been sacrificed to the animosities of the several contending parties, and without entring into the dispute which of them are more or less in the right, it is pretty sure, that whilst these opposite sets of angry men are playing at foot-ball, they will break all the windows, and do more hurt than their pretended zeal for the nation will ever make amends for." [1]

There was general agreement in admitting the power of party ; the historian's task is to ascertain, from conflicting evidence, the source of that power and the benefits, if any, it conferred on the nation.   Bolingbroke had, as usual, a ready and plausible explanation of the origin of parties ; he based the division on economic and political lines—a quarrel of land against banks, of patriots against aliens :

" We supposed the Tory party to be the bulk of the landed interest, and to have no contrary influence blended into its composition.   We supposed the Whigs to be the remains of a party formed against the ill designs of the Court under King Charles II., nursed up into strength and applied to contrary uses by King William III., and yet still so weak as to lean for support on the Presbyterians and the other sectaries, on the Bank and the other corporations, on the Dutch and the other allies." [2]

For Swift and Defoe, however, the vital issue was religious. Swift found he could not be a Whig " and wear a gown " when Whig and Presbyterian were synonymous terms ; modern historians, such as Trevelyan and Feiling, follow them in making religion the permanent line of cleavage in party history.[3]   Differences of constitutional principle are less clearly marked ; on such points both parties were opportunists, subordinating all things to their religious and economic aims.[4]

(a) *The Rise and Fall of the Whig Junto*

The Whigs must be put on trial first, since they obtained the greatest benefits from the Revolution and built upon it half a

[1] Cautions for Choice of Members in Parliament (*Works*, p. 160).

[2] *Letter to Wyndham.*

[3] Cf. Trevelyan, Romanes Lecture (1926) on the Two Party System in English History.

[4] Ranke, V, p. 291, makes some fine-drawn constitutional distinctions.

century's monopoly of power. In spite of the Jacobite intrigues of timid and discontented individuals like Shrewsbury and Russell, the party as a whole was committed as no other section of the nation to the Revolutionary system and the revised Succession. Hence arose its value to William and George of Hanover, its importunate demands upon them, and its conviction that it alone could save the Protestant Constitution.[1]

They were in organisation a new party, quite distinct from Shaftesbury's political machine; the highly respectable conspirators of 1688 were careful to avoid contamination with the survivors of the failures of 1679 and 1685. There is hardly a sign of permanent organisation before the Junto of 1695; yet the forces that were knit and disciplined by Wharton, Somers, Russell and Montague had been dominant in English politics since 1640. Pym had been the organiser of the alliance of nobles and merchants, Manchester and Hollis his successors; Shaftesbury, Monmouth and James II. in turn had tried to lead the party astray to extremes of democracy or despotism; but they survived seduction and proscription alike, and found in 1688 their Tory rivals borrowing their principles and seeking their aid. In William of Orange they thought they had discovered an ideal leader; but " they loved him, not as a King, but as a party leader, and it was not difficult to foresee that their enthusiasm would cool fast if he should refuse to be the mere leader of their party, and should attempt to be King of the whole nation." [2] The ungrateful desertion of William to the Tories in 1690 taught them to seek leadership within and not above their ranks; from that year dates the planning of a self-dependent organisation and policy which would be strong enough to control the government, whatever King or Queen might reign.

It is, on first thoughts, strange that the Whigs should have gained most from the Revolution. James' chief and immediate attack had been directed against their rivals, and he had offered the Whigs the satisfaction of present revenge and a share, at least for a time, in the spoils of a Royal and Catholic victory. It was the political

---

[1] Halifax sneered at the " pretenders to exorbitant merit in the late Revolution," who " presently cry out, The Original Contract is broken, if their merit is not rewarded, at their own rate too " (*Works*, pp. 160-1).

[2] Macaulay, *History*, ch. 11.

monopoly of Anglican squire and parson that was at stake in 1688, and that monopoly was no less odious to the Whigs than to James. The Tories, as the injured party, had most to defend and most to restore ; their leaders, Danby and Bishop Compton, set rebellion on foot, and the participation of Tory magnates such as Halifax and Seymour was the decisive factor in its success. Yet it is not difficult to explain why the Whigs stole from them the fruits of victory. It was inevitable that control of the movement should pass to the party which was more hardened to rebellion and less sensitive to personal loyalties ; while the shame of bearing arms against a lawful King seemed to paralyse Tory political faculties, their temporary and unwelcome allies throve on treason, revived their shattered organisation, and returned a majority to the Lower House of the Convention. Moreover, although no stage of the Revolution bore the mark of a party movement, the Whigs had a right to expect some return for their renunciation of James' bribes and their magnanimous defence of Bishops and Tests. It is therefore not surprising that the Whigs dominated the settlement of the Convention, despite the prominence of Danby, Halifax and Nottingham ; when Regency was rejected and the Original Compact was given the force of law, an indelible stamp of Whiggery was set on the English Constitution. Similarly, while the legislation of the Convention Parliament served national as well as party interests, its abrupt dissolution was due to the revival of the Whigs' suppressed passions of revenge. Not only was Oates beatified and pensioned, but the question of indemnity was turned, as in 1660, into a hunt for victims ; even Halifax was in danger from the avengers of Sidney and Russell, whose lives he had tried to save. The Corporation Bill of January 1690 was designed not only to undo the work of 1683, but also to break up the Tory party by disfranchising for seven years all persons concerned in the surrender of the borough charters. But William averted a Whig monopoly by " dishing " them with the decision, if not the grace, of Charles II. ; for he at once dissolved the Convention Parliament and called the moderate Tories into office.

In 1694 William came back to the Whigs. Danby's second Ministry had failed to give him the necessary support either at home or abroad, and the death of Mary removed the only hold he had on Tory affections. This, together with defeat in the Netherlands, ended William's independence of party; Whig money and Whig votes alone could ensure his title and his European designs. This time the Whigs were resolved to rely, not on Royal favour, but on their own organisation; they built their power on a solid majority at the elections of 1695, on the leadership of the Junto, on the National Bank and the National Association to protect the King's life. These last two institutions revealed at once the strength and the unscrupulousness of the party.

The Bank provided a base more permanent, if less tangible, than votes—the power of credit; it linked inseparably the fortunes of Whig finance with the national interests of the Protestant Succession and with the personal interests of William.[1] The consequent financial measures of the Junto had in them a mixture of selfish and national motives. In the interest of national commerce they carried out at State expense the urgent task of re-coinage, and they preserved the Bank amid the shocks of the transition from the old to the new coinage, despite the malicious attacks of the goldsmiths and the rivalry of the Land Bank of 1696; what was more vital, they raised for William the funds necessary to bring Louis to a stand at the Treaty of Ryswick. In their vindictive opposition to the Scottish Darien Company and to the Irish woollen trade, they represented prejudices which were common to the whole nation; in their " rigging " of the East India Company they were only undoing a shady scheme of Danby's and substituting a scheme of Montague's—equally partisan but financially sounder.

The Whigs, under the guidance of Montague and Godolphin, were at their best in finance; their plans, however selfishly conceived, had the combined virtues of prudence and imagination which made them beneficial to the whole nation. But moderation and foresight were less marked in their general policy. True, they ended the censorship of the Press in 1695, and they passed in 1696 an Act reforming treason trials; but in 1696 also, they revived

[1] Cf. Macaulay, *History*, ch. 20 : " It is hardly too much to say that, during many years, the weight of the Bank, which was constantly in the scale of the Whigs, almost counterbalanced the weight of the Church, which was as constantly in the scale of the Tories."

for the last time in English history the arbitrary weapon of Attainder, by which a man could be condemned by Parliament without trial for offences unknown to the law.[1] The same year provided the most striking example of their use of national emergencies for sectional ends. The assassination plots of 1695-6 had produced a spontaneous wave of hatred of France and loyalty to William; an Association to protect his life, on the Elizabethan model, was enthusiastically taken up throughout the country.[2] The Whigs could not resist the obvious temptation. They converted the voluntary movement into a compulsory test by which all officials, great and small, were bound to unqualified acceptance of the Revolution settlement; further, all private persons were threatened with electoral disqualification and the disabilities of Recusants if they refused the test. All Jacobites and hesitant Tories, even the " de facto " school of Nottingham, were to be excluded from public life, if they did not commit themselves to Whig doctrine and leadership; the general proscription of Toryism, which had failed in 1690, seemed inevitable in 1696. But Harley, the rising Tory manager, found a loophole; he turned the principle of " occasional conformity " against the Whigs, who had introduced it into politics to save the Dissenters from the penalties of the Test Acts. He persuaded the bulk of the Tories to subscribe for the occasion to all the old oaths and new engagements. So the Whig plan was defeated; but they had secured this gain: that the Tories, despite the dubious value of a forced engagement, were committed more closely to the new régime. On the other hand, they had provided a most dangerous precedent of party vengeance—a precedent for which Bolingbroke was grateful in 1710, and their failure brought upon them and upon William, their tool, a violent reaction.

After 1696 the Junto declined from unpopularity without and divisions within. The Peace of 1697 made their services no longer indispensable and their domination intolerable to all parties; their

[1] For the Treasons Act, cf. Grant Robertson, pp. 140-4, and Burnet, II, p. 141; the chief point was the necessity of two witnesses to prove the commission of a treasonable act or acts. Sir John Fenwick was condemned by attainder because two witnesses could not be found to prove his treason (cf. Macaulay, ch. 22).

[2] Cf. Macaulay's vivid account (ch. 21), and heavy satire on the Lords, who escaped the contagion and examined minutely the words of the engagement for fear—afterwards justified—of a Whig trick.

followers deserted to the Country Party which Harley was working to link with moderate Toryism ; their King became a source of weakness rather than of strength owing to the national dislike of his Dutch friends and secret diplomacy. The elections of 1698 destroyed their majority and organisation, and for the rest of William's reign a hostile Commons sought their disgrace and punishment. Yet their work was not all undone ; for the Act of Settlement, though " a thinly veiled vote of censure " [1] on William and the Junto, so completed the work of 1688 and treated monarchy so roughly that Swift in 1711 advanced the Act as a proof of the Republicanism of the Whigs.[2]

Perhaps the chief reason why the party measures of this reign did go far beyond the limits of national interest is that the Whigs were careful not to raise any religious storms. There was no attempt to revive William's comprehension scheme of 1689 ; shrewd politicians preferred the unostentatious way of " occasional conformity." Though the term " Presbyterian " was usually applied by foreign observers to the men posterity calls Whigs, there is no evidence that they desired religious reconstruction, or any religion at all save the " religion of the magistrate." They had no love for noisy gatherings of the clergy, whether in Presbytery or Convocation ; their aim was to keep Dissent quiet by minimum concessions and lax enforcement, and to muzzle the Anglicans by a Latitudinarian episcopate. Thus the " high-fliers " were impotent, even in those happy shires where there was " scarce a Presbyterian in the whole county, except the Bishop." [3] The Junto rendered valuable service to the nation by postponing the outbreak of clerical fury until the new constitution took some root.

(b) Tory Opposition and Adaptation : 1689-1702

What did the Tories contribute to the national interest in the limited scope allowed them in William's reign ? Theirs was an

[1] Grant Robertson, p. 151 (introduction to Act of Settlement).

[2] Cf. *Examiner*, No. 36 (Trevelyan : *Select Docts.*, p. 60) : " They " (the Whigs) . . . " have therefore taken care (as a particular mark of their veneration for the illustrious House of Hanover) to clip it " (the Prerogative) " closer against next reign ; which, consequently, they would be glad to see done in the present : . . . the majority of them . . . would allow that they prefer a commonwealth before a monarchy."

[3] Addison : *Freeholder*, Nos. 14 and 22 (Trevelyan : *Select Docts.*, p. 72).

unhappy position ; after the shock James gave to their confidence and organisation, they succeeded in pulling their world about their ears in a desperate attempt at recovery. The Revolution destroyed their cohesion and, what was far worse, their self-respect ; they were uneasy and ashamed in their new allegiance, even with the reservations they attached to it. The confusion and bewilderment of the party in the new conditions is illustrated by the desire of some to disown, or at least minimise, their party's share in the Revolution, while Swift on the other hand complained that the Tories who had made the Revolution were deprived of their just reward :

" This " (the insolence of Dissent) " was the more unexpected, because the Revolution being wholly brought about by Church of England hands, they hoped one good consequence of it, would be the relieving us from the encroachments of Dissenters, as well as those of Papists." [1]

The very act of rebellion by non-resisting loyalists put them out of joint, and from the day when they saw control of the sorry business passing in the Convention to the Whigs, all their energies were given to suspicion and obstruction. They had two objects, both defensive ; one, to protect themselves from Whig proscription on the charge of Jacobitism : the other, to adapt their creed and methods to a provisional settlement while hoping for better days.

The first chance of adaptation came in 1690, when William, tired of Whig arrogance and determined on power, sought the Tories as natural supporters of monarchy. Halifax and Nottingham soon abandoned the experiment, but Danby, while changing his titles with confusing frequency, remained steadfast in control of the movement he had started, and in service to the master whom he had favoured since 1677. The experiment failed through mal-administration, failures in the land war, and inefficiency at sea,[2] and it was disastrous to Tory organisation and morale. Office had the effect of demoralising them and dividing them from their leaders ; they felt themselves to be in a false position in upholding a dubious Prerogative and a foreign Court. The dreaded accusa-

---

[1] *Examiner*, No. 37 (Trevelyan : *Select Docts.*, p 65).

[2] Russell, the victor of La Hogue (1692), was replaced by Tory Admirals who lost the great Smyrna convoy in 1693.

tion of Jacobitism came in 1696 to complete the disintegration;
Mr. Feiling points out that it was virtually a new party which
gradually assumed the name of Tory in the middle years of the reign
under the leadership of Clarges, Foley and Harley.[1] Harley just
succeeded in saving the old remnants by committing them to
William's title and by linking them to the " country " movement.

Historic Toryism—the Cavalier tradition—was scrapped by this
ex-Presbyterian Whig for a programme of immediate limitations
on the Executive; in opposition to the Whig King, Harley revived
the Whig ancestral doctrines of Parliamentary independence and
strict definition of royal rights. He won over from the old Tories
and the landed Whigs a heterogeneous following, which gathered
strength and cohesion under his leadership. With their aid the
reviving Tories instituted a Land Bank, pressed for a landed
Commons, denounced the alien scourges of Popery and Dutch
favourites, reduced the army, humiliated the King and the Lords,
brought down the Junto and William's European schemes, and
crowned their work by the Act of Settlement—the Magna Carta of
legislative obstruction and executive impotence. It is very doubtful whether all this can be fairly ascribed to the historic Tory party;
for between 1697 and 1702 old allegiances were in abeyance, old
creeds in process of revision, party machinery out of action.
Conservatives of both parties were alarmed by the growth of Court
influence and of the complexity and expense of government; they
would follow anyone, save a Jacobite, who advocated an entirely
English policy. Harley seized the occasion, and carried his followers with him into the Tory ranks in the next reign; but as
yet he and they were only Tories in embryo. However, though
their principles were strangely similar to Shaftesbury's and their
personnel was largely ex-Whig, they were the founders of the new
Tory party. Their service to Toryism was that they offered it a
career free from the burden of Jacobitism and attached to national
interests, though they can be criticised for responding too easily to
popular prejudices; their service to the nation was that they confirmed the Protestant Succession by the Act of Settlement, and thus
raised it above the level of a Whig expedient.

[1] Cf. Feiling, chs. 10-12.

Thus the nation benefited—was indeed preserved from imminent disaster—by William's labours, the brilliance of the Whig Junto, and the adaptability of Harley. Party rule had given some coherence to government, and it had not the power to do its worst; its excesses were checked by weak organisation, the hostility of the King, and the interventions of the "country" members. Men hoped it was a passing evil, which an English Queen and a national war would finally eradicate.

II. The Merciless Rule of Party : 1702-1714

(a) *The Failure of Coalition* : 1702-5

Notwithstanding William's real successes and the national agreement on the Protestant Succession, England was faced with grave dangers in 1702. The menace of France seemed greater than ever, with the overrated forces of Spain at her disposal; and William's death and the disorganisation of parties left England apparently without leadership and government adequate for the crisis. Moreover, the Succession was less secure in reality than on paper; for Louis, who had abandoned James II. in 1697, recognised his son as James III., while, against this young and healthy claimant, Protestantism and national union depended on the life of a sickly and childless woman.

It fell to the lot of the Tories to face the problems of the new reign, for they reaped an immediate advantage from the accession of a direct and Anglican Stuart. They dropped the uncongenial role of anti-monarchists which they had played against William; but they soon found themselves committed to less pleasing reversals of policy. They were loaded with their old aversions—the Bank, standing armies, European alliances: they had to carry out William's policy with William's chosen agents, Marlborough and Godolphin: they had, in deference to Anne's wishes, to share office with the Whigs. No one party in 1702 was ready or capable to conduct a large-scale war; but before long the control of affairs was bound to drift into the hands of that party which accepted full responsibility for the war and conducted it wholeheartedly. Now the Tories felt a growing distaste for the growing European entanglements, and as they wished to avoid being principals abroad, so did they become auxiliaries at home; the due penalty fell on them when in 1705 they threatened to destroy national unity in wartime by attacking Dissent on the issue of Occasional Conformity. The result was both disgrace and division; Harley broke with Rochester and Nottingham and stood by the Queen and the war.

Though Harley remained in office until 1708, the coalition really ended in 1705; [1] from then on, Anne and Marlborough reluctantly entrusted the direction of the war to the Whigs, since they alone were sound and united on the vital issue. War and peace ceased to be national aims and became party symbols; the war that made England a first-class power was carried through in the midst of the fiercest and most organised party struggle that the nation had known short of civil war. To what extent did the war become a mere party war, regardless of national interest? To what extent did the Whigs use their power for the common good?

(b) *The Fruits of Whig Supremacy*: 1705-9

Contemporary evidence is one mass of charges and counter-charges against the integrity of both parties; for both literature and the press—not then divorced—were absorbed and organised for party service. Every Tory was a Jacobite, every Dissenter a revolutionary: [2] the Whigs were Dutch pensioners and Blenheim spelt the ruin of the Constitution. If there can be no smoke without flame, then some of the accusations must be treated with respect, even after a generous discount is made for partisan bias. Marl-borough, more detached than most, wrote in 1703: "All parties are alike, unreasonable and unjust"; [3] and a year later he counted even the ravaged States of Germany happy in "not knowing the detested names of Whig and Tory." [4] He chose the Whigs per-force, as William had—not because of any moral superiority, but because he vowed "to have no friends but such as will support the

---

[1] Feiling, p. 381, dates a marked rise in party heat from 1705.

[2] The temper of the time is best revealed in the Tory acceptance as genuine of Defoe's not too subtle satire, *The Shortest Way with Dissenters*, which urged them to "pull up this heretical weed of sedition," since "the poison of their nature makes it a charity to our neighbours to destroy those creatures" (Trevelyan: *Select Docts.*, pp. 52-8).

[3] Letter to the Duchess (Trevelyan: *Select Docts.*, p. 156).   [4] *Ibid.* p. 170.

Queen and government." [1]   The Whigs undoubtedly throve on war, as the Tories on peace ; but it is not so clear that the nation throve accordingly.   The charge against the Whigs, framed ably and unsparingly by Swift, falls under two heads : one, from 1704 they unjustifiably extended the scope of the war to serve Dutch and Austrian, not English interests : two, that from 1709 they prolonged the war on the issue of the Spanish throne for no conceivable reason save that of clinging to office. [2]

(i) *Blenheim and the Extension of the War.*   The first charge is entirely bound up with the aims of Marlborough, and the second is closely linked with them.   The Whigs did not plan Blenheim ; but they accepted and supported the policy of the General, who was as yet more independent of them than William had been. We need not therefore fall into the fallacy detected by Dr. Johnson—" You know it is ridiculous for a Whig to pretend to be honest " [3]—and assume that their motives were entirely disinterested ; but the testimony of Sarah Churchill, an acute though not impartial observer, deserves to be recorded in their favour :

When " the interest of the Church, that is, of High-Churchmen, was to be preferred before the interest of the Queen or of the nation, or the preservation of the liberties of Europe . . . the Whigs did indeed begin to be favoured, and with good reason.   For when they saw that my lord Marlborough prosecuted the common cause with such hearty diligence and such unexpected success, they, notwithstanding the partiality which had been shown to their opposites, universally forgot their resentments, and no longer considering themselves as an oppressed party, ran in with the loudest acclamations, extolling his merits and services." [4]

Blenheim frightened the Tories and made the war the chief business of the Whigs ; it was the sign and effect of a radical change in the aims of the Grand Alliance of 1701, a change wholly alien to Tory principles of diplomacy and strategy.   The original defensive alliance with the Dutch and Austrians to protect the English Succession and English trade was converted by Marlborough in

[1] Letter to the Duchess, 1705 (Trevelyan, *Select Docts.*, p. 172).
[2] Cf. Swift's *Conduct of the Allies*, a brilliant and damaging indictment.
[3] Boswell, *Journal of a Tour to the Hebrides*, Oct. 21, 1773.
[4] Conduct of the Duchess (Trevelyan : *Select Docts.*, pp. 198-207).

1703 into an European offensive encircling France, Bavaria, and the
Iberian Peninsula. In the Treaty which brought Portugal into
the alliance it was agreed that Spain was to go to the Austrian
Archduke Charles, and that peace was not to be made until the
French were driven out of Spain.[1] The new war-aim of " no peace
without Spain " involved a general attack on the French protecto-
rates and extended co-operation on land with the Austrians; for
Austria must be freed from Bavarian pressure, and the ring round
France must be completed by English troops holding the Upper
Rhine and Danube as well as the Scheldt and threatening the
Pyrenees frontier from Portugal and Barcelona. Donauworth
and Blenheim broke French power in Germany and cleared the
way for a triple offensive in Flanders, Italy and Spain; the victories
of Ramillies, Turin and Barcelona followed, and justified the new
policy by bringing Louis to the verge of disaster. Yet the " honourable and safe peace " that Marlborough professed to desire was
not concluded in 1706, and the reason lay in Spain; the occupation
of Madrid and the enthronement of the Archduke provoked Louis'
family pride and stiffened his resistance. Swift denounced the
Whigs as both fools and knaves for sacrificing English interests to
Austria—for making Englishmen " the dupes and bubbles of
Europe " for " the aggrandizing of a particular family " (the
Churchills) and the profit of " moneyed men . . . whose perpetual
harvest is war, and whose beneficial way of traffic must very much
decline by a peace." [2]

It is more charitable, and at the same time more probable, to
suppose that the Whigs were led into the Spanish impasse by the
theory of the balance of power, coupled with a political miscalculation. The proposal to substitute Charles of Hapsburg for Philip
of Bourbon on the Spanish throne averted the danger of French

[1] For the Treaty of Grand Alliance and the Treaty with Portugal, cf. Trevelyan :
Select Docts., pp. 5-10 and 15-19; the clauses containing the new policy are the
first and twenty-first of the Portuguese Treaty. The twenty-first runs : " Neither
peace, nor truce, shall be made, but by mutual consent of all the Confederates ; and
they shall not be made at any time while the most Christian King's grandson, the
Dauphin's second son, or any other Prince of the House of France, remains in Spain."
" Most Christian " was a title borne by the Kings of France since 1469 ; " Dauphin "
was a title borne by the eldest son of the King as lord of the county of Dauphiné.

[2] *Conduct of the Allies.*

domination in Europe without creating a Hapsburg ascendancy, since the accession of Charles to the Empire was a remote contingency until it unexpectedly occurred in 1711. The miscalculation was over the Spanish attitude towards their candidate; yet, in so far as they neglected national feeling, they were in accordance with an age in which Kings were shuffled as cards in a pack; and in this case they were supporting a true Hapsburg, of the House that had made Spain the leader of Europe, against a Bourbon, the traditional enemy of Spain. Their policy was ruined in execution, as Swift rightly complained, by the failure of the Allies to bear a fair share of the burdens of war; but his alternative, a policy of naval raids and land defensive, would have left the Allies to the mercy of France and made them worse than useless to England. A Tory " auxiliary " war could have produced nothing but a dangerous isolation and a precarious truce like that of Ryswick; the French menace to the English Crown, Empire and religion could only be removed by offensive co-operation with European allies, however greedy and unreliable. Swift was right in declaring that it was " a war of the General and the Ministry, and not of the Prince and people " ; for Marlborough and the Whig leaders alone realised the dangers of a premature withdrawal from the struggle. Marlborough had to cheat the Dutch into action, while Godolphin and Harley beguiled the Parliament into paying for the stream of victories; but their methods were justified by the terms of surrender offered by Louis in 1709.

(ii) *Spain and the Prolongation of the War.* The case against the Whigs' prolongation of the war after 1709 is much stronger. From 1708 they were a purely party Ministry; they had forced on Anne the dismissal of Harley and St. John and the appointment of the young Sunderland, Marlborough's son-in-law, as Secretary of State. The Tories, once more united in opposition, took up the cry of peace to spite the Whigs, and the Whigs, fearing the reaction of peace on the analogy of 1697, found new arguments for war and new dangers in peace. They stiffened their terms to Louis and entrenched their position at home. Party itself seemed to be narrowing to a family ring; when Marlborough demanded from Anne the Cromwellian security of a life Commandership-in-chief, the war seemed to have as its main object not the Protestant but the Churchill Succession. The shadow of the overmighty subject fell across the land.

Even moneyed interests were neglected by the Dutch Barrier Treaty of 1709, which Marlborough considered necessary to bind the Dutch to the war against Louis' offers ; [1] Swift had an easy score :

" We have conquered Flanders for them, and are in a worse condition, as to our trade there, than before the war began." [2]

But the real weak spot was the Spanish obsession of the Ministry in blind defiance of facts. [3]   Since they regarded a Hapsburg Spain as the cornerstone of their European settlement, the English defeat at Almanza in 1707 nullified all their victories ; and yet they refused to modify their plans or to recognise the impossibility of their task with useless allies against a growing national resistance. Brihuega in 1710 confirmed the decision of Almanza, and in the next year, when the Archduke became Emperor, success promised worse evils than failure, owing to the threat to the balance of power caused by the union of Spain with the Empire.   This was the ' reductio ad absurdum ' of Whig policy, even though it occurred after their fall ; but apart from this, there was no sound answer to Swift's questions :

" Did those who insisted on such wild demands ever intend a peace ?   Was there no way to provide for the safety of Britain or the security of its trade, but by the French King turning his arms to beat his grandson out of Spain ? " [4]

It was the one cause of the continuance of an expensive war, the main burden of which, as Swift showed, fell on landowners and posterity, while " usurers and stockjobbers " profited by the fluctuations of credit, the funding of loans and the high rate of interest.   War, as always, created its own interests and perquisites for politicians and generals, who would naturally judge the national

[1] Cf. Trevelyan : *E.U.S.*, pp. 499-500, and *Select Docts.*, p. 189.

[2] *Conduct of the Allies.*

[3] Cf. Trevelyan : *Select Docts.*, p. 190 for Marlborough's view, and pp. 176-7 and 187-9 for letters bearing on Spanish difficulties.

[4] *Conduct of the Allies.*

welfare as a reflection of their own, and would consider their own services indispensable to the nation. Meanwhile the whole of Europe longed for peace, and the Allies needed more and more stiffening by promises of English money and troops ; and when the victories and bonfires died away after Malplaquet, Englishmen asked (not without Swift's prompting) whether the " visionary prospects " of absolute security were worth the price, and whether Franco-Spanish union was such a fearful bogey after all. Swift reminded them that the death of the aged Louis might solve the problem, and added the decisive argument : " These at least are probabilities, and cheaper by six million a year than recovering Spain or continuing the war." [1]   There is, in fact, no defence save that of human frailty for the Whig war policy after 1708— " the new romantic views " of the House of Churchill—even if we do not accept all of Swift's charges or agree with the Tory strategy, the " old, reasonable, sober design " of 1702-3.

(iii) *Whig Domestic Policy and the Scottish Union.*   The great Whig Ministry fell in 1710 because it neglected England for Europe ; in its absorption in building an European system under Whig control it forgot that unpopularity at home was sapping the real basis of its power.   It lost touch with the Queen and people, who cared little for high diplomacy, but much for low taxes ; the Sacheverell explosion warned the Whigs too late of their error in " mistaking the echo of a London coffeehouse for the voice of the kingdom." [2]   Under stress of war the National Debt rose from £16,000,000 in 1701 to £53,000,000 in 1714, and this reckless use of public credit aroused problems and temptations that proved too much for Whig and Tory financiers alike until Walpole took control.

There were, however, two measures, passed by the Whigs to secure their position and plans, which are of permanent value ; it is perhaps significant that both were passed before the Ministry became exclusively Whig.   The first was the Regency Act of 1705, which provided constitutional methods for the change of dynasty

[1] He asked : " Is it likely that Philip will be directed by a brother against his own interest and that of his subjects ?   Have not those two realms their separate maxims of policy ? "   (*Conduct of the Allies.*)

[2] *Conduct of the Allies.*

on Anne's death, and included also a fundamental revision of the Act of Settlement.[1] The latter's " place " clause was. deprived of its sting ; in future, ministers and officials, with certain limitations that a new Statute could override, were admitted to the Commons. Thus the advantages of unified government, linking Legislature and Executive, were ensured ; a workable Constitution was evolved and the indispensable foundation of Cabinet government was laid.

After knitting the Constitution together, the Whigs accomplished the far greater feat of uniting England with Scotland. Few, except devout Johnsonians, will deny that the Union of 1707 was one of the greatest services conferred on the two nations by any Ministry. Though the Whigs cannot claim the sole credit—Anne, Marlborough and Harley must have their share [2]—it was an integral part of their grand design. It was for that reason not wholly disinterested ; it was, like the Tory Act of Irish Union, a product of war emergency and party interest. But in method and result the contrast of 1707 with 1800 is complete. The tact of the Whig negotiators, the delicate management of Scottish susceptibilities and the scrupulous observance of Scottish interests, the speedy acceptance of the entire English scheme, are all tributes to the statesmanship of the English Ministers, in particular Somers and Godolphin. Despite " a great backwardness in the Parliament of Scotland for an union with England of any kind whatsoever," [3] despite the High Tory propaganda against the recognition of Presbyterianism and the admission to Parliament of Scottish Peers and merchants, they solved the perennial Scottish problem, not by the methods of Flodden and Pinkie, nor by those of Laud and Cromwell, but by common agreement after the plan of Francis Bacon. They destroyed the French and Jacobite hopes that had been raised by the Scottish Act of Security of 1703, they ensured

[1] Anne was old, ill, and had no children living ; so a new dynasty was inevitable. For the Act, cf. Grant Robertson, pp. 179-186.

[2] Next to the preservation of the Church, it was Anne's dearest wish ; Marlborough wrote to Godolphin in 1706 : " The Union must be supported ; and I hope the reasonable men of the other party will not oppose the enlarging of the bottom, so that it may be able to support itself " (Trevelyan : *Select Docts.*, p. 197). For the Act, cf. Grant Robertson, pp. 162-179, and Trevelyan : *Select Docts.*, Section VI.

[3] *Memoirs* of Sir John Clerk, a Scottish Commissioner for the Treaty, in Trevelyan : *Select Docts.*, p. 215.

the Protestant Succession in both countries, and they created a large free-trade unit to which Adam Smith ascribed much of British economic power.   When both nations gained so much, it is unnecessary to disparage Whig motives or to grudge them the immediate benefits the party received, especially since they thereby increased the Anglican fury which was soon to rend them.

(c) The Tory Settlement : Peace and the Church : 1710-4

The sudden fall of the Whigs at the end of 1710 was due to many causes, some of them petty enough.   In one year the Churchills fell from favour, and Harley replaced them by Abigail Masham ; that was the Court Revolution.   At the same time the war went badly and the Whigs lost confidence ; their nervousness took the form of bullying Anne and impeaching Sacheverell.   They offended at once Anne's pride and her religion ; so she dismissed them, called in Harley, and secured confirmation of her actions from the electorate.   The Whigs, bent on their war, had forgotten Anne and Harley ; these two set about restoring peace abroad and Anglicanism at home by a national and moderate settlement.   Yet moderation was difficult with a High Tory Commons, hot for revenge, distrustful of Harley and compromise ; if they found a leader, national settlement would give way to party revenge.

(i) *The National Settlement of the Queen and Harley.*   Harley began with two measures to check the excessive influence of money and Dissent.   The Acts imposing a landed qualification on M.P.'s and punishing the practice of Occasional Conformity represented a general reaction toward the conservatism so marked in 1689 and 1701—the theory that the supremacy of land and the Church was the " fundamental " of the English Constitution.   But these measures were subsidiary to the great question of the peace.   By Utrecht the Tories stood and fell, as the Whigs by the war ; " the peace," wrote Bolingbroke, " had been judged with reason to be the only solid foundation whereupon we could erect a Tory system." [1]

Such a motive renders the peace suspect, and Bolingbroke later admitted " the badness of the peace " as one cause of the Tory

[1] *Letter to Wyndham.*

collapse. Advantages and allies were sacrificed by men who regarded Marlborough, not Louis, as their enemy ; yet moderate terms are sound policy, if peace is to last, and pity need not be wasted on the " Grand Allies," who had only been kept faithful by bribes.[1]   The nation wanted speedy relief from the burdens of war, and the twelve new Peers who carried the Treaty in the Lords represented, not only a party manœuvre, but the will of the nation. The Tories gave it also the nucleus of an Empire and a durable European settlement; above all, they enabled the approaching change of dynasty to be effected without French interference or other risks of war.   Such were the achievements of Harley's " moderate or comprehensive scheme " ; in it the Tories played the legitimate role of a party, in organising and enforcing the will of the majority.[2]

(ii) *Bolingbroke and the Tory Revenge.*   But the 150 hot Tories of the " October Club "[3] were not satisfied with Harley, whose moderation, Whig connections, and dislike of organised parties made him suspect.   The jealousy of his younger and more brilliant colleague, Bolingbroke, gave the malcontents their leader.   He resolved to play " a Whig game " in a very different sense from Harley's : to erect a Tory Junto in logical succession to Whig rule and to place the Crown in the gift of the Tory party.   In contrast to Harley, the keynote of his policy was unsettlement.   Like Shaftesbury in 1679-81, he concealed his ultimate aims behind a policy of revenge and monopoly; he confessed that, beyond filling " the employments of this Kingdom down to the meanest with Tories, few or none of us had any settled resolutions."[4]   The immediate programme was to harry all opposing interests : Dissent, the Bank, the merchants, the Hanoverians, and Harley's moderate group ; so that in the confusion the true Tory party, rid of Whig and crypto-Whig encumbrances, might dictate terms to any new King and establish its power on a permanent basis.

[1] Pity should be reserved for the minor allies, the Catalans and Camisards, who were abandoned through Tory indifference and the exigencies of a speedy peace.

[2] Cf. Feiling, p. 424, who insists strongly that " the Ministry of 1710 was always a coalition."

[3] So called from the elections of October 1710, which sent 150 Tory novices to Parliament.

[4] *Letter to Wyndham.*   Cf. *supra*, p. 185.

The methods adopted were examples of party venom at its worst. The Schism Act cut at the roots of the Toleration Act; the dismissal of Harley by a Court intrigue ruined the national Toryism which had revived the party and made it of national utility; the Commercial Treaty with France was inspired less by the dawning spirit of Free Trade than by spite against Whig merchants and desire for French support. All three failed; the Schism Act, because, as it was aimed at the education of the young, it could only be effective in the next generation: the fall of Harley, because it came too late— " The Earl of Oxford was removed on Tuesday; the Queen died on Sunday " : [1] the Treaty, because Whigs and moderate Tories united to defeat a measure which offended commercial doctrine and national prejudice.

The fatal charge, however, against Bolingbroke's " ginger group " was that of Jacobitism. It was a charge that every Tory feared owing to the qualified nature of his allegiance to imported Kings. Though Rochester and Nottingham at times showed remarkable zeal for the Hanoverian claims, the taunt of Jacobite never failed, and indeed received new vigour from the incrimination of Harley's secretary in 1708. Yet before 1713 the party as a whole officially supported the settlement it had helped to make, and before Bolingbroke no responsible Tory leader, and no considerable party group, ever attempted to reopen the question of the return of the Catholic Stuarts. Bolingbroke himself declared that he took up the Pretender only as the instrument of Tory revenge; his chief regret was that, instead of making James their tool, they became his : that instead of wrecking the settlement of 1689, they only succeeded in wrecking their own party.[2]

The cause of Tory ruin was the obstinate Popery of the Pretender. Bolingbroke worked to commit the Queen and Government to recognising James III. without any precise assurances of Protestant guarantees; the " true-born English " and Anglican party took the disastrous step of intriguing for French aid and pinning their cause to a Prince who had " all the superstition of a

---

[1] Letter to Swift from Bolingbroke, quoted by Trevelyan : *E.U.S.*, p. 515.

[2] Cf. *Letter to Wyndham.*

Capuchin." [1] This does not imply that they were anxious for a return of Stuart despotism; it was because party government seemed so strong and personal government seemed so obsolete that Bolingbroke thought he could alter the Succession to suit party purposes. In fact, his real miscalculation was that he underrated the remaining powers and importance of Royal persons; he tried to make Anne his slave and expected that either James III. or George I. would accept a Tory dictatorship. But all in turn escaped the trap, and the Tories alone were caught; if the Whigs, as Bolingbroke claimed, drove the Tories into the arms of the Pretender, no less certainly did the Tories drive Anne and George I. into the arms of the Whigs.

The "unsettlement" plot failed because Anne refused to endanger her Church. Under Whig guidance the Hanoverians came to the throne on the national issue of defence against France and Popery. When Anne sent for Shrewsbury instead of for Bolingbroke to replace Harley, she showed that, despite her leaning to her own family and her dislike of Whigs and Hanoverians, she accepted the national view of the situation. Shrewsbury represented not only moderate Whiggery, but the Revolution itself— land, aristocracy, and the trimming tradition of Halifax; he was as colourless and reluctant a partisan as Harley. Anne signified that she and the nation must submit to guidance by party organisations, for lack of a possible alternative; but she set a limit to their claims and ambitions by exiling from office the men who had lost the confidence of the nation and had forgotten all but private ends. The failure of the coalitions in 1705 and 1711 had proved that party government was inevitable for effective administration either in war or peace; the retribution for party excesses in 1710 and 1714 proved that moderation and responsibility to public opinion were indispensable conditions of successful party rule, as well as of national safety. Anne's reign owes its importance largely to the fact that it was the age of apprenticeship for English political parties.

[1] Cf. three vigorous and influential tracts, published in 1713, for which Defoe was imprisoned until Harley's favour protected him. They are: (i) *What if the Pretender should come?* (ii) *Reasons against the Succession of the House of Hanover,* (iii) *What if the Queen should die?*

(*d*) *Parties and the Individual*

The ordinary, non-political Englishman was exposed to all the risks of party experiments and feuds ; he saw his fate and that of the nation tossed about between the rivals with a general lack of scruple or consistency ; disaster was averted only by a seeming miracle in 1714. What, then, did he gain from the new methods and masters of government ?

His taxes were increased, in spite of the convenient device of handing down part of the burden to his descendants as a public debt ; no despot would dare to extract such sums as his official representatives voted on his behalf. Charles II. and James II. had given him fifteen years of peace : the Revolution had brought twenty-five years of war and alarms of war. Parties were as careless of national interests and private rights as the Stuart Kings ; they were often more oppressive, since the doctrine of State offences was extended beyond the person of the King to the shibboleths of party, as in Sacheverell's case. The subject has a right to petition the King, but if the men of Kent petitioned an angry Parliament, the Bill of Rights gave them no protection ; Defoe found that excessive bail could still be demanded if it was necessary to muzzle a pamphleteer of the other party ; the burgesses of Aylesbury discovered that elections were free—but only against Royal, not against party interference ; the good Churchman Dammaree learnt to his cost that the burning of conventicles was no longer a work of constitutional loyalty, but high treason and insurrection against an Anglican Queen ; John Tutchin, a critic of naval administration, was indicted for seditious libel on the ground that " if people should not be called to account for possessing the people with an ill opinion of the government, no government can subsist." [1] It is clear from these examples that the liberties gained by the Revolution had very strict limits and some strange qualifications. Undoubtedly " interests "—landowners, patrons, merchants,—were protected, though some precariously : *e.g.* bankers and Dissenters. The upper classes in town and country, who made the settlement, had no quarrel with it save over the division of the spoils ; but amid the demands and feuds of overbearing factions the unprotected citizen

[1] Cf. cases in Grant Robertson, pp. 407-439.

had little chance, unless he were a faithful or watchful dependent. It was an age of monopoly in politics, trade and religion; the independent, or " interloper," went to the wall.

On the other hand, the substitution of an intelligent and commercially-minded oligarchy for the folly and caprices of the Stuarts brought unified government and national prosperity. The oligarchy gave its subjects Empire and glory, to satisfy their pride; it gave them commercial and agricultural wealth, in which they might have a modest share, unless they were master-craftsmen, smallholders or squatters, the necessary victims of capitalist evolution. It had no mind to give them either economic independence or political power; as Rousseau observed, a Septennial Parliament reduced the electoral system to a farce, particularly since the new Riot Act hampered the only other weapon of public opinion. Yet the irresponsibility of Hanoverian Parliaments was less dangerous to liberty, even though more outrageous, than the irresponsibility of Stuart Kings; for it was but the abuse of a representative principle which could always be revived, while arbitrary Prerogative was a complete denial of the principle itself. The machinery of oligarchy could also be the machinery of democracy; it was a flexible instrument, adaptable for use by all classes, in turn or together, available for oppression or for emancipation. The chief national service of the Whig and Tory magnates in the reigns of William III. and Anne was that they created the modern English Constitution, tested it by the strain of their quarrels, and bequeathed it, with all its merits and imperfections, to the Anglo-Saxon world.

(For suggestions for further reading, see pp. 183-4.)

IX

THE UNITING OF THE KINGDOMS

THE story of Scotland and Ireland in the seventeenth century is one of conquest and union; the difference between them is that Scotland, after suffering a temporary conquest by England, was linked to her neighbour by a free and permanent union, while Ireland, after alternate periods of conquest and revolt, was bound to England by a permanent conquest without the benefits of union. The expansion of England was thus the supreme interest in the external relations of both countries, and it also exercised a constant influence on their purely domestic history. Even in separate histories of Scotland or Ireland the English question must be the central theme of the historian; in this chapter it must be the sole theme. The course of domestic events in both countries was more bloody and confused than in England and cannot be compressed with profit into a few pages; a short survey must confine itself to tracing the chequered progress of the union of the British Isles in one State. The achievement of union altered the destinies both of Great Britain and of Europe. It ranks with—and indeed was a necessary condition of—the parallel achievement of English union under the sovereignty of Parliament; for the English Parliament had to absorb or control the rival Parliaments and administrations if it was to maintain supremacy over the Monarchy. Union converted England from a small to a large power, strong in men, wealth and strategic security; it gave Scotland order, peace, and a share in English trade and Empire; [1] it crushed for two centuries the

---

[1] A vivid sketch of Scottish life in the seventeenth century is given in Hume Brown: *History of Scotland*, Vol. III, ch. 2. It emphasises Scottish poverty and economic backwardness both in agriculture and industry.

spirit and prosperity of Ireland; it was the foundation of British economic supremacy in Europe and of the victory over France in the duel for Empire.

I. The Uniting of England and Scotland

Scotland must take precedence in the history of union, less because it provided in 1603 a bond of dynasty (for the Stuart line was as often a cause of division),[1] than because it gives the clue to union. The common interest was fear of Popery, and above all, fear of foreign Popery threatening Reformation and independence together. It is true that religion, like dynasty, worked both ways;[2] for the rigid theological spirit was hostile to the worldly compromise that alone made union possible, and the spirit of trade and barter was more noticeable in the negotiations of 1707 than the spirit of religion. Nevertheless, the Scots surrendered their political independence, not because they wished to be included in the tariff walls of the Navigation Code, but because they wished to secure the Presbyterian religion and the political liberties that had grown up with it.

The years between 1603 and 1707 were strewn with abortive schemes of union. There was the Parliamentary plan of James I. and Bacon which the English Commons rejected in 1607: the Church plan of James I., Charles I. and Laud which was ruined by the Bishops' Wars and brought ruin on its authors: the Solemn League and Covenant (1643) which was shattered by the execution of Charles I.: the Cromwellian conquest and union which ended with the departure of the garrison in 1660: the despotic plan of James II., based on toleration and free trade, which the Revolution frustrated: and the negotiations of William III. which were checked by the Darien disaster and interrupted by his death. This series of failures revealed obstacles of religion, race, temper and interests which made the success of 1707 the more remarkable. Well into the next century the English dislike of the Scots was shown by the

---

[1] *E.g.*, between 1649-60 and in 1689 (Killiecrankie), 1703 (Act of Security), and 1715.

[2] Cf. P. Hume Brown, Vol. II, pp. 376-7 and 454.

unpopularity of Bute and the diatribes of Johnson and Wilkes, who made of it a link of mutual respect ; in the seventeenth, there was no doubt that the two nations regarded each other with the distrust of ignorance and fear. Scotland, from the time of Edward I. and even earlier, was the traditional enemy, a French client-state on England's flanks. Between them lay the Border, a ' no man's land ' of raid and counter-raid, which made communication risky and difficult ; and though James I. altered its name to " the Middle Shires," it was not so easy to turn it from a barrier to a link.[1] Tradition was reinforced by trading jealousy and religious divergence ; for while England was Protestant before Scotland, the Scottish Church was " Reformed " in the Continental sense when the Anglican Church clung to the relics of its past. Formal religious harmony only prevailed for the two years of 1643-4 ; it died with the rise of Cromwell, who in English rather than Puritan fashion confessed a " carnal " preference for Cavaliers over Scots.

Yet we must remember that from 1603 there were some permanent links between the countries except in the Civil Wars ; they had in common a King, an Executive, and the rights of English citizenship.[2] Throughout the century Scotland was governed by a Council controlled from London (either a Royal Privy Council or a Republican Council of State), which always contained the leading English Ministers ; even Charles II., who elevated separatism into a State policy, maintained executive unity.[3] And since the semi-English Council could pack and dominate the Scottish Parliament, it follows that the accession of James VI. to the English throne deprived Scotland of independence in her Legislature, Executive and foreign policy.[4] At once she assumed something of the character of a province—though it might be argued that the only change was from a French to an English province. She suffered a succession of absentee Kings ; James VI. returned but once (1617),

---

[1] Cf. D. L. W. Tough, *The Last Years of a Frontier.*

[2] By the decision of the English Courts in ' Calvin's Case ' (1608) all Scots born since 1603 (" Post-Nati ") had the rights of English subjects.

[3] Lauderdale advised Charles to foster divisions and thus to prevent a repetition of common resistance as in 1640-5 ; cf. Burnet, I, p. 107.

[4] Cf. Hume Brown, II, p. 240.

Charles I. came twice (1633 and 1641), Charles II. once when England was barred to him (1650), and James VII., as King, not at all. The Stuarts found their new Kingdom at once more comfortable, more profitable and more engrossing. They never felt homesick; they only took the desperate step of visiting Scotland when some great affair demanded their presence, and they left their old subjects to the mercy of bailiffs—a Spottiswoode, a Sharp, or a Lauderdale.

The first union scheme (1604-7), born of James' impatience and Bacon's optimism, was a weakly and premature child; its interest lies in that it anticipates in method, terms and spirit the final solution.[1] James dropped the Parliamentary union when it became a cause of friction rather than of harmony, and turned to the more promising alternative of ecclesiastical union by and for Royal Supremacy. This was the plan which increasingly occupied the energies of James, Charles and Laud; it was in intent the cornerstone of the first Stuart despotism, in effect the mine which blew despotism to pieces. James made two contribution s; he converted the secular machinery of State from a limited to an absolute government, and he restored the Episcopal system in the Church with certain additions on the Tudor model. Of his political power in Scotland he boasted with reason:

" Here I sit and govern it with my pen; I write and it is done; and by a Clerk of the Council I govern Scotland now—which others could not do by the sword." [2]

His nominated Privy Council had absolute control of all officials, including those of the Royal Burghs, and it arranged in Royal interests elections to Parliament or to the General Assembly of the Kirk. He summoned and dissolved Parliaments at pleasure, and he secured the initiative in legislation by obtaining in 1609 virtual nomination of the " Lords of the Articles." [3] James used these powers to establish order in the remotest parts of Scotland for the

[1] Cf. Hume Brown, II, pp. 246-8, and Gardiner, I, pp. 324-340.

[2] Hume Brown, II, p. 240; James was pointing the moral to the English Parliament.

[3] These were a body of 24 (8 from each of the three Estates of clergy, lords, and burghs) chosen to prepare the business of Parliament; the nobles nominated 8 Bishops, the Bishops nominated 8 nobles, and the 16 nominated 8 commissioners for the barons and burghs. Thus the Bishops, being King's men, could ensure a favourable Committee for the King.

first time in history; turbulent clans such as the Armstrongs and Macgregors were broken up, " Jeddart Justice " tamed the Border, and a system of Justices of the Peace and Constables was imported from England to keep the countryside in hand.[1] But the secret of James' success was his control of the nobles who had been the real rulers of Scotland for centuries; before he came to England he had crushed the overmighty, and he cemented his victory by bribing them with Church lands resumed by the Act of 1587. The fundamental condition of Scottish despotism was the separation of the nobles from the Kirk; James by fulfilling it was able to undo the work of Knox and crush the Kirk in isolation.

James began his remodelling of the Scottish Church by suppressing General Assemblies and exiling the Presbyterian leaders, in particular the Melvilles; then by Parliaments and Conventions of clergy he gradually restored the Bishops to their offices and jurisdictions, and fortified them with two High Commission Courts (1610); he then felt strong enough to restore the General Assembly as his tool, and obtained from the Glasgow Assembly (1612) decrees conferring on the Bishops complete diocesan control and forbidding General Assemblies to meet without Royal summons. Thus by 1612 the machinery of the Royal Episcopal Church was complete, and James proceeded cautiously on the second and more delicate stage of remodelling the doctrine and ritual of the Church. He knew his people and was sensitive to danger, so he went no further than obtaining the ratification by Assembly and Parliament of the " Five Articles of Perth "; [2] he left to Charles and Laud the curious problem of an Episcopal hierarchy imposed on a Presbyterian personnel and discipline.

It was not until 1633, the year that Laud became Archbishop of Canterbury, that Charles took up the plan where James left it, but in the meantime he did one thing to make its failure inevitable. The Act of Revocation (1625), which resumed all grants of Crown and Church lands made since 1542—before the

[1] Cf. Hume Brown, II, pp. 253-264 and 277.

[2] The Articles prescribed : (i) kneeling at Communion : (ii) and (iii) Private Communion and Baptism in cases of necessity : (iv) observance of the festivals of the Church: (v) Confirmation by Bishops. Cf. Hume Brown, II, pp. 265-271. Cf. Ch. I, for James' fear of Laud's intervention in the Kirk.

Reformation, broke the alliance of Crown and nobles and revived that alliance of Kirk and nobles which had carried through the Reformation and the Revolution against Mary Stuart.[1] Imagine the consequences in England if Mary Tudor had resumed all the monastic lands on her accession. When at last, in 1633, Charles visited Scotland and was crowned with Anglican pomp, he brought with him a man whose reputation had preceded him and put the taint of Popery on all Charles' acts. What James had feared came to pass when Laud's unquiet spirit was let loose on Scotland. At once the Privy Council was packed with Bishops, the High Commission was enlarged in power, and the Royal Prerogative was used to sweep away the whole work of Knox without the consent of any representative body of the Church. The Royal Book of Canons (1636) and Laud's Liturgy (1637) imposed on the Kirk Royal Supremacy and Arminian ritual; the self-governing national Church was faced with an alien despotism, reeking of Popery. The national protest was organised into triumphant revolution with startling rapidity. The Bishops fled to England and safety ; the Protestors replied to Charles' threats by setting up a provisional government and binding the nation together by a Solemn Covenant against Popery (1638) ;[2] first the General Assembly and then the Parliament regained freedom of spirit and action ; finally the Covenanters raised money and arms to resist the punitive expedition of their lawful King. The two Bishops' Wars (1639-40) were little more than half-hearted skirmishes in the Royalist North, around the Royal Castles and on the Border ; but they served to reveal to Scots and English alike the total collapse of Royal power, when an improvised rebel army swept into Northern England and forced their King first to treat and then to make complete surrender. The Treaty of Ripon (Oct. 1640) sealed the failure of the first Stuart attempt at Anglo-Scottish union by the bonds of despotism and Episcopacy.

The irony of the Royal failure was that it did indeed produce union—not the union of Kingdoms, but that of insurgent Parlia-

---

[1] The Act was called at the time " the ground stone of all the mischief that followed after " (Hume Brown, II, p. 287).

[2] It was based on the Negative Confession of Faith authorised by James VI. in 1581, and claimed to be in defence of the King and true religion.

ments.   Forty years of Royal unification were succeeded by twenty
years of effort by their subjects to the same end.   The result was
the same ; the failure of Parliamentary alliance led to a second conquest of Scotland, with a similar temporary success and violent
reaction.

The Scottish revolt not only called the Long Parliament into
being, but it provided a guarantee for its policy and independence ;
it gave Charles' opponents the power of the sword.   Pym took
care not to give the King money to pay off the Scots before August
1641, when the destruction of the Prerogative system was finished ;
the need of security for those who lent money for the purpose
produced the Act taking from the King the power of dissolution of
Parliament.[1]   From August 1641 to June 1643 Scotland was officially neutral while England plunged into Civil war ; but while the
King's bid for Scottish support in the summer of 1641 came to
naught owing to the " Incident," the appeal of the Parliament two
years later led to the Solemn League and Covenant, which the
English ratified in September 1643.[2]   Politically the union was
imperfect ; Parliaments and administration were separate, the only
link being the Committee of both Kingdoms ; [3] the armies had
separate commanders, though the English Treasury paid for both.
The bond of union was to be true religion, " according to the word
of God and the example of the best reformed Churches."

In war the effect of the alliance was decisive.   Leslie's troops,
trained and led by veterans of the Thirty Years' War, confident in
their recent triumphs, were the nearest approach to a skilled force
that had yet appeared on either side ; whichever party they joined
had an overwhelming advantage in numbers and striking force.
Immediately they hemmed in the Royalist North and prevented
the triple advance on London which had threatened defeat for the
Parliament since the beginning of the 1643 campaign ; at Nantwich
they destroyed the Royalist reinforcements which Ormonde had
sent from Ireland after the Cessation of September 1643, and cut

[1] Cf. Gardiner : *Hist.*, IX, pp. 359-360.

[2] Cf. Gardiner : *Docts.*, pp. 267-71, for the Covenant : for the Incident, cf. Hume
Brown, II, pp. 323-6.

[3] Cf. Gardiner: *Docts.*, pp. 271-4.

off the Royalists in Wales from those of the North; finally they shared—how much, is disputed—in the victory of Marston Moor, which lost the North for Charles and broke up his best weapons, Rupert's horse and Newcastle's foot. Thereafter their value declined, though they held down the North and crushed at Philiphaugh (1645) Montrose's dangerous but tardy venture to raise Scotland for her own King; for the English Parliament had created an Army sufficient unto itself and hostile to the Scots through religious and national prejudice.

Consequently, when the military crisis was over, the weakness of the political alliance became manifest; gratitude and the memory of common service was soon forgotten after the English and Independent victory of Naseby. The new masters of England rejected the Scottish interpretation of the League and Covenant, and cared little for the Presbyterian divines of the Westminster Assembly, who since 1643 had sought to frame a common national worship. So the Scots, with their own house in urgent need of order, declined in 1646 the thankless task of arbitration between two parties, who only agreed in refusing the Scottish solution—Presbyterian Monarchy and war upon heretics. Their surrender of Charles to the English in 1646 has brought upon them natural but unmerited abuse from contemporaries and posterity alike; but three facts must be stated in their defence. First, they would have defended him against the world if he had accepted the Covenant—a condition they had openly maintained since 1638; secondly, far from being heavily bribed to give him up, they only received a portion of the arrears of their expenses which the Parliament had agreed to pay in the League and Covenant; thirdly, they made Charles' personal safety a condition of the surrender. Further, regicide came in a sudden spasm of fury two years later; it took by surprise not only Scotland but England, even Cromwell himself by his own profession; and the Scots' immediate proclamation of Charles II, in rash defiance of superior force, is their own vindication.

Union broke down in 1646 and conquest followed in 1651; between these years Scottish relations with England were determined by obscure party intrigues. The removal of despotism

restored the Reformed religion, but it also revived older forces—
the ambitions and feuds of the nobility. The internal unity of
Scotland was new, artificial, and imposed from above; liberty
released feudal disruption, racial differences between Highlander
and Lowlander, besides the religious divisions of Presbyterian,
Episcopalian and Catholic. Three parties arose in turn in defence
of the Stuarts, and it is difficult to decide whether they represented
general causes or personal factions. The first was the party of
Hamilton, the " Trimmer " of Scotland, who made the " Engagement " with Charles I. and led a coalition of Royalists and moderate
Presbyterians to disaster at Preston in the Second Civil War
(1648).[1] The second was Montrose's desperate rally of the Scottish
North in 1650, against the strict Covenanters and in favour of
Charles II. whom the Covenanters had proclaimed; this ended with
the defeat of Carbisdale and the execution of Montrose as a traitor.
The third was the remains of the national movement of 1638, now
identified with the power of the Campbell Clan. The Earl of
Argyle, as head of the Campbells and leader of the Kirk, became the
ruler of Scotland after the failure of Hamilton. His first expedient,
an alliance with Cromwell, fell through with the death of Charles I.;
his next alliance, with Charles II., was even more unnatural.
However, he crushed Montrose with ease, surrounded the convert
King with chaplains and restrictions, and at Dunbar came very near
to complete success. In 1650 Cromwell failed to pierce Leslie's
defence of Edinburgh, and was trapped in retreat at Dunbar with
an inferior and enfeebled force; defeat was only converted into
victory by the incredible tactical mistakes of the Scottish Council
of War and the poor fighting qualities of the Scottish troops.[2]
Dunbar ended at once Argyle's domination and national independence; the raid which led to Worcester was only an incident in the
Cromwellian conquest.

A few conclusions emerge clearly from the welter of this decade
of independence. First, Scotland, far from being ready for amal-
gamation in a larger unit, could not even maintain the unity of a

[1] The Engagement stated that Charles was to receive Scottish support on terms
of suppressing all sects and establishing Presbyterianism for three years. Cf.
Gardiner : *Docts.*, pp. 347-52.

[2] Cf. Hume Brown, II, pp. 352-360, and Firth : *Cromwell*, ch. 14.

nation. From 1640 her history, like that of England in the same years, is a story of disintegration in Church and State. By 1651 the nobles were alienated from the Kirk and quarrelling among themselves ; and the arrival of Charles II. created a fatal split in the Kirk between the " Protesters " against him and the " Resolutioners " in his favour. So in Scotland as in England a divided nation lay at the mercy of the one united and armed force in either country. Secondly, though union by alliance had failed, isolation had proved equally impracticable. Much as English and Scots hated each other, geography drew them together. Risings in either land spread magically to the ends of the other ; no party was sure of power in the one, unless it could control its neighbour. It was a marriage of necessity ; the theologians had failed to elevate it into a marriage of love ; it remained for statesmen to patch it up into a marriage of convenience.

For the next eight years (1651-9) Scotland was happy in having no history. Even the Highlands were subdued by 1654, and the nation, freed from the cares of independence by Monk's garrison of 8000 men, settled down to free trade with England, party struggles in the Kirk, and provincial prosperity. Peace brought wealth despite heavy taxes, and besides material progress there was a marked " plenty of the means of grace." [1] The changes in English politics had little effect, for the Army kept continuity under the supervision of a Council sent from England ; and both the Rump and the Protector were set on a corporate union. Economic union was established, and Cromwell had some Scottish " representatives " nominated to both his Parliaments ; [2] but the Scots showed a natural lack of enthusiasm for a system by which their spokesmen were chiefly foreign officials, and they would have none of Cromwell's ' fundamental ' condition of union—the deadly sin of religious toleration. Thus, since the material benefits incidental to strong and good government could not heal the wounds of national pride and religious zeal, union by conquest could only produce reaction when the garrison marched away. Cromwell prophesied

---

[1] Quoted in Hume Brown, II, p. 378.

[2] Also in Barebone's Assembly and Richard Cromwell's Parliament; the Instrument of Government assigned Scotland 30 members (cl. 9 and 10), and Ireland a like number.

his own failure when he said : " That you have by force I look upon it as nothing." [1]

Restoration is an accurate description of what happened in Scotland in the years following 1660. Unlike the English Presbyterians, the Scots could claim no active share in bringing back their King ; they awaited his pleasure and could make no terms. Charles II. restored a separate Privy Council and Parliament, but these were tools of despotism wielded from London by Clarendon and Lauderdale ; the English Parliament broke the economic union by excluding Scotland from the Navigation Act of 1660, and left Scotland out of the political settlement of the Act of Indemnity. Scotland was politically separated from England in order that Charles might use his docile against his refractory subjects ; but there was to be a very real union of despotic policy, working through the chosen instrument of the Church. Charles, ever lavish with promises, announced that he would " protect and preserve the government of the Church of Scotland, as it is settled by law, without violation " ; [2] but he was also a practical joker, and his first step was to make the Scottish Parliament annul all Acts passed since 1633. This " Rescissory Act " (1661) made Episcopacy the only government settled by law ; so the Bishops reappeared under the Primacy of James Sharp, a repentant Covenanter, and with them the High Commission and lay patronage. The rest of Charles II.'s reign is a dreary story of persecution, directed by Lauderdale and Sharp until 1679 and thenceforward by James of York ; now and then it was relaxed a little from laziness or policy, while at times it waxed fiercer, after the ineffectual risings of 1666 and 1679 (Pentland Hills and Bothwell Brig). It began with the execution of the Covenant leaders, Argyle, Guthrie and Johnston of Warringtoun ; there followed the ejection of anti-Episcopal clergy, the fining of lay absentees from the parish services, the use of torture by the Privy Council against suspected rebels, the quartering of Highland militia upon disaffected districts (particularly the South-West, home of the Whigs), the harrying of field-meetings under the Conventicles Act of 1670, and the application of the full Catholic Penal Code against Protestant

[1] Speech of July 16, 1647.   [2] Hume Brown, II, p. 383.

' recusants." The work of men such as Graham of Claverhouse, Dalziel and "Bluidy" Mackenzie was thorough and successful; such isolated incidents as the murder of Archbishop Sharp in 1679 only help to prove that resistance was confined to a small and desperate group. At the end of the reign the "Cameronians" alone were left—the followers of Richard Cameron who declared war upon Charles and his agents; and they did little but alienate their compatriots and provide a heroic but futile army of martyrs.[1] The miserable failure of Argyle's invasion in 1685 showed that Scotland could not free herself from despotism by her isolated efforts.

In 1688 England returned the compliment of 1640 by ridding Scotland of James VII. James himself helped her by his last manœuvre. The King who, as Duke of York, had raised persecution to its climax proclaimed in 1686 full toleration to all except the self-outlawed Cameronians. Although this miraculous change of heart was accepted more credulously by the Scottish than English Dissenters, the restored clergy soon regained their independent spirit; the Kirk returned to politics to meet the Catholic menace, made acute by the birth of a Catholic heir. As in 1660, the withdrawal of the arms of despotism in 1688 swept away the system without a trace, and a Scottish Convention after England's example offered the Crown to William and Mary, coupled with a Claim of Right.

Scotland now embarked on its last period of independent alliance with England. Yet its troubles were not over. While the English had slowly learned to guide their quarrels into the milder channels of party politics, the Scots, with their dummy Parliament, still clung to the ruder method of fighting them out. The Highlanders, led by Dundee (Graham of Claverhouse), fell upon the Lowlanders for their treachery towards James and were only checked at Killiecrankie (1689) for lack of a leader when Dundee fell. Then in revenge, the Scottish supporters of William, guided by Dalrymple, William's Scottish adviser, issued "letters of fire and sword" against the Highland chiefs who failed to take the Oath of Allegiance, and they seized the occasion to make an example of the Mac-

[1] The most notable were in 1685, John Brown of Priesthill and the two women martyrs of Wigtown.

donalds for their tardy submission. The Campbells were set on their old enemies, and the Massacre of Glencoe was the result (1692).[1] Then the General Assembly, revived after a long lapse since 1653, added to the disturbance by its ejection of the Episcopalian clergy and its quarrels with William over Church government and Royal Supremacy.[2] Finally, commercial enterprise and the new secular spirit brought an economic disaster and a quarrel with England.[3] The tragedy of the Darien scheme (1695-9) cannot be described here, but its political effects must be recorded.[4] From its beginning Paterson's enterprise was invested with national pride and hope ; a capital of £400,000 was enthusiastically raised from a poor nation whose annual revenue was £160,000 ; so when the crazy scheme ended in inevitable disaster, it was natural to vent the anger and blame on the old enemy. The English King, Parliament and East India Company had consistently opposed the venture, and they were held responsible for this crushing blow to Scotland's infant credit. England was guilty in motive, though not in fact ; and the quarrel revealed to William and to politicians of both countries that the alliance of 1689 had broken down.

William's political testament to Anne was the necessity of an " incorporating " union, but her first attempt at negotiation only increased the friction.[5] However, two facts—the French War and Anne's lack of heirs—turned convenience into urgent necessity ; the alliance of Louis XIV. and a Catholic Pretender made separation the hope of Jacobitism. In the crisis relations became worse before they improved, for from opposite poles Presbyterians and Catholics united against the Anglican policy of Anne. The Scottish Parliament, in the exuberance of its new freedom and in the extravagance of raw parties, showed its spite by encouraging French wines, by declaring its independent right to decide entry or non-entry into war, and by passing the famous Act of Security (1703). When

---

[1] Cf. Hume Brown, III, pp. 16-21.

[2] William's plan for a compromise with Episcopalians was rejected and he was forced to renounce the doctrine of Royal Supremacy.

[3] Hume Brown characterised the years after 1689 as the " Age of Secular Interests."

[4] Cf. J. S. Barbour, *William Paterson and the Darien Company*, and Hume Brown, III, pp. 26-39.

[5] A joint Commission sat in 1702-3.

Scotland by this Act threatened to choose its own ruler on the principle that he or she must not be the ruler of England except under certain conditions, the English Government's first thought was of reprisals. But its Aliens Act (1705), imposing loss of citizenship and non-importation on the Scots if the Hanoverian Succession was not accepted, was followed by calmer reflection that the way of security lay in removing grievances and offering benefits on condition of union. Admittedly the hope was Utopian and the atmosphere could hardly be more unfavourable; but Anne had the merit of obstinacy, Godolphin of management and Somers of imagination. Two forces carried the Union through against the indifference of the English and the violent protests of the Scots: the divisions and cross-currents of Scottish political parties and a united English Ministry making full use of the large powers remaining to the Monarchy. The scheme prepared by a carefully chosen joint Commission was first ratified by the Scottish Parliament by a small majority of nobles and then by a large majority in the English Parliament; the Scots added to it the chief guarantee of its permanence—an Act of Security safeguarding the Presbyterian Church " without any alteration . . . in all succeeding generations." The Treaty established the Hanoverian Succession in both countries—this was the fundamental. It abolished the Scottish Council and Parliament, and gave the Scots 45 seats in the Commons and 16 in the Lords of the Parliament of Great Britain: free trade: some customs exemptions: a grant of £400,000 to compensate for Darien losses, national debts and future liabilities: and a proportional share of British taxation. Scottish justice, burghal and baronial jurisdiction were to be left intact.[1]

Thus in 1707 Scotland was surrendered to the mercy of an omnipotent Parliament in which it was represented by a permanent minority; its fortunes were subject to the whims of none too scrupulous parties and to the needs of English policy. Some of the financial and judicial clauses were broken almost as soon as made; but there was no remedy against overwhelming force. Why, then, did the Scottish Parliament commit political suicide? Bribery

[1] For a summary of the intricate story of the negotiations, cf. Hume Brown, III, pp. 75-128; for the Treaty, cf. Grant Robertson, and Trevelyan: *Select Docts.*, pp. 210-249. Cf. also Ch. VIII.

will not explain it, nor will commercial and financial concessions which appeased a small class. Popular prejudice was rampant against it; the Commissioners and representatives who passed it went in fear of their lives from Edinburgh mobs. The answer is that it was accepted as the lesser evil by the intelligent and interested oligarchy which governed Scotland. The nobles, the clergy and the officials had their interests protected more safely than was possible either under precarious independence or under a Stuart restoration; they preferred the mercy of Whigs and Tories to the mercy of their own enemies or a Catholic King.[1] For the rest of Anne's reign there was a flood of disputes and gloomy prophecies in both countries on the fate of the Union, but at the first test in 1715 the framework held and the prophets were confounded. There could be little enthusiasm for the English connection; there could be none in the Lowlands—for there lay the Scotland that counted in history—for a Catholic Stuart surrounded by Highlanders. Popery, despotism and the clans had been the curses of Scottish history in the seventeenth century; England, with all its faults, had none of these.

II. The Conquest of Ireland

In the union of England and Scotland geography and religion overcame the wilfulness of man; the presence of a third factor produced another kind of union between England and Ireland. This factor was fear. Fear inspired desperate revolt and savage repression, which degraded victors and vanquished in equal measure. Geography demanded union; for England barred Ireland's way to Europe, and Ireland under hostile influence threatened England's flank and commerce. But since the English Reformation religion fixed a gulf broader than the Irish Sea between the peoples. In Ireland Englishmen saw the Counter-Reformation gathering for an attack, and they saw that attack directed by the national enemy, Spain.

The Tudor policy—holding strongly the Channel coast and the

[1] The nobles were led by the Earls of Argyle, Queensberry and Mar (Mar later recanted and led the '15): the clergy by Carstairs, the friend of William III.: the officials by the Earls of Stair (Dalrymple) and Seafield.

Dublin " Pale " and elsewhere letting sleeping Irishmen lie—broke down utterly in 1595 with the revolt of the Northern clans of O'Neill and O'Donnell under the two Hughs, the Earls of Tyrone and Tyrconnel.   They raised the whole of Celtic Ireland and forced Elizabeth in nine years of war to undertake a systematic conquest of the island.   Thus James I. was faced with the problem and expense of a permanent armed occupation.   It was comparatively easy to control the Dublin administration ; the Royal Deputy or Lieutenant had complete command of the Executive officials and could usually procure a subservient Parliament ; moreover by Poyning's Law (1494) no measures could be placed before the Irish Parliament which had not been previously approved by the English Council.   The two great problems were to break up the political solidarity of the tribes and the religious solidarity of the Catholic Church.

There were three sustained attacks on the Irish tribes and Church —those of the early Stuarts, Cromwell, and William III ; between them were the attempts of Charles I. and James II. to win Irish support by conciliation.   The same methods appeared in all three schemes of conquest—eviction or restriction of Irish landowners and a Penal Code against Catholics.

In the first attack (1603-41) religious persecution played a minor part except in spasms, as after Gunpowder Plot ; priests were often in danger as foreign agents, but laymen were only forced to swell the revenues by " recusancy " fines.   Catholics sat in Parliament, though they were excluded from office by the Oath of Supremacy ; Stuart policy, while rejecting open indulgence in the form of repeal or " Graces," [1] was that of the blind eye.   But since this religious policy could not hope to inspire loyalty and would be fortunate to secure acquiescence, drastic steps were needed to erect English political ascendancy.   Expense made impossible the upkeep of a large army ; surplus revenues were unknown before 1660, for the customs, which formed the main source, were kept down by trade restrictions framed to protect English industries from Irish competition.   The only alternative was a militia strengthened by a

[1] Charles in 1628 promised to enact relief from the Oaths and security of land tenure in return for grants ; but though he took the money, he refused to confirm the " Graces " in 1634.

professional nucleus; and a militia demanded a large resident English population. "Plantation," then, was the solution; for it was not only a military bulwark but a source of profit to the Crown and a method of breaking into the tribal countryside. England was full of colonising fever, and the precedent was there, set by a Catholic Queen; Mary had planted Leix and Offaly, west of Dublin, and re-named them Queen's County and King's County.

The first and most lasting result of this agrarian policy was the planting of Ulster in 1609 with English and Scottish settlers. It is probably the most disastrous single event in Irish history, and its baneful effects grew with the centuries; nor is it safe to assume that their end is in sight. However, the Plantation, after a slow start, soon fulfilled its object as a Protestant stronghold; the City of London developed the port of Derry and the Scots filled the countryside. They incidentally created a new religious problem for the Stuarts, in that they were too Protestant by far; but militant Presbyterianism at least produced good soldiers and farmers who would neither be corrupted nor frightened away by Papists.[1] When a generation had proved the success of the Ulster experiment in substituting English for Irish ascendancy in the rebel North, Wentworth began to plan a further extension. He proposed to spread the English garrison right across Ireland, to Connaught in the West. He faked a claim for the Crown from the marriage in 1333 of Lionel of Clarence to an Irish heiress, and by packing and intimidation of juries he secured general recognition of the Crown's claim (1636). Though nothing more was done, it was this threat to all security of tenure which hung over the Irish when the Stuart despotism fell in 1640.

The recall of Wentworth and the disbanding of his Army meant the end of strong government at the very time when it aroused limitless fears. The conquest was as yet incomplete, the garrison still hopelessly outnumbered. The Irish no less than the Scots could seize the opportunity offered by Charles' domestic difficulties to undo the past and prevent the coming enslavement. Plotting

---

[1] By 1640 it was reckoned that there were 100,000 Scots and 20,000 English in Ulster; Gardiner: *Hist.*, X, pp. 68-9.

was easy in the state of intrigue and confusion that existed in Ireland; so under cover of simultaneous but independent Royalist plots, Phelim O'Neill and his friends were able to rouse the North against their oppressors and supplanters. They failed to surprise Dublin (October 1641), but they swept the rest of the country except a few towns; and by the end of 1642 they had a brilliant leader in Owen Roe O'Neill and new allies in the Anglo-Irish nobility of the Pale, who feared the indiscriminate revenge of the Puritan Parliament.

The success of the revolt against a paralysed opposition was naturally rapid; but the vengeance on the Ulster planters laid up for the rebels and for their posterity a terrible retribution. The "Ulster Massacre" fatally determined the policy of England towards Ireland for over a century, whatever government was in power. Its immediate effect in England, after the first panic rage was over, was to precipitate civil war over the question of the punitive army; but both King and Parliament vied in protestations of revenge as soon as their own differences were settled. It is a comparatively unimportant question whether the deaths by sword or destitution were exaggerated or whether the violent expulsion of the intruders was justified; what is historically important is that all England believed that the Irish people were guilty of a hideous and wholesale massacre of defenceless Protestants, and that all England demanded that the perpetrators should be wiped out and their race so chained as to prevent another outbreak. The Ulster Massacre may be a myth, but it was none the less a historical fact to the seventeenth century.[1]

However, while the English parties fought for the possession of the sword of vengeance, Ireland regained total independence for the first time since the English occupation. The Confederation of Kilkenny (1642) set up a government of Assembly and Councils, hampered by Celtic and Anglo-Irish quarrels; vigour was supplied by Owen Roe and the Papal Nuncio Rinuccini, who arrived in 1645. While the Parliamentarians made sporadic efforts at resis-

[1] There are no reliable figures, for all accounts have been distorted by propagandist bias; a modern Nationalist text-book accepts 4000 as slain and 7-8000 dead of exposure, etc. (Hayden and Moonan, *Short History of the Irish People*, p. 297, based on Gardiner's estimate, *Hist.*, X, 68-9).

tance, the Royalists under Ormonde, appointed Lord Lieutenant by Charles I. in 1643, proceeded by way of a truce and a secret agreement to a full Irish alliance.[1] But Ireland proved no exception to the disintegrating tendencies of the age ; her independence, like that of Scotland, was ruined by her own divisions. The offers of Charles I. caused an open breach between the Council with its Anglo-Irish majority and the anti-Stuart party led by Owen Roe and the Nuncio (1646) ; so the English fringe was saved, and Ormonde even surrendered Dublin to the Parliament in 1647 to save it from the Irish. The national movement was wrecked by the long duel between Owen Roe O'Neill, head of the tribes, and James Butler, Duke of Ormonde, symbol of the Protestant feudal ascendancy ; and when Owen Roe yielded the direction of the Irish movement to Ormonde in 1649 it was too late ; for the wrath of Cromwell was at hand.

Racial and religious divisions are sufficient to explain the failure of the resistance to the New Model Army ;[2] we should rather wonder at the stoutness of the defence by scattered and half-trained troops, especially after the warning of Drogheda. Clonmel, Limerick and Galway held out for months, and the task of repression took nearly three years. There was atonement in blood at once ; the massacres of Drogheda and Wexford have festered in Irish traditions as did the Ulster massacres in Anglo-Scottish memories, and no amount of whitewashing can disguise their historical effects.[3] Yet the atonement in kind was even more thorough and permanent. The landed settlement of 1652 not only restored the plantation system but extended it to the whole island east of the River Shannon ; Connaught, the scene of Wentworth's plans, was designed as an Irish reservation. It was not to be a mere change of large landowners or an infiltration of planters as in Ulster, but a complete displacement of population, involving the

[1] The Cessation of Arms, 1643 ; the secret Glamorgan Treaty, 1645 ; the Ormonde Peace, 1646.

[2] From 1648-50 Scots Presbyterians added to the mixture of Royalist parties.

[3] Cromwell made no attempt to deny or deplore the slaughter. In his letter of September 17, 1649, to Speaker Lenthall he wrote : " I am persuaded that this is a righteous judgement of God upon these barbarous wretches, who have imbrued their hands in so much innocent blood ; and that it will tend to prevent the effusion of blood for the future " (letter CV in Carlyle's collection).

transplantation of all Irish landowners worth above £10 a year who could not prove a " constant affection " to the Parliament ; and a large section of the South-East, all land south of the River Boyne and west of the River Barrow, was to be entirely cleared of native inhabitants.

The design was not fully carried out, partly from the vast difficulties of wholesale eviction, but mainly owing to the lack of immigrants. Many of the soldiers who had been promised land instead of arrears of pay sold their expectations to their officers for ready cash ; so that a large part of the settlement was undertaken by capitalists, both officers and London merchants who as early as 1641 had been promised shares in Irish land in return for loans to the Parliament. Thus vengeance was tempered with exploitation ; for the adventurers needed Irish labour. The results were that, on the one hand, the political and economic ascendancy of the English landed interest was secured : on the other hand, a large Irish majority was left in every province, sufficient to cause a permanent fear of rebellion and to absorb by marriage and environment the English smallholders.[1] Ireland was enslaved, but the Irish problem was still unsolved.

The second conquest survived with its main features untouched until the reign of James II. ; for the Restoration only brought to power the other English party which had sworn vengeance for 1641. Also it was the conquerors, not the conquered, who restored the power of Charles II. in Ireland, and the preservation of their vested interests was their reward. A Royal Declaration in November 1660 denounced the Irish in words that Cromwell might have used, and the Act of Settlement (1662), while making some transfers of land as between Protestants—from Republicans to Cavaliers, maintained the 1652 policy of agrarian depression of Catholics.[2] There was also continuity in religious policy until the scare of the Popish Plot in 1678 ; Ormonde, who ruled Ireland from 1660 to 1685 except for the years 1670-7, followed Cromwell's generals

---

[1] It is conjectured that about 90,000 Irish either emigrated or were transplanted to Connaught or transported to the Colonies ; but a 1659 census shows a vast Irish majority everywhere, even 5 to 2 in Ulster.

[2] Charles promised to reinstate all Catholics who could prove innocence of rebellion, but Parliament in 1663 refused to hear any more appeals.

in letting the laity alone and making occasional raids on priests. Yet the Restoration brought some changes for the worse to Ireland. The Anglican Establishment recovered its estates and political power, but it was poorly staffed and no adequate provision was made for the lower clergy.[1]   The political and economic union of the Protectorate was abandoned ; no Irish members or Peers came to Westminster, and Irish trade was excluded from the Navigation system by a series of enactments ; in 1667 the English Parliament attacked Ireland's staple export when it forbade the importation into England of Irish cattle.   These measures showed that the English distrust of Ireland had not been affected by the conquest ; the natives were feared as potential traitors, and the settlers were disliked either as Cromwellians and Presbyterians or as competitors.   The results of the settlement were minutely described in 1672 by Sir William Petty, economist, official and promoter of plantations ;   the remedies he advocated were free trade, Parliamentary union, reform of land tenures, and the diminishing of the numbers of priests and alehouses.[2]   He estimated the population of Ireland as 1,100,000, of whom 300,000 were Protestants (200,000 English and 100,000 Scots) ;   since 1652 the Protestants owned 5,000,000 acres of cultivable land and the Irish 2,250,000 acres ; three-quarters of the Irish lived in abject poverty in " nasty cabbins " ;   trade, though recovering, was backward owing to poverty, under-population, and the English embargoes and high duties, and what there was was in the hands of the settlers ;   there was a standing army of 6000, a militia of 24,000, and a mob of corrupt officials ;   the fundamental line of division in the country was between those " vested " and " divested " of Irish land as owned in 1641.

Such was the condition of Ireland which the Irish made a last effort to remedy on the accession of a Catholic King.   In the reaction from the Popish Plot, which took as its chief and innocent victim Oliver Plunkett, Catholic Archbishop of Armagh, there was

---

[1] Cf. Swift's *Letter to a Young Clergyman*, for some interesting sidelights on the Church of Ireland.

[2] Cf. ' The Political Anatomy of Ireland,' in C. H. Hull's edition of the *Economic Writings* of Sir William Petty.

a period of toleration and expectation; and James II. did not belie their hopes.   Though he sent an Anglican Lord Lieutenant in his brother-in-law Clarendon, he put his trust in Richard Talbot, created Earl of Tyrconnel and made Lieutenant-General of the Irish forces, and through him secured the appointment of Catholics to civil and military posts in increasing numbers.   By revoking the Charters of the boroughs and nominating Catholic officials he tamed the oldest Protestant strongholds, and in 1687 he appointed Tyrconnel as the first Catholic Lord Lieutenant since the Reformation.

These proceedings in Ireland and the introduction of Irish troops into England were among the main causes of the Revolution of 1688.   The effect of that Revolution was to separate Ireland from England as in 1641 and to make James dependent on Irish loyalty. To secure their support toleration was not enough; the Catholic Parliament called to Dublin in 1689 demanded and obtained a share of the tithes for the Catholic clergy, the independence of the Irish Courts and Parliament, and above all personal revenge and landed restoration.   An Act of Attainder proscribed 1800 of James' opponents, while the repeal of the Acts of Settlement was meant to restore the Irish landed ascendancy to its position before 1641. The Battle of the Boyne made this but a paper programme, but it reveals the grievances and bitterness of the unending feud.

William III. has the credit of the third and most permanent conquest of Ireland, though he must be acquitted of the blame for the final settlement; James, however, by his irresolution and desertion and Louis XIV. by his inadequate support contributed to the disaster.   The brave resistance of Derry and Enniskillen in the North tends to obscure the fact that Ireland was virtually abandoned by the English until 1690, and that, if Louis had made proper use of the command of the seas secured by the victory of Beachy Head (1690), Ireland might have been made impregnable against an English attack.   As it was, French officers and money could not produce at short notice an Irish army fit to oppose William and his Generals in the field.   When William advanced from Ulster in full force upon Dublin, the Jacobite army, inferior in number and training, could not hold the line of the Boyne against successive attacks, though they resisted bravely the first onslaught.[1]   The victory of the Boyne (July 1, 1690) won back Dublin and Eastern Ireland ; the Jacobites retired behind the Shannon to their bases at Athlone, Limerick and Galway, while their King retired to France. The deserted Irish were doomed to piecemeal reduction in the Cromwellian manner, and the exploits of Sarsfield and St. Ruth only postponed the end and infuriated their enemies.   A last pitched battle at Aughrim in Connaught (July 12, 1691), and the fall of Limerick after two long sieges prepared the way for a final reckoning with Ireland.

Ireland lay condemned of three crimes : support of despotism, assault on Protestantism and alliance with the English national foe. The English Parliament did not intend to let her escape due punishment because a Dutch General had allowed the garrison of Limerick to make terms for all their compatriots.   The first and second Articles of Limerick stated that the Irish Catholics should enjoy such religious privileges as they had under Charles II., and that James' followers should enjoy their estates, privileges and offices as under Charles II. if they took the new Oath of Allegiance.[2] The Irish Parliament of 1692, from which Catholics were excluded by an English Statute (1691) in defiance of the Articles, proceeded to define the reign of Charles II. as a period of full application of the Penal Code, and acted accordingly.   The indemnity and toleration promised at Limerick were repudiated ; Catholics were driven from Parliament and offices and were disarmed ; there was a further confiscation of Jacobite lands ; and in 1695 a beginning was made with a new Penal Code.   None except secular priests were allowed, and those under stringent regulation ; Catholic laymen were deprived of political franchise and of access to the professions of law, the army, teaching and bookselling ; restrictions were put on their right to buy or inherit land or to own horses ; conversions were encouraged by giving Protestant converts sole rights of heirship, while Protestants who became Catholics or married Catholics forfeited land and rights.[3]   The finishing touch was economic proscription.   The woollen industry was ruined by high export

[1] Cf. Macaulay, ch. 16.   [2] For the Articles (1691), cf. Macaulay, ch. 17.
[3] Acts of 1695, 1697 and 1704.

duties (1698) and the prohibition of export of woollen goods to any place but England (1699) ; Irish trade was confined to fish, linen goods and provisions.[1]   This time the settlement was effective ; Ireland gave no further trouble until the days of England's embarrassment with America.

The story of conquest is one of remarkable continuity, with the exception of two Stuart Kings in extremities ; James I., Wentworth, Cromwell, Ormonde and William III., agreeing in little else, carried through the same Irish policy to its end.   They all feared Popery for the alien loyalty it imposed and the hostile alliance it invited, and they saw but one preventive—a Protestant garrison rooted in the land.   Such a policy led logically to union after conquest, for the interests of the garrison were sacrificed by political and economic separation.   Yet union never came because it was impossible to extirpate the enemy or to control the commerical jealousies of London ; the taint of the outcast island fell upon the most English and Protestant of its immigrants.   Sooner or later the inhabitants of Ireland would discover that, despite their differences, England had forged for them a bond of union in their common exclusion.

III. Great Britain

By standards of immediate advantage the Union which was no union was the more successful.   Ireland lay quiet during a generation of war, but Scotland disturbed the peace of England with a series of Jacobite revolts.   Yet there can be no doubt that the courageous experiment of 1707 was far more beneficial to both partners than the old policy of fear.   Englishmen and Scots in their own and in each other's countries embarked on careers of triumphant energy in war, trade, government and culture ; while the fetters of 1692 produced a lethargy fatal to all who dwelt in Ireland. Gaelic letters expired under suppression at home, and no successors arose to Hugh O'Neill, Owen Roe and Sarsfield ; but the Irish Colleges and Brigades abroad showed that Ireland had vitality enough, if the English conquest had not driven it into exile. England was to learn its strength at Fontenoy and in America.

[1] Provisions and stock could not be exported to England since 1667.

The forces which demanded the union of the three countries in a single State were the defence of Protestantism and the danger of Catholic Imperialism, either Spanish or French. These considerations drew England and Scotland together and made Ireland the sacrifice. The forces against union were religious difference, racial dislike and economic jealousy ; and of the three, commerce proved the toughest obstacle. The growth of English mercantilism nearly overruled national and religious security; it prevented a real Irish union, and its failure to prevent Scottish union was due only to fear of France and the enlightened despotism of the Whig Junto.

Union was inevitable in the seventeenth century; the only question was upon what terms—alliance or conquest. Three factors made isolation impossible : England's superiority in strength over Scotland and Ireland,[1] England's weakness against a Continental combination, and the failure in both Scotland and Ireland of internal unity and self-sufficiency. The fact that England alone in the century evolved unity and order out of division made her the dominant partner who could dictate the terms. The Scots bowed to the inevitable ; the Irish chose to be broken by it.

SUGGESTIONS FOR FURTHER READING

Scotland :

DICKINSON, W. C., DONALDSON, G. and MILNE, A. : *Source Book of Scottish History.* (Nelson, 1952–61)

MACKIE, R. L. : *Short History of Scotland.* (O.U.P., 1931)

RAIT, R. S. : *History of Scotland.* (O.U.P., H.U.L., 1946)

BROWN, P. HUME : *History of Scotland,* Vols. I and II. (C.U.P.)

MATHIESON, W. : *Politics and Religion in Scotland.* 2 Vols. (Maclehose, 1902)

FIRTH, SIR CHARLES : *Scotland and the Commonwealth, Letters and Papers.*
Scotland and the Protectorate, Letters and Papers. (Scottish Historical Society)

---

[1] England's population was over 5 millions, Ireland's over 1 million, Scotland's under 1 million. Scotland's wealth was estimated at one-thirtieth to one-fiftieth of England's. Cf. Hume Brown, Vol. III, *Scotland on the Eve of Union.*

BUCHAN, J. : *Montrose.* (O.U.P., 1957)
FOSTER, W. R. : *Bishop and Presbytery.* (S.P.C.K., 1958)
PRYDE, G. S. : *The Treaty of Union.* (Nelson, 1950)
DICEY, A. V. and RAIT, R. S. : *Thoughts on the Union.* (Macmillan, 1920)
DEFOE, DANIEL : *History of the Union.*

Ireland :

BECKETT, J. C. : *A Short History of Ireland.* (Hutchinson, 1958)
   Protestant Dissent in Ireland, 1687–1780. (Faber, 1948)
O'BRIEN, G. : *The Economic History of Ireland in the Seventeenth Century.* (Dublin, 1919)
BAGWELL, R. : *Ireland under the Stuarts.* 3 Vols. (Longmans, 1909–16)
DUNLOP, R. : *Ireland under the Commonwealth.* 2 Vols. (Manchester U.P., 1913)
MOODY, T. W. : *The Londonderry Plantation, 1609–41.* (Belfast, 1939)
KEARNEY, H. F. : *Strafford in Ireland 1633–41.* (Manchester U.P., 1959)
MACLYSAGHT, E. : *Irish Life in the Seventeenth Century after Cromwell.* (Dublin, Talbot Press, 1939)
SIMMS, J. C. : *The Williamite Confiscations in Ireland, 1690–1730.* (Faber, 1956)

X

ENGLAND AND EUROPE

MODERN English Ministries, however much they may denounce their predecessors' domestic administration, affect great zeal for the "continuity of foreign policy." But history proves that this is no remarkable achievement; for one of its most constant phenomena is the similarity despite themselves of the foreign policy of governments who are totally and consciously opposed in every respect. Examples may be taken from France and Russia before and after their Revolutions; England in the seventeenth century provides plenty of them. The landmarks of her internal history were not as a rule the landmarks of her foreign relations. Foreign policy, therefore, should not be surveyed reign by reign; nor, for other reasons, should it be surveyed country by country. The seventeenth century still retained some traces of the unity of Christendom, and its leaders' energies were devoted to building some kind of States-system to replace the medieval ideal of unity. The great issues—religion, trade and dynasty—were rarely confined to two nations at any one time; if they did not affect the whole of Europe, they affected wide regions—the Baltic, the Mediterranean, the West and the East. Two European movements, the Counter-Reformation and the Imperialism of Louis XIV., dominated English foreign policy. There were two cross-currents, trade and dynasty. These four provide the clues to events which were often strangely unaffected by internal revolutions. Until 1689 English relations with Europe were generally peaceful, except for the two war periods of 1624-9 and 1651-72; from 1689 to 1714 there was almost continuous war.

I. ENGLAND AND THE COUNTER-REFORMATION: 1603-1659

In this period Spain was the enemy, France and, in lesser degree, the Dutch our allies. This grouping was the Tudor legacy to the Stuarts, based on a common fear of the Hapsburg threat to national independence. England was vulnerable in her Catholic population, Ireland, her navy and foreign trade; long after the danger had passed with Spain's decline, the fear remained. In fact, English policy until late in the century was vitiated by two cardinal mistakes: overestimation of the power of Spain and underestimation of the power of France. Fear of Spain overcame, except at rare intervals, religious differences with France and commercial disputes with the Dutch. England was linked to both by a political and a dynastic alliance, and when the Commonwealth broke the dynastic alliance by the execution of Charles I., Cromwell did not rest until he had resurrected the old bulwarks against Spain.

The Counter-Reformation reached its political climax in the Thirty Years' War, which from its start in Southern Germany drew into its vortex the whole of Europe. English diplomacy first tried to avert the war or end it by mediation, then for a few years committed England to take a part, then withdrew for lack of means and troubles at home, and finally returned to the aftermath,—the Franco-Spanish war which continued for eleven years (1648-59) after the Peace of Westphalia.

James I., lover of peace and a stranger to the English vendetta against Spain, guided English policy in the years when the Catholic reformers were preparing their attack. There is no reason to suppose that he was blind to the Spanish danger, for his acts show that he had as profound a belief as his subjects in the power of Spain. But he made another over-estimate—of his own diplomatic genius. He proposed to counter Spanish intrigue by the method, cheaper than war, of conciliation and alliance. At first it was a sound plan, accepted by Cecil since England could afford no other; nor did it endanger Protestantism when Spain, France and Austria were exhausted and quiescent. Moreover, in spite of the peace made with Spain in 1604, the Dutch were not deserted; James remained their protector and maintained English garrisons in Dutch service.[1]   The alliance was unpopular in England because of the milder treatment of Catholics and the restrictions on buccaneering ; but James triumphed over opposition by doing without Parliaments and by diverting venturers' energy to Ulster and the northern coasts of America.   Until the arrival of the Spanish Ambassador Gondomar (1614) James' policy was not one of subservience to Spain, but of balance.   On occasions he could act as a vigorous Protestant leader ; in 1609-10 he joined with Henry IV. and Oldenbarneveldt, the Dutch statesman, to prevent Hapsburg designs on the strategically important Duchies of Julich and Cleves on the Lower Rhine, and in 1613 he made the fateful match of his daughter Elizabeth with Frederick, Count of the Bavarian Palatinate and head of the Calvinist " Protestant Union."   But with Cecil dead (1612) and Bacon discredited by the failure of the " Addled Parliament " (1614) to give James the promised support, the King turned to the able Spaniard who flattered his despotic fancies and offered Spanish help for their accomplishment.   From 1616 the King became more pro-Spanish and his subjects more anti-Spanish every year.   When the Parliament of 1621 boldly expressed the popular wish for war against Spain and a Protestant marriage for Charles, James had for years tried to conclude a Spanish marriage.   He only abandoned hope when the theatrical journey of Charles and Buckingham to Madrid exposed the real dislike of Spain for her heretic client.   For Spain James had sacrificed Raleigh in 1617 after his disastrous raid on the Spanish possessions in the Orinoco, although he had authorised the expedition in the full knowledge that it must lead to a clash ; [2] for Spain James had left his son-in-law and the Protestants he led to the consequences of their rashness.   His motives, though generally impugned, may have been sound in each case, but the net results of deference to Spain were a breach with his subjects, and a snub from his ally.   Even if James had no pride, his son and favourite were only too sensitive ; their anger restored the Monarchy to its old popular rôle and restored England to the Protestant Union.

[1] There were interested reasons, for until 1616 he possessed Flushing and Brill as " cautionary towns."

[2] Cf. Gardiner, *Hist.*, II, pp. 370-81 and III, ch. 25 ; *C.M.H.*, IV, pp. 754-5 ; and *D.N.B.*, article on Raleigh.

Even on its own merits, James' policy of balance was bound to fail in the crisis of 1618. It was futile to adopt a judicial attitude towards Frederick's acceptance of the Crown of Bohemia as if it were an isolated incident; this false move made by the nervous Calvinists was seized as a Heaven-sent occasion by the Catholic offensive. Even before Ravaillac's religious dagger had removed the great obstacle—Henry of Navarre, leagues and counter-leagues had been forming; since 1610 Pope Paul V., Philip III. of Spain, Maximilian, Duke of Bavaria and Ferdinand of Styria, with the Jesuits everywhere, were waiting and planning the destruction of the Calvinists. The Lutherans in the North were safe for the time, for they were harmless, almost respectable, and protected by the Augsburg settlement of 1555; but the aggressive Calvinists had no status for their religion or for the land they had seized. By 1618 their isolation was complete; the Lutherans, following their founder's example, were hostile or indifferent, while France and England under Anne of Austria and James had deserted them. All that was needed was a young and vigorous German leader, and he was found when Ferdinand of Styria was chosen by the childless Emperor Matthias to succeed to the Hapsburg dominions (1617). Ferdinand was elected King of Bohemia in 1617 and Holy Roman Emperor in 1619, and between those dates he had begun the Thirty Years' War by driving the Bohemian Protestants to revolt. The rebels offered the Bohemian Crown to Frederick of the Palatinate; Frederick by accepting it exposed not only his old and new dominions, but also the Protestant Union and the religious balance of power to the righteous vengeance of Ferdinand, enforced by the joint Hapsburg and Catholic power. Thus, whatever Frederick's deserts, it was vital to the safety of Protestant Europe that his punishment should not be made the pretext of the great Catholic Plot.

Geography did not give England immunity from danger in 1618. Though England was an island, there was another island on her flank; Ireland, as well as the English Catholics, made it impossible for her to ignore the plot. Public opinion naturally but wrongly held Spain to be the arch-plotter, and as wrongly acclaimed Frederick as a Protestant hero—and an English hero by marriage. Fear and sympathy swept across the Channel and broke down James' long resistance. In 1624 Buckingham led a willing people into the Thirty Years' War.

Posterity should be grateful to James for delaying our entry and to Charles for his early withdrawal; thanks to them, and to insularity (not then a myth in strategy), England escaped the devastation which crippled Germany for a century. The actual intervention was neither glorious nor effective. Though Parliament asked for the familiar naval attack on Spain, the Stuarts were bent on rescuing their relatives by military operations, and since they possessed no trained army they wasted their money on mercenaries like Mansfeld and Christian of Denmark. The plan failed utterly, and its failure and expense made Charles dependent on a disappointed Parliament; its one result, a marriage alliance with France, only aggravated the quarrel with Parliament in its militant Protestant mood. Buckingham made another throw for popularity by adopting the naval crusade, and the sequel was the hasty and disastrous attack on Cadiz (1625). Charles' counter-Armada was as ill-equipped and led as Philip's had been, and Buckingham though brave and energetic, was the equal of Medina Sidonia in inexperience of the sea; Charles had not the money, trained crews, nor organisation for such an undertaking after a generation of peace. Cadiz did not fall, and the Spanish treasure fleet escaped, while the cost and disgrace of failure further alienated King and subjects.[1] Then Buckingham in desperation took up the rôle of indiscriminate Protestant champion; France was to be challenged for Richelieu's attempt to disarm the Huguenots. The French marriage had not gone well, for Charles was unable in the heated state of Protestant feeling to honour the secret clause promising toleration to Catholics, and had treated his young wife and her attendants with some asperity. Yet Richelieu from policy was conciliatory, and nothing could justify the madness of interfering in the internal politics of an old ally and of attacking two superior powers at once. The story of Cadiz was repeated on the Ile de Rhé, for the expedition to relieve La Rochelle was made with even scantier resources; in 1626 the Commons had refused any grants,

[1] Cf. Gardiner: *Hist.*, VI, ch. 55.

so the stores were rotten, the troops unpaid and mutinous, and of no military value. La Rochelle fell while Buckingham's army rotted away on the island outside (1628) ; its leader had returned to face the judgment of Parliament and escaped their vengeance by death at the hand of an aggrieved sailor.

Buckingham cannot be held responsible for England's entry into the war ; that was determined by the national will. But his energy and confidence directed the war efforts, and his incompetence and misjudgment of national resources brought intervention to an inglorious end. Protestant Europe owes nothing to him ; it was saved by another foreign champion and the feuds of its enemies. England, however, gained from the war the Petition of Right ; the strain of war showed King and Commons that the problem of internal government must be settled before England could take any effective action abroad. Charles, without Buckingham's energy or any supplies from Parliament, patched up the French alliance and made peace with Spain (1630). England had proved a worthless ally and a harmless foe ; she withdrew from European history for twenty years, and the combatants hardly noticed the disappearance of a second-rate power.

For the next ten years Charles made spasmodic appeals for Frederick and occasional plots with Spain against the Dutch, both without effect. He did, however, lay the foundation of future strength by the creation of the " shipmoney " fleet for the protection of English trade against piracy and the Dutch. It was the lack of a trained Navy which had brought failure in 1624-9, and it was Charles' legacy which saved the Long Parliament and made it feared abroad. Yet Charles did little with it, despite the emergency he proclaimed. He asserted, with the backing of Selden's *Mare Clausum* (1636), English sovereignty in the Channel and tried to pick a quarrel with Richelieu. He forced the Dutch herring-boats to pay tribute, but he was unable to prevent Tromp in 1639 from destroying a Spanish fleet in English territorial waters. Then Scotland ended his futile demonstrations, and he was only too glad in 1641 to arrange the marriage of his daughter Mary with William II. of Orange, who became head of the Dutch Republic in 1647.

The Civil Wars exposed England to intervention such as she had inflicted under Buckingham. Spain and the Papacy were interested in Ireland, while France and Holland were linked to Charles by dynastic ties. Three things saved her : the continuance of the war against Spain by France and the Dutch, when the rest of Europe sank exhausted into peace : the reluctance of Continental statesmen to risk war in such an unpromising cause : and the Parliamentary command of the sea. Richelieu was not sorry to see Charles in trouble after all the pinpricks he had received, and he had not scrupled to revive the old French policy of setting Scotland against England.[1]

So, in spite of Henrietta's begging tour, England was left to fight her quarrels undisturbed. By 1645 it was too late for intervention ; the New Model Army made French diplomacy in favour of Charles as futile as Stuart diplomacy had been in favour of Frederick. The growing colonies of exiles found France and Holland looking to their own defence instead of planning a chivalrous rescue. In 1649 the murder of a crowned King made the English Republic an outlaw among nations, and exalted intervention to a sacred duty for his Royal kin ; but France was in the throes of a minority, and William of Holland's plans to avenge his father-in-law were cut short by his own death in 1650 and the deposition of the Orange House from power. The envoys of the Republic were either not received or were murdered, as Dorislaus in Holland ; that was the most that Europe could effect.

But the Puritan Commonwealth did not intend to let Europe alone ; it resolved to take up the work that Buckingham had mismanaged and Charles neglected, even before it had completed the conquest of Scotland and Ireland. Union was its policy abroad as at home ; Protestantism was to be secured by the fusion of England and the Dutch Republic in one great power. In 1651 an Embassy was sent to the Hague to settle old differences and to arrange " an intimate alliance and union." [2] Unfortunately for the Puritans, their foreign policy was almost fifty years out of date.

[1] Cf. Ranke, II, p. 156.
[2] Cf. Edmundson, *History of Holland*, pp. 212-5.

Holland [1] was no longer an English Protectorate but a thriving nation, jealous of its hard-won freedom and commercial enterprise, suspicious of English political domination, and unwilling to share her trading Empire with a poorer rival. The Dutch rejection of union led the Puritans to abandon idealism in diplomacy, and to revive the Stuart naval claims, fortified by the Act of Navigation ; the war that followed postponed until 1654 the English return to the attack on the Counter-Reformation.

In 1654 the Protectorate restored idealism, not without a spice of Jingoism, to foreign policy. Cromwell's first care was to end the Dutch war which divided and discredited Protestantism. He tried in vain to persuade the Dutch to a full union, but he succeeded in making a temporary settlement of the old grievances (much in England's favour) and in binding the new Dutch leader De Witt to the perpetual exclusion of the Orange House from office.[2] He obtained peace, not an active alliance ; for co-operation in his Protestant crusade against Spain he had to turn to France, the old Catholic ally of England. Cromwell in fact adopted the methods of James I. which his party had denounced so bitterly ; he made friends with the Catholics in order to protect the Protestants. Mazarin, continuing the traditional French policy of supporting Catholicism at home and Protestantism abroad, welcomed his alliance (1655) and humoured his ideals. At Cromwell's request Mazarin secured toleration for the Huguenots in the South of France and Savoy (the Vaudois whom Milton immortalised), and he expelled Charles and James Stuart from France. In return Cromwell gladly helped to complete the French victory over Spain ; England crowned a century's struggle by wresting from her Jamaica (1655) and Dunkirk (1658).[3] The war involved ruinous expense with no commensurate results ; for sand-silted Dunkirk was no Calais, and Jamaica, with future prosperity undreamt of, was a poor reward

---

[1] Holland is used as a convenient term for the Dutch Republic, though it was only one, if the most powerful, of the seven States of the Union.

[2] For the somewhat shady negotiations between Cromwell and De Witt, cf Edmundson, *op. cit.*, pp. 220-4.

[3] For Cromwell's defence of his Spanish war, cf. speech on Sept. 17, 1656 : He gives three grounds : (1) Spain is the "natural enemy " ; (2) Spain is " Anti-Christ " ; (3) The Papists in England are " Spaniolised."

for the failure of the expedition of Penn and Venables to take Hispaniola.[1] Nevertheless the English navy ruled the Channel, the Atlantic and the Mediterranean, where Blake chastised the pirates of Algiers and terrorised the Pope ; the New Model Army survived the test of the Spanish infantry at the Battle of the Dunes (1658) and won the respect of Europe. The ascendancy of Spain, the inveterate foe who harboured the Stuarts and would even ally with Anabaptists if she could strike at England, was broken for ever. Cromwell's England was a first-class power, as it had not been since the days of Henry V.

On a short view Cromwell's foreign policy must be judged a great success. Clarendon, Burnet, and Pepys all testify to the general fear of him—a fear which took Charles II. some years to dispel.[2] National pride, even that of the Cavaliers, was satisfied ; but that is all. Protestant union was obsolete and could not be resurrected by schemes for a World Council ; [3] there was nothing permanent in temporary French concessions, a Dutch peace and an ineffective Swedish alliance. In fact, Protestantism did not need protection as long as Bourbons and Hapsburgs were kept quarrelling ; and Cromwell, by speeding Bourbon ascendancy, helped to remove the vital guarantee. England's European prestige disappeared with the disintegration of the Puritan Army, but Richelieu and Mazarin laid a foundation for French power which even Marlborough failed to uproot. Cromwell as a foreign statesman was a Tudor, born a hundred years too late ; he must be condemned for allowing religion and prejudice to blind him to the real issues of his time—trade and the balance of power. Yet who would not prefer the last of the Elizabethans to the diplomatic jugglers who followed ?

[1] Both generals were dismissed for their conduct ; cf. Venables' *Narrative* (ed. Firth).

[2] Cf. Clar. : *Hist.*, VI, p. 94 : Burnet, I, p. 81 ; Pepys' *Diary*, July 12, 1667.

[3] Cf. Burnet's account of Cromwell's ideal of a Protestant federation, I, pp. 77-8. Cromwell had a great admiration of Sweden and wished to make a close alliance with her.

II. ENGLAND AND THE ASCENDANCY OF FRANCE: 1660-1714

For the next half-century France dominated the scene, as patron or enemy: Spain was her poor relation, and Holland the buffer-state. During the whole period, except for occasional quarrels, Louis XIV. was the protector of the Stuart House; but under the changed conditions of the Restoration this did not necessarily involve a national alliance with France. In the time of the early Stuarts and Cromwell there was but one foreign policy—that of the ruler. There was often general opposition leading to obstruction, but no constitutional means of enforcing a positive alternative; for example, when Protestant feeling was fully aroused, Buckingham was able to direct the war according to his whims. From 1660, however, Parliament's claim to have a voice in general policy could not be denied, and there was a regular Parliamentary policy, formulated by political parties and executed by the Ministers drawn from those parties. Thus foreign affairs between 1660 and 1688 were complicated by the existence of two rival policies of King and Parliament, and between 1689 and 1714 by Whig and Tory policies.[1] Much of the confusion in English relations with Europe was due to this fact; for none in England or abroad was sure which policy would prevail at any given time or what new incident or person would turn the balance. So foreign Chanceries had to gamble prudently and cover their bets by preparing alternative schemes if the favourite fell by the way. The Anglo-Dutch alliance of 1668, the Franco-Whig alliance of 1678, and the neutrality of Louis XIV. in 1688 were covering schemes of this nature.

English policy can be conveniently divided into three phases: the coincidence of Royal friendship with France with Parliamentary hate of the Dutch (1660-74): the clash between Royal friendship with France and the Protestant alliance with the House of Orange (1674-88): the Anglo-Dutch alliance against France and the exiled Stuarts (1689-1713). Much of the story has already been told, for English internal history cannot be explained without it;[2] it remains to place England in her European setting and to show the

---

[1] There was also William's private policy, illustrated by the Partition Treaties.
[2] Cf. Chs. V-VIII.

European effects of the English diplomatic revolution of 1677—the attack on France begun by Danby's Orange alliance.

It was fortunate for English liberties that the Stuart alliance with France was renewed after and not before the Restoration.[1] Charles owed nothing to France, Spain or Holland for his return ; France and Holland, despite marriage ties, had refused him asylum, and Spain had fulfilled none of her promises except to give him refuge at Brussels.   Yet it was necessary to make a settlement of old disputes and to make some foreign friendships, for the rest of Europe was faced with the ominous alliance of former foes in the Treaty of the Pyrenees (1659).   Spain had yielded to France and now accepted her alliance by the fateful marriage of Philip IV.'s eldest daughter, Maria Teresa, to Louis XIV., with a clause stating that Maria was to renounce all claims to the Spanish throne when and if her dowry was paid.   All thing conspired to turn Charles to the rising sun of France ; national tradition, his French parentage and education, the personal charm of the young Louis, and the death of Mazarin, the regicides' ally (1661).   The Courts were linked by the marriage of Hénrietta, Charles' dearly loved sister, to Louis' brother, the Duke of Orleans (1661) ; in the following year Charles at Louis' suggestion married Catherine of Braganza, daughter of the King of Portugal.   This matrimonial settlement had important results, soon and late.   Henrietta was the intermediary in the Secret Treaty of Dover, and Catherine, besides bringing Bombay and Tangier as her dowry, cemented the Portugese alliance which has been one of the permanent features of British policy—witness the Portugese troops in France in the Great War.[2]   The immediate effect was to bring England and Portugal into the ring of French client-states which Henry IV. and Richelieu had built up against the Hapsburg menace.   The sale of Dunkirk to France followed as a natural consequence (1662).   This was not the sinister transaction that later events made it appear to be.   The expense of maintenance was formidable, and Charles was faced with the debts of his exile, for which a not too generous Parliament had failed to provide.[3]

[1] Cf. Ranke, III, p. 335, and Clar.: *S.P.*, III, p. 511.

[2] Cromwell began the connection by an alliance in 1654.

[3] Lister, *Life and Letters of Clarendon*, Vol. III, letter cv, gives Monk's report on the cost of upkeep.   Cf. Stone, pp. 9-11.

Monk and Montague, Cromwell's General and Admiral, recommended the sale on technical grounds ; Clarendon, who incurred all the odium (it figured in both his Impeachments), was only concerned with bargaining for a good price.   Sale at five million livres was a good bargain for the King and a good riddance for the country, but it gave France a first step into Spanish Flanders and heralded that attack which threatened Dutch independence and English commerce.[1]

It is natural to connect the Second Dutch War which followed with French inspiration ; but such a conjecture anticipates the development of Louis' plans.   The Dutch had made a close alliance with France in 1662 and were still regarded as one of the French client-states, until they showed their independence and, according to Louis, their ingratitude in 1668.   The Second Dutch War was a thoroughly English design.   It was a trade war, as Clarendon admitted with disgust ; it arose out of the accumulation of grievances which successive treaties had only aggravated.   Louis even declared war against England in 1666, but his subsequent actions brought the war to a sudden close.   In 1667 he enforced his claim to the Spanish Netherlands in right of his wife, who, he asserted, succeeded on the death of her father Philip IV. (1665) to a large portion of them by the Brabantine " Law of Devolution."   The invasion of Flanders made both Dutch and English realise the new danger and hastened the conclusion of peace at Breda.   Peace was quickly followed by alliance.   What Cromwell had failed to bring about, the common action of the three Protestant powers of England, Holland and Sweden, came to pass under a crypto-Catholic King and Ministry.   The Triple Alliance forced Louis to halt at the Treaty of Aix (1668) ; he had to be content with a string of towns on the Franco-Spanish Netherlands frontier.   The chief credit must go to William Temple, but the consent of Charles and Arlington (Clarendon's successor in 1667) shows that English policy was not yet subservient to French—though their motives may have been nothing more elevated than spite at Louis' hostility in 1666, a hope that Louis would bid high for their support, or even Arlington's Dutch wife.[2]

[1] Cf. Lister, *op. cit.*, III, letter cxiv, and Clar. : *S.P.*, Vol. III, supplement, p. xxv.
[2] Edmundson, *op. cit.*, pp. 244-5, and Stone, pp. 25-7.

The Triple Alliance is a landmark in European history because it was the first of several combinations to restore the balance of power after France had upset it ; it is a landmark in English diplomacy because it divides the first from the second of Charles' French alliances.   It achieved its immediate purpose, but it could not hope to be permanent.   Charles, like Louis, wanted revenge on the Dutch ; they excluded his Orange relatives from their proper offices, they had escaped defeat in 1667 and their Medway raid had caused a popular outcry which had shaken his throne.   A successful Dutch War would restore his prestige and would give him both weapons and cover for his hidden ambition of a Catholic despotism on the French model.   It was therefore easy for Louis XIV. to detach England from her unnatural allies.   The Secret Treaty of Dover, with its special clause promising French help for an English Counter-Reformation, concerns the internal rather than the external relations of England.[1]   If any effort had been made to enforce it, France would have had a clear path to European domination while England was paralysed by civil war ; but since it produced nothing but an abortive Declaration of Indulgence, more money for Charles to waste and Louise de Kerouaille to waste it on, it is unimportant when compared with the open Treaty of 1671, which caused the Third Dutch War.

The Third Dutch War (1672-4) has certain similarities with the Second—the same pretexts, the same *agent provocateur* in Sir George Downing, the same indecisive result.   But it could not be honestly claimed as a true English war, though the claim was made in Parliament : " This is an English and no other war." [2]   The French invasion of Holland and the heroic resistance of the Dutch behind their flooded dykes aroused England to a danger far graver than the competition of Dutch merchants.   The murder of De Witt (1672) had removed an enemy and restored to Holland a dynasty which was Stuart and Protestant, while the marriage of James of York and Mary of Modena (1673) brought the possibility of a Catholic dynasty at home.   Englishmen felt they were playing the Jesuits' game in taking the Dutch on the flank.   They resolved to stop the suicidal waste of Protestant money and men in such

---

[1] Cf. Ch. VI, and Stone, pp. 27-31.   [2] Stone, p. 37.

fierce and useless battles as that of Southwold Bay (1672) ; so the
Parliament drove the Cabal out of office and forced Charles to
make peace at the Treaty of Westminster (1674).[1] Protestantism
was secured at home by the Test Act and relieved abroad by the
Treaty ; the French control of England was broken, and William
of Orange entered English history.   Three years later Danby
cemented the Protestant alliance by the marriage of William to
Mary, elder daughter of James of York and heiress to the English
Crown.

For the next fifteen years (1674-88) England was at peace and
had little interest in or influence on European affairs.   It was the
age of the double policy, and since the policies neutralised each other
England ceased to count.   Louis no longer expected aid from
Charles ; he was content with England's isolation and neutrality
while he developed his Eastern frontier and Spanish designs.   He
gained his end first by betraying Danby in 1678 and throwing
England into internal discord over the Popish Plot, and then by
renewing Charles' pension in 1681.   He thus paralysed the Anglo-
Dutch alliance based on the Orange marriage.   The Cavalier Parliament in 1678 voted for a large army and fleet to help the Dutch ;
but in a few months they rescinded their vote through distrust of
the designs of Charles II., and impeached Danby the war minister.
It was a farcical and degrading position, due largely to Louis'
supplying of Charles and the Whigs with money and information
against each other.   Danby fell because he was the double
policy incarnate ; he transmitted Charles' demands for money and
a French alliance at the same time that he engineered the Dutch
marriage and proclaimed " Confusion to all that are not for a war
with France." [2]   Yet some good came out of chaos.   Louis made
peace at Nymwegen in 1678, leaving Holland intact and restoring
part of the Spanish Netherlands ; he made some gains at Spain's
expense, but he was baulked of complete success by the mere threat
of Anglo-Dutch co-operation.

The last ten years of Stuart rule were years of growing suspense
in Europe.   Louis was nibbling up Alsace and in 1685 he terrified

---

[1] Cf. Stone, pp. 39-40.   [2] *C.M.H.*, V, p. 219 (useful summary of the
intrigues); cf. Stone, pp. 41-50, for documents.

Protestantism by the expulsion of the Huguenots; he added religious to territorial and economic aggression, and revived the spirit of Philip II. as if he already ruled from Madrid. Everything hung on the heirs of the two Charles II.'s; a Catholic succession in England endangered the Anglo-Dutch alliance, the sole hope of Protestantism, and a French succession in Spain put Europe at Bourbon mercy. Louis was waiting for Charles of Spain to die, and the English and Dutch were waiting for James II. to die without Catholic heirs. On June 10, 1688, the suspense was ended and the storm came. The birth of the " Old Pretender " brought the English Revolution and made Danby's Dutch marriage the key to European history. Louis made his most fatal miscalculation in allowing William to sail for England while he conducted a minor operation in the Rhineland; England had been so insignificant for the last ten years that he forgot the checks which he had experienced in 1668 and 1678 through the temporary union of the two maritime powers. But in 1688, instead of the civil war and paralysis he expected, the union lasted twenty-five years and became the head of a pan-European combination against France.

England under William of Orange returned to the position of a first-class power which Cromwell had created for her, and as a result of that union which Cromwell had failed to achieve. It was a favourite cry of the Tory " Little Englanders " that William sacrificed English to Dutch interests, and that England gained little from her expensive connection. But it was the Dutch who made the sacrifices. After a few years of war they found the burden of naval upkeep too great, and in return for English naval protection they surrendered that naval supremacy for which they had striven for a century. After William's death their army was commanded by an English General; it was one of the pawns in Marlborough's intricate game. They gained no commercial advantage from the union; England tightened instead of relaxing the Navigation Code and hampered Dutch trade in wartime by imposing the English view of blockade and contraband on a nation that had always believed in taking its enemy's money.[1] The wars were the foundation of

[1] Cf. G. N. Clark, *The Dutch Alliance and the War Against French Trade* (1688-97).

English greatness, but they doomed the Dutch to the obscurity of a minor power.

In the War of the League of Augsburg—or of the English Succession—England gained much more than appeared at the indecisive Peace of Ryswick (1697), at which all conquests were restored and the Protestant Succession was secured for William's lifetime only. First, the counter-Revolution had been defeated in war and politics ; the English and Scottish Jacobites were tamed and leaderless, and Ireland had been finally conquered. Secondly, the naval victory of La Hogue (1692) not only wiped out the disgrace of Beachy Head (1690) but gave England control of the seas ; for Louis, like the Dutch, scrapped his battle-fleet and confined French naval operations to commerce raids by privateers.[1] Thirdly, William, after a series of defeats (Steinkirk and Neerwinden) and a solitary success (the recapture of Namur, 1695), had brought Louis' armies to a stand, and forced him to a peace which for the first time in his career brought him no gain. Louis in 1697 did not repeat the mistake of 1688 in risking disaster for petty aims ; he yielded scraps of Spanish land because he had his eye on the whole—for Charles II. of Spain could not prolong the miracle of his life much longer.

Peace came as a great relief to England. Foreign policy to most Englishmen meant two unpopular things : taxes and the Dutch connection. It was only at rare intervals that the nation took any deep interest in European affairs, and then it soon returned to its own problems. William, looking at France from the exposed Dutch frontier, saw in the peace an opportunity to build up a diplomatic barrier against the renewal of war ; but Parliament wished to be quit of Europe, and felt so secure in control of the sea and Ireland that it cut down the army to 7000. When it heard of the diplomatic entanglements to which William and the Whig Junto had committed the nation, it fell with fury on the Ministers and heaped insults on the King. Then, while weakening its defences, it enacted a full settlement of the Protestant Succession which was a direct challenge to James II. and Louis, his protector.

[1] It was the age of Jean Bart ; sea-power did not prevent heavy trade losses, cf. Clark, *op. cit.*, p. 62.

Thus the Partition Treaties of 1698 and 1700 are no part of English history, for William would have had no English support in enforcing his schemes for the division of the Spanish Empire. Their part in European history was cut short by Charles II, who, on the last of his deathbeds, willed his united Empire to Philip of Anjou, Louis' second grandson. Not even Louis' acceptance of the will aroused England from her insular lethargy; what brought England back to European leadership was Louis' proclamation of James III. in 1701. It was French interference in English internal politics, in the vital question of the English, not the Spanish Succession, that provoked a national war against France and converted William's Grand Alliance from a paper scheme to a striking force.[1]

The course and expansion of the war, as it affected the English government and parties, has been described above;[2] what must be considered here is the impact of England upon Europe. In addition to the Dutch alliance she revived the connection with Portugal (1703) and made a new ally in Hapsburg Austria. As a result of the Austrian alliance Marlborough saved Vienna and revived English military prestige at the Battle of Blenheim (1704); as a joint result of the Austrian and Portugese alliances, the Whigs undertook the first English Peninsular War (if we exclude the Black Prince's raid). The intervention in Spain on behalf of the Austrian claimant was the one great failure of the war, both in strategy and diplomacy, and it was fatal to its authors; none the less, it revived Cromwell's policy of naval ascendancy in the Mediterranean, which Charles II. had dropped with the evacuation of Tangier on grounds of expense (1683). In place of Tangier, the Rock of Gibraltar was seized, on the Spanish side of the Straits, and in the same year (1704) the sea-fight of Malaga confirmed British supremacy. The French were penned in Toulon, which was attacked in vain—though the French fleet was sunk to avoid capture; and in 1708 the island of Minorca was captured as a valuable naval base. British sea-power extended from the Atlantic to the Mediterranean, and the way of trade was open to the West and to the East.

[1] For the Treaty, cf. Trevelyan: *Select Docts.*, pp. 5-10 and Ch. VIII; for a summary of the negotiations of 1698-1701, cf. Ogg, *Europe in the Seventeenth Century*, pp. 260-9, and *C.M.H.*, V, ch. 13.

[2] Ch. VIII.

The main front of the war, however, was in the Netherlands ; there went most of the men and money. Marlborough's task was to protect Holland from French invasion and to expel the French from the Spanish Netherlands which they garrisoned ; for England's safety the Flemish coast must be cleared. After Blenheim Marlborough settled to the work, and in seven years of fighting (1704-11) drove the French back to their own frontier, marking the stages of clearance by the victories of Ramillies, Oudenarde, Malplaquet and Bouchain. The first two of these battles reduced Louis to ask for terms of peace ; the last two put France the aggressor in danger of invasion. The French troops under Villars made a desperate resistance on their own frontier and inflicted heavy losses at Malplaquet (1709) ; but in 1711 Marlborough's genius won what was perhaps his greatest, if least sensational triumph, when he forced Villars' elaborate frontier defences without a battle and opened the way to Paris. Paris was only saved by his dismissal (Dec. 1711) and the Tory withdrawal ; the war ended with a French counter-attack on the Dutch and Austrians at Denain (1712), which drove the Allies back from the frontier and preserved France from invasion.

Marlborough was also mainly responsible for the successful diplomacy of the war, which drew a ring of enemies around France and brought in Portugal, Savoy and Brandenburg. But every new alliance meant a subsidy and a new war-aim, and there was a growing feeling in England, fostered by the Tories, that she would never see the end of the expense of fighting other people's battles.[1] So, directly Louis showed signs of reason, the old insular policy revived in force. In 1710 the Whigs' dilemma in Spain and their defeat at home made a separate withdrawal the only possible course, for none but Marlborough could keep the Allies together and carry out the plan of campaign. England had nothing more to fight for except the expensive luxury of humiliating France ; her safety was securely based on sea-power, the Scottish Union and the exhaustion of France. The Tories honoured the Barrier Treaty (1709), by which England guaranteed to the Dutch the armed occupation of a line of towns on the French frontier of the Spanish

[1] Cf. Swift's *Conduct of the Allies*, and Ch. VIII.

(or, from 1714, Austrian) Netherlands ; but they refused to support the Utopian scheme of an Austro-Spanish Empire, and they left the Emperor Charles VI. to make his own terms. They obtained from Spain the Mediterranean gains of the war and a limited share in Spanish-American trade ; the South Sea Company was allowed to send one ship a year to the Spanish Colonies and was given a thirty years' monopoly of the import of negroes, on condition of supplying the Colonies with 4800 negroes a year. France at last made full recognition of the English Protestant Succession, and expelled the Stuarts from France ; Louis promised to dismantle the fortifications of Dunkirk and ceded Acadia (Nova Scotia), Newfoundland with fishing rights reserved, and St. Kitt's in the West Indies ; both Louis and his grandson swore never to unite their Kingdoms.[1]

The Peace of Utrecht, in spite of its failure to secure any effective separation of France and Spain, was for England as for Europe a moderate and sound settlement. It did not give England the maximum of gain, but it did give her as much as she could absorb. It gave her security—not only the security of the Hanoverian Succession and sea-power, but the security of the absence in France of any desire for revenge. The Tory proposal of a commercial alliance failed, and the political alliance of the Whigs and the Regent Orleans after 1715 was of short duration ; but France was at least neutral and inclined to peace for a generation. The work of William and Marlborough in restoring the balance of power was not lost even by Tory carelessness, for France had experienced the weight of English arms and wealth, and the memory would make her walk delicately for some time. Whether she wished it or not, England was now a permanent force in Europe ; the withdrawal of 1713, unlike those of 1629 and 1660, was not due to loss of strength but to transference of interest to a wider sphere—from Europe to India and America.

[1] Cf. *C.M.H.*, V, pp. 437-446, and Ogg, *op. cit.*, pp. 276-9.

III. Trade and the Dutch

During the course of the century France became the major political interest of English political diplomacy ; in other respects her influence was not so marked, except on the fashions of the Restoration Court and the political ideas of Charles II. and James II. In trade France was not a serious competitor before the economic reconstruction of Colbert (1661-71) ; and then her competition was met by absolute prohibition of import (1678) or by high duties. In economic life the Dutch were at once the rivals and the models of England ; the second half of the seventeenth century has been called the age of " conscious imitation of the Dutch." [1] The connection produced a series of precarious alliances punctuating a century-long quarrel over trade—a quarrel which defied the needs of religion and politics. There were good grounds for union : common fear of first Spain and then France ; the defence of Protestantism as in 1610, 1624, 1674 and 1688 ; Stuart-Orange kinship, except during the Republican rule of Jan de Witt (1650-72). At the beginning of the century Holland was emerging from a period of English protection which the truce with Spain (1609) made more irksome than useful ; at its end it fell again under English protection, which saved it from France at the cost of its power and wealth. In between these two protectorates, Holland upheld its political independence and economic ascendancy from a series of English attacks, culminating in the wars of 1651-4, 1665-7 and 1672-4.

Two of the quarrels arose over the still vexed question of the freedom of the seas. England, holding the doctrine of the " Mare Clausum," insisted on all foreign ships saluting the flag " in any of the seas from Cape Finisterre to the middle point of the land Van Staten in Norway." [2] Whether genuine or not, it was a most effective *casus belli* and appeared in every English indictment of the Dutch until they yielded it in 1674. The practical corollary of this ceremony was the right of search claimed by England over neutral shipping in time of war—the claim that caused war with

[1] By Cunningham ; cf. discussion in Clark, *Seventeenth Century*, p. 15.
[2] Stone, p. 39 (from Treaty of Westminster).

the United States in 1812 and aroused dangerous friction in 1914-6. The confiscation of Dutch ships and cargo for carrying contraband crippled Dutch trade, which depended for its life on freedom to trade with their own and other people's enemies. As England lay astride the vital shipping routes, the Dutch (taking Grotius' *Mare Liberum* as their authority) could not consent to such restrictions, except under duress in 1654. Even William III. could not secure an agreement. In 1689 the Dutch Union under English pressure forbade trade with France ; but their merchants defied the ban, and the Dutch smugglers were a constant source of friction between the two governments.

Trade disputes covered almost every side of commercial life. In the woollen trade, the English resented the Dutch control of the finishing processes. Holland would buy any quantity of rough cloth (" whites "), but when James I. tried in 1614-6 to establish a complete cloth industry in all processes, she helped to ruin the experiment by an absolute refusal to buy English finished cloth ; it was long before the English clothiers rid themselves of dependence on the Dutch market. The fisheries caused yet more trouble. In spite of Burleigh's efforts and the retention of the weekly fast, Englishmen when they took to the sea preferred trading or piracy to fishing, and they left the rich harvest of their own waters to the Dutch.[1] James I. and Charles I. tried to discourage this alien exploitation of English wealth by imposing tribute, and the Navigation Act of 1651 struck at the staple industry of the States of Holland and Zealand by prohibiting the English fisheries to aliens ; Cromwell in 1654 reopened the trade but insisted on an annual tribute. The Navigation Code began its long career in 1651 as a purely anti-Dutch measure. As a direct attack it was not a great success owing to the ease of evasion, but, besides being a standing cause of friction, it gave to English shipping the stimulus of protection. The strength of commercial jealousy can be gauged by the remarkable fact that the Code was not relaxed in the time of closest alliance (1689-1714).

The great quarrel, however, was over the markets of Asia and

---

[1] Cf. Mun's complaint (*England's Treasure*, etc., ch. 19). The West Country fishermen were absorbed in the Newfoundland fisheries.

America. In America, the Dutch settlement of New Amsterdam on the Hudson River (1614) divided the English colonists and infringed English claims; this quarrel was settled by the cession after conquest of the colony in 1667. Thus New Amsterdam became New York, in honour of the High Admiral, James of York, and from its Anglo-Dutch beginnings advanced to its Irish-Hebrew maturity. In South America England for a time supported the Portuguese against the Dutch occupation of Brazil, fought in Guiana, and lost Surinam (1667).[1] There were battles over whales in Spitzbergen, slaves in Guinea and spices in the Moluccas. The feud of the English and Dutch East India Companies, founded in 1600 and 1602 respectively, led to unofficial war in the Tropics for fifty years, and then involved the home governments in three mercantilist wars. The Dutch Company from the start had political support and ambitions and a capital nearly twenty times as large as that of the English Company; under a line of able and ruthless governors such as Jan Koen and Pieter Carpentier it established an armed trading Empire in the Malay Archipelago with its centre at Java. All interlopers were kept out by force until in 1619 James I. secured the admission of English merchants to a share of the spice trade; but the agreement was ended at Amboyna in 1623, when the Dutch officials tortured and executed eighteen English settlers for alleged conspiracy. The Stuarts did not let the " massacre " of their merchants affect their policy, but Amboyna became the war-cry of the Commonwealth in 1651; Cromwell in 1654 secured indemnity and punishment of the officials. After 1660 Charles II. sent George Downing to the Hague with instructions—unknown to Clarendon—to pick a quarrel and prevent a Dutch-Portuguese settlement; " the several injuries, affronts and spoils done by the East and West India Companies . . . upon the ships, goods and persons of our subjects . . . amounting to vast sums " were made the chief pretext of war in 1665.[2] Yet this government support, designed more to embarrass the Dutch Republic than to help the merchants, did little to affect Dutch

[1] For the Portuguese question and the preliminaries of the Second Dutch War, cf. Downing's letters to Clarendon in Lister, *op. cit.*, Vol. III.

[2] Stone, pp. 11-12.

supremacy in the East Indies ; and after 1660 the English Company retired to the Indian mainland, where they had no such strong competition until the French came with Lally and Dupleix. Thus the East was portioned out between the Dutch and English, as was South America between the Portuguese and Spanish, and North America between the English and French.

Though greed was the root of the Anglo-Dutch wars and stalemate their result—for the Dutch lost more by allying with England than by fighting with her—the actual conduct of the wars was more worthy of the combatants. They produced a race of great sailors : Blake, Monk, Rupert, James of York, de Ruyter, Martin and Cornelis Tromp. In each war were sea-fights in which the losers deserved equal credit with the victors : the three days' fight off Portland between Blake and Martin Tromp in February 1653, the Four Days' Battle off the North Foreland in June 1666 between de Ruyter and Monk and Rupert, the battle of Southwold Bay in June 1672 between de Ruyter and the Anglo-French fleet under James of York and D'Estrées. The Dutch had none the worst of the battles, and they never experienced such disgrace as they inflicted when they burned the English Navy in its own docks in 1667 ; [1] but they lost more heavily by war from the fact that they had more trade to lose, and that trade was their life-blood. In the end the unequal fight against a great land power and a great sea power was bound to end in either defeat or exhaustion ; with the English crippling their trade and fisheries and the French ravaging their lands and forcing them to flood their farms, with a crushing load of taxes, not even Dutch enterprise and financial skill could avert the inevitable decline. They defeated one enemy and allied with the other, but the reward of independence was insignificance.

In the seventeenth century England rose from a second-rate to a first-rate power ; despite lapses into nonentity and even dependence. Some of the political effects of her irregular advance have been described ; it is less easy to assess the social and cultural

---

[1] It did not prevent the English securing the balance of advantage from the Treaty of Breda.

effects.   It is clear that England received far more than she gave.
She led the way in the creation of a professional navy, and the Dutch
were forced to follow; so the "armament-race" began.   To
science she contributed Bacon, Boyle, Harvey and Newton: to
political thought Locke and the theory of toleration and a Parliamentary Monarchy.   In economics she was a pioneer of free money,
in industry she excelled in the making of clocks and fine instruments.[1]   It is doubtful whether her literature, her chief glory, was
well known in Europe.   From abroad England received late her
Renaissance in painting and architecture; landlords home from
the Grand Tour would have none but Palladian houses, and the
Courts of Charles I. and II. welcomed European painters, among
them Vandyck, Rubens and Lely.   Yet a good deal of foreign
influence was superficial and spread no farther than the manners
and clothes of Whitehall.   In industry, however, the impression
was deeper.   Dutch and Huguenot cloth and silk workers taught
the art of fine manufacture, and Dutch engineers supervised large
drainage schemes.   Banking and exchange were learned from
Genoa and Amsterdam, and English visitors admired and copied
the Dutch art of comfortable living.   In spite of all, England was
still a barbarous island on the fringe of Europe, suspicious of
foreigners and left to herself.   She owed little to Europe for her
great achievements in the seventeenth century: her literature and
music, her Constitution, her Navy and her Colonies.[2]

SUGGESTIONS FOR FURTHER READING

CLARK, G. N.: *Seventeenth Century Europe.*   (O.U.P., 1947)
OGG, D.: *Europe in the Seventeenth Century.*   (Black, 1960)
FREIDRICH, C.: *The Age of the Baroque, 1610–60.*   (Harper,
   1951)

[1] Cf. Clark, *Seventeenth Century*, pp. 18-9, who sees a certain significance in English
skill in such work; for "the clock is the modern idol."

[2] Cf. Clark, *op. cit.*, for a brilliant survey of European Civilisation and England's
contribution to it.

NUSSBAUM, F. L. : *The Triumph of Science and Reason, 1660–85.* (Harper, 1951)

WOLFF, S. B. : *The Emergence of the Great Powers, 1685–1715.* (Harper, 1951)

TREVOR ROPER, HOBSBAWM and OTHERS : *The Crisis of the Seventeenth Century. A Collection of Essays from Past and Present.* (Routledge, 1965)

The New Cambridge Modern History, Vols. IV, V, VI.

BELOFF, M. : *The Age of Absolutism, 1660–1815.* (Hutchinson, 1954)

GREEN, R. W. (Ed.) : *Protestantism and Capitalism.* (Heath/ Harrap, 1959)

HAZARD, P. : *The European Mind, 1680–1715.* (Hollis and Carter, 1953)

COBBAN, A. : *In Search of Humanity.* (Cape, 1960)

France :

LOUGH, J. : *An Introduction to Seventeenth Century France.* (Longmans, 1954)

LEWIS, W. H. : *The Splendid Century.* (Eyre and Spottiswoode, 1953)

Spain :

ELLIOTT, J. H. : *Imperial Spain.* (Arnold, 1963)

LIVERMORE, H. V. : *History of Spain.* (Allen and Unwin, 1958) *History of Portugal.* (C.U.P., 1947)

The Netherlands :

GEYL, P. : *History of the Netherlands in the Seventeenth Century, 1609–1648* and *1648–1715.* 2 Vols. (Williams and Norgate, 1961–4)

Germany :

HOLBORN, H. : *History of Modern Germany*, Vol. 1. (Knopf, 1954)

WEDGWOOD, C. V. : *The Thirty Years War.* (Cape, 1938)

XI

THE FOUNDATIONS OF THE BRITISH EMPIRE

" EMPIRE " is a convenient but misleading term to describe the overseas possessions of England in the seventeenth century. There was then but one true Empire—the Holy Roman Empire. The word has always implied unity, either of conquest or policy or sentiment; and no such unity can be traced in the growth of forts, trading posts, fishing grounds and plantations which England accumulated in this period. There are traces of an Imperial policy in Tudor times, based largely on a fear of over-population; but this motive ceased when in the Stuart age the opposite fear of under-population became prevalent. For Imperialism proper, a policy of political and territorial expansion undertaken by the State, we must wait until the middle of the eighteenth century. One of the most remarkable features of seventeenth-century colonisation is the lack of State support. The State as such planted no colonies except Jamaica; all it contributed was dubious reinforcement from its criminal classes. At times it was aroused from indifference to hostility, as for instance in Newfoundland and New England. National policy was exclusively directed to the encouragement of trade and shipping, and settlements were tolerated in so far as they contributed or were subordinated to these ends. There remained but one of the Elizabethan colonising motives. The search for a passage to Cathay through or around the American continents was virtually abandoned, though it figured in the plans of Raleigh's Orinoco expedition and in the early instructions of the Virginia Company; so the need of a half-way house disappeared. Similarly, after Raleigh's failure at Guiana and a half-hearted search

in Virginia, the hope of gold and silver mines faded away.[1]   The
surviving motive was national rivalry.   The first abortive plantations, Newfoundland (1583) and Virginia (1585), were planned as
bases of attack against Spain and posts of defence for English fishing
and trading fleets.   Fear of France saved the later Newfoundland
settlement in 1675 and prompted the seizure of Acadia, while
jealousy of Spain and the Dutch led to the conquest of Jamaica and
New York.   The choice of the early sites was in itself a hostile act,
for the north coast was claimed by France since Cartier's expedition
of 1534, and America south of latitude 40 had been reserved to Spain
by Pope Alexander VI.[2]   This policy did not necessarily involve
State support or responsibility ;   for the useful convention that
colonial disputes were not *casus belli* survived until 1651, when
the English Commonwealth made traders' rights an affair of national
honour.

In 1603 England possessed a few dependencies : Ireland, the
Channel Islands and the Isle of Man.   In 1714 she had partially
converted her Irish dependency into a colony : she had gained as
dependencies, without permanent settlers, Gibraltar and Minorca
in Europe ; Bombay, Madras, Surat and Calcutta in India and Hudson's Bay in Canada : she had gained as " plantations " Newfoundland, Nova Scotia (Acadia), twelve of the thirteen Independence colonies (excluding Georgia), Bermuda, and in the West
Indies the Bahamas, the Leeward Islands, Barbados and Jamaica.
She had gained and lost Dunkirk, Tangier and Surinam (now Dutch
Guiana).   Private occupation or conquest from natives accounted
for most of the gains, except French Newfoundland (Placentia),
Nova Scotia, New Netherland (New York), and Jamaica.

Some of these acquisitions, as the Indian and Hudson's Bay
stations, were instruments of trade rather than of Empire.   The
large Companies eschewed politics and discouraged settlers ; they
were founders of Empire despite themselves.   It was not until

---

[1] Captain John Smith, the real founder of Virginia, was contemptuous of mines
from the first, and pointed the contrast between bankrupt Spain and Holland, enriched
by fishing, " the chiefest Mine " (cf. *Travels and Works*, ed. Arber and Bradley,
pp. 708-9).

[2] The Treaty of Tordesillas (1494) between Spain and Portugal made a final
longtitudinal division between the two powers ; in fact Portugal was content with
Brazil, and Spain neglected the outer West Indies and lands north of Florida.

the next century that the portent arose which Adam Smith never tired of denouncing, of merchants who also aspired to be sovereigns.[1] In the seventeenth century traders and settlers were rival interests, and it was the traders who had the ear of the State. Hence the story of the founding of the Empire is not that of the London Companies nor of the mercantile system ; it is a story of private enterprise in face of trading opposition and State indifference.[2] Even the " venturers " who financed the colonising expeditions deserve but faint praise, for they either exposed their settlers by neglect or nearly throttled them by their demands for quick profit. The real foundations—the plantation of English communities and institutions—were laid, not by traders and politicians, but by the motley bands of " planters " : outsiders in commerce, outcasts in religion or politics, felons or paupers.

I. Newfoundland and Nova Scotia

Any account of the Empire should begin with the first English discovery. In 1497, John Cabot, with Henry VII.'s commission and Bristol ships, discovered Newfoundland and claimed it for England. There was no permanent occupation until 1610, but its seas and its shores became the home of large international fisheries ; its value was realised by Elizabeth's government on the theory that " it is the long voyages that increase and maintain great shipping." [3] So the West Country seamen fished the Great Banks and left their own seas to the Dutch. In 1610 London and Bristol merchants joined, with Bacon's patronage, to plant a permanent colony in addition to the migratory fishermen who camped there in the summer. Though the settlement did not end in tragedy as Gilbert's scheme had done, it had a poor and precarious existence. During the seventeenth century it was " something more than a fishing ground and something less than a colony." [4] The floating population of fishermen always greatly outnumbered the settlers,

[1] Cf. Adam Smith, *Wealth of Nations,* II, pp. 68 and 127-137.

[2] Cf. Ch. XII for the Navigation Acts and the economic system applied to the Colonies, and Chs. X and XII for the history of the Companies.

[3] Lucas, V, pt. IV. (Newfoundland), p. 31.

[4] Lucas, V, pt. IV, preface, p. vii.

and the home fishing companies, resenting the settlers' competition, persuaded the State to prohibit immigration and to confine the fisheries to their own ships.   Charles II.'s Trade Council had their own objections of depopulation and the smuggling activities of the Newfoundlanders, and ordered the dissolution of the colony in 1675.   It survived only because the Navy insisted on its retention as a base against the French development of Canada ; but no garrison was placed there till 1697, and its chief town, St. John, suffered several disastrous raids from its French neighbour Placentia.   Its future was not assured until the French evacuated the island in 1713, retaining Cape Breton Island and fishing rights ; then it became of double importance, as a fishing centre and as the gate to Canada. It has this other point of interest, that it had no organised government before 1697, and no resident clergy between 1629 and 1697 ; it was a plantation without Church or State—a marvel in the age of Plymouth and Boston.[1]

If Newfoundland was the gate to the Dominion of Canada, Nova Scotia was its beginning.   The French settlement of Acadia on the isolated peninsula south-west of Newfoundland had been neglected much as its English neighbour ; it provided its own simple needs, but formed no part of the great colonial design of Richelieu and Colbert.   Gilbert on his last voyage (1583) first directed English attention to that region ; the next attempt was the first of the two unlucky Scotch Colonial ventures, the scheme of Sir William Alexander to found a Nova Scotia in 1621.[2]   Where both alone had failed, the power of England and Scotland together prevailed ; but it was a cheap conquest, easily made by a Massachusetts force in 1710.   The occupation of Newfoundland, Nova Scotia and Hudson's Bay was the foundation of British Canada. Louis XIV. strove in vain at Utrecht to avoid the cession of Acadia because he saw too late that it was a valuable wedge between the English settlements, and that its loss meant the closing of the St. Lawrence estuary and the naval blockade of Canada.

[1] Lucas, V, pt. IV, p. 86.
[2] Hume Brown, II, p. 273.   The other failure was Darien (1698-9).   For further information on Nova Scotia, cf. Lucas, Vol. V, pt. I, pp. 173-80.   Cromwell also seized it in 1654, but Charles II returned it to France in 1667.   Alexander in return for his losses gained the title of Viscount Canada.

But for the blindness of Charles I. Canada itself might have been held without difficulty. In 1628 Alexander and some London merchants, incorporated as " Adventurers to Canada," sent three brothers Kirke in three ships to plunder the French. The Kirkes not only destroyed the French squadron but captured Quebec, and the great Champlain with it, in 1629. But Charles gave it back in 1632 for part of Henrietta's dowry, and two later attacks, in 1690 and 1711, failed against the strengthened colony.[1]

II. The West Indies

The islands of the Caribbean Sea, which run in a vast chain from Florida to the mouth of the Orinoco, were the first evidence that Columbus supplied of the New World. Within six years (1492-8) he explored them and claimed them for Spain, and none came to dispute that claim for over a century. It was not that Spain guarded them closely ; after a rapid conquest that passed like a plague, she swept on to the mines of the Spanish Main and left empty all but the big islands of the inner ring (Hispaniola, Cuba, Jamaica, Porto Rico). England's first entry was ominous and not too creditable ; Hawkins combined piracy with the trade in slaves from West Africa (1562). The Elizabethans came to trade, plunder and fight the Spaniard, not to settle ; and the tradition of piracy continued and throve until the end of the seventeenth century with the Buccaneers, who, from English bases such as the Virgin Isles and later Jamaica, destroyed the trade and crippled the power of Spain.[2]

The first step south to the West Indies was the colonisation of Bermuda (1612) by the Virginia Company, as the result of the shipwreck of its Governor, Sir George Somers, on the island (1609). As the map shows and as its inhabitants insist, Bermuda is far from being in the West Indies ; but it has proved a useful link for ship-

[1] The 1690 attack was led by William Phipps with a Massachusetts force ; the 1711 attack was the Tory fleet, with five regiments of veterans led by General Hill the Court favourite ; after losing 1000 men by wreck in the St. Lawrence it went home tamely without approaching Quebec. Cf. Lucas, Vol. V, pt. I, pp. 123-146.

[2] Cf. Lucas, Vol. II (West Indies), pp. 53-6 : " To them Jamaica owed its strength and prosperity as an English island." Cf. also *Encyclopedia Britannica* and Esquemeling, *Buccaneers of America* (contemporary accounts by buccaneers).

ping and trade between the islands and the North American mainland. It proved of no great value except as a naval base, but geography and climate have endeared it to tourists and smugglers.

England's share of the West Indies is the majority of the small islands of the outer ring and Jamaica in the inner group. By 1714 she had the Bahamas at the Floridan end of the ring, the Leeward Isles in the centre (east of Porto Rico), and Barbados at the south end (chief of the Windward group); the centres of colonisation were St. Kitts (chief of the Leeward group) and Barbados. The only other island of importance, except Jamaica, was Antigua. British enterprise was confined to the islands with two exceptions. There was a series of settlements in Guiana, carrying on the plans that were fatal to Raleigh in 1617; [1] in 1667, however, the last of them, Surinam, was ceded to the Dutch, and the British did not return till 1803. There was a growing trade in logwood and mahogany from Honduras, which led to a British protectorate over the Mosquito Indians (1655-70) and later to a settlement; but the attempt in 1630 to occupy the island of Old Providence near the Mosquito Coast was soon abandoned. [2] These failures apart, English settlers spread and throve with a rapidity and good fortune in striking contrast with the slow progress and heavy losses of the northern settlers; there were but thirty odd years between the first settlement of St. Kitts in 1623 and the conquest of Jamaica in 1655, the last important addition before 1763.

There is a certain monotony and similarity in the history of these islands. Most of them achieved speedy prosperity by one means—a sugar crop worked by imported slave labour, and most of them became increasingly dependent on the supply and energy of their slaves and a protected market for their sugar. The white population grew fast, but the black grew faster; by 1668 Barbados, the most populous, had about 20,000 whites and 40,000 negroes. [3] Hence slave revolts became one of the recurring incidents that disturbed their peace; others were hurricanes, earthquakes such as

[1] Guiana was supposed to be the gate to Eldorado; for Raleigh's fate, cf. *supra*, Ch. X; Gardiner: *Hist.*, ch. 25; and *D.N.B.*

[2] Surinam was the scene of the Restoration Tragedy *Oroonoko* by Thomas Southerne; Pym and Warwick were prominent members of the Providence Company.

[3] Lucas, II, p. 188.

that which destroyed Port Royal (the old capital of Jamaica) in
1692, quarrels with the French (who shared St. Kitts until 1713
and held Martinique and Guadeloupe), and their own share in the
Civil Wars. The proprietor of all the islands by Charles I.'s
grant of 1627 was the Earl of Carlisle, who sold his claims to Lord
Willoughby of Parham, a leading Parliamentarian who turned
Royalist in the Second Civil War. Barbados and other colonies
followed him in declaring for Charles II., and the Rump sent a
punitive squadron under Ayscue. Barbados, led by Willoughby,
defied both a commercial boycott and Ayscue's fleet until 1652,
and then surrendered on good terms. Besides claiming free trade
with the Dutch in spite of the new Navigation Act, they stipulated
that they were not to be taxed save by their own Assembly—a precedent which might have been useful in the following century.[1]
Barbados stands out in vigour and independence ; in 1655 it sent
a contingent of 3500 to Cromwell's expedition, it helped to plant
Carolina, Surinam and Jamaica, it gained its freedom from its proprietors in 1663, and took an active part in the French Wars after
1688. For all that it was forced to be a dumping ground for English
undesirables ; Barbados was the favourite place for the transportation of rebels, felons, Irish and vagrants.

Jamaica comes second to Barbados in importance and surpasses
it in interest. It is connected with great names ; it was the patri-
mony of Columbus, the consolation prize of Cromwell, and the
base of the great Welsh Buccaneer Morgan, who became its
Lieutenant-Governor. It had been wasted and practically deserted
by the Spanish when the disgruntled and disgraced expedition of
Penn and Venables seized it after the failure to take Hispaniola,
and Spain made no serious effort to recover it. Cromwell took great
pains to people it, not only from home but by draining other colonies ; [2] Charles II. encouraged it by transportations and a grant
of a representative Assembly, which was soon sturdy enough to
defeat the application of Poyning's Law to Jamaica (1678).[3]   It

---

[1] Lucas, II, p. 186.

[2] Lucas, II, p. 101 ; they came from Scotland, Ireland, New England, and the other
West Indian Islands.

[3] *I.e.*, no law to be passed without the previous assent of the English Privy Council.

became the trading centre of the English West Indies, the chosen home of the Buccaneers, and chief exploiter of the wood industry of Honduras ; its population grew rapidly to nearly 20,000 in twenty years. Kingston, built after the earthquake of 1692, became the chief naval base of the Caribbean ; with these advantages it overtook Barbados in the next century.

The West Indian colonies have so declined in wealth and importance by comparison with those of the mainland of North America that it becomes difficult to realise their predominance in the seventeenth century. They began to show large profits and greater promise much earlier ; they gave much less trouble since they were Episcopal and mildly Royalist in beliefs ; their produce did not compete with English goods, they encouraged shipping and they damaged Spain. They were the oases of Empire, while the mainland was as yet a desert ; most Englishmen of that time, except some refractory Whigs, would have cheerfully exchanged the whole of North America for one of the larger islands. The later advance of the Northern Colonies and their infinitely greater possibilities must not obscure the fact that the tropical settlements, like tropical beauties, matured more quickly and had livelier charms—while they lasted. But after 1660 the white population remained stationary and was increasingly outnumbered by negroes ; the total population in 1713 is estimated at 200,000, of whom three-quarters were negroes.[1]

One of the consequences of English settlement in the West Indies was the development of West African trade. In one sense it can be said that the foundations of our African Empire were laid in the seventeenth century ; for in 1618 forts were built on the coast of Gambia (south of Cape Verde) and the Gold Coast, and the Royal African Company of 1672 made a line of forts, directed from Cape Coast Castle by a " General of Guinea." But the government had no political designs other than harrying the French and Dutch traders, and the Companies, as in Newfoundland and Hudson's Bay, had no wish for competitive settlers. So trade was a bar to Empire, and the peculiar nature of the slave trade, which involved a state of war, made settlement almost impossible. The early

[1] *Camb. Hist. Brit. Emp.*, I, p. 267.

Companies of 1588 and 1618 did not follow the example of Hawkins, whose coat of arms, conferred by Elizabeth, was a negro in chains ; but when after 1640 the West Indian planters demanded cheap tropical labour for sugar, the Royal Companies of 1662 and 1672 readily supplied their growing needs.   So West Africa from 1660 to 1806 became, not a colony, but a West Indian dependency, ravaged and exploited for the benefit of colonies across the Atlantic.[1]

III. The North American Colonies

(a) *The Pioneers* : *Jamestown and Plymouth*

Whether we accept the usual division of the mainland settlements into New England, Middle Colonies and Southern Colonies, or whether we trace to its origins the great division of 1861 between the " free " and " slave " States, we should give a first and separate place to the two pioneer settlements which faced the unknown and showed the way.   Their early struggles illustrate the typical difficulties of the settlers, but in a more acute form ; their courage was unique, for their imitators had better support and the advantage of their experience ; and the differences in their history were significant of the future development of North and South.

Until 1620 Virginia was a name for the whole of North America between latitudes 30 and 45, from north of Florida to the Bay of Fundy and from the Atlantic to the Pacific ; in that year the Council of New England (which meant in effect Sir Ferdinand Gorges) took over the northern sector, the line of division being latitude 40 which runs through Philadelphia.   Raleigh's tragic settlements of 1584-7 were in what was later North Carolina ; it was the expedition of 1606-7 that founded the present State of Virginia.   It was a private commercial venture of London merchants, seeking gold and a way to the East ; the " adventurers " stayed at home and sent 100 " planters " to make their profits—mainly gentlemen with a sprinkling of soldiers, artisans and labourers.   Captain John Smith, the real founder of Virginia, complained loud and often of " ignorant projectors and undertakers . . . every year trying new conclusions . . . till they had consumed more than two

[1] Cf. Lucas, Vol. III, pp. 70-104.

hundred thousand pounds and near eight thousand men's lives . . .
doating of gold and the South Sea . . . making religion their colour,
when all their aim was nothing but present profit . . . " [1]

He also criticised the kind of settlers they sent : too many gold-
workers and fine craftsmen, too many " idle charges " of gentlemen and their families :

" one hundred good labourers (were) better than a thousand such
gallants as were sent me, that would do nothing but complain, curse
and despair, when they saw our miseries and all things so clean
contrary to the report in England." [2]

He cured some of the swearing by pouring a can of water down the
offender's sleeve for each oath, with the result that " a man could
scarce hear an oath in a week." [3] But he failed to inspire sufficient
energy in the planters for the work of fortification and cultivation,
and he wasted his own energies in quarrels with the Company and
its Governors over policy. His chief success was with the
the Indians ; he won the respectful fear of most and the friendship
of some ; he declared that he owed his life to the affection of an
Indian chief's daughter.[4]

Yet the Indians were not the greatest danger. They were too
few, too divided, too weakly armed to do any serious damage
beyond theft or the murder of stragglers or small parties ; they do
not appear to have been supplied with fire-arms by contraband
traders as early as in the North ; and when they awoke to fear for
their hunting-grounds owing to the expansion of the settlement,
they struck too late. The massacre of 350 outlying settlers in
March 1622 was due to false security—" a careless neglect of their

---

[1] " Advertisements, or the Pathway to Experience to erect a Plantation " ; in Arber
and Bradley, *Travels and Works of Captain John Smith*, II, pp. 925-931.

[2] Smith, *op. cit.*, II, p. 929.   [3] Smith, *op. cit.*, I, p. 126.

[4] The romance of Pocahontas was probably a romance of Smith's imagination, but
the story of his rescue makes good reading (*Works*, II, p. 400). The verified story of
Pocahontas is almost as romantic. She was taken as a hostage and married to a
planter, John Rolfe ; the marriage gave the colony safety and supplies from the
Indians. She visited England, was received as a Princess at James I.'s Court and died
in England. She left a son from whom Virginian families are proud to claim descent.
But the precedent was not followed ; English and Indians could not live in community,
and there was no general intermarriage. However Rolfe's initiative had greater
effects in another sphere. He was the first to plant tobacco, and thus decided the
whole future of Virginia.

own safeties "[1]—and left 1000 survivors; the settlement was by then firmly established and only needed adequate precautions and strong government. The one important result of the massacre was that it filled the cup of the planters' grievances against their exploiters in London and led with other causes to the revocation of the Company's Charter by the Crown. In 1624 Virginia became a Crown Colony, and the State took over responsibility for its defence; it ceased to be a commercial experiment and became the head of a North American Empire.[2]

The real menace to the infant settlement lay in the neglect of the promoters, the quarrels of the planters, the lack of food and the malarial swamps around Jamestown—to-day a damp and desolate region. In 1609 the settlers in despair took to ship and abandoned the colony, only to meet a large supply fleet down the river which gave them new courage. Thenceforward their condition improved, despite great hardships and appalling losses; and Rolfe's discovery of a profitable crop in tobacco assured their prosperity for all James I.'s dislike of their produce.[3]

The early story of Plymouth was one of similar hardships, casualties and Indian relations; but there the resemblance ends. The hundred "Pilgrims" of the Mayflower who landed on the tip of Cape Cod in 1620 made a success of their venture by their unaided resources and by persistent courage and unity. They intended to join the Virginian settlements, but the winds drove them north; they might have had the guidance of John Smith, but to his disgust they found his books and maps cheaper.[4] So the new venture took place in a different scene and spirit, separated from the old by 500 miles and the Dutch between them. They were at first dependent on the inevitable adventurers who supplied the capital and fondly hoped for quick and rich returns; but after seven years of loss, bickering and some sharp practice the promoters

[1] Smith, *op. cit.*, II, p. 577.

[2] In 1619 the planters held an Assembly to make local regulations—the first American legislature. In 1619 also the first negro slaves were bought from a Dutch trader.

[3] He wrote a "Counterblast to Tobacco" and tried in vain to persuade the planters to grow more varied and useful crops.

[4] He ascribed their early disasters to their "humourous ignorance" in refusing to employ him, but admired their "infinite patience" and "good husbandry" (*Works*, II, pp. 926 and 941-3).

sold out to the settlers for £1800.[1]   Plymouth never became a great fishing or trading centre nor attained importance through wealth, population or political influence ; its sole distinction was in brave, honest and simple living.   They had few gentlemen among them, perhaps only Edward Winslow and Miles Standish, and no men of wealth ; they were the ideal colonists—chiefly farmers from Scrooby and Gainsborough.   They had left England to avoid the growing rigour of persecution in 1608 and had found religious liberty in Leyden ; they left Leyden because of the dreary prospect of poverty before their children and of the fear of losing their Englishry in alien exile ; they sailed to provide a home for their children that would be free, Protestant and English, and to spread the Gospel among the heathen.[2]   They were a picked band, unlike the motley Virginian parties swept up by the Company ; they were self-chosen, with no illusions about the risks, united by religious fervour and years of common exile.   They had inadequate stores and tools, dubious support, a still more dubious title to their lands, and no Crown Charter.   James I., in a moment of good temper, winked at their voyage ; that was all the guarantee they had of State protection or against State interference.

They were both lucky and unlucky in their final choice of site on the mainland across Cape Cod Bay.   Unlucky, in choosing a backwater, with no deep harbour or river highway inland, and soil exhausted by Indian cultivation ; they were doomed to immediate poverty and later insignificance.   Lucky, in a healthy if severe climate and the absence of Indians ; the remnant (50) that survived the scurvy and exposure of the first winter established themselves unmolested, and were never in great danger until 1638, by which time they could call on Boston for help against the Indians.   They were wise as well as fortunate in their Indian relations ; by fair trading and honourable alliance they won the friendship of the neighbouring Wampanoag tribe, whose leader Massasoit protected them against the warlike Narragansetts and Massachusetts on either

[1] Bradford's *History of Plymouth* is overloaded with these unending disputes ; the Pilgrims were steadily unfortunate in their choice of backers and agents.

[2] In their " Compact " of 1620 they stated their aims : " For the glory of God, and advancement of the Christian faith, and honour of our King and country " (Bradford, *History of Plymouth*, I, p. 191).   However, their missionary work was negligible.

side of them. Two events marked their early progress; in 1623 they gave up communal corn-growing and secured themselves against famine by the increased production of private enterprise, and in 1627 they rid themselves of English exploitation and interference and gained full possession of their properties. Their government was simple and helpful : a Governor with wide powers elected annually by the freemen, a General Assembly of freemen as the supreme Legislature and Judiciary, and justice based on English procedure and evangelical discipline. There was a voluntary Church separate from the State; Church membership was not necessary either for residence or citizenship, though the unregenerate were punished or deported if they gave trouble or wide offence.[1] It was not a full democracy, nor was there full toleration; there were quarrels and backslidings, and worldly passions as the failure of communism shows. An aura of sanctity has veiled these failings of humanity, but even without the veil their record is one to wonder at. They had all the qualities of English decency; they were pious, humble, mild, hardworking, adaptable and prudent. They had the courage of endurance in loneliness; there were few called Timorous or Mistrust in their Pilgrim's Progress.

The Massachusetts colony soon outstripped, surrounded and dominated them; after the Confederation of New England of 1643 Plymouth became more and more a protectorate of Boston, and was at last absorbed in 1691. The Pilgrims gave to their orthodox Puritan neighbours the Congregational form of church government, but they failed to give them its tolerant spirit; in fact they received the virus of persecution and followed Boston in harrying the Quakers in 1657. The Mayflower generation contained sober if unambitious statesmen in Bradford and Brewster, who gave continuity, harmony and strength to leadership; but it produced no distinguished successors in any field, and the scattered settlements of Plymouth modestly retired from history.[2]

---

[1] Cf. Bradford's account of Lyford (1624) the adulterous clergyman, Morton (1628) " the lord of misrule " and the " increase of sin " in 1642.

[2] Brewster died in 1643 and Bradford in 1657; they had held the offices of Elder and Governor respectively almost without break. An interesting feature in a religious community was the lack of prominent clergy, although in Leyden their minister, John Robinson, was their guide in the affairs of both worlds; it may account for the lack of religious disputes and persecution.

Nevertheless their aims had been achieved. They had secured freedom and peace of religion and politics—and not for themselves alone. They made it possible for Puritanism to revive abroad, and yet to remain English; they gave English citizens an English alternative to despotism. By their allegiance they honoured their King more than he deserved; their settlement saved New England from becoming New Netherland by Dutch expansion from their posts on the Hudson (1614). By their conduct they honoured their country, and they cannot be blamed that their more powerful neighbours of Massachusetts and Connecticut neglected their example of tolerance and modesty.

(b) New England

There is a distinct gap between the pioneers and the " Great Migration" of 1629-40. European war absorbed men and interest and restricted trade; Puritans were immersed in home politics; venturers and planters alike were discouraged by the risks, hardships and appalling casualties of settlement. In 1629, however, peace and the Royal victory over Parliament gave a double impetus to colonisation; capital was freed and the wrath of Charles I. and Laud raised emigrants in plenty. Most of them went to the Puritan North; Virginia had to wait a little longer for her refugees. Over 20,000 were added by 1640 to the few hundred settlers of Plymouth Colony; then emigration on a large scale stopped, and New England grew from its own fecundity. The majority settled under the jurisdiction of the Massachusetts Bay Company; Massachusetts at once took the leadership of New England which she has retained ever since. She had the preponderance in wealth and population; she had the two chief ports in Boston and Salem; she was the channel of immigration, the founder and protector of other settlements; she was the dominant influence in policy, religion and education.

Unlike its predecessors, the settlement of 1628-9 was well planned, well equipped and well supported. The promoters, wealthy and influential Puritans, obtained a Royal Charter without awkward restrictions, and resolved to lead their own settlers and govern them on the spot. This unity of interest between venturers and planters, so lacking in Virginia and Plymouth, was the decisive factor in the success of the scheme. Another advantage was that they were orthodox State Puritans, deeply attached to the national Church and anxious to reform and dominate it; thus they were sure of support from a large and wealthy class, even though, as John Robinson had prophesied, the very fact of emigration made them Separatists despite themselves. The new settlers were not the humble men of Plymouth, but men of substance and education, trained to government and full of ambition. There was, therefore, in and around Boston more organisation and efficiency, less democracy and toleration; it was a rigid and oligarchic Church-State. In government, John Winthrop, the first Governor, was a born autocrat who only grudgingly admitted the colonists to a share of control; in religion a succession of able clergy ruled the Church— Higginson, Cotton, Hooker, Harvard and the Mathers. The freemen, chosen from the Church members alone, composed the General Court which made the laws and chose the Governor and his Board of Assistants. Toleration was impossible in such a theocracy; Thomas Dudley, founder and Deputy-Governor, wrote:

> " Let men of God in courts and churches watch
> O'er such as do a toleration hatch,
> Lest that ill egg bring forth a cockatrice
> To poison all with heresy and vice." [1]

Not only were the godless disciplined or expelled, but there was no room for the over-godly. Roger Williams, who denounced all religious establishments or compulsion, was expelled in 1636, and Anne Hutchinson, prophetess of the " inner light " and disturber of the peace, was banished in 1637 with her " Antinomian " followers; later Massachusetts was rebuked by Charles II. for her ruthless harrying of the Quakers. English ballads of the time sneered at the " Christian liberty " of New England:

> " A Synagogue unspotted, pure,
> Where lusts and pleasures dwell secure ". [2]

[1] Quoted in John Fiske, *The Beginnings of New England*, p. 103 (ed. 1889).

[2] Firth, *Ballads Relating to America* (1563-1759), p. 29, from " The Summons to New England." Cf. also " The Zealous Puritan " (p. 25) and " A West Countryman's Voyage to New England " (p. 32).

But, far from being a home of licence and communism with no discipline but the Law of Nature, the stern laws of England were fortified by the sterner laws of Moses, and the discomforts of nature pressed less hardly on human frailty than the strict rule of Winthrop and his clergy.

Such a rule proved a tonic to industry and prosperity. In a few years there was a closely organised ring of towns around Massachusetts Bay and the mouth of the Charles River, and soon, with the constant stream of immigrants, the settlers spread inland. When the Indians resisted the encroachment on their hunting-grounds, they were severely crushed in the Pequot War of 1638 and gave no serious trouble for forty years. The fertile valley of the Connecticut River was occupied in defiance of both Indians and Dutch, and the English expansion was secured by the Confederation in 1643 of Massachusetts, New Plymouth, Connecticut and Newhaven. This completes the first stage in the growth of Massachusetts—establishment and organisation, and with it ends the first great immigration. It was already the strongest colony on the North American mainland,—self-supporting and fiercely independent.

Once in 1634 Charles I. had threatened to interfere and reduce it to order and orthodoxy by making Laud President of a Council for New England ; but the fall of despotism and the Civil Wars averted the danger. The colony took no part in the wars, though it was sympathetic to the Parliament and lost some settlers who returned to fight ; it recognised the changing Puritan governments, while protesting against the claim of Parliament to succeed to Royal sovereignty over the colonies.[1] Protectorate and Restoration had little direct effect across the Atlantic ; Cromwell and Charles II. were content with formal submission, knowing its pride and anxious to avoid fresh troubles. The one English change that affected them directly—the Navigation Code—was met by wholesale evasion. So from 1640 to 1675 New England throve in peace and gathered strength to meet the coming storm.

In 1675 danger threatened from three quarters. Disobedience to the Navigation Laws offended English pride and damaged her

[1] Cf. Channing, *History of United States*, I, p. 489 ; Fiske, *op. cit.*, p. 161-2.

revenues ; the Indians were restive at the settlers' advance and had
mastered the use of firearms ; James of York had become a colonial
potentate and wished to extend the sphere of Royal power and
profit from New York to New England. The Indians struck first
after warnings unheeded. Massasoit's son, " King Philip," swept
the Western borders of Massachusetts and Connecticut with fire
and massacre ; New England was only saved by two years of hard
fighting (1675-6) and the savage extermination of three tribes,
including the Narragansetts. Fortunately the great Iroquois
Confederacy, which ruled the interior from the Great Lakes to the
borders of Virginia, remained faithful to its English alliance. But
almost without breathing-space came the attack of the Stuarts.
In 1684 Charles revoked the Charter of Massachusetts, nominally
on the grounds of encroachment on the rights of the proprietors
of Maine and New Hampshire, actually because of its political
independence and violation of the Navigation Acts. It became a
Royal province with a Royal Governor, Andros, sent to enforce
English laws and Customs and to set up an Episcopal Church ; by
1688 it was absorbed in a Royal Dominion extending from Maine
to New Jersey.

The second English Revolution of the century, unlike the first,
had a vital effect on New England ; it ruined the unity of despotism
and restored the colonies to their separate lives and a large measure
of freedom. In 1691 Massachusetts received a new Charter as a
reward for its revolt against the Stuarts ; the Company disappeared
and representative institutions were put on a new basis.[1] Home
control was not abandoned, for the Crown appointed the Governor
to a Royal province and retained the right of veto on colonial laws ;
but the colonists had the right of legislation and taxation vested
in their Assembly. The franchise was based on property, not on
Churchmanship, and the Toleration Act was embodied in the laws
of the Colony. Massachusetts became the " model " constitution :
a Crown-appointed Governor and Executive with an elected
Assembly for laws and taxes ; it was the fashionable theory of the
division of powers which the English Constitution escaped by
accident. The Revolution settlement confirmed Massachusetts' hold

[1] Cf. Macdonald, *Select Charters Illustrative of American History* (1606-1775), p. 205.

on Plymouth and Maine and its claim to Acadia, but it also confirmed and tightened the Navigation Acts in 1696.

The growth of English trade and commercial wars necessarily brought England and her colonies into contact and collision, whether Stuarts or Parliament ruled ; the history of New England, and of Massachusetts especially, from 1689 to 1713 was merged in the world-struggle with France. It is a story of raid and counter-raid, equally ineffective, which did little but ravage frontier settlements and cause a permanent fear and hate of the Indians whom both sides used as their pawns. English efforts were spoiled by lack of unity and incompetent Governors ; but Massachusetts took a striking part, and her forces conquered Acadia and besieged Quebec. The great struggle, however, was still to come ; for these local operations did nothing to check the vast encircling movement which the French were planning from the St. Lawrence to the Mississippi.

In 1713 the Bay Colony had over 50,000 inhabitants of a total of less than 100,000 in New England. Its prosperity was firmly based on fisheries, shipping and trade ; and while Boston and Salem were accumulating mercantile wealth, the farms of the colony were producing a hardy and prolific population. The real strength of Massachusetts lay in its smallholders ; the number of tenants, servants and slaves was small compared with Virginia ; there was no negro or " poor white " problem. Slavery was not forbidden as in Rhode Island ; but there was no economic demand for it and a considerable volume of public opinion against it. For reasons of safety Indian slaves were not allowed ; on the other hand the earlier attempts to convert the Indians had little success and were thwarted by the epidemic warfare since 1675. The decline of the missionary spirit may be connected with the growth of the secular spirit which affected Puritan New England no less than Presbyterian Scotland and Anglican England. Politics were secularised with the disappearance of the Church franchise ; the growth of wealth and European connections sapped the isolated purity of a " Bible Commonwealth " ; liberal theology took root, despite the anathemas of the Mathers, and invaded Harvard College to such an extent that the conservatives founded Yale College (1716)

in the more evangelical air of Newhaven. By the end of the century
the sound educational policy of the Colony had borne fruit;
Harvard, founded only seven years from its birth (1636), had given
New England an intellectual centre and Massachusetts intellectual
leadership, and it was fed by a compulsory system of elementary
and grammar schools set up in 1647. There is one dark stain on
the picture—the Salem witch trials of 1688. The murder of twenty
women on ludicrous evidence at the instigation of Cotton and
Increase Mather and with the approval of Governor Phipps, seems
a curious commentary on the tale of intellectual progress; but
it was the last, if worst outbreak of primitive religion, and the quick
reaction showed that the days of theocracy were over.[1] After the
1689 Revolution the absorbing interests were secular: war with
the French, expanding trade, evasion of the Navigation Acts,
quarrels over the salary of the Royal Governor—in fact, the preliminaries to the conquest of Canada and American Independence.

The rest of New England can only be treated summarily. In
the main the other settlements followed more slowly the progress of
Massachusetts, but certain differences must be noted. In the north,
Maine and New Hampshire suffered from incompetent proprietors
and French and Indian attacks; Maine was given to Massachusetts
in 1691, but New Hampshire, lying between them, was erected into
a separate but insignificant province in 1679. To the south,
Plymouth in decline, " like an ancient mother grown old and for-
saken of her children," [2] was absorbed in Massachusetts in 1691.
Connecticut was founded in 1639 by Thomas Hooker, leading
his Newtown congregation from the outskirts of Boston; according to John Fiske, the constitution that Hooker framed

" was the first written constitution known to history, that created a

---

[1] Cf. J. A. Doyle, *The English in America* : The Puritan Colonies, II, pp. 384-400.
He suggests that the second generation of New Englanders degenerated as their
leaders died and they lost touch with the outside world; hence " the weaker and
meaner elements in the Puritan creed " became more prominent and produced a
growth of credulity and cruelty, as in the career of Cotton Mather. Thus came the
witch-hunt, while at the same time the genuine love of learning and the renewed
connection with Europe (through trade and politics) was creating a public opinion
which eventually overcame the rule of superstition, although it was powerless
against sudden popular frenzies (*op. cit.*, II, pp. 111-14).

[2] Doyle, *op. cit.*, II, p. 22. This was Bradford's complaint when the younger
settlers moved out to more promising sites.

government, and it marked the beginnings of American democracy, of which Thomas Hooker deserves more than any other man to be called the father." [1]

The colony was otherwise not important in this period ; it had two growing towns, Hartford and Newhaven, but no good harbours for trade, so that it was confined to agriculture ; it was distinguished for its religious conservatism, which had one good effect—the founding of Yale College.

Rhode Island on Narragansett Bay was still weaker and less influential ; it was the pariah of New England, but its story is in some ways the most interesting of all. It was weak through its scattered settlements and internal jealousies, and through the hostility of its orthodox neighbours who blocked its expansion. There was however good soil and abundance of good harbours, Newport in particular ; by 1700 its prosperity was assured by smugglers, privateers and pirates. But its undying fame is due to Roger Williams, its founder, and to the political ideals he bequeathed to his settlement. He was an ardent and bellicose idealist, whose gospel was the complete separation of the Church from the world and full toleration of all believers. On both counts he was banished from theocratic Massachusetts, where Church and State combined to brand toleration as a wile of Satan against the truth ; even Plymouth could not stomach his fiery radicalism, for he advocated religious peace, not with the calm of the sceptic, but with the devouring zeal of the fanatic. So in the winter of 1635-6 he settled on the coast south of Cape Cod and founded the town of Providence as a refuge for religious outcasts ; in 1638 Anne Hutchinson brought her followers to Rhode Island opposite. [2] It

---

[1] Fiske, *The Beginnings of New England*, p. 127. The constitution made no mention of the English Crown nor of a religious franchise. For the " Fundamental Orders of Connecticut," cf. W. Macdonald, *Select Charters Illustrative of American History*, 1606-1775, pp. 60-5. The constitution was confirmed by Royal Charter in 1663 (when Newhaven was incorporated), and remained in force until 1818. It was a federal republic ; " all attributes of sovereignty not expressly granted to the General Court remained, as of original right, in the towns " (Fiske, p. 128) ; for this reason, " the government of the United States is in lineal descent more nearly related to that of Connecticut than to that of any of the other thirteen colonies " (Fiske, pp. 127-8). Such decentralisation was an illustrious precedent, but in pioneer times it was an obvious source of weakness.

[2] She soon moved to Long Island and was murdered by Indians in 1642.

was not the first American experiment in toleration, for Protestants and Catholic had lived side by side in Maryland since 1633 ; but it was the first public declaration of the full doctrine, and it remained the policy of Rhode Island when Maryland submitted to Protestant ascendancy. In two other respects the small colony set a high example to its neighbours : in friendship and mission work with the Indians and in its refusal to legalise slavery. But the example from a tainted source was rejected by the orthodox ; the weakness of the colony deprived it of influence, though it also preserved it from hostile intervention.[1] The destiny of New England was shaped, not by Roger Williams, but by Bradford, Winthrop and Hooker.

(c) *The Southern Colonies*

The story of the southern colonies is less complex than that of New England ; there was less trouble with England, less religious divergence and constitutional experiment, no foreign complications. There were similar recurrent troubles over Indians and Navigation Acts ; there was, too, one dominating influence—Virginia. The two fundamental differences between North and South were religion and economics. The Southern settlements, Maryland apart, were officially Anglican and were not intended as religious commonwealths, and they developed as interior plantations, not trading stations on the coast.[2]

Of the minor settlements, Carolina, the most southerly, was in 1713 in its infancy. The district in which the first English colony was planted was neglected for nearly eighty years after the tragedy of 1585 ; but soon after 1660 settlers began to come south from Virginia, while at the same time the courtiers of Charles II. turned to plantation as a source of revenue. The Virginian emigrants slowly and painfully developed into the State of North Carolina ; the English proprietors, of whom Shaftesbury was the most active, founded a settlement at Charleston (1670), which soon forged ahead

[1] It even obtained a Charter from Charles II. in 1663.

[2] New England soil is stony and poor, unfit for heavy crops and large plantations ; in Virginia and Carolina there is good, rich soil behind the swamps of the tidewater region ; " as the conditions of life were ever driving the Virginian and the Marylander inland, so they were ever holding back the New Englander and keeping him to the sea " (Doyle, *op. cit.*, II, p. 35).

of the squatters to its north.   South Carolina was well backed by
its founders, although they had many quarrels with the planters
and nearly strangled the infant colony by the most cumbrous and
ludicrous constitution that the fancy of Shaftesbury and Locke
could devise ; fortunately it remained a paper draft.[1]   Charleston
became a busy port, strong enough to defy a Franco-Spanish siege
in 1706 ; rice-growing became the staple industry, and large plantations flourished on slave labour.   The colony in 1719 consisted
of 9000 whites and 12,000 negroes.[2]

Maryland, lying north of Virginia at the head of Chesapeake
Bay, was the outcast colony of the South, as Rhode Island of the
North.   It was founded in 1633 as the private domain of Lord
Baltimore and as a refuge for Catholics, and a succession of able
proprietors managed to secure both profit and toleration through
all the political changes at home and despite Protestant threats from
both Virginia and New England.   The Baltimores, though
absentee landlords, steered their American estates into a safe obscurity and encouraged immigrants of every creed ; business trium-
phing over religion, they made no effort to preserve a Catholic
majority.   The Proprietorship survived the Puritan and Whig
Revolutions to fall with the rest of British supremacy ; it was a
unique relic of primitive colonisation.   Yet in spite of this private
exploitation the settlers of all creeds prospered, and as long as they
paid their quit-rents and tobacco tax, they were left in peace and
allowed self-government.   There were no serious Indian wars,
but a number of boundary quarrels with Virginia which led to
Virginian attacks under cover of the English Parliamentary cause ;
later, when France became the enemy, the Maryland Catholics
were denounced as Jesuitical traitors, although the Baltimores from
the first had discouraged any active Catholic clergy.   Hence the
Revolution of 1689 in Maryland brought the seizure of power by the
Protestant majority, the end of full toleration, and the deposition
of the Proprietor until the Baltimore family became Protestant in
1715.   From 1689 Maryland was a typical Southern State, back-

[1] Cf. Macdonald, *Select Charters*, pp. 149-168; the aim was to erect a feudal " county
palatine," and to " avoid erecting a numerous democracy."

[2] *Camb. Hist. Brit. Emp.*, I, p. 395.   After 1685 there was a considerable immigration of Huguenots.

ward in towns and education, with a life based on tobacco, large plantations and slave labour ; in 1689 its population was estimated at 20,000.[1]

The first American colony in time and rank was Virginia. Massachusetts in its first decade threatened to outstrip it in growth, but the introduction of negroes to supply the lack of white labour after 1642 kept Virginia ahead, and the restored Monarchy took great pains to supply it with plentiful and cheap labour from the vagrant and criminal classes.   So the population rose from 3000 in 1628 to 58,000 in 1689 and was nearing 100,000 in 1714.   It was also the province dearest to the English government, the most loyal and the most profitable ; and its Anglican landed oligarchy was the nearest American counterpart to English society.

The history of Virginia from 1624, when it became a Royal Province, to 1714 was uneventful, compared with its early struggles or with the history of New England.   Three times, in 1622, 1644, and 1676, the Indians ravaged the outlying settlements and took toll of about 300 lives ; but the normal relations were those of friendship and trade, and the Virginian Assembly evolved an Indian code of laws for the mutual protection and agreement of settlers and natives.[2]   Virginia's central position saved her from French or Spanish troubles ; the only foreign attack that she experienced was Dutch raids on shipping in the Anglo-Dutch wars. Conflict with England was rare ; in 1652 the Virginians, after proclaiming Charles II., were reduced to submission by a trade boycott and a Parliamentary squadron ; they made some ineffectual protests against the Navigation Acts ;[3] and they resisted more successfully Charles II.'s grant of the whole colony to his favourites, Arlington and Culpeper.   The Whig Revolution changed little ; it meant, as elsewhere, more English and fewer colonial-born officials and a tightening of the Navigation Acts.   The scattered planters, absorbed in their estates and lacking the political incentive of town life, took but an occasional interest in politics ; for years

---

[1] Figures of population in 1689 are given in Channing, II, p. 222.

[2] Cf. Doyle, *The English in America* (Virginia, etc.), pp. 319-321 ; Indian lands, lives and freedom were guaranteed by law (consolidating Act of 1662).

[3] Cf. the protest of 1663, in Bland : *Docts.*, pp. 672-4.

they left government to the irascible Cavalier, Sir William Berkeley, who was Governor from 1640-52 and 1660-77. Two fears alone could rouse them—taxes and Indians. In 1652 the Assembly obtained in the terms of their surrender to Parliament the recognition of their sole right to tax, and that right was jealously preserved against Stuart and Whig Governors alike. The only serious crisis was produced in 1676 by Berkeley's unpopularity and feeble measures against Indian attacks ; Nathaniel Bacon led a revolt of small planters against the governing clique, and established a temporary despotism which was justified by his repression of the Indians. Bacon's death from exhaustion restored the oligarchy to power and led to stricter control by the English government.

Virginian politics are unimportant in comparison with the economic evolution of the colony. Virginia was the model Southern State with large plantations worked by indentured or slave labour ; its history is the history of tobacco. Politicians and economists deplored the dependence of the colony on a luxury, but it became the staple crop, and the chief interest of the colony lay in its marketing and price. Tobacco took the place of money as the chief currency, and took the place of politics as the chief interest of the Colonial Assembly.

It was the competition of the Maryland tobacco-planters which inspired the Virginians to pick quarrels over religion and boundaries ; the " enumeration " of tobacco in 1660 as a commodity which could only be exported to England was far more vital to Virginians than the restoration of King and Church.[1] Tobacco determined not only the prosperity but the social structure of the colony. It needed large estates, and large estates needed capital and cheap labour ; so a landed oligarchy grew up and prevented any healthy development of smallholders. The majority of the white population was composed of labourers with small hope of independence ; they were paupers and felons supplied by the English government, or wretches kidnapped by enterprising shippers who " spirited " them aboard. They were condemned to serve the planters virtually as serfs for a period of years, and their complaints

[1] In compensation for the restriction, they had a monopoly of Empire markets, while tobacco-growing was forbidden in England.

have survived in ballads. " The Trapann'd Maiden " bewails her harsh mistress, the beds of straw, the spiders, the hard fate of drinking "the water clear, which makes me pale and wan," the heavy field work ; and the lad who was " lagged " to Virginia by " hard-hearted judges so cruel " declares :

> " My bones are quite rotten, my feet are quite sore,
> I'm parched with fever, and am at death's door,
> But if ever I live to see seven years more,
>   Then I'll bid adieu to Virginia." [1]

It would be unfair to accuse the planters generally of harshness, though the system was obviously open to abuses that no laws could check ; the real evil was in the social divisions created of " poor whites " and idle planters. It was inevitable that, as the demand for labour increased and the English supplies failed to keep pace, the planters should seek the obvious remedy of full-time slave labour on the West Indian model. In the second half of the century the negroes entered American history ; they solved the immediate problem, but they created another which eventually brought material and moral disaster to Virginia.[2]

The scattered country life not only militated against political or commercial centres, but it was unfavourable to education. The richer planters could send their sons to England, but the mass was illiterate, and there was no provision for higher education until William and Mary College was founded in 1692, as a very modest beginning. At the same time the Church was redeemed from neglect and poverty by the labours of John Blair ; previously the only aspect of religion that aroused interest was the harrying of Puritan immigrants and attacks on the Maryland Catholics. Nevertheless Virginian society had a grace and dignity of its own ; life on the country estates was generous, patriarchal and self-sufficient ; the Southern aristocracy became natural leaders, proud of their independence and quick to resent wrongs. As Burke pointed out, the presence of slavery made freedom " a kind of rank or privilege " ; " in such a people, the haughtiness of domination com-

---

[1] Firth, *American Ballads*, p. 73 ; for the " Trapann'd Maiden," cf. pp. 51-3.

[2] The first negroes were imported in 1619   in 1662 slavery was made hereditary.

bines with the spirit of freedom, fortifies it, and renders it invincible." [1]

(d) The Middle Colonies

North and South were not linked until they had embarked on widely different careers; and when the intervening lands were occupied by English settlers, the settlements were of such a kind that they proved more of barriers than links. Until 1664 the Dutch had provided the barrier. In 1609 the Dutch East India Company sent Henry Hudson to find a new way to the East; he found instead the river that bears his name, and the Dutch occupied the Hudson valley for trade in furs; in 1614 they built a fort on an islet at its mouth—Manhattan Island, the site of New York City. They ranged up the valley towards Canada, and south towards Virginia, absorbing a Swedish colony (founded 1638) at the mouth of the Delaware River; but they were traders first, and colonisation was slow until they admitted colonists from England. As the English flocked in and around the colony, the Dutch grasp relaxed; and it fell without a blow to James of York's expedition in 1664—the second English colonial conquest.

The conversion of New Netherland into New York had important consequences. The English seaboard was complete and the way inland was barred to outsiders; Dutch sea-power and smugglers were removed; New York, from its central position and control of the inland route to Canada, became the strategic key of North America; the Proprietorship of James Stuart made it the base of Stuart colonial despotism. The conquest was eventually divided into four colonies: New York (from the coast to Lake Erie), New Jersey and Delaware (the coastal region from the Hudson to the Delaware rivers), and Pennsylvania (inland west of the Delaware river). The small settlements of New Jersey and Delaware soon fell under Quaker control and do not need separate treatment here, but the other two grew rapidly in population and importance.

New York was under the absolute rule of James of York until 1688; it was governed well and tactfully, with toleration for all

---

[1] *Speech on Conciliation with America* (1775). For Southern society and slavery, cf. Doyle, *English in America* (Virginia), ch. 13.

religions, and was the model for the Dominion of New England which James established under Andros in 1686. But his fall produced, as nowhere else in America, a bloodstained revolution. A popular movement under Jacob Leisler used the English Revolution to gain democratic control, and then fell foul of William III.'s agents ; its forcible repression left the colony rent with faction and suspect in England. Hence the fall of the Stuarts, while it naturally ended the toleration of Catholics, did not bring complete freedom to New York ; it remained a Royal province, subject to English Governors with considerable powers. It was, moreover, unfortunate in its new Governors, Lord Bellomont the busy intriguer and Lord Cornbury the embezzler ; but the Colonial Assembly had some check on these abuses through its control of taxation. Yet political quarrels were not so troublesome as economic, for New York felt acutely the revived enforcement in 1696 of the Navigation Code. It was a natural magnet for trade with its fine harbour, its great river highway and its access to the Great Lakes and the interior ; it had risen by trade—legitimate fur trade, tobacco-smuggling from Virginia and Maryland, slave-trading, privateering and even piracy.[1] A community of this kind found more restriction than protection in English mercantilism, and unlike the other colonies it had a large element not bound to England by blood. The Dutch minority was rich and powerful, and a new foreign strain was added in 1710, when 3000 German exiles from the Palatinate were imported, the advance-guard of a great immigration. Thus the years 1689-1714 brought to New York all the ingredients of American Independence.

Though it was less populous (20,000 in 1689) than either Massachusetts or Virginia, it took a leading part in the rivalry with the French. James II. learned from his management of the colony the need of united action against Canada, and Jacob Leisler in 1690 called the first Colonial Congress for the same purpose. New York's hinterland was threatened by the explorations of Frontenac and La Salle ; it possessed the Lake Champlain route to Canada by which French and English could strike directly at each other ;

[1] Privateers, licensed to plunder enemy commerce, easily slipped into piracy. Captain Kidd, sent by Bellomont to suppress piracy, practised it and became almost its patron saint (cf. Channing, II, pp. 268-70).

and it inherited from the Dutch a permanent alliance with the great Iroquois Confederacy which the French were attempting to destroy with the aid of the Algonquins.   It was thus vitally concerned with the French encircling movement from Canada across the Great Lakes, down the Ohio and Mississippi rivers to the Gulf of Mexico, where Mobile was founded in 1702.   Frontenac saw its importance and planned an attack in 1690, but did no more than destroy the frontier station of Schenectady ;   the strength of the Iroquois and the difficulties of the route diverted his attacks to New England.[1] From the same difficulties Leisler's counter-attack in 1690 broke down, and twenty years of futile raids ended in 1713 with an uneasy balance of power that left neither side safe or contented.

Pennsylvania was the last of the " holy experiments " in colonisa- tion, and the last but one of the proprietary colonies ;   it was founded in 1681 by William Penn as a refuge for the Quakers in payment for a Crown debt to his father.   After half a century of persecution in new and old England, the Quakers found, not only a safe and fertile abode, but a State of their own framing ;   and their rule was extended by Penn's purchase over New Jersey (until 1702) and Delaware (until 1776).   Their lives were free from Indian and French complications ;   for Penn by his honest dealing won the friendship of the Indians as no other Englishman of his age, and the Quaker objections to force precluded them from military operations despite the pressure of the English Government and of their own neighbours. So they were able to concentrate on godliness and prosperity ;   their only danger was the hostility of the adjoining settlements against their peculiar tenets and unholy connection with the Catholic Stuarts.[2]   The settlement grew fast in wealth and numbers, with an immediate success that no other colony had attained ;   there were 12,000 in 1689, and the great city of Phila- delphia on the Delaware was planned and founded.   Penn ensured this success by his untiring search for settlers all over Europe and by his careful choice of men of industry, substance and religion ;

---

[1] The most famous was the raid on Deerfield, Mass., in 1704.

[2] Penn was a close friend of James II. and supported his English policy whole- heartedly ; so he naturally fell under suspicion in 1689 and was deprived of his pro- vince.   But besides being a good Quaker and a sound business man he was also a shrewd courtier, and was restored to his Proprietorship in 1694.

but he was not so fortunate in his search for an ideal government. His famous "Frame of Government" (1682), for all its sound principles and details, precipitated a long quarrel which ended in the permanent alienation of Proprietor and settlers ; the final solution, the Charter of Privileges of 1701, was the normal Colonial constitution with powers divided between an appointed Governor and Council and an elected Assembly.[1] Even toleration was whittled down ; all who acknowledged " one Almighty God " were allowed to settle, but only Christians were admitted to citizenship and in 1705 Catholics were excluded from the Assembly. Yet, in spite of external jealousy, intestine quarrels, and the handicaps of the Quaker creed in military and judicial matters,[2] Pennsylvania in 1713 ranked with the greater colonies and showed the way to progress ; for it was the first mainly inland settlement. William Penn can hardly be called a founder of Empire, since his colony in spite of its contribution to English wealth only added to the divisions that weakened the political power of English domination ; but he must be called a founder of America. He brought a fine stock to its population and he planted firmly the principles of religious and civil liberty.

IV. The Foundations of Independence

By 1713 the English nation across the Atlantic consisted of 400,000 people ; 50,000 of these were in the West Indies, owning a negro population of 150,000.[3] The variety of the population was as impressive as its size : white and black : English, Scotch, Irish, Dutch, German : Huguenot, Anglican, Puritan, Quaker, Catholic : landlord, smallholder, servant and slave. They were spread in a thin line of settlements from Newfoundland to Barbados, over 3000 miles apart ; their climates, their needs, their characteristics, their enemies differed widely as a consequence.

---

[1] The successive " Frames of Government " and the Charter are given in Macdonald's *Select Charters*.

[2] The Quakers found difficulty in erecting a system of justice because of their objection to oaths. One of the reasons for the successful petition of the people of New Jersey for separate government was their fear of unsworn magistrates and juries.

[3] *Camb. Hist. Brit. Emp.*, I, p. 267.

Such diversity was a rich seed-bed for new nations, but it was inimical to unity of government or sentiment. It created a problem for English Governments which they only grasped late and slowly. The State had evaded responsibility for the infant settlements, and had neither encouraged nor shaped their growth ; but from 1650 their numbers and wealth had forced England to improvise a colonial policy for their regulation and protection. There were three motives at work : to prevent other nations seizing the colonies, to prevent the colonists injuring home industries, and to obtain for England the major share of the value created by the colonists' unaided labours. Colonial policy was therefore mainly military (or naval) and economic ; but to enforce either aspect, it was necessary to establish a firm constitutional control of the colonial governments. But the problem created by diversity was aggravated by two factors. There was distance, and " all the causes which weaken authority by distance " ; " the Ocean remains," said Burke, " you cannot pump this dry." [1] Then there was the delay in taking control ; by 1650 the colonists were set in their ways, used to independence, without habits of submission or cause for gratitude. The " Old Colonial System " had the weakness of an afterthought ; it did not, as in France, create the Empire, but was created by it.

Control was chiefly a mainland problem ; the West Indian islands were bound by economic dependence on a protected sugar market and by fear of slave revolts and French and Spanish attacks. One only of these bonds affected the mainland—the threat of France to New England and New York ; it failed to secure unity, but it did ensure dependence until the threat was removed in 1763. There were three attempts at partial union, two by the colonists themselves in 1643 and 1690 and one imposed by James II. from 1686-8 ; none were permanent or effective. After 1689 the home Government gave up hope of political unity, and concentrated on economic unity and constitutional uniformity. The net result was to produce unity of another kind ; a unity of grievances that was the foundation of American Independence.

The Navigation Code (1651-96), regulating the external and

[1] *Speech on Conciliation* (*Works*, ed. Payne, I, pp. 191-2).

inter-colonial trade of America, was the heart of the system; its enforcement was the main colonial interest of Crown and Parliament. The chief duty of Boards of Trade and colonial Governors was to erect and supervise a growing establishment of Customs officials and Admiralty Courts. Yet the effect of economic grievances on Independence has been variously estimated. Burke and Pitt saw no danger in trade restraints, while modern " economic historians " see in the Stamp Act only the occasion of a long-smouldering revolt against economic oppression; the latest tendency is to emphasise constitutional and social differences—" two opposed theories of government and . . . two opposed types of character." [1] It can be said that in 1714 the colonists accepted the benefits of the Navigation Acts, grumbled at and evaded their restrictions, and made no serious attempt to question the principle of English regulation of trade. After 1714 came a period of lax enforcement while American wealth and population doubled every twenty years; so when the seventeenth century system was revived in revolutionary conditions, it was at once more oppressive and less traditional, a relic of an outgrown tutelage.

In addition to the extension of the English mercantile system to the Colonies, they were also vitally affected by the English Revolution—the transference of power from King to Parliament. They were founded, not by the Crown, but under the Crown; they held their Charters from the King, and were subject to the King's Privy Council. On Tudor principles, the King alone was supreme over foreign trade, policy and plantations; the Stuarts in 1649 lost their power to Parliament, which, as " the supreme authority of this nation," claimed the government of " the people of England and of all the dominions and territories thereunto belonging." [2] This meant that one of the Legislatures hitherto subject to the Crown seized control, not only of the Crown, but of the other subject Legislatures; the English Parliament, instead of being *primus*

---

[1] For a summary of the opposing views, cf. Egerton, *The American Revolution*, chs. 1 and 3. Among American historians, Channing (*op. cit.*) holds the economic interpretation, and C. H. McIlwain (*The American Revolution*) emphasises the constitutional factor.

[2] Gardiner: *Docts.*, p. 388 (Act Declaring a Commonwealth); McIlwain (*op. cit.*, p. 26) holds this innovation to be the main cause of the American Revolution.

inter pares, stepped into the King's place as master of its fellow assemblies. Events showed that the colonists had no great attachment for the Stuart Kings; they accepted the Revolution of 1649 and actively aided that of 1688 with Revolutions of their own. But the sovereignty of Parliament meant less, not more freedom for them, as for many of the King's subjects; for the new claims of Parliament were as infinite as the old Prerogative, and were enforced with a more jealous spirit. One of the benefits of Royal neglect was Royal liberality; the Stuarts had been careless with their privileges. But the new masters, servants themselves of the merchants, were not so generous; the Declaration of Rights did not extend to America, and from 1689 colonial government was tightened by home supervision and imported officials. The greatest change was in taxation; the King had not taxed without the colonists' consent, but Parliament claimed to consent for them. The King had treated them as " foreign plantations " ; Parliament included them within the realm, as part of a unitary State.

Professor Pollard has said :

" The American Revolution of 1776 is the second volume of the English Revolution of 1688." [1]

The sovereignty of Parliament, finally established in 1689, involved a constitutional revolution in the relations of England and her colonies which had some immediate effects and the seeds of ultimate catastrophe. It substituted unity for federalism, and it threatened to take away those " rights of Englishmen " which despotism had conferred. The Americans between 1763 and 1776 idealised the Prerogative and looked back to the years before 1689 as to a Golden Age. It was the Long Parliament which set the precedent of tyranny with the boycott Act of 1650 ; [2] the " free Parliaments " of William and Anne laid the foundations for the Parliamentary Imperialism of the Stamp and Declaratory Acts. By 1714 there was not as yet an American nation to meet the challenge of Parlia-

---

[1] *Factors in American History*, p. 11.

[2] The Act prohibited trade with (Royalist) Barbados, Bermuda, Virginia and Antigua, restricted alien trade with the plantations, and empowered the Council of State to settle the colonial governments ; its preamble declared the full doctrine of Parliamentary sovereignty over the plantations. Cf. *Camb. Hist. Brit. Emp.*, I, pp. 215-6.

mentary supremacy; but it needed only fifty years of common danger and common grievances to weld the colonists into a people who would no longer endure the subjection of a " dominion thereunto belonging."

SUGGESTIONS FOR FURTHER READING

General :

Cambridge History of the British Empire, Vol. I (useful for reference, and good chapters on Navigation Acts, wars and constitutions; chapters on internal history of colonies are difficult in arrangement and compression; no maps; full bibliography).

CARRINGTON, C. E.: *The British Overseas.* (C.U.P., 1950)

WILLIAMSON, J. A.: *A Short History of British Expansion.* 2 Vols. (Macmillan, 1943)

EGERTON, H. E.: *A Short History of British Colonial Policy, 1606–1909.* (Methuen, 1945)

BEER, G. L.: *The Origins of the British Colonial System, 1578– 1660.* 2 Vols. (New York, 1933)
The Old Colonial Systems, 1660–1754. (New York, 1933)

INNES, A. D.: *The Maritime and Colonial Expansion of England under the Stuarts, 1603–1714.* (Low, 1931)

PARRY, J. H.: *Europe and a Wider World, 1415–1714.* (Hutchinson, 1949)

LUCAS, SIR C. P.: *Historical Geography of the British Colonies.* (O.U.P., 1887–1931)

American Colonies :

Chronicles of the Pilgrim Fathers. (Dent, Everyman Library)

NETTLES, C. P.: *The Roots of American Civilisation.* (Crofts, 1938)

MORISON, S. E. and COMMAGER, H. S.: *The Growth of the American Republic.* (O.U.P., 1950)

COMMAGER, H. S. (Ed.): *Documents of American History, 1492– 1940.* (New York, 1948)

West Indies :

PARRY, J. H. and SHERLOCK, P. M. : *A Short History of the West Indies.*   (Macmillan, 1956)
BURN, W. L. : *The British West Indies.*   (Hutchinson U.L., 1951)
NEWTON, A. P. : *European Nations in the West Indies, 1493–1688.*   (Black, 1933)

XII

ECONOMIC ORGANISATION AND DEVELOPMENT

THE " economic interpretation of history " has become a modern
fetish; yet though Karl Marx is credited with its invention, the
seventeenth century had at least one Marxian before Marx.   Harrington insisted that the economic organisation of society alone
did and should determine its political organisation :

" As is the proportion or balance of dominion or property in
land, such is the nature of the empire." [1]

We need not on this method ascribe all historical events to economic
causes.   The grievances either of landowners or merchants were
not the decisive factors in causing the outbreak of rebellion against
Stuart despotism : but we must admit that the ultimate failure of
despotism, whether of King or Protector, was due to its economic
dependence on a landed and commercial oligarchy.   That is to say,
economic power does not always start a revolution, but it always
decides its fate.   To understand the political victory of the English
oligarchs, either in 1660 or in 1688, we must examine the wealth of
the nation—its growth, its distribution, and its relations with the
State.

I. THE GROWTH OF NATIONAL PROSPERITY

Despite the lack of adequate statistics, contemporary and modern
observers are agreed that England in the seventeenth century grew
steadily in wealth and population ; that the nation waxed fat and
insolent was a typical Royalist excuse for the fall of the Monarchy.

[1] Introduction to *Oceana* (1656 : dedicated to Cromwell).

Clarendon found no other explanation of the Rebellion necessary but " the same natural causes and means which have usually attended kingdoms swoln with long plenty, pride and excess, towards some signal mortification, and castigation of Heaven " ; [1] and he looked back sadly to the golden days of Charles' personal government, when a wise King, combining *imperium et libertas*, maintained the peace and happiness of his three Kingdoms at a time when the rest of Europe was stricken " by the rage and fury of arms." England became " the Exchange of Christendom "—" the country rich, and, which is more, fully enjoying the pleasure of its own wealth, and so the easier corrupted with the pride and wantonness of it ".[2] The wars and uncertainty of the years 1640-1660 destroyed this picture and diminished the national wealth ; but the fact that England could provide such huge armaments and recover so quickly after 1660 is in itself evidence of great natural reserves. And apart from these years there was no serious break in development ; for the twenty years of war that followed the Revolution of 1688 secured, as they passed, English maritime and mercantile supremacy, and forced the nation to develop the resources and machinery of national credit. One of the major indictments of the Tories was that the Whig merchants throve on war and threatened to upset the balance of power between Land and Banks ; " we have been fighting," wrote Swift,

" to enrich usurers and stock-jobbers, and to cultivate the pernicious designs of a faction by destroying the landed interest." [3]

Though no total figures of national wealth are available for comparison, there is ample evidence of increase and expansion. The simplest proof lies in the increase of the customs duties between 1603 and 1689, before the period of heavy taxation ; even when allowance is made for the decline in the value of money (which was considerable in the first half of the century) and for adjustments and increases in rates (as in 1608 and 1629), the figures show a remarkable expansion of trade. The yield was £127,000 in 1604 : nearly £500,000 in 1641 : nearly £1,000,000 in 1689 (excluding over £600,000 from excise, imposed since the Civil

[1] Clar.: *Hist.*, I, p. 2.   [2] Clar.: *Hist.*, I, pp. 94-5.   [3] *Conduct of the Allies.*

War).[1]   These figures indicate a growth of both consumption and production; Englishmen were spending more on luxuries— the standard of living was rising, at least in the upper and middle classes; and they were making more to pay for their new wants. Coffee, tea, tobacco, newspapers and public coaches soon passed out of the sphere of luxuries into that of necessities; the extravagance of James I., not the simplicity of Charles I. or Cromwell, set the standard for the entertainments of Court, nobles and merchants.   Manor houses, centres of rural economy, were replaced by palaces—imitation Courts and an incubus on the land; Jacobean gave way to Palladian, and Blenheim was the result, the *magnum opus* of inflated architecture.[2]   Even the merchants were alarmed at the extravagance of the Restoration age; Thomas Mun, while admitting that " all kind of Bounty and Pomp is not to be avoided (for if we should become so frugal that we should use few or no Forraign wares, how then shall we vent our own commodities)," [3] lamented the wasteful idleness of his countrymen in contrast with the industry of their hated Dutch rivals :

" This great plenty which we enjoy, makes us a people not only vicious and excessive, wastful of the means we have, but also improvident and careless of much other wealth that shamefully we lose " (*i.e.* fishing).

He particularly denounced " unnecessary wants of silks, sugars, spices, fruits " and the idle habits

" of late years besotting ourselves with pipe and pot, in a beastly manner, sucking smoak and drinking healths, until death stares many in the face." [4]

Nevertheless, this increase in consumption, however misdirected, could only be the effect of increased wealth in the past, even if it

[1] Cf. Dowell, *History of Taxation*, Vol. I, (Book VIII, ch. 1), and Vol. II (Book II ch. 1).

[2] Many of them were physical as well as economic burdens ; cf. Abel Evans' epitaph on Vanbrugh, architect of Castle Howard and Blenheim ;

> " Lie heavy on him, earth, for he
> Laid many a heavy load on thee."

[3] Mun : *England's Treasure by Forraign Trade*, ch. 15 (p. 60 of Oxford reprint of 1664 ed.).

[4] Mun : *op. cit.* ch. 19, pp. 71-2.

were also the cause of diminished wealth in the future; and the event belied Mun's fears, for the disfranchised Puritans soon equalled the Dutch in industry and thrift.[1]

One factor which affected consumption and production alike was a considerable growth in population, which stimulated the staple industries of corn and wool. The growth was much less than in the two following centuries, and cannot be estimated accurately; but an increase of a million from $4\frac{1}{2}$ millions in 1600 to $5\frac{1}{2}$ in 1700 may be accepted as tolerably near the truth.[2] Even more significant, however, was the growth of an economic spirit; there was a great development of economic theory and organisation, and the art of government became deeply concerned with and influenced by economic interests. England, hitherto economically backward, began to deserve the title of a nation of shopkeepers.

The clearest sign of economic progress was the substitution of the theory of the " Balance of Trade " for the theory known as " Bullionism." One of the first recommendations of Charles II.'s new Council of Trade was to allow free export of money; it became Statute in 1663 and remained permanently in force with a few interruptions. Free trade in money was now possible because money was no longer the sole, indispensable medium of exchange; it was a commodity which, like any other, could be bought and sold on credit. With the growing use of bills of exchange English commerce advanced from the cash to the credit stage; not only private but public finance was reorganised on the new basis with the aid of the goldsmiths, the brokers who gathered round the Royal Exchange, the Bank of England and the National Debt. The Restoration, in fact, brought a financial revolution to England which put her ahead of all other nations except always the Dutch; by the beginning of the eighteenth century London displaced Amsterdam as the centre of world finance. The economic advisers of the Privy Council, whether of Charles II. or of William III., grasped the two decisive causes of the flow of money into the country—the encouragement of trade and a enlightened monetary policy.

---

[1] Cf. Tawney, *Religion and the Rise of Capitalism*, ch. 4; the accumulation of capital by Puritan abstinence was one cause of the Industrial Revolution.

[2] G. N. Clark, *The Seventeenth Century*, ch. 1. The increase would have been more but for the emigration of thousands of the most virile stock in the country.

They began by removing artificial restrictions on the export of money as unnecessary and ineffective ; in 1666 they encouraged its import by instituting free coinage of bullion by the Mint, instead of the usual charge called " seignorage." [1]   Even the Stop of the Exchequer in 1672, when Charles II. refused to return the principal he had borrowed from the goldsmiths and paid them annual interest instead, was the foundation of the national credit system, though it caused a temporary economic and political crisis.[2]   In 1694 the foundation of the Bank of England, for the two objects of organising a permanent National Debt and of issuing paper money (in the form of Exchequer Bills) on public security, made a permanent and stable basis for English finance ; [3] and in 1696 the government undertook, at the public expense, the urgent public duty of re-coinage, to remedy the scarcity of good coin and the diversity in exchange value of coins of the same denomination.[4]

Parallel with this remarkable series of monetary reforms, there was a similar advance in scientific investigation of the sources and causes of wealth.   It was admitted that trade produced money more effectively than mines or laws ; the·burning question was what kinds of trade and what regulation of trade would best advance national prosperity.   The solution which won favour with merchants and governments was the theory of the balance of trade : that the wealth of a nation was the excess of its exports over its imports.   This was the gospel according to Thomas Mun :

" The ordinary means to increase our wealth and treasure is by Forraign Trade, wherein we must ever observe this rule ; to sell more to strangers yearly than we consume of theirs in value . . . because that part of our stock which is not returned in us in wares must necessarily be brought home in treasure." [5]

The theory of the balance of trade was a distinct advance, but it created its own fresh problems.   First there was the difficulty of drawing up the balance ; though Mun was supremely confident of its possibility in an age of rudimentary statistics and bureaucracy, it is now agreed that " the difficulty of calculating the balance

---

[1] Cf. Bland : *Docts.*, pp. 674-5 ; and for the whole subject, W. A. Shaw, *History of the Currency*.

[2] Cf. Clark, *op. cit.*, p. 44.   [3] Cf. Bland : *Docts.*, pp. 676-7, and Chs. VII and VIII.

[4] Cf. Bland : *Docts.*, pp. 677-8.   [5] Mun : *op. cit.*, ch. 2, p. 5.

renders it useless as a criterion of employment." [1] In fact, the politicians did not attempt the task ; they used the theory as proved to encourage exports and discourage certain kinds of imports, and to guide them in making commercial treaties.[2] The second difficulty, which had to be faced, was the vexed question of imports. Imports were suspect, since they took money out of the country and competed with home manufactures. Yet, since commerce is exchange, we must buy from other countries in order to " vent our own commodities " ; yet we must not buy too much, else we become poorer (in some mysterious way), and we must be careful what kind of goods we buy. This line of argument led to the elaborate tariff tangle which Adam Smith found so easy to ridicule ; its objects, though not always its effects, were to confine imports to raw materials (excluding corn) and such other goods as English industry did not produce; its effects were most clearly seen in the Colonial tariff system included in the Navigation Acts. Its defects, both in plan and execution, are obvious ; Adam Smith showed that it gave the import and export merchants a monopoly at the expense of producers and consumers alike, and that it diverted capital from the home trade, which, though it did not figure in the mythical balance, was the real foundation of national prosperity. For it was the internal freedom of trade and industry, expanded by the Scottish Union of 1707, which was the cause of economic progress, and not " the wretched spirit of monopoly," by which

" the sneaking arts of underling tradesmen are thus erected into political maxims for the conduct of a great empire." [3]

Yet the merit of the theory was that it convinced English governments that their business was to foster trade instead of vain efforts to hoard bullion.

Another sign of the times was the collapse of the restrictions placed both by Statute and public opinion on trade in money.

[1] Cunningham, *Growth of English Industry*, etc., Vol. II, pp. 399-400 ; cf. Adam Smith, Bk. IV, ch. 3 (Everyman Edition, Vol. I, pp. 417-9). In 1696 an Inspector-General of Exports and Imports was appointed to draw up regular balances.

[2] *E.g.*, Portuguese Treaty (1703) and rejected French Treaty (1713).

[3] Adam Smith, I, p. 436 : for advantages of Union and free trade, cf. II, pp. 382 and 427.

The sin of " usury " became the respectable operation of " interest."
The old laws were not repealed ; Henry VIII. had begun the method
of fixing a maximum rate, and the Stuarts reduced it from 10 per
cent. at the beginning to 5 per cent. at the end of the period, following and not dictating the market rate.   Ecclesiastical prejudice
was still hostile until late in the century, but was powerless after
the fall of the Church Courts in 1641 ; and whereas Anglican sentiment remained conservative, the Puritans shook off the restrictions
of Calvin and their early teachers and developed what Mr. Tawney
calls " the religion of trade." [1]   The " godly discipline " of Baxter
gave place to the " economic individualism " which arose when
Puritans treated their business careers as a " calling " from God,
under the guidance of Dr. Nicholas Barbon, company promoter
and son of Praise-God Barebones.[2]   With Anglicanism muzzled
and Puritanism converted, the way was clear for the free and
beneficent activities of capitalism.

II. The Chief Sources of Wealth : Land : Cloth : Foreign Trade : Colonies

(a) *Land.*—In the seventeenth century England possessed two
great industries only : agriculture and cloth.   Of these two, cloth
was the better organised and made the greater progress during the
century ; but land was by far the larger interest in either economic or
political strength.   The two were connected by their common interest
in wool, which made them economic rivals, as sellers and buyers ;
but though the grazier might complain of the clothier's prices,
grazing land rose in value from the increased demand for cloth.
However, the most marked improvement in agriculture was in
tillage, or " husbandry " as the Tudor Statutes preferred to call it ;
the progress of enclosed farming, of drainage, and of the science
of rotation of crops made a beginning for the " Agricultural
Revolution " of the next century—the era of scientific and capitalist

---

[1] Cf. Tawney, *Religion and the Rise of Capitalism*, ch. 4 ; he describes the process
as " the transition from the anabaptist to the company promoter " (p. 248)

[2] Tawney, *op. cit.*, p. 247 ; cf. also p. 244, Richard Steele, *The Tradesman's Calling.*

farming. To this movement the seventeenth century made one vital contribution ; in its course land regained the political power which it had lost with the collapse of feudal government, and the landlords gave England what Disraeli called a " territorial constitution." [1] Once they were freed from the rebukes and fines of a Privy Council which refused to make a proper discrimination between rich and poor (except to fine the rich more heavily), they began to consolidate their ascendancy in both local and central government. As Sir Charles Firth has shown, their influence was often decisive in the counties during the Civil War, and Harrington's doctrine of the balance of land and power was proved by the " men of estates " who filled the Cavalier Parliament.[2] The Restoration brought an end to restrictions on enclosures and the internal corn trade, and it began the age of " strict settlements " tying up large estates. The Revolution completed their triumph ; the Corn Law of 1689 gave them an export bounty for their corn, besides maintaining high import duties on foreign corn, while in 1710 their control of Parliament was revealed by the Statute imposing a high landed qualification on all Members of Parliament, burgesses as well as knights of the shire. Meanwhile, their control of agricultural labour was absolute ; the restored Privy Council left the regulation of prices and wages to the employers as Justices of the Peace, and Parliament in 1662 passed the iniquitous Act of Settlement, which virtually bound the labourer to the soil by giving the Justices power to refuse admittance into any parish to any labourer who could not give security against parish relief.[3] The landlord had passed from the Purgatory of Star Chamber into an economic Paradise.

[1] Disraeli, defending the Corn Laws in 1846, still argued that Parliament should give " preponderance " to agriculture over other industries. Bland : *Docts.*, pp. 709-11.

[2] Cf. Chs. III (p. 69) and V (p. 114).

[3] Cf. Bland : *Docts.*, pp. 647-9, and Adam Smith, I, p. 128 : " There is scarce a poor man in England of forty years of age, I will venture to say, who has not in some part of his life felt himself most cruelly oppressed by this ill-contrived law of settlements." Tawney notes after 1660 a change of public opinion towards poverty, and ascribes it partly to the Puritan belief that it was the result of sin (*Religion and the Rise of Capitalism*, p. 267) ; cf. also Defoe's pamphlet, " Giving Alms No Charity " (extracts in Bland : *Docts.*, pp. 649-650—" There is a general taint of slothfulness upon our poor.").

Given these advantages, it is perhaps surprising that there was not more progress made. The chief improvement was in the substitution of enclosed for common fields. There had been in Tudor times a fierce outcry, supported by the Monarchy, against enclosure, mainly because the landlords, in converting arable land into pasture for sheep, pulled down houses, depopulated the countryside, turned contented peasants into rebellious vagrants, and threatened the national supply of corn and men. The Tudors attacked enclosures as dangerous to " husbandry," and their policy was summed up in the Preamble to the Act of 1597-8 " for the Maintenance of Husbandry and Tillage " :

" Whereas the strength and flourishing estate of this kingdom hath been always and is greatly upheld and advanced by the maintenance of the plough and tillage, being the occasion of the increase and multiplying of people both for service in the wars and in times of peace, being also a principal means that people are set on work . . . ; and whereas by the same means . . . the greater part of the subjects are preserved from extreme poverty in a competent estate of maintenance and means to live, and the wealth of the nation is kept dispersed and distributed in many hands, where it is more ready to answer all necessary charges for the service of the realm ; and whereas also the said husbandry and tillage is a cause that the realm doth more stand upon itself, without depending upon foreign countries. . . ." [1]

These can be taken as the aims of the Stuarts also, though they had to face a different aspect of the problem. By the end of the sixteenth century the glut of wool and the decline in corn output made tillage as profitable as pasture. Henceforward, most enclosure was for purposes of tillage ; that is to say, the enclosure movement was no longer hostile to agriculture, but a necessary step in its progress. The economic superiority of enclosed fields over open fields was undoubted ; the farmer whose land was scattered in strips among those of his neighbours was bound to customary arrangements with no possibility of experiment or initiative, and good land was infected by bad cultivation of adjoining strips ;

---

[1] Bland : *Docts.*, pp. 268-270 ; for the whole problem, cf. Tawney, *The Agrarian Problem in the Sixteenth Century.* The Statute of Artificers (1563) was also designed to secure a regular supply of labour for the land.

enclosure halved his labour and gave him freedom and protection.[1] "Depopulation" was no longer the issue, since labourers were needed in the enclosed fields; what moved Charles I. and Laud to harry the enclosers was a mixture of fiscal motives and a genuine desire to preserve a rural middle class. They regarded the over-mighty landlord and the dependent labourer as social diseases, and their ideal was "to keep the plough in the hand of the owners and not mere hirelings."[2] Yet, despite a series of Commissions (1632, 1635, 1636) and heavy fines, their activities only afford evidence of the persistence of enclosure with the connivance of the landowning Justices of the Peace; and after 1641 there was nothing to check the movement except the disturbances of the Civil Wars. In 1649 the Levellers were taught by Cromwell that the Puritan victory meant freedom to enclose, not freedom of the commons; the Diggers at St. George's Hill, Surrey, who threw down the sacred fences of private property, were dispersed by armed force, and the restrictive proposals of Leicester City Council (in 1649) and of Major-General Whalley (in 1656) were both rejected by the reigning Parliament. In fact, the dispossession of conservative Cavalier magnates and the consequent outbreak of speculation in land by officers and merchants gave a fillip to the commercialisation of agriculture. The Law lent its aid, as is proved by the growing number of Chancery decrees ratifying enclosures; in the reign of Anne Parliament began to sanction enclosure by private Acts.[3]

Up to the end of the sixteenth century the movement had affected chiefly the Midlands and the South-West, and a conservative estimate has put the area enclosed at 500,000 acres;[4] in Stuart times

[1] The arguments of Thomas Tusser, in *Five Hundred Points of Good Husbandry* (1523), are applicable to the whole period 1500-1800:

> "More profit is quieter found,
> Where pastures in several be,
> Of one silly acre of ground
> Than champion maketh of three.
> Again what a joy is it known
> When men may be bold of their own.'

("Champion" was a term for open-field farming.)

[2] Harrington, Introduction to *Oceana*.

[3] Cf. Gonner, *Common Land and Enclosure*, pp. 54-6 and 181-3.

[4] Gay, *Quarterly Journal of Economics*, Vol. XVII.

it continued in these districts (provoking serious riots in the North Midlands in 1607), and spread to the Eastern counties, where a beginning was made in the draining of marsh and fen, and to the North, in Durham and Yorkshire.[1]   There is no body of statistics available for the seventeenth as for the sixteenth and eighteenth centuries, but it is clear, first, that a large area was enclosed, and secondly, that the greater part of cultivable land was not enclosed before the middle of the next century.   The movement had two economic effects—increased production of corn and the introduction of new crops.   A growing population increased the demand for corn : enclosure supplied the need : and further stimulus was given by the disappearance in 1641 of the Council restrictions on internal trade and by the protective tariffs imposed after 1660.[2] But enclosure was also a necessary preliminary to scientific farming by rotation of crops ; for the old system confined farming to the staple heavy crops, which exhausted the soil unless it lay fallow at frequent intervals.   On enclosed land variety was possible ; light crops could alternate with heavy, and the soil could rest without being entirely unproductive.   Progress was slow before the eighteenth century, but clover and turnips were introduced into the fields, and land which had hitherto been regarded as useless was drained and cultivated.   The drainage schemes of Charles I. and the Dutch engineer Vermuyden in Hatfield Chase (Yorkshire), Lincolnshire and the Great Level around Ely were the most ambitious attempts at improvement ; but politics, lack of capital, and the opposition of the fenmen impeded progress.[3]   Land in the seventeenth century gained one condition of progress—freedom of internal production and trade ; it was left for the next century to provide the second condition—the application of capital on a large scale.

(*b*) *Cloth*.—" Our clothing," wrote Mun, " is the greatest wealth and best employment of the poor of this Kingdome," but he deplored,

[1] Gonner, *op. cit.*, pp. 179-181 ; Leonard, *R.H.S.T.*, New Series, Vol. XIX ; for the 1607 riots, cf. Gay, *R.H.S.T.*, New Series, Vol. XVIII.

[2] For regulation by Council, cf. Leonard, *History of Poor Relief*, and Bland, *Docts.*, pp. 383, 390, 391.

[3] For Cromwell's support of the commoners against the Earl of Bedford, cf. Firth, *Cromwell*, pp. 32-4.

on grounds of national defence, that the nation should "trust so wholly
to the making of cloth" to the neglect of tillage and fishing.[1]   It
was a highly organised national industry, supported by capital
and State encouragement, which during the century freed itself
from gild and town restrictions ; it was the pioneer of the " domestic " or " factor " system, by which spinners and weavers in their
homes were supplied with wool or yarn by merchants who undertook the marketing of the cloth.   There was considerable variety
of organisation in different districts, but the two general features
of the industry were the scattered, unorganised craftsmen and
the dominance of the capitalist *entrepreneur*.   A State Paper of
1615 describes how the " breeders of wool," except a few " men
of great estate," were dependent on the clothiers both for marketing
wool and for borrowing money to buy sheep, and how the clothiers
controlled both production and sale.   There was the " rich clothier
that buyeth his wool of the grower in the wool countries . . .
and in the winter time hath it spun by his own spinsters and
woven by his own weavers and fulled by his own tuckers, and
all at the lowest rate of wages " ; then the " meaner clothier "
that " borrows the most part of it at the market, and sets many
poor on work " ; then the clothiers with small capital, who " buy
but little or no wool, but do weekly buy their yarn in the markets,
and presently make it into cloth and sell it for ready money " ; then
the " thousands of poor people " engaged in the " new drapery."[2]
This survey brings out the contrast between the organised control
of the merchant clothier and the unorganised dependence of most
of the wool growers and wool workers ; for even those who did
not work for wages were at the mercy of the " wool chapman " for
supplies, credit and profits.   The degree of dependence varied with
districts, being greater in the West and lesser in the North ; for
enclosure in the West deprived the peasant of land and common
rights which had enabled him to exist without money from spinning
and weaving, while until the great enclosing wave of the late
eighteenth century the Northern smallholding craftsmen preserved
a precarious independence.   Defoe in 1724 gave almost an idyllic
picture of the " domestic system " in the West Riding which

[1] Mun, *op. cit.*, p. 73.   [2] Bland : *Docts.*, pp. 354-5.

would apply equally to the seventeenth as to the eighteenth century :

" Though we met few people without doors, yet within we saw the houses full of lusty fellows, some at the dye-vat, some at the loom, others dressing the cloths ; the women and children carding or spinning ; all employed from the youngest to the oldest ; scarce anything above four years old, but its hands were sufficient for its own support.   Nor a beggar to be seen, nor an idle person, except here and there in an almshouse. . . .   The people in general live long ; they enjoy a good air ; and under such circumstances hard labour is naturally attended with the blessing of health, if not riches." [1]

Against this must be set the conclusions of modern experience : that unregulated child labour always leads to grave abuse, and that the worst " sweated " industries are not factory, but domestic industries.   Further, the craftsmen lost during the century the protection of Gild and State.   The workers in the " new drapery " had not the benefit of gild incorporation, since the Judges interpreted the Statute of Apprentices as inapplicable to new trades ; the old gilds fell under the control of the rich merchants and manufacturers ; and the fall of Stuart despotism in 1641 meant the disappearance of the State regulation of employment, wages and prices, which the Privy Council had enforced through reluctant Justices of the Peace on resentful employers.[2]

Nevertheless, this freeing of capital from old restraints was one of the two important causes of the progress of the industry.   And not only was internal freedom secured, but the export trade was also freed from the old monopoly of the Royal Chartered Companies.   There was one important restriction from 1660 to 1825 —on the export of raw wool, which had been the chief medieval export ; but with the growth of a native cloth industry wool had to be kept in the country, both to give the English clothier a closed market and to cripple foreign clothiers in their supplies.   The medieval Kings had given control of the export trade in wool and cloth to two companies of merchants incorporated by Royal

---

[1] Bland : *Docts.*, p. 483 (from *A Tour through Great Britain*) ; cf. also Defoe's account of the organisation of the industry, *op. cit.*, pp. 483-7.

[2] Cf. E. M. Leonard, *op. cit.*, and Bland : *Docts.*, pp. 342, 345, 351, 356, 357.

Charter—the Merchant Staplers for wool and the Merchant Venturers for cloth. These were " regulated " companies, as distinct from the later joint-stock companies ; that is to say, there was no common stock, but each merchant traded with his own capital and ship, subject to company regulations fixing depots of trade, profits and amount of cargo. In origin and intention the Companies were not exclusive, since any merchant could join on payment of the admission fees ; but during the sixteenth century, the Venturers in particular had established a virtual monopoly by raising the fee and attacking provincial companies such as the Venturers of Newcastle, Bristol and Exeter. In 1604 the Venturers were at the peak of their power ; they had obtained the revocation of the privileges of their foreign rivals, the German Hansa, they had the controlling interest in the declining Staplers, and they had the support of the Crown. But the Commons in that year extended their attack on monopoly from internal to foreign trade, and passed a Bill (later dropped) " for the enlargement of trade " :

" It is against the natural right and liberty of the subjects of England to restrain it into the hands of some few . . . for . . . the Governors of these Companies, by their monopolising orders, have so handled the matter, as that the mass of the whole trade of all the realm is in the hands of some two hundred persons at the most." [1]

The pressure of opinion led the State to fix maximum admission fees and later to reduce them ; so that the monopoly passed away and, while the Companies flourished, the trade was " enlarged." [2]

The other cause of progress was advance in cloth manufacture. Until the end of the sixteenth century the industry was mainly confined to coarse cloth, and the chief export was " white " or half-finished cloth which was dyed and made up in the Netherlands. Then the persecution of Philip II. drove many skilled clothworkers to England, and the " new drapery " began in Norwich, Colchester, and the towns of the South and East coasts. England began to produce a variety of fine cloths, and James I. enthusiastically supported the new development. His aid was in fact ill-judged and premature ; in 1614 he revoked the privileges of the Venturers,

---

[1] Bland : *Docts.*, p. 444 ; the whole document is most illuminating (pp. 443-453).
[2] Cf. Cunningham, *op. cit.*, II, pp. 223-234.

forbade the export of "whites," and attempted to divert the whole cloth industry into making finished cloth under the direction of a Chartered Company floated by Alderman Cockayne of London.[1] But the project lacked capital, organisation, and a sufficient supply of skilled workmen; the Dutch retaliated by refusing to take English finished cloth, and the whole industry came to a standstill for lack of markets and productive power.[2] The scheme was dropped, the Venturers were restored, and the industry was left to develop by more gradual and natural methods. The State still protected it in several ways: by prohibiting the export of wool, by heavy duties on the import of foreign cloths, by suppressing woollen manufactures in Ireland and the Colonies, and even by ordering that everyone must be buried in woollen shrouds (1680); but the chief stimulus came from the freeing of capital from State and Gild bonds both in production and marketing.[3]

(c) *Foreign Trade.*—Before the Industrial Revolution, however, the main sphere of capital, other than that sunk in land, was foreign trade; and it was in the seventeenth century that England challenged and succeeded the Dutch as the carriers of the world. Foreign trade appealed to the instincts of adventure and gain; it was fostered by the State as providing revenues for government, and ships and sailors for defence; it brought treasure into the country, and stimulated employment at home; by the " balance of trade " theory it was the sole source of national prosperity. The approved method of conducting it was by chartered companies; Bacon wrote:

" I did ever think that trading in companies is most agreeable to the English nature, which wanteth that same general vein of a Republic which runneth in the Dutch and serveth them instead of a company." [4]

The Tudor age saw the foundation of the regulated companies— besides the cloth companies there were the Eastland and Levant

---

[1] Cf. Bland : *Docts.*, pp. 454-460, and Unwin, *Industrial Organisation in the Six-teenth and Seventeenth Centuries*, ch. 7.

[2] Cf. Bland : *Docts.*, pp. 460-1, for desperate remedies proposed by Sir Julius Caesar, on the principle that " ' *Salus reipublicae suprema lex est,*' *which is a sufficient answer to all cavillers and peevish lawyers.*"

[3] Cf. Unwin, *Industrial Organisation*, etc., pp. 194-5.

[4] This reference is taken from old lecture notes and I cannot now trace it in Bacon's *Works*; I give it with reserve as a penetrating observation.

companies ; the Stuart age was the great period of the joint-stock companies, the East India, Royal African and Hudson Bay companies.[1] The new form of organisation was necessitated by the expansion of markets and the consequent increase of distances and risks. It was no longer possible for traders to venture all their limited capital in ships that were away for years and might never return ; capital must be increased and the risks must be divided. Therefore non-traders must be invited to invest a part of their wealth in cargoes that brought high profit as compensation for risk and slow returns ; the functions of capitalist and trader were specialised. The distinctive features of the new companies were a " common stock " divided into shares : a personnel of shareholders who lent the money, of governors who appointed the agents, controlled policy and apportioned the dividends, and of servants who did the work of trade and navigation : and a regional monopoly protected by Royal Charter.[2] Organisation evolved gradually ; the East India Company at first was " floated " for a single voyage (1600), at the end of which the capital with profits was returned to the lenders, and it was not until 1657 that a permanent capital was organised with transferable shares. But the monopoly was there from the first, despite the growth of anti-monopolist feeling, and all the attacks of the " interlopers " failed in the end to prevent exclusive trade in India and Northern Canada.

After a series of failures, the African trade in ivory, gold and above all, slaves was handed over by Charles II. in 1672 to the sole exploitation of the Royal African Company, under the direct patronage of James of York ; but though the trade flourished, so did interlopers, and the monopoly fell, soon after its patron, in 1698. The Hudson Bay Company, founded in 1670, again with Royal patronage—its first governors were Prince Rupert and James of York—opened up a profitable and serviceable trade in importing furs and naval stores, and was used as a political weapon against the

---

[1] " In passing from the sixteenth to the seventeenth century, we pass from an age of great men and little Companies to an age of little men and great Companies " (Lucas, Vol. V, Part IV, p. 45).

[2] The differences between the new and old companies may be summarised thus : increased capital, stricter monopoly, specialisation of function, common trading and policy, wider markets.

French; but its great days came after the Treaty of Utrecht. Attention in a short survey, therefore, must be confined to the East India Company and the American plantation companies; though we must remember the foundation in 1711 of the ill-omened South Sea Company, and the " Assiento " clause of Utrecht which gave it a fatal stimulus.

The East India Company grew from a simple trading company into a political power that dominated India and influenced both Imperial and domestic politics; the prominence of the tea duty on the eve of the American revolt makes it plausible to argue that the Company gave us India only to lose America for us. The Restoration was the turning-point in its fortunes and ambitions. Before 1660 it had tried with varying success to open trade in Persia, China and the Far East in general; it even experimented with a north-west passage to China, in order to develop an export trade of English cloth in temperate climates; but after 1660 it confined its energies to India, with factories at Surat, Madras, Calcutta and Bombay.[1] Its early career was hampered by lack of permanent organisation, by interlopers and by lack of State support, for James I. and Charles I. did little to protect it from the Dutch and left unavenged the murder of its traders at Amboyna in 1623; Charles even supported a rival company, and the Commonwealth threw open the trade until 1657. Charles II, however, took up their quarrels; he not only revived the Navigation Act against the Dutch carrying trade, but he used the disputes of the English and Dutch East India Companies to force the Second Dutch War. In 1663 the free export of bullion benefited them directly, since they could not use English exports in tropical trade; and the new theories of Mun justified them against the old charge that by exporting bullion they impoverished the country. Mun argued that " remote trades " such as the Indian were by far the most profitable to the nation in creating a favourable balance of trade; for

" if we send one hundred thousand pounds into the East-Indies to buy pepper there, and bring it hither, and from hence sent it for Italy or Turkey, it must yield at least seven hundred thousand

[1] Bombay was the most valuable part of the dowry of Katherine of Portugal, the wife of Charles II.

pounds in those places . . . all which . . . the King and the Kingdom gets." [1]

The close alliance of the Company, directed by Sir Josiah Child,
with the Court brought upon it the storms of the Revolution, but
wealth and " lobbying " triumphed in the end. The interlopers,
who had been handled so roughly with Royal permission, secured
in 1694 a resolution of the Commons :

" That all subjects of England have equal right to trade to the
East Indies unless prohibited by Act of Parliament." [2]

But party intrigues soon converted the movement for free trade
into the struggle of rival monopolist groups, Whig and Tory,
and in 1708 the two Companies amalgamated and the monopoly
was restored in return for a loan to the government. There were
two important results of the quarrel ; Parliament took from the
Crown the power of granting Charters and making terms, and the
Company became a permanent creditor of the nation with all the
consequent influence on politics. Henceforward politics rather
than trade became the chief interest of the directors ; profits
dwindled while territories, debts and abuses increased, until the
Company became an easy prey to the devastating criticisms of
Adam Smith, who denounced them for preferring " the little and
transitory profit of the monopolist to the great and permanent
revenue of the sovereign." [3] However they supplied the growing
demand for spices, tea, coffee and fine cloth, and though they did
little by direct export to encourage English manufactures, they were
protected for their wealth, shipping and favourable influence on the
balance of trade.

(*d*) *Colonies.*—The fourth great source of wealth came from the
colonies and plantations. Their political growth and organisation has
already been described ; it remains to show what profit England drew
from them and how they were fitted into the national economic

---

[1] Mun, *op. cit.*, ch. 4, pp. 15-16.

[2] Cunningham, II, p. 268. For the treatment of interlopers, cf. Bland : *Docts.*,
p. 675.

[3] Adam Smith, II, p. 134 ; cf. his genera conclusion : " The government of an
exclusive company of merchants is perhaps the worst of all governments for any
country whatsoever " (II, 68).

system. We must be careful not to ante-date economic Imperialism ; the State did little for years but grant a Charter and remit a part or all of the Customs as an encouragement to trade.   In fact throughout the century there ran a debate whether colonies were useful or harmful to the nation ; it was urged against them that they, and New England in particular, competed with English farmers and manufacturers and that they all drained an under-populated country of man power.   Plantations fell under the same suspicion as enclosures ; immigration, not emigration, was the traditional policy. However, emigration was tolerated for a variety of reasons.   The Elizabethan motives were the desire for mines which would provide bullion independently of foreign supplies, the needs of depots and harbours for fishing and the Eastern trade, the fostering of shipping and the hate of Spain.[1]   The Stuarts added reasons of internal policy ; population was to them a matter of quality as well as of quantity, and they were prepared to expedite the emigration of undesirables.   This use of the colonies as a dumping-ground and as a " safety-valve for Dissent " [2] explains two facts : why they were left in their infancy to their own efforts, and why jealous restrictions were put upon them when they began to thrive.

At first development was in the hands of companies or proprietors who invested capital in the hope of large, if slow returns ; but except in the West Indies, climate, soil and native opposition reduced the colonists' rewards to a bare living for many years. Even the rapid growth of tobacco planting in Virginia did not save the Virginia Company of 1606 from bankruptcy in 1632 after sinking £200,000 in capital ; [3] the Bermuda Company expired in 1684 ; the London merchants who financed the voyage of the *Mayflower* cut their losses in 1627 and left the Plymouth Colony to develop as a community for righteous living rather than as a factory for commercial profit ; the Massachusetts Bay Company in its first year (1629) transferred its headquarters from London to New England and evolved rapidly from a commercial joint-stock company into a political oligarchy, though the Company forms

[1] Cf. Bland : *Docts.*, pp. 434-8, for Gilbert's views on Colonies.

[2] Egerton, *Short History of Colonial Policy*, p. 47.

[3] *Cambridge History of British Empire*, I, p. 151.

were retained until 1684.   As with the companies, so was it with
the proprietors with the exception of Penn and the Baltimores of
Maryland, who combined the arts of business and diplomacy;
private exploitation was abandoned as ruinous.

The period of national, as distinct from private, exploitation
begins with the victorious commonwealth ; for the Rump claimed
for Parliament all the Imperial authority of the Crown.[1]   There
had been earlier shipping regulations for the colonial trade (in 1624
and 1646), but in 1649 the merchants were for the first time able
to obtain a systematic commercial policy from the State.   From
1650, while other policies and governments changed, these two
aims were consistently followed : to develop English and colonial
shipping at the expense of the Dutch, and to regulate colonial trade
and manufacture for the exclusive benefit of England.   The colonies
were treated as an integral part of the national economic organisation ; the first ' Empire Crusade ' had begun.

Both these aims, " defence " and " opulence " in Adam Smith's
words, were embodied in the Navigation Code.[2]   The earlier Acts
(1650 and 1651) dealt with shipping alone, but the very first proclaimed the absolute power of Parliament over colonial trade and
government.[3]   They confined to English, Irish or colonial ships
all trade except that between Europe and the Empire ; foreign goods
could only be imported in English ships or in ships of the countries
(being European) which produced them.   At the Restoration,
which London did so much to bring about, the London merchants
found the Privy Council of Charles II. as sympathetic as the Council
of the Rump and Protector ;   Clarendon and Shaftesbury continued
the policy of supervision by committees and encouragement by
Statute.   The Act of 1660 did little more for shipping than
strengthen in detail the Act of 1651 ; for instance, an English ship
was defined as one owned by English subjects and manned by a crew
of which three-quarters were English subjects.[4]   In 1662 an Act laid

[1] Cf. McIlwaine, *The American Revolution*, and Ch. XI.

[2] Cf. *Camb. Hist. Brit. Emp.*, I, chs. 7 and 9.

[3] Cf. *Camb. Hist. Brit. Emp.*, I, pp. 215-6, and Gardiner : *Docts.*, pp. 468-71 (1651).

[4] One important change was the exclusion of Scotland from shipping protection.
Cf. Bland : *Docts.*, p. 670.

down that ships must be English-built as well as English-owned ; finally after thirty years of feeble enforcement and persistent evasion the comprehensive Act of 1696 imposed heavy penalties on colonial Governors for negligence and on shippers for false certificates, and instituted a complete system of registry for ships.[1] The shipping Code was now complete, and effective enforcement was for the first time possible. It is difficult to estimate its effect on English sea-power ; the number of Acts, Proclamations and complaints testify to general evasion, while the undoubted growth of the mercantile marine may have been mainly due to other causes, such as the exhaustion of the Dutch and the natural growth of English wealth. Yet Adam Smith, no lover of the system, admitted that :

" As defence is of much more importance than opulence, the Act of Navigation is perhaps the wisest of all the commercial regulations of England." [2]

However, from 1660 the Code was also designed, by regulations of increasing and bewildering complexity, to increase wealth by monopoly ; it was restrictive as well as protective for the colonies. The policy is best outlined in the Preamble of the Act of 1663 : to keep the Colonies in " firmer dependence," to make them beneficial to English shipping and manufactures, to give England a monopoly of the colonial products she needed, and to make her a " staple " or depot for exchange between the colonies and Europe.[3] The chief Acts were those of 1660, 1663, 1671, 1673 and 1696. The methods may be summarised as follows : certain " enumerated " colonial exports, such as sugar, tobacco, cotton-wool, dye-woods, could only be imported to England, and had to pay English duties even when sent to other Colonies ; other exports could not be imported direct to Europe north of Spain (thus excluding Scotland and Ireland, France and Holland), while the rest could be exported freely save for shipping restrictions ; some exports, such as naval stores, were encouraged by bounties,[4] while others, like wool, cloth, and corn, were barred from England by prohibition or high duties ;

[1] Summary in *Camb. Hist. Brit. Emp.*, I, pp. 285-8.   [2] Adam Smith, I, p. 408.
[3] *Camb. Hist. Brit. Emp.*, I, p. 275.
[4] Bounties were sums paid by the State to exporters to assure them profit and to reduce the selling price abroad.

nearly all European goods had to be shipped to English ports and
pay English duties before reaching the Colonies ; and to enforce
this cumbrous system a network of Courts, Customs, bonds and
penalties was set up. Adam Smith exploded it as a means to
wealth and the American Revolution discredited it as a political
expedient. However, the system had a century of active life, in
spite of periods of lax enforcement and Colonial evasion, because
it provided a measure of protection. But when their shipping
was established and the Dutch and French dangers removed, the
Colonies did not need protection and resented exploitation ; and
in 1764 the tightening of restriction came into fatal collision with
a rapidly expanding trade. Nevertheless the rapid growth of
Colonial wealth and population was a decisive factor in English
prosperity, whether monopoly hindered or not.

III. The National Economic System

The methods adopted by the European States for the regulation
of trade and industry between the sixteenth and eighteenth centuries
are often described by the general term of " Mercantilism." It
is convenient thus to distinguish the age of national restrictions
from the earlier age of municipal commerce and the nineteenth
century of free trade ; but it is dangerous to read into the mass of
regulations any consistent principles. There is no one set of
mercantilist principles ; it is unwise to define Mercantilism more
closely than as the economic aspect of nationalism. There was one
motive common to most States—jealousy of other States ; the
result was that wealth was judged by comparative, not absolute
standards. The great aim was economic self-sufficiency, particularly in food, money, raw materials and necessary manufactures ;
but there was always an admixture of private motives, such as the
King's need of revenue and the merchants' desire for monopoly.
The professed object of regulation was the subordination of private
gain to common good, but it often resulted in the corruption of the
State by strong private interests ; this was equally true of Royal
grants to courtiers and Parliamentary grants to companies. Adam
Smith pointed out that the effect was often contrary to the design ;

that what was meant to protect corn-growers and manufacturers ended in benefiting corn-factors and merchants at the producers' expense.[1]   The system proved too complex for its administrators, too ambitious for its purpose (regulations were altered and suspended with confusing frequency), and too tempting for human frailty ; it was a mass of inconsistencies rather than of principles. The East India Company, for instance, was licensed to export bullion when its export was forbidden, and it was allowed to import luxuries and foreign cloth when fashionable theory denounced all save necessary imports and in particular imports which competed with English manufactures.

Moreover there were two mercantilist systems in England, divided by the turn of the century.   James I. and Charles I. left foreign trade to haphazard experiments with but occasional interventions such as the disastrous scheme of 1614 ; but they continued with renewed vigour the Tudor regulation of internal trade in the interests of the consumer.   Production was subordinated to the needs of a steady, cheap supply of good quality, and the accumulation of capital was discouraged in order to maintain a wide distribution of wealth.   They inherited the spirit as well as the machinery of the gilds ;   "grinding the faces of the poor " was to them a criminal offence cognisable in Star Chamber.[2]   Their paternal socialism is shown by a flood of Privy Council instructions to Justices of the Peace, as for example :

" We do hereby require you to call before you such clothiers as you shall think fitting, and to deal effectually with them for the employment of such weavers, spinners and other persons as are now out of work . . . this being the rule by which both the wool-grower, the clothier and merchant must be governed, that whosoever had a part of the gain in profitable times . . . must now in the decay of trade . . . bear a part of the public losses." [3]

A good test of an economic system is its treatment of its victims and surplus ; nothing illustrates better the contrast between Royal and Parliamentary economics than the change after 1641 in the administration of the Poor Laws.   Elizabeth's servants had by

[1] Adam Smith, Book IV, *passim.*
[2] Bland : *Docts.*, pp. 391-6, and Leonard, *op. cit.*
[3] Bland : *Docts.*, pp. 382-3.

hard work and experiment drawn up a comprehensive Code (1601) ;
the early Stuarts were alone in attempting to enforce it as a whole.
The Council of Charles I., particularly in the non-Parliamentary
years, grappled with unemployment from all angles.   It sought to
prevent it by regulating prices and supplies and by compelling
employers to retain their men even at a loss ; it sought to remedy
it by " setting the poor on work " with materials provided by the
Justices of the Peace and by punishing beggars and vagrants ; and
it ensured relief, not only to the aged and impotent, but to the able-
bodied who could find no work.   The Star Chamber had terrors
for lazy Justices and recalcitrant employers, but none for the poor
unless they were active Puritans.   Hence the collapse of the Prerogative involved the fall of the Poor Law Code in its preventive
and remedial aspects ; relief alone was left to the caprice or humanity
of the local Bench.   One significant addition was made ; the Act
of Settlement (1662), by restricting the movement of labourers,
protected parishes against possible burdens on their poor rates ; a
state not far from serfdom was made the condition of poor relief.[1]
Apart from a series of Settlement Laws, the only other government
remedy was the occasional transportation of vagrants to the
Colonies.[2]   The new rulers of England, being employers, rejected
the Royal doctrine of the responsibility of employers for poverty ;
under Puritan inspiration, they traced responsibility to the idleness
or sins of the labourers.[3]   The State therefore abandoned the attempt
to save men from the consequences of their own folly ; it left the
industrious poor to the employers and grudgingly maintained those
whom industry rejected.

Thus after 1649 the power of the State was turned to other ends
and spheres.   Production took the place of consumption as the
State's chief care ;[4]   the increase of wealth was studied more than

[1] For the Poor Law Act, cf. Bland : *Docts.*, pp. 380-1 ; for its administration, cf.
E. M. Leonard, *Early History of English Poor Relief* ; for Settlement Act, cf. Bland :
Docts., pp. 647-9.

[2] *Camb. Hist. Brit. Emp.*, I, p. 236, and *supra*, Ch. XI.

[3] Cf. Tawney, *op. cit.*, pp. 263-273 ; Bland : *Docts.*, p. 649.

[4] Cf. Adam Smith's criticism, II, pp. 155-6: " Consumption is the sole end and
purpose of all production. . . .   But in the mercantile system the interest of the
consumer is almost constantly sacrificed to that of the producer."

its uses and distribution; systematic regulation was applied to foreign, instead of internal trade. Contemptuous neglect gave the home trade its freedom; the reaction was so extreme that one economist could write:

" By what is consumed at home, one loseth only what another gets, and the nation in general is not at all the richer; but all foreign consumption is a clear and certain profit." [1]

The plan was to encourage agriculture, manufactures, and the export and carrying trades in one comprehensive system; but since London was the seat of government and finance together, the system was worked out under the direction of merchants rather than producers. When merchants became politicians, government became capitalised; and an aggressive economic policy brought over a hundred years of trade warfare—from the First Dutch War to the Treaty of Versailles (1783). The consumer, the taxpayer, the English and colonial producer paid for the upkeep of two myths, the balance of trade and the balance of power; hence the costs of war and bureaucracy must be set against the profits of monopoly. It was not a genuine Imperial policy, for the Empire was excluded from its full benefits; though the scope of regulation was extended from 1650, its parochial temper remained untouched. Yet, while the system produced the American Revolution, the wealth and energy which it vainly tried to discipline laid the foundations of a greater change. For good or ill, the seventeenth century created the capital, financial organisation and internal freedom which made possible the Industrial Revolution.

SUGGESTIONS FOR FURTHER READING

MUN, THOMAS: *England's Treasure in Foreign Trade.* (Blackwell)
SMITH, ADAM: *Wealth of Nations.* (Dent)
CLAPMAN, J. H.: *Concise Economic History of Britain to 1750.* (C.U.P., 1951)
LIPSON, E.: *Economic History of England,* Vols. II and III. (Black, 1961)
CLARK, G. N.: *The Wealth of England, 1495-1760.* (O.U.P., 1946)

[1] *Camb. Hist. Brit. Emp.,* I, p. 563.

318 *The English Revolution*

FISHER, F. J. (Ed.) : *Essays on the Economic and Social History of Tudor and Stuart England.* (C.U.P., 1961)

CARUS WILSON, E. N. (Ed.) : *Essays in Economic History.* (Arnold, 1955)

ERNLE, LORD : *English Farming Past and Present.* (Heinemann, 1961)

CAMPBELL, N. : *The English Yeoman under Elizabeth and the Early Stuarts.* (Yale, 1945).

TREVOR ROPER, H. R. : *The Gentry, 1540–1640.* (Supplement to the *E.H.R.*, 1953)

ZAGORIN, P. : ' The Social Interpretations of the English Revolution'. *Journal of Economic History*, xix, no. 3.

HABBAKKUK, H. J. : 'English Land Ownership, 1680–1740'. *E.H.R.*, x.

UNWIN, G. : *Industrial Organisation in the Sixteenth and Seventeenth Centuries.* (O.U.P., 1904)

HEATON, A. : *The Yorkshire Woollen and Worsted Industry.* (O.U.P., 1920)

NEF, J. U. : *The Rise of the British Coal Industry.* (Routledge, 1932)

COURT, W. H. B. : *The Rise of the Midland Industries, 1600–1838.* (O.U.P., 1938)

RAMSAY, G. D. : *English Overseas Trade during the Centuries of Emergence.* (Macmillan, 1957)

WILLAN, J. S. : *The English Coasting Trade, 1600–1750.* (Manchester U.P., 1938)

River Navigation in England, 1600–1750. (O.U.P., 1936)

JACKMAN, W. T. : *History of Transportation.* 2 Vols. (C.U.P., 1916)

SCOTT, W. R. : *The Constitution of English, Scottish and Irish Joint Stock Companies to 1720.* 3 Vols. (C.U.P., 1916)

SUPPLE, B. : *Commercial Crisis and Change in England, 1600–42.* (C.U.P., 1959)

RICHARDS, R. D. : *Early History of Banking in England.* (King, 1929)

CLAPHAM, J. H. : *The Bank of England.* 2 Vols. (C.U.P., 1944)

TAWNEY, R. H. : *Religion and the Rise of Capitalism.* (Murray, 1926)

WILSON, C. H. : *Mercantilism.* (Historical Association Pamphlet)

LEONARD, E. M. : *The Early History of Poor Relief.* (C.U.P., 1900)

XIII

ENGLISH POLITICAL THOUGHT IN THE
SEVENTEENTH CENTURY

THE seventeenth century was not only the most dramatic age in the history of English political action : it has also a strong claim to be considered the greatest age of English political thought. The age of Bacon, Milton, Hobbes, Halifax and Locke need not fear comparison with that of Ockham and Wycliffe, or that of Mill, Spencer, Bosanquet and T. H. Green. The English Revolution produced a rich crop of ideas, no less than of men ; for the men who made or opposed such vital changes in Church and State guided and justified their acts by complete systems of political principles. And though the men died and their work was often undone, their ideas remained to mould law and opinion in England, North America and France. They gave us our political habits, still more our dogmas and catchwords—the " Fundamentals " of toleration, the rights of property, the liberties of the subject, limited Monarchy, the rule of law, the tradition of compromise.

One preliminary warning is necessary for the student. The habit of thinking in centuries, or any other arbitrary unit of time, is dangerous for the historian because of its very convenience ; and it is nowhere so dangerous as in the history of ideas. Although a fair case can be made for treating the seventeenth century as a true historical unit in English political, constitutional and economic history,[1] there is no such unity in the civilisation of the century. In manners, language, ideas, there are in the century two ages, which might almost be described as medieval and modern ; and the cultural watershed between them is the Restoration, which restored

[1] The unit of time in which Parliament established constitutional supremacy, and the upper middle class established political and economic control.

little in politics and less in thought.   At the opening of the century, theories of government, as propounded by Hooker and James I., were founded on scholastic theology; at its close, in the days of Bolingbroke, Swift and Defoe, they had assumed the lay and ephemeral character of party programmes.   This change from Scriptural authority to reason, from Divine Right to contract, marks a complete revolution in thinking.   There was indeed continuity; Divine Right died hard, and in its final form—for it was an elastic doctrine—received a new impetus in 1660, while Locke ostentatiously based his views on those of Hooker.   Nevertheless, the effective basis of society was transferred from religion to secular utility.

We must begin with definition.   " Political thought " is a vague term, which includes the unending speculations of men about the nature, the end, and the proper conduct of organised society. According to Aristotle, it is the head and sum of all human wisdom ; what then can be left out ?   We are learning in the twentieth century that the study of politics cannot profitably be divorced from the study of economics ; certainly in the Mercantilist seventeenth they were closely bound together, and one influential writer, Harrington, had as his main thesis that balance of property determines balance of power.   Religion cannot be left out in the age of Laud, Cromwell, and Sancroft; Figgis declared that all the political theories of the century were theories of Divine Right.[1]   Then for the first half of the century law and lawyers dominated men's views on politics, with the result that the student of political thought finds himself entangled in the meshes of the Common Law.[2]   But since it is a hard fate to be condemned to read all the sermons and lawbooks of the age, it is best to begin with a few outstanding works on politics, provided that we remember that there were no watertight compartments between politics, religion and economics.[3]

---

[1] Cf. Figgis's *Divine Right of Kings*, p. 177.

[2] Cf. Sir W. Holdsworth's account of the rival theories of law in his *History of English Law*, Vol. VI.

[3] The first half of the century was in many respects the close of the English Middle Ages, and retained the medieval longing for unity expressed in Dante's phrase : " Totum humanum genus ordinatur ad unum."   The Tudor and early Stuart monarchs in practice, and Hooker in theory, saw in the State the director of all earthly activities, preparing its members for the next world as well as this.   From this

Some of the treatises can be read with pleasure ; Milton, Hobbes, and Halifax excelled in a great age of prose-writers.   Others are illuminating historical documents, written to justify the past ; even the most abstract in form, such as Hobbes' *Leviathan* or Locke's *Second Treatise*, are closely linked with and coloured by contemporary politics.   Others were historical forces ; the Divine Right of Kings and the natural rights of subjects inspired men to action as strongly as did concrete grievances.   Besides these claims to interest, most of the writers assert that their ideas have a permanent value and contain the secret of good government everywhere and for all time.   The student must consider this claim, for the modern world cannot afford to neglect any help in the solution of its problems.   He may be sceptical that the agrarian seventeenth century could offer any solution useful to the industrial twentieth century, but he will discover that its thinkers discussed many questions that still agitate the minds of men : Milton attacked the censorship, Mun and North debated free trade, Hobbes and Locke probed the rights of property.   Above all, the sovereignty of the State, the main battle-ground of modern political theorists, was first introduced to English thought in the seventeenth century.

The leading writers can be grouped, for all their variety, in rival schools of thought, though men like Hobbes and Halifax stood alone and aloof.   One of the first warnings that the student needs is that these divisions of thought often cut across party labels.   Royalists and Parliamentarians, Anglicans and Presbyterians had many beliefs in common—the necessity of Kingship, of a compulsory national Church, of government by men of property.   On the other hand, there were fundamental differences among Royalists and Puritans themselves.   James I. introduced the doctrine of Divine Hereditary Right, Hobbes would have none of it, and Filmer altered its basis to one of natural right ; some Puritans appealed to Scripture like their adversaries, some to utility, others to natural rights.   More-

comprehensive ideal sprang the perpetual interference with individuals and groups, intolerance, and the passion for reform ; it was the main impulse of political thinking. It was only the disillusionment of experience which drove men to separate politics from the rest of life, and to set limits to State action ; it was only after the Restoration had failed to restore harmony that men discovered the virtues of variety. Hooker's *Ecclesiastical Polity* was the epitaph of English unity ; cf. his great panegyric of Law (*Works*, ed. 1841, Vol. I, p. 285).

over, the ideas changed and fused at times ; though Divine and natural right seem logically opposed, as in the crisis of 1688, Figgis proved that natural right was but Divine Right disguised.[1]   It was a dogma, claiming like its rival absolute and eternal validity, which was based on the scholastic theory of the Law of Nature as a branch of the Law of God ; hence the real justification of natural rights was that they were sanctioned by God as effectively as claims based on Scripture.   Some fundamental divisions, however, can be traced throughout, and it is the purpose of this chapter to provide the clues.   It will deal first with theories of the State, and then with those of the individual or section within society : that is, with theories of government and theories of liberty.

In examining both sets of views, it is important to notice what the various writers drew from a common stock—the generally accepted principles of the age [2]—and what caused divergencies between them. Much of the difference can be explained by human temperament ; perhaps the truest distinction is that between the optimists and the pessimists.   This psychological antithesis often coincides with others ; it may be that it is their source.   The pessimists usually advocated absolute Monarchy, restrictions on individual freedom, the repression of privileged or non-conforming groups, the rule of tradition and the enforcement of a State religion ; the optimists distrusted little save a strong executive, were ready to experiment with representative government and religious toleration, and pre-ferred utility to tradition, mixed government to sovereignty, civil liberty to religious uniformity.[3]   Distrust of human nature was the inspiration of Divine Right and of Presbyterian theocracy alike, for the theologians regarded men as corrupt and liable to degenerate unless put under strict correction.   Hobbes, too, though he hated

[1] The converse also held, particularly in Filmer's case.   His main argument rested on the identity of the two ; cf. Figgis, *op. cit.*, p. 155 : " Filmer's theory of Divine Right was expressed in a syllogism :

What is natural to man exists by Divine Right.
Kingship is natural to man.
Therefore Kingship exists by Divine Right."

[2] Cf. Figgis, *op. cit.*, p. 221, on the universal notion of non-resistance to authority, and p. 245, on the universal respect for law and government.

[3] Hobbes, as is the way with men of genius, cuts across this classification ; though a pessimist he despised tradition, and founded his theory of sovereignty solely on grounds of utility (*Leviathan*, ch. 20).

theologians, had a profound belief in original sin and in the natural malevolence of mankind ; whereas those, like Hooker and Locke, who believed in the perfectibility and natural benevolence of man, were prepared to take risks and allow the individual opportunities for progress.

I. The Powers of the State

Englishmen are often accused by foreigners of a lack of intellectual curiosity, and they as often accept the criticism with complacency and even pride.   Political speculation played but a small part in our early history ; the names of Wycliffe and Sir Thomas More stand out in isolation.   At the beginning of the seventeenth century Hooker and Bacon devoted a little of their time and wisdom to politics ; but Bacon in his *Essays* and *Life of Henry VII.* was content to justify or at most to touch up the existing system, and Hooker was more concerned with the national Church than the State.   Serious political theory was introduced from Scotland by James I., and though it caused some irritation to the lawyers in the Commons, it made little impression for some years ; the *Trew Law of Free Monarchies* cannot be regarded as a best seller of the age. Even though the Arminian school of clergy who sought the protection of Charles I. developed a theory of despotism which the Royalist Judges tried to incorporate in the Common Law, it never took firm root, nor was it fully worked out ; the fight over the Prerogative was one of legal and historical precedents, not one of rival political theories.   It was only when war had shattered the traditional organisation of society that men began to ask fundamental questions about the nature and purpose of government ; Englishmen became political theorists because the urgent task of reconstruction after 1645 compelled them to adopt some general principles, old or new, to help them in that task.

The shocks of civil war and regicide set men debating about institutions and traditions that had been instinctively obeyed for centuries.   The immediate question was : Monarchy or Commonwealth ? but though England was a Republic in name for eleven years, it was not the great political issue of the century.   For the establishment of the Commonwealth by an armed minority was

not the result of a reasoned objection to Monarchy, but of a conviction, born of events, that the Stuart line was tainted ; hence no
other solution was possible unless or until a man fit to be King
appeared in the land.   The doctrinaire Republicans were the minority of a minority ; despite the support of Harrington, the admirer
of Venice, and Milton, the admirer of Republican Greece and Israel,
they were isolated in a nation which demanded a Constitution with
" somewhat monarchical " in it, whether Protector or King.   The
main body of political thought accepted Monarchy as the necessary
executive of the State ; differing limits were set to its powers, but
the main problems went deeper, to probe the functions of government as such, whatever form it might take.

Three fundamental questions were debated : the ORIGIN, the
FORM, and the LIMITS of the powers of the State.   Can the rulers
demand unquestioning obedience from their subjects, or are their
powers derived from the free consent of the people ?   Should the
powers of government be concentrated in the hands of a single
person or body of persons, or should they be divided between
independent persons or bodies of persons ?   Should any ruler or
rulers have unlimited powers over subjects, or are there any rights
or duties of men which the State cannot infringe or impede ?

The origin of government was ascribed either to Divine command or to human invention.   Those who upheld Divine sanction
for the powers of rulers taught that subjects had a duty of unconditional obedience; monarchy on earth was the pattern of monarchy
in Heaven.   Those who based government on human foundations
were divided on the question of obedience.   If authority was their
ideal, they proved the legitimacy of a strong Executive from history
or nature.   Bacon and Strafford appealed to Tudor history,
Charles I.'s lawyers to legal precedent, Filmer to the patriarchal
household, and Hobbes to the quarrelsome nature of man ; they
agreed that obedience, which was traditional, was imposed from
above and could not be questioned or withdrawn.   If, on the other
hand, liberty was the ideal, the argument was that the State had
been founded by the agreement of a free people, and that subjects
could not alienate their historic and natural right of choosing or
changing the rulers they had appointed for their own convenience :

such were the views of Selden, Lilburne, Milton, Harrington, Sidney and Locke. In general, the defenders of absolute Monarchy, with the doubtful exception of Hobbes, based government on command, either human or divine, while the advocates of representative government made contract and consent the only valid sources of political power.[1]

On the second question—the proper form of government—the believers in authority naturally insisted that government, to be effective must be unified : that " mixed Monarchy " or division of powers led direct to anarchy.   Hobbes asked : " For what is it to divide the power of a Common-wealth, but to dissolve it ; for powers divided mutually destroy each other." [2]   He and James I. declared without qualification that confusion and rebellion were certain unless all rights were derived from, and revocable by one supreme authority ; their fundamental doctrine was the necessity of sovereignty.[3]   A united and all-powerful Executive alone could free the State from the fatal medieval diseases of the overmighty subject, the unruly corporation and the interfering Papacy.   There is no doubt that the monarchists performed a national service in emphasising the function of the Monarchy as the nation's bulwark against sectional interests and foreign intervention ; such was the *raison d'être* of the Tudor Monarchy, and the dangers still existed in Stuart times.   James rightly said :

" He is but a titular king that reigneth only at another's discretion, and whose princely head the Pope hath power to bare of his royall crowne " [4] ;

---

[1] Hobbes ostentatiously based his absolutist system on a social contract in the hope of spiking the enemy's guns, but his trick had the further purpose of disguising the true basis of the system—force.

[2] *Leviathan*, ch. 29 (p. 251 of Clarendon Press reprint, 1909).

[3] " As . . . the king is overlord of the whole land, so is he master over every person that inhabiteth the same, having power over the life and death of every one of them : for although a just prince will not take the life of any of his subjects without a clear law, yet the same laws whereby he taketh them are made by himself or by his predecessors ; and so the power flows always from himself." (*True Law of Free Monarchies*, extract in Prothero, pp. 400-1).   " And because, if the essential rights of sovereignty . . . be taken away, the Common-wealth is thereby dissolved, and every man returneth into the condition and calamity of a war with every other man (which is the greatest evil that can happen in this life), it is the office of the Sovereign to maintain those rights entire. . . .   For he that deserteth the means, deserteth the ends." (*Leviathan*, ch. 30, p. 258.)

[4] Cf. Hearnshaw, *Social and Political Ideas of the Sixteenth and Seventeenth Centuries*, p. 127.

and Hobbes attacked with equal vigour the " ghostly power " of the " Kingdom of Darkness " and the " great number of corporations " :

" which are as it were many lesser Common-wealths in the bowels of a greater, like worms in the entrails of a natural man." [1]

But the opponents of absolutism saw its abuses greater than its uses, and held no man strong enough to resist the temptation of misusing such concentrated and arbitrary powers. Since they preferred liberty to slavery, they advocated division instead of unity of powers, limitation rather than efficiency of government. The chief motive of the constitutional struggle of the century was the hope of finding a fair division of powers between Crown and Parliament which could prevent " arbitrariness " in either. The constitutionalists, whether oligarchs or democrats, saw in the King, not a " mortal God " to be worshipped, but a public official to be respected or rebuked as his conduct warranted. " A king," said Selden, " is a thing men have made for their own sakes, for quietness' sake " ; [2] while Halifax wrote :

" If the people were designed to be the sole property of the supream Magistrate, sure God would have made them of a differing and subordinate species ; as he hath the beasts." [3]

Not only Kings were suspect ; the defenders of liberty smelt tyranny everywhere. Cromwell and Lilburne, who agreed on little else, both denounced the tyranny of the Long Parliament, and the whole democratic movement of the century aimed at a system of checks and balances, whereby the supremacy of the people and the freedom of the individual could be protected against the excesses of their officials and representatives.[4] Though the cumbrous apparatus of written constitutions and the devices of Ireton, Lambert and Harrington were discarded by later thinkers, Locke finally summed up the popular views in his *Treatises of Civil Government*, where he stated that the legislative and executive power should be in distinct hands " in all moderated monarchies and well-framed governments " :

[1] *Leviathan*, ch. 29, p. 257.   [2] Selden, *Table Talk*.
[3] *Works*, ed. Raleigh, p. 223.   [4] Cf. Gooch, *English Democratic Ideas*.

" because it may be too great a temptation to human frailty, apt to grasp at power, for the same persons who have the power of making laws to have also in their hands the power to execute them, whereby they may exempt themselves from obedience to the laws they make, and suit the law, both in its making and execution, to their own private advantage, and thereby come to have a distinct interest from the rest of the community, contrary to the end of society and government." [1]

It is obvious that this criticism applies as much to Puritan and Hanoverian Parliaments as to Stuart Kings ; hence the conclusion that no form of government (no " determinate body of persons," to use Austin's jargon) can be intrusted with supreme power, which belongs to the community alone, " but not as considered under any form of government." [2]

The widest difference, however, between the defenders of authority and of liberty arose on the third question—the proper scope of government. The former saw in the State a living force, greater and more worthy than the individuals it protected and directed ; it was at once the guardian and the sum total of the happiness of its citizens, and the King was its incarnate symbol. Their view of the State was organic, paternalist and collectivist. The Divine Right of Kings, from James I. to Filmer, had its main strength in the argument that the King was the father of his people ; Filmer wrote :

" All power on earth is either derived or usurped from the fatherly power, there being no other original to be found of any power whatsoever." [3]

The collectivist aspect was best put by Hobbes, in defining his Commonwealth, his *Leviathan or Mortal God*; it was " more than consent or concord," for it was " a real unity of them all in one and the same person," the Sovereign—

" One Person, of whose acts a great multitude, by mutual covenants one with another, have made themselves every one the author, to the end that he may use the strength and means of them all, as he shall think expedient, for their peace and common defence." [4]

[1] Locke, *Second Treatise*, pp. 189 and 190 (Everyman Edition).
[2] Locke, *op. cit.*, p. 193.   [3] Quoted by Locke, *First Treatise*, p. 52.
[4] *Leviathan*, ch. 17, pp. 131-2.

Such was the ideal of the all-powerful State, with unlimited powers for the public good concentrated in the hands of the Monarch ; it was the ideal of all impatient reformers—Bacon, Strafford, Laud and Cromwell. But it underestimated the pride and intelligence of English subjects as grossly as it overestimated the ability and immunity from temptation of the ruler, whether King or Protector ; and it fell before the views of those who distrusted the State, both as the guardian of the individual and as the complete expression of the community. The Revolution of 1688 enthroned the theory of the State as a necessary evil—not a soul but a piece of machinery. The community appointed a set of officials for certain restricted purposes such as police, defence, justice ; such officials needed constant and suspicious supervision, lest they should exceed their narrow scope and interfere in the general life of the community, as directed by its free and rational members.[1] The private individual, not the sovereign, was the basis of society, and government was his servant, to preserve his life and goods—his natural rights.   Locke wrote :

" The great and chief end of men uniting into commonwealths, and putting themselves under government, is the preservation of their property." [2]

Hence the power of government was limited, " in the utmost bounds of it," to the common good, and the right of interpreting what was the common good was reserved for the community alone : " The people shall be judge." [3]   Distrust of the State became a political axiom ; indeed, for the next century and a half, it became one of the strongest political instincts of Englishmen.   Hence the scope of the central government was greatly contracted ; religion, industry, literature, local government and property were all in more or less degrees safeguarded from its malign influence, and the age of toleration and *laissez faire* was inaugurated.   As a political force the State, the organised machinery of society, declined before the growth of Individualism on the one hand, and of the general idea of Society—the whole community above both State and individual—on the other.   This distinction between

[1] Cf. Locke's definition of " political power " in his *Second Treatise*, ch. 1.

[2] *Second Treatise*, ch. 9, p. 180 ; cf. also ch. 8.

[3] *Second Treatise*, ch. 19, p. 241 ; cf. also conclusion of Treatise, p. 242.

State and Society, which Locke first impressed on English politics, is perhaps the most valuable contribution of English seventeenth-century thought to modern political theory.[1]

II. THE INDIVIDUAL AND SOCIETY

Thus while the State was freed from its medieval foes of unruly corporations and external interventions, it was weakened in its claim on the obedience and affections of the individual. The individual was, in theory, the clear gainer from the theories of politics which prevailed in the battle of books. The seventeenth century saw the foundation of the modern doctrine of Individualism. This doctrine grew out of three closely connected roots—religious, economic, and political. The Puritan ordered his religious life, and in consequence his earthly conduct, in virtue of a close personal communion with God ; the thriving merchant was impatient of the obsolete restrictions of Canon Law and Royal Council on production, interest and exchange ; both distrusted the State which hampered and persecuted religious and economic progress.[2] They appealed from the social obligations thrust upon them to the two medieval patrons of Individualism, the English Common Law and the scholastic Law of Nature. The one protected their property and " birthright "—a term of infinite elasticity : the other sanctioned their resistance to mere positive laws. It seems strange that the Middle Ages, in which the ideas of community and unity were dominant, should have fathered this alien doctrine ; but reasons can be found, partly in the very nature of medieval thought, but more especially in the form in which that thought was transmitted to the post-Reformation world. The Common Law, since it was the weapon of the King against feudal immunities, protected the rights of the King's subject against the feudal group ; it defined his rights no less clearly than his duties to the King. So long as feudal duties were fulfilled—and after the thirteenth century this meant little more than the payment of feudal dues—

---

[1] Cf. *Second Treatise*, ch. 10 and ch. 19, p. 224 : " He that will, with any clearness, speak of the dissolution of government, ought in the first place to distinguish between the dissolution of the society and the dissolution of the government."

[2] Cf. Tawney, *Religion and the Rise of Capitalism*, ch. 4.

property and inheritance was secured ; so that when in 1660 feudal dues were abolished with their tenures, the rights of property remained without the duties, and the way was clear for Locke to place private property before and above the State, its master and not its servant. Similarly, the Law of Nature, while it was the link uniting God and men, Church and State, community and community, gave the individual rights and duties outside and above a man-made State ; for it was, first and foremost, the principle of reason implanted by God in the mind of each man, by which he might discern right and wrong in himself, in others, and in the State. Thus the precedents of Common Law, derived from history, defied the new science of government, and the principles of Natural Law, derived from God, overrode the positive laws of erring men.

The individualism of the century expressed itself in two magic phrases, the Original Compact and Fundamentals. "We are born free as we are born rational," wrote Locke ; "I think," said Colonel Rainborough, leader of the Agitators of 1647,

" it is clear that every man who is to live under a government ought first by his own consent to put himself under that government ; and I do think the poorest man in England is not strictly bound to that government that he hath not had a voice to put himself under." [1]

Two conclusions arise from these premises : government must be based on consent (either original, actual, or implied), and government must be strictly limited in scope, to avoid infringement of man's inalienable rights.

(*a*) *The Original Compact.*—To attain and justify their first aim— government by consent, the individualists turned to the idea of a primitive agreement either between man and man or between the community and its chosen ruler ; they adapted and developed the main controversial weapon of the anti-monarchic writers of the preceding century. When free men, in the unknown past, decided to form a community, they appointed officials to protect their pre-existing and inalienable rights ; the State was the product and servant of the individual, and not the individual of the State. It is no longer necessary to point out the historical fallacy of this theory, though it must not be forgotten that feudal Europe and seventeenth-century

[1] Gooch, *English Democratic Ideas*, p. 138.

America provided many examples of the social, if not the original contract; Maine's *Ancient Law* and the growing study of anthropology have sufficiently demonstrated that the individual as distinct from his family, group, or tribe, was not the founder of society, but the last and most painfully delivered child of civilisation. What is more important is to estimate the political value of the myth.

We must be careful not to antedate its influence. In the first half of the century the opposition to Monarchy gathered, fought and won on practical and immediate issues ; what theory there was, derived not from philosophy but from Common Law and Protestant theology. The Original Compact emerges as a political force immediately on the conclusion of the first Civil War—when the problem of reconstruction divided the victors into rulers and subjects. What was the new liberty ? Was it no more than a change of masters, as Lilburne and Winstanley lamented, and Halifax later defined ? [1] It is to the credit of the Original Compact alone that the persecuting Presbyter did not step into the place of the persecuting Bishop, and that the arbitrary Parliament did not exercise all the powers of the arbitrary King. The clergy, the Rump and the Protector were never allowed to forget the existence of the imperishable rights of the People ; those rights were often neglected and violated, but they had stout and vocal defenders, and the governors themselves had to praise them with their lips, and excuse or minimise their infraction. It is true that their task was the easier for the lack of definition of the word " People " ; it was—and is—a satisfying and elastic term for political jerrymandering. But though it meant to most Republicans the " best people," people of interest and property, it was capable of expansion ; at its narrowest it was wider than the ruling oligarchy, and thus involved some conception of responsibility in the government.

That it was the official doctrine of the Commonwealth is shown both by the Declaration of the Commons of January 4, 1649,

---

[1] The last and most brilliant apologist of Divine Right put into the mouth of a Hottentot a criticism of the 1688 Revolution which is equally pertinent to the Puritan Revolution: " That is, you are not at the mercy of one man, but of five hundred. O delicate freedom ! " (Leslie, *A Battle Royal*, p. 142 ; extracts in Figgis, *op. cit.,* pp. 393-5.)

and by that treatise of Milton which obtained for him the post of Latin Secretary to the Commonwealth. In *The Tenure of Kings and Magistrates* the theory appears as a justification of tyrannicide. It is worth recording at length, since it contains the germs of the views of Hobbes and Locke, and it reveals the religious origin of natural rights :

" No man, who knows aught, can be so stupid to deny, that all men naturally were born free, being the image and resemblance of God himself, and were, by privilege above all the creatures, born to command, and not to obey : and that they lived so, till from the root of Adam's transgression falling among themselves to do wrong and violence, and foreseeing that such courses must needs tend to the destruction of them all, they agreed by common league to bind each other from mutual injury, and jointly to defend themselves against any that gave disturbance or opposition to such agreement. Hence came cities, towns, and commonwealths. And because no faith in all was found sufficiently binding, they saw it needful to ordain some authority that might restrain by force and punishment what was violated against peace and common right.

This authority and power of self-defence and preservation being originally and naturally in every one of them, and unitedly in them all ; for ease, for order, and lest each man should be his own partial judge, they communicated and derived either to one, whom for the eminence of his wisdom and integrity they chose above the rest, or to more than one, whom they thought of equal deserving ; . . . not to be their lords and masters . . . but to be their deputies and commissioners, to execute, by virtue of their intrusted power, that justice, which else every man by the bond of nature and of covenant must have executed for himself, and for one other. And to him that shall consider well, why among free persons one man by civil right should bear authority and jurisdiction over another, no other end or reason can be imaginable." [1]

All the ingredients from which Whig, Republican and democratic systems were composed are found here. Its contemporary and practical value was that it provided a standard and authority by which to judge monarchy, but its permanent and philosophic value is that it provides a standard by which all governments may be judged, and erects a refuge for the individual against all kinds of

[1] *Prose Works*, Vol. II, pp. 8-10 (Bohn) ; pp. 66-7 in " The Prose of Milton," selected by R. Garnett.

State tyranny. It did not fall with the rest of Republican ideals and experiments ; it survived to become the Whig foundation for limited Monarchy, and the safeguard of the private and public liberties of the ordinary Englishman.

This last claim needs substantiation, for both Parliamentary practice and Hobbes' arguments seem to refute it. Parliament in the Interregnum and in William III.'s reign did much to prove Hobbes' point that " mixed government " meant weak government, and as such favoured powerful interests at the expense of the ordinary freeman : that natural rights, by preventing organised tyranny, exposed the individual to the worse tyranny of anarchy. [1] Hobbes was as much an individualist as he was a pessimist ; he advocated despotism as the only sure way to preserve life and security. He used the " original contract " to prove his case ;

" The motive and end for which this renouncing and transferring of Right is introduced is nothing else but the security of a man's person, in his life and in the means of so preserving life, as not to be weary of it." [2]

He reserved only one inalienable natural right which the Sovereign could not touch—the right to life :

" A man cannot lay down the right of resisting them that assault him by force, to take away his life. . . . The same may be said of Wounds, and Chayns, and Imprisonment." [3]

Yet though Hobbes grasped the vital point that law and government are indispensable guardians of civil liberty, his ingenious arguments defeated their own object. He claimed that his was an infallible formula for a strong State ; whereas in fact such a State would have two radical defects. First, no community can hold together which is avowedly based on fear and suspicion ; society cannot be created out of anti-social instincts. Secondly, since the real basis of Hobbes' State is not contract but force, it is essential that there should be force in abundance ; yet Hobbes, by granting the right of resistance to the rebel and criminal and depriving the State of the right of life and death, made his Leviathan weakest at

---

[1] Cf. *Leviathan*, ch. 29.   [2] *Leviathan*, ch. 14, p. 102.
[3] *Leviathan*, ch. 14, pp. 101-2.

that joint where it should be strongest.[1]   The monstrous tyranny was not monstrous enough ; Leviathan had feet of clay.

Hobbes then sacrificed the individual—in all except bare life, and yet he did not save the State.   Now the chief virtues of the liberal advocates of Natural Rights, and the real reasons why they safeguarded the liberty of the individual without endangering society, are to be found in their disagreement with Hobbes on two points of social instincts and the value of force.   They rejected Hobbes' crabbed view of human nature which coloured his whole thought, and they rejected his dogma that government by force was the sole guarantee of the safety of the individual.

On the first point, the strength of Milton, Sidney and Locke was that, though for form's sake they appealed to the mythical rights of their ancestors, in reality they directed their arguments to the reasoning power of living men.   Milton was less impressed by the noble savage than the noble Puritan ; in 1644 he appealed to the Parliament to have confidence in " God's Englishmen " :

" Consider what nation it is whereof ye are, and whereof ye are the governors ; a nation not slow and dull, but of a quick, ingenious, and piercing spirit ; acute to invent, subtile and sinewy to discourse, not beneath the reach of any point the highest that human capacity can soar to." [2]

Locke offers no other argument for the stability of his system than the known reasonableness and conservatism of men.   Men will not stir to upset government unless that government, framed by reason for the public good, has already been uprooted by delinquent officials " who set up force again in opposition to the laws " ; for " people are not so easily got out of their old forms as some are apt to suggest." [3]   They both relied on the social instincts of men to guide the State and hold before it the purpose of its being—the welfare of society and the happiness of the individuals who constitute society.

The second point of disagreement with Hobbes is even more

[1] Cf. *Leviathan*, ch. 21, pp. 167-8 : " If the Sovereign command a man (though justly condemned) to kill, wound or main himself, or not·to resist those that assault him . . . yet hath that man the liberty to disobey."   It follows that the State has no right to conscript soldiers.

[2] *Areopagitica : Works*, II, p. 90.   [3] Locke, *Second Treatise*, ch. 19, p. 230.

important. Without a distinction of State and society freedom is in constant danger of destruction. If there is no alternative between obedience to the government or constitution of the moment and sheer anarchy, then Hobbes is right in holding obedience the lesser evil. If Kings, magistrates, and policemen embody the whole of communal life and aims, the duty of non-resistance becomes clear, and the liberty of subjects dwindles to " the Silence of the Law " : [1]

" All that is done by him " (i.e. the Prince) " in Vertue of his Power, is done by the Authority of every Subject, and consequently, he that brings an action against the Sovereign, brings it against himselfe" [2]

In modern dress, this means that no man has the right of conscience to protest against and resist any law of any temporary government ; that there is no moral or political appeal from Parliament or officialdom. Locke solves the dilemma, not by his defence of abstract individual rights, but by his introduction to English politics of the idea of Society as the controlling, though unorganised force. The power of rulers " in the utmost bounds of it is limited to the public good of the society " ; [3] as it controls the government, so it has power over the individuals who, in one way or another, have consented to join it :

" The power that every individual gave the Society when he entered into it can never revert to the individuals again, as long as the society last, but will always remain in the community." [4]

Hence " the community may be said in this respect " (*i.e.* the power to alter or remove the legislature) " to be always the supreme power, but not as considered under any form of government." [5] Sovereignty is rejected by Locke, except the vague control of society ; and that is a force as indefinite as public opinion or Rousseau's general will, unless it is provoked to revolution. Yet the value of Locke's distinction between State and Society is that it ensures the responsibility of government, and emphasises the connection of men with each other apart from the artificial bonds

---

[1] *Leviathan*, ch. 21, p. 168.   [2] *Leviathan*, ch. 21, p. 169.
[3] *Second Treatise*, ch. 11, p. 185.   [4] *Second Treatise*, ch. 19, pp. 241-2
[5] *Second Treatise*. ch. 13, p. 193.

of the State. He points out that men derive their rights and duties from the sum of their common ties and affections, and that if obedience to the State conflicts with the deeper claims of society, the individual has the right, or rather has the duty, to resist the lesser authority, in order to obey the greater. Such is the teaching of liberal thought in every age, and such was the theory of the English Revolution.

(b) *Fundamental Rights.*—The century was rich with ingenious devices for model societies; the details and mechanics of State-building were studied with a care that had not been known since the time of Aristotle and the Greek law-givers whom he criticised. Their interest, however, is mainly antiquarian, since most of them died with the death of Harrington's Rota Club in 1660. Yet at times academic constitutions were put to the test of practice. The American plantations were considered fit subjects for the political experiments of Shaftesbury, Locke and Penn, and some of Harrington's less fantastic ideas were embodied in their laws.[1] England herself suffered a more remarkable, if more ephemeral, set of constitutions under the Commonwealth and Protectorate. These have already been discussed in some detail in relation to the political history of Puritanism; it remains to indicate their permanent value in the development of political ideas. [2]

From the Heads of the Proposals to the Humble Petition and Advice there is a whole cycle of political experiments. The moderate changes proposed by Ireton accelerated into radical reform which was, in its turn, checked by the return to conservatism of Cromwell's civilian advisers; but for all these contrasts, there was one unchanging feature in the written constitutions of the period. In the heart of each was a list of " Fundamentals "— rights of man which no government, however justly framed, could infringe. Their number and content altered, but the principle remained; and one right—the liberty of conscience—was always to be found among them.[3] Liberty of conscience even survived the wreck through the Declaration of Breda; it was only the fate

[1] Cf. Russell Smith, *Harrington and His Oceana*, chs. 7 and 8, and Gooch and Laski, *English Democratic Ideas*, etc., pp. 305-7 (Second Edition).

[2] Cf. Ch. IV, and Gooch and Laski, *op. cit.*

[3] Cf. Gardiner : *Docts.*, Nos. 71, 74, 81, 97, 102.

of the Royal pledge that finally convinced politicians of the superiority of a living Parliament to a written document. Yet though Fundamentals died under the " horrid arbitrariness " of every Stuart Parliament, whether Royalist or Republican, they lived on in popular thought, for they represented and fortified the hardy individualism of the century. Fundamentals, or Natural Rights, formed the basis of the English brand of liberty which made England unique and envied in the eighteenth century. The individual's right to property, to free speech, movement and trade was gradually recognised by the Common Law, and gradually admitted by a theoretically omnipotent Parliament; and yet there were no constitutional safeguards but the strength of public opinion. It may be objected that such liberty was the perquisite of a minority at the expense of a majority; but despite its restrictions and abuses, it enabled its possessors to do great things, and of its very nature it could not remain for ever in the possession of a few. And, whatever its civil imperfections, in religion it provided a theory of toleration which in the end triumphed over all fears and obstacles.

There is one other important effect of the doctrine of Fundamentals which must be noticed in the shortest survey. Where there are Fundamentals, there can be no sovereignty ; even though written constitutions be destroyed and Parliament be without formal checks, a popular belief in certain fundamental rights prevents complete concentration of powers in the hands of any official body. In the time of the Commonwealth, Fundamentals were proclaimed by the sanction of the " Sovereignty of the People " ; and though, in logic, they are inconsistent with any form of sovereignty, however vague, in the history of English political thought they helped to maintain the supremacy of the community as a whole over its appointed governors. Hence the main body of thinkers rejected the theory of Sovereignty which James I., Hobbes and Filmer proclaimed ; hence there was little trace of the modern or Austinian doctrine that all powers are concentrated in, and all rights derived from the central authority of the State. Hobbes has been called the founder of the doctrine of sovereignty, and there is no doubt that he was working towards it ; but he missed the way through his individualism and his starting-point of Natural

Rights, and his solution was rejected by Royalists and Parliamentarians alike. The art of government undoubtedly suffered from the lack of moral authority or reasoned theory to support it; but the danger of despotism was too great and the inexperience of the rulers too marked to inspire the trust necessary for the acceptance of any theory of sovereignty. Englishmen obtained efficient government, not by theory, but, as is their custom, by entrusting Parliament by degrees with increasing functions in proportion as Parliament appeared competent to fulfil them. That is why, when in the eighteenth century party and Cabinet government were exercising *de facto* sovereignty, England was taken by French and American theorists as the model of a constitution with divided powers and a limited Executive.

III. The Victory of Secular Thought

When we have disentangled some of the chief issues and schools of Stuart political thought, we can then ask whether any marked change or progress can be found in its method or conclusions. Did men at the end of the century have a better understanding of the proper aims and conduct of rulers and subjects than they had at its beginning? Was there any gain in the substitution of the " Treatises of Civil Government " for the " Trew Law of Free Monarchies," or any change other than the triumph of the Divine Right of Property over the Divine Right of Kings?

The most striking change was the disappearance of the theological setting, coincident with the decline of the political leadership of the clergy, both Anglican and Puritan. Theocracy was out of fashion after the experiments of Laud, the Westminster Assembly and the Independent Saints. Hobbes and the secular Republicans, such as Lilburne and Harrington, were the unpopular pioneers of the view that was gradually adopted after the Restoration: that the only concern of the State with religion was to keep it in its place and to prevent it from disturbing political peace and order. Hobbes observed that " The most frequent pretext of Sedition, and Civill Warre, in Christian Common-wealths hath a long time proceeded from a difficulty, not yet sufficiently resolved, of obeying at once,

both God, and Man." Since the difficulty arose from the failure
to distinguish between what was, and what was not necessary to
eternal salvation, he solved it by declaring that "All that is necessary to Salvation, is contained in two Vertues, Faith in Christ, and
Obedience to Laws." [1] His bitterness against " unpleasing priests "
was possibly less significant than the cold sneers of Halifax; the
claims of Bishop and Presbyter appeared ludicrously obsolete to
the man who wrote: "The Clergy in this sense, of Divine
Institution; that God hath made mankind so weak that it must
be deceived." [2] Locke had not enough interest to sneer; in
his *Civil Government* he omitted the Church from discussion as
irrelevant, and in his *Letter Concerning Toleration* he relegated all
religious organisations to the insignificance of "voluntary
societies," and gave them freedom as a consolation.

"The commonwealth," he wrote, "seems to me to be a
society of men constituted only for the procuring, preserving and
advancing their own civil interests . . . the whole jurisdiction
of the magistrate reaches only to these civil concernments . . .
the care of souls is not committed to the civil magistrate." [3]

But the corollary of toleration is this:

"Nothing ought nor can be transacted in this society " (*i.e.* the
church) "relating to the possession of civil and worldly goods.
No force is here to be made use of upon any occasion whatsoever.
Force belongs wholly to the civil magistrate, and the possession of
all outward goods is subject to his jurisdiction." [4]

Locke's exceptions to the rule of toleration prove that he was prepared to protect religious freedom only because and in so far as
organised religion was powerless to persecute opponents or to
endanger the interests of lay society.

Thus the theorists of the 1688 Revolution, and the politicians
whose schemes they justified and rationalised, converted political
theory from a theological to a purely secular business; it was
considered sufficient for the State to direct men's conduct in this

---

[1] *Leviathan*, ch. 43, pp. 457-8.   [2] *Works*, p. 221.
[3] *Of Civil Government and Toleration* (Cassell's National Library Edition),
pp. 147-8.
[4] *Of Civil Government and Toleration* (Cassell's), p. 153.

world, without preparing them for the next. With the fall of religion from political power came the disuse of her maxims as the stock-in-trade of political arguments. For the first half of the century the construction of a political theory was largely a matter of counting texts, or of stealing them from the other side ; but Hobbes by his juggling revealed the absurdity of the method, and opened the eyes of his opponents to its dangers. Hobbes drew the sting of the theologians by arguing that since Scripture derives its authority in this world from the sovereign of the Christian commonwealth, which is the only true Church, the sovereign alone has the power of interpretation.[1] It was not surprising that texts became suspect, and that Filmer, in refounding the doctrine of Divine Right, used the Bible, not as an armoury of Divine commands, but as historical evidence of the naturalness of Kingship in primitive society. In Locke's arguments the texts have disappeared ; his Bible was Hooker's *Ecclesiastical Polity*, which transmits, from Aristotle through Aquinas to Locke, the method of testing the organisation of society by principles of reason and natural development.

The victory of secular unity and rationalist method brought to the State temporal peace instead of eternal salvation. Whether that may be counted gain or not, there were some losses involved in the process. In certain respects Locke was inferior to Hooker, even to James I. ; the rejection of Divine Right and of sovereignty removed dangers and absurdities from English life and thought, but it also discredited some valuable principles. Figgis has proved that Divine Right was a doctrine evoked by, and responsive to real political problems ; that it was a working and useful theory and did not lose its influence or value until its work was done. It was needed to save England from the theocratic encroachments of Popery and Presbytery ; it provided the necessary moral and mystic authority for the central Executive ; and it taught that the foundations of society were more than convenience and contract—that society was a moral organism, united by tradition

---

[1] *Leviathan*, ch. 33, pp. 300-2. For his identification of Church and State, cf. *Leviathan*, ch. 39, p. 362 : " Temporall and Spirituall Government, are but two words brought into the world, to make men see double, and mistake their Lawfull Soveraign."

and loyalties which could not be violated or disregarded with impunity. In the reaction against Divine Right both the necessary powers of government and the social instincts of men were belittled ; rights were put before obligations, convenience before loyalty, and the individual before the community. The philosophic conservatism of Bolingbroke and Burke was needed to restore dignity to the Constitution, by reviving the mystical and traditional elements of society. Until then, the State—that is, the coercive and administrative machinery of society—was discredited, and its organs fell into decay and corruption. The substitution of the contractual for the organic theory of politics weakened the sense of political obligations from the middle of the seventeenth to the middle of the nineteenth century.

We must reject the claims of any of these authors to provide a permanent solution for every political ill, but we learn from their wisdom and their mistakes alike. The individualist can use the arguments that destroyed medieval restrictions to stem the rise of bureaucracy. The socialist may find some trenchant definitions in Hobbes, inspiration in Winstanley, and a labour theory of value in Locke. Above all, we would do well to revive the sensitive plant of toleration with the ideas of Milton and Locke ; for the objects of persecution change, but its spirit seems immortal. Perhaps the modern age, with the confidence of its new knowledge, needs more than any other to be warned against the dangers of claiming infallibility, which is the beginning of persecution. It is to the credit of seventeenth-century England that a chosen few pursued toleration as an ideal and public opinion recognised it as a necessity. If we remember nothing else of the thought of the century, we ought never to forget Milton's cry :

" Give me the liberty to know, to utter, and to argue freely according to conscience, above all liberties." [1]

[1] *Areopagitica.*

SUGGESTIONS FOR FURTHER READING

SABINE, G.: *History of Political Theory.* (Harrap, 1951)

ALLEN, J. W.: *English Political Thought 1603–60.* (Methuen, 1938)

GOOCH, C. P.: *Political Thought in England, Bacon to Halifax.* (O.U.P., H.U.L., 1914)

LASKI, H.: *Political Thought in England, Locke to Bentham.* (O.U.P., H.U.L., 1920)

ZAGORIN, P.: *History of Political Thought in the English Revolution.* (Routledge, 1954)

HILL, C.: *Intellectual Origins of the Puritan Revolution.* (O.U.P., 1965)

WOODHOUSE, A. S. P.: *Puritanism and Liberty.* (Dent, 1951)

FIGGIS, J. N.: *Divine Right of Kings.* (C.U.P., 1914)

GOUGH, J. W.: *Fundamental Law in English Constitutional History.* (O.U.P., 1955)
The Social Contract. (O.U.P. 1957)

MACPHERSON, C. B.: *Political Theory of Possessive Individualism.* (O.U.P., 1962)

FRANK, J.: *The Levellers.* (Harvard and O.U.P., 1955)

GIBB, M. A.: *John Lilburne.* (Drummond, 1948)

ASHLEY, M. P.: *John Wildman.* (Cape, 1947)

BRAILSFORD, H. H.: *The Levellers and the English Revolution.* (Cresset, 1965)

FILMER: *Patriarcha.*

HARRINGTON, J.: *Oceana.*

HOBBS, T.: *Leviathan.* (Blackwell, 1946)

LOCKE, J.: *Second Treatise Concerning Civil Government.* (Blackwell)

MILTON, J.: *Prose Works.* (Bohn)

WINSTANLEY: *New Law of Righteousness*

CONCLUSION

In the course of the seventeenth century England experienced a revolution in politics which determined her character and rôle until the middle of the nineteenth century, if not later. Oligarchy replaced despotism, and the Commons succeeded the Crown as the motive force of government. This political revolution had marked consequences beyond the limited sphere of English central government; it vitally affected local government, organised religion, economic development, and English relations with Scotland, Ireland, Europe and the English colonies. There is no one date at which the revolution can be said to have arrived. Despite Macaulay, the claim of 1688 must be rejected; for it lies half-way between beginning and end. Moreover, the rising of 1688 was in spirit and design a restoration; it is no paradox to assert that it worked less revolutionary changes than 1660. But 1660 looks back to 1640; there, if anywhere, is the decisive date. The work of the first year of the Long Parliament cleared the ground for oligarchy; it was that work which, though jeopardised by the quarrels of the parties of 1641, was revived in 1660 and finally confirmed in 1688 by the united action of both parties. The English Revolution, then, began in 1640, was confirmed in 1660 and 1688, and was worked out in detail between 1689 and 1714.

Such is the main theme of this book. Much else of importance has been omitted; the scope of the book has been limited to a study of the State and its agents—that is, to a fragment of national life and to a minority of the nation. The history of society and culture has been excluded for the reason that it would be improper to treat the major subject as an appendix to the minor. But the student of history must never forget that, though it is necessary to begin with the framework of society, to stop there is to stop short of the real stuff of history. He who knows Shaftesbury and knows not Purcell, Grinling Gibbons and Wren, knows little of Stuart England ; a knowledge of the Constitution does not compensate for ignorance of *Paradise Lost*. A Queen Anne house is a more worthy and enduring monument than the follies of politicians who may have lived in it. The State at its best is but the means to the " good life " of its citizens ; history should observe the due proportion of means and end, and study the life more than the mechanism of society.

INDEX

This has been arranged where possible under main headings; *e.g.* for *Hampden's Case* see under *Cases* and not *Hampden*; for *Triennial Act* see under *Parliament, Acts of,* where it will be found in its chronological order.

Abbot, Archbishop, 29
Acadia. *See* Nova Scotia
Africa, West. *See under* Guinea
Agitators (Army), 83, 330
Agreement of the People (1647), 83
Aix-la-Chapelle, Treaty of (1668), 138, 245
Alexander VI., Pope, and America, 260
Alexander, Sir William, and Nova Scotia, 262-3
Almanza, battle of (1707), 199
Amboyna, massacre at (1623), 255, 309
America. *See under* Colonies, American
Amsterdam, 257, 296
Andrewes, Bishop, 49, 53
Andros, Governor, 275, 285
Anglesey, 1st Earl of, 128
Anne, Queen, at Revolution (1688), 156, 157; reign of, 162, 164-71, 174 n. 2, 194-207; and Scotland, 201, 220-1
Anne of Austria, Queen of France, 237
Architecture, English, 257, 295, 344
Argyle, 8th Earl of, 92, 216; execution of, 218
Argyle, 9th Earl of, rising of, 153, 219
Arlington, Henry Bennet, Earl of, 126, 128, 129, 138-40, 245; and Virginia, 281
Armada, Spanish, 6, 7
Arminians, 26, 29, 49-51, 54-5, 90; political theory of, 323
Army, English, before 1645, 24, 32, 35, 50, 62, 64-5, 68-78; New Model, 64, 68, 70, 76-87, 90-111, 114, 115, 117, 215, 217, 226-7; and Europe, 240-2; landed settlement of, 110, 226-7, 302; (1660-1688), 118, 130, 132, 141-2, 149, 153, 157, 247; (1689-1714), 162, 170, 177, 230, 249, 251
Army Plot (1641), 35

Arundel, Earl of, 40
Association, Eastern, 67, 69, 71, 72, 74; National (1696), 164, 189-90
Attainder, Acts of, 190 and n. 1
Atterbury, Bishop, 174
Aughrim, battle of (1691), 230
Austin, John, views of, 327, 337
Austria, alliance with (1701), 196, 197, 250
Ayscue, Admiral, in West Indies, 265

Bacon, Francis, 4, 5, 20-2, 39, 58, 236, 257; and Scotland, 201, 209, 211; political theory of, 1, 323, 324, 328
Bacon, Nathaniel, of Virginia, 282
Baltimore family, the. *See* Maryland
Banbury, in 1st Civil War, 69, 73
Bancroft, Archbishop, 53-4
Bank of England, 177, 180, 189, 203, 257 294, 296-7
Barbon, Dr. Nicholas, 299
Barcelona, capture of (1705), 197
" Barebones " Assembly, 95-6, 217 n. 2
" Barebones," Praise-God, 299
Barrier Treaty (1709), 199, 251
Barrow, Henry, 52
Bastwick, John, 30
Bavaria, in Spanish Succession War, 197
Baxter, Richard, 119 n. 1, 124 n. 3, 299
Beachy Head, naval battle of (1690), 229, 249
Bedford, 1st Duke of, 70
Bedloe, William, 142
Bellomont, Lord, 285
Berkeley, Sir William, 282
Bermuda, 260, 263-4, 290 n. 2, 311
Bishops. *See under* Church, English
Blair, John, of Virginia, 283
Blake, Admiral, 107, 242, 256
Blenheim, Battle of (1704), 196-7, 250